Beyond Good Company
Next Generation Corporate Citizenship

Bradley K. Googins, Philip H. Mirvis, and Steven A. Rochlin

palgrave
macmillan

First published in 2007 by
PALGRAVE MACMILLAN™
175 Fifth Avenue, New York, N.Y. 10010 and
Houndmills, Basingstoke, Hampshire, England RG21 6XS.
Companies and representatives throughout the world.

PALGRAVE MACMILLAN is the global academic imprint of the Palgrave
Macmillan division of St. Martin's Press, LLC and of Palgrave Macmillan Ltd.
Macmillan® is a registered trademark in the United States, United Kingdom and other
countries. Palgrave is a registered trademark in the European Union and other countries.

ISBN-13: 978-1-4039-8483-8
ISBN-10: 1-4039-8483-2

Library of Congress Cataloging-in-Publication Data
Googins, Bradley K.
   Beyond Good Company: Next Generation Corporate Citizenship / by Bradley K.
   Googins, Philip H. Mirvis, and Steven A. Rochlin.
         p. cm.
   Includes bibliographical references and index.
   ISBN 1-4039-8483-2 (alk. paper)
   1. Social responsibility of business. I. Mirvis, Philip H., 1951- II. Rochlin, Steven A.
III. Title.
   HD60.G663 2007
   658.4'08—dc22   2007018522

Design by Scribe, Inc.

First edition: December 2007

10 9 8 7 6 5 4 3 2 1

Printed in the United States of America.

To Edmund M. Burke and J. Donald Monan, SJ

Contents

Acknowledgments

We have dedicated this book to the combined vision and dedication of Ed Burke, the founding director of the Boston College Center for Corporate Community Relations and J. Donald Monan, S.J., former president of Boston College. More than twenty-five years ago, Ed Burke, former dean of the School of Social Work, had the prescience to realize that the role of business was changing and executives needed to learn how to manage new societal expectations related to the communities in which they manufacture, sell, and source. Father Monan's support and recognition that Ed's vision was an opportunity to express Jesuit values beyond the campus of Boston College has been the bedrock of our organization and has allowed it to grow in size and scope and evolve into the Center for Corporate Citizenship. We also want to thank the Carroll School of Management for supporting the Center, especially the early leadership of Jack Neuhauser that provided the fertile ground and entrepreneurial space that inspired thinking, learning, and networking. This has continued to the present with Dean Andy Boynton who allows us the flexibility to be responsive to the world's leading companies.

Most of the others we want to thank stand on the shoulders of Ed Burke—from those who helped build the Center's premiere executive education program, beginning with Nancy Goldberg and Tamara Bliss followed by David Abdow, Billy Brittingham, and Chris Pinney. An effective education program requires a foundation of solid research and through the years the Center has built that capacity. The many years of research are present on every page of this book and reflect the hard work of so many, including Guy Morgan, Kwang Ryu, David Wood, Belinda Hoff, Vesela Veleva, Jonathan Levine, Julie Manga, Mick Blowfield, Kathleen Witter, Kristen Zecchi, Sapna Shah, Platon Coutsoukis, and Janet Boguslaw.

The Ford Foundation, with the leadership of Frank DeGiovanni and Michele Kahane, was instrumental in helping the Center build its research credentials. A strong research cornerstone for the Center has been the biennial State of Corporate Citizenship survey work that would not be possible without the support of The Hitachi Foundation and the efforts of Barbara Dyer and Mark Popovich. Another research project that has strengthened the field of corporate citizenship and shaped this book is the Global Leadership Network that the Center created with Simon Zadek and AccountAbility. The GLN that was inspired by Stan Litow at IBM with support from Bob Corcoran of GE, Shizuo (Ricky) Fukada of Omron, Mitch Jackson of FedEx, Geoffrey Bush of Diageo, Rodolfo Santiago Larrea Vega of CEMEX, Mark Murphy of Cargill, Kathy Reed of 3M, David Jerome of GM, and Helen Kerrison of Manpower. Others, including the World Bank's International Finance Corporation, continue to support this work. The Executive Forum research community was also instrumental to the content of this book and we want to especially thank Reeta Roy, Kevin Callahan, and Susan Beverly of Abbott; Gene Endicott of Agilent; Allyson Peerman and Phil Trowbridge of AMD; Theresa Fay-Bustillos of Levi Strauss & Co.; Hazel Gillespie and David Stuart of PetroCanada; Laurie Regelbrugge of Unocal; and Chris Lloyd and Susan Sullivan of Verizon for their participation.

The Center is proud to be known as a place where business comes to unite, not compete. Our membership team, with the leadership of Cheryl Kiser, has created a supportive environment we call "In Good Company." Other colleagues supporting our 350 member companies include Seema Bharwani, Eileen Blinstrub, Susan Fonseca, Eve Kristiansen, Kit Manning, Lisa Medolo, Colleen Olphert, Karen O'Malley, Chris Ryan, Josh Shortlidge, and Susan Thomas.

The academic community has also informed and supported our work and this book. The insights of many have been invaluable, especially Sandra Waddock, Jane Nelson, Jim Walsh, David Vogel, and Dave Cooperrider, not to mention graduate students Keith Cox, Mona Amodeo, and Guy Vaccaro. We have built a world-class faculty for our executive education program that includes: Ron Brown, Ken Freitas, Myriam Laberge, Lawrence Moore, Celina Pagani-Tousignant, Ann Pomykal, Richard Pringle, Susan Santos, Ann Svendsen, Dick Trabert, and Eric Young.

The dynamics of the twenty-first century have required the Center team to have a global reach, which we have done by creating partnerships with so many around the world including Susanne Lang, Michael Buersch, and Frank Heuberger in Germany; Derrick de Jongh in South Africa; David Halley in the United Kingdom; Ricardo Young and Mariana Pereira in Brazil; Dante Pesce in Chile; Simon Pickard in Belgium; and Francisco Roman, Jr. in The Philippines.

Leadership is a key component of next generation corporate citizenship. The Center has been fortunate to be influenced by some extraordinary executives who have chaired our International Advisory Board. For their demonstrated leadership and commitment to making this a better world through this service, we thank Dick Trabert, formerly of Merck, Mary O'Malley of Prudential, Lew Karabatsos, formerly of HP, Theresa Fay-Bustillos of Levi Strauss & Co., and Edgar Rodriquez of CEMEX.

This book was also informed by hundreds of other men and women inside business who have provided us their knowledge and perspective. While space does not allow us to name everyone, we must acknowledge Paula Baker, Raymond Baxter, John Bloomfield, Jennifer Brown, Alice Campbell, Carolyn Casey, Evern Cooper, Ann Cramer, Sasha Dichter, Mary Franco, Nathan Garvis, Adrian Godfrey, Michelle Grogg, Barbara Haight, Greg Hall, Lisa Hamilton, Tanya Hayes, Deborah Holmes, Rose Jackson Flenorl, David Gonzalez, Stephen Jordan, Donna Klein, Kimmo Lipponen, Kevin Martinez, Joan McDade, Ria Messer, Bo Miller, Bob Morris, Nancy Nielsen, Donna Obuch, Pat O'Reilly, Douglas Pinkham, Karen Proctor, Ralph Reid, Jerry Ring, Martin Sandelin, Johanna Schneider, Brad Simmons, Helen Smith Price, Laura Tew, Dave Thomas, Kevin Thompson, John Weiser, Allen White, and Bill Valentino.

And finally, we thank a few other key players that made this book possible: Research assistant Sylvia Ciesluk never failed to find facts, figures, and the most appropriate example to illustrate a point; Sharon Sabin for her first-rate chart-making skills; and Leslie Stephen for her spot-on copy editing. Lastly, our appreciation to Peggy Connolly for managing to keep the project on track and the authors focused, grounded, and well-prepared.

Bradley K. Googins
Philip H. Mirvis
Steven A. Rochlin

September 2007
Chestnut Hill, MA

Introduction

From Margins to Mainstream

A select set of big businesses and entrepreneurs are moving beyond the tiresome terrain where shareholders' interests are pitted against other corporate responsibilities. At this socio-commercial frontier, companies are using time-tested strengths—risk management, R&D, market prospecting, innovation, brand differentiation, and continuous improvement—to bring corporate citizenship from the margins of their agenda into their mainstream business. In so doing, they are enlisting their employees, suppliers, and customers in a new mission and working together with other companies and nonprofit partners around the globe.

Consider some examples of how business is applying its know-how and imagination to a diverse set of activities that have, to this point, been lumped under labels of social responsibility, environmental sustainability, or corporate citizenship (the inclusive term used here):

- In light of pricey energy and the threat of global warming, GE launched its "ecomagination" campaign and is investing $20 billion in technologies to reduce its customers' energy consumption and carbon emissions;
- Drawing on its open-sourcing philosophy, IBM is applying know-how from its philanthropic "reinventing education" efforts to social problems having to do with health, transportation, and crowded urban life and inviting thousands of stakeholders to use its tools;
- In a bid to expand markets and shrink the digital divide, AMD, Nokia, HP, and others are reaching millions of poor people with inexpensive software, cell phones, and hand-held PCs;
- Faced with local competition and the glare of global critics, P&G and Unilever have new business models to deliver purified water and fortified foods to the "bottom of the pyramid";
- Recognizing problems and seeing opportunities, Starbucks and Green Mountain Coffee have, along with non-governmental organization (NGO) partners, created a market for "fair trade" coffee that brings benefits to subsistence farmers and serves a growing segment of ethical consumers;
- Seeking a first-mover advantage, Goldman Sachs created an environmental, social, and governance index that documented how those firms with the strongest ratings outperformed the overall market and industry peers from

August 2005 to July 2007. Now other investment banks and consulting firms are establishing practices and gaining credibility in these domains.
• Meanwhile, Johnson & Johnson is tackling the dire nursing shortage while Manpower is training millions of hard-to-employ youth; and
• Novo Nordisk, Novartis, and other big healthcare products companies are sharing patents and working with generics to greatly increase access to life-saving medicines.

These companies plus others are moving beyond legal compliance, checkbook philanthropy, and even stakeholder management to define the next generation of corporate citizenship. The players range from old-timers in new hands, like Ben & Jerry's and the Body Shop, to new entrants like salesforce.com, touting e-based "compassionate capitalism," to late-to-the-game Wal-Mart, rapidly greening its Chinese suppliers and its own facilities and offerings, to emerging market powerhouses like CEMEX (Mexico) that has aspirations to "make a better world."

The Facts up Close: What this Book Is About

The Boston College Center for Corporate Citizenship (the Center) has been studying and working with these companies for decades.[1] The Center, neither as critic of nor cheerleader for business, has amassed a database of evidence—including personal, in-depth interviews with the CEOs of these and many other global businesses, hands-on case studies of what's behind these efforts and what they can and cannot deliver, plus multiyear surveys of business leaders—to present a clear-eyed and, we believe, compelling case that an increasing number of companies and their values-driven leaders are redefining the business-of-business today.

Nevertheless, most everyone familiar with decision making in corporate boardrooms and executive suites—or who manages or works in an office, plant, or retail outlet—has to take this sort of testimony with a cautionary grain of salt. After all, most of the work dealing with issues raised by employees, customers, suppliers, NGOs, regulatory bodies, and the media is handled by diverse corporate staff functions and addressed through policies, programs, and reporting. Meanwhile, business managers are busy activating strategies to gain competitive advantage, using disciplined processes to drive quality improvement, cost reduction, and innovation, and relying on sophisticated measurement systems to ensure efficiency and support improvement. Thus the work of citizenship in most companies is, at best, an "add-on" to the business agenda.

A slew of recent articles, books, conference reports, and surveys contend that business is entering an era of stakeholder capitalism and thought leaders tout the prospect of solving the world's problems through business-driven solutions. At the same time, skeptics rightly point to the "limits of virtue" in markets even as critics question to what extent corporate social investments constitute anything more than window dressing.[2] And a public mistrustful of business, not to mention many of our fellow business professors and M.B.A. students, remind us that for all the talk, "Saying it's so, don't necessarily make it so."

What are the facts? We've spent years not only polling executives but also talking with hundreds of them face to face about the role of business; and we have studied their companies individually and collectively to see to what extent they "walk the new talk." Our research unfolds in several key themes developed in the three parts of this book.

Part I: A Movement Afoot

Part I provides a big-picture overview of next generation citizenship, drawing on our interviews with CEOs and other top leaders, national surveys, select case studies, and a model of stages in the development of corporate citizenship presented in a brief in the *Harvard Business Review* and a more developed article in the *California Management Review*.[3]

Attitudes about corporate citizenship and the role of business are changing.
Executives today are confronted with a paradox. On the one hand, the public holds business leaders in low regard, mistrusts what they say and the motives behind what they do, and sees big companies as too powerful and far more interested in profits than in the welfare of people or health of the planet. Most executives are aware of these perceptions and lament how the financial fiascos at Enron, Tyco, WorldCom, and elsewhere have exacerbated them. On the other hand, executives also understand that the public has increasingly high expectations that business should behave more responsibly, concern itself with environmental sustainability, use its resources and talents to improve society, and address itself to social issues as broad as the gap between rich and poor and as specific as the spread of HIV/AIDS.

To delve into this subject, we interviewed over the past two years nearly fifty executives from twenty-five of the world's largest companies, including the CEO and another top official at GE, IBM, Citigroup, Verizon, State Street, Baxter, Ernst & Young, Aramark, Johnson Controls, Nestlé, Lloyds TSB, Raytheon, Timberland, and others. In a "view from the top" we learn that most top executives agree that companies have a broader set of responsibilities in society beyond maximizing profits. But they have different and nuanced views on citizenship and the role of business in society: some see it in moral terms, some as risk management, and some as a matter of "doing well by doing good." A vanguard, as we shall see in Chapter 2, takes a holistic view of their role in society that portends fundamental changes in their corporate cultures, operating practices, and commercial strategy.

Practices are changing fast too.
Have you noticed the Dove soap ads that feature a variety of women and adolescent girls, in all shapes and sizes, worrying over freckles, fat, and other imperfections in their bodies? This campaign tries to counter the skinny-model body image so commonly purveyed and to make Dove relevant to a broader sampling

of women who want to express their "inner beauty." Have you read or heard about Project Shakti in India where poor, rural women have banded together to sell soap, toothpaste, and such to villagers who have never had access to such high-quality health-and-hygiene products? This campaign, supported by microlending, has turned underprivileged women into entrepreneurs and people at the "bottom of the pyramid" into consumers. Is this corporate citizenship? Or business strategy? Unilever, the company behind these two efforts, thinks that the answer is both of them.

We spent nearly a year working with Unilever, and its new CEO Patrick Cescau, featured in a January 29, 2007 *Business Week* cover story that invited readers to "imagine a world in which eco-friendly and socially responsible practices actually help a company's bottom line."[4] In Chapter 3 we begin our look at Unilever's transformation from "good company" to what we called in *HBR* the "best of the good."[5] We also look at the growing set of players pushing business to adopt a broader and bolder citizenship profile.

"New rules" for business success are emerging.
Climate change; global commerce and its uneven benefits; an obesity pandemic in the offing; continuous breakthroughs in information, communication, and soon biotechnology; and over four billion people living in poverty—all of these factors, and many more, are part of the new business landscape. The business leaders we talked to realize that societal factors impinge in many ways on how they do business. The most visionary leaders are taking account of these factors as they contemplate core strategy and design business models. In so doing, they are defining a new set of rules on how to compete responsibly and successfully as a twenty-first-century company. In Chapter 4 we will list some of these rules and consider how they apply to America's most- and least-admired corporation, Wal-Mart, a company that, according to Marc Gunther writing in *Fortune*, is becoming a "green machine."[6]

Companies are at different stages in the development of citizenship.
To pull the big picture together, in Chapter 5 we lay out in stages how companies develop their thinking and practice in this arena. To preview, many companies are content with playing the conventional business game—making money while complying with laws or conforming to industry standards. By comparison, a growing segment is beginning to play by this new set of rules for business success. They are less defensive and more responsive in dealing with social, ethical, and environmental issues raised about their activities and have a range of policies and programs that address universal and particular concerns. In business matters their executives factor in the interests and views of multiple stakeholders and typically exceed the legal requirements when it comes to employment practices, product safety, and the natural environment. However laudable these efforts may be, they are typically conceived of and managed as matters of compliance, philanthropy, stakeholder relations, or operational improvement.

Our interests are at the leading edge of development where we have identified a select number of companies that embody the next generation of corporate citizenship. Here firms adopt a strategic longer-term view of the business-society relationship and bring a socio-commercial mindset to their products, processes, and purpose.

Part II: Repurposing the Enterprise

Part II is based on the Center's studies of companies moving toward more advanced stages of citizenship and looks at how these firms are repurposing themselves in relationship to society. Business readers consider: Is your company taking appropriate and effective actions on transparency, internal governance, community economic development, work–family balance, environmental sustainability, human rights protection, and ethical investor relationships? In most firms, these subjects are handled without any real enterprise-wide perspective or oversight, and absent coordination or even coherence.

The Center has created several multiyear, multicompany learning forums where senior executives meet regularly with one another to share ideas, discuss tactics, and mark progress on getting their corporate act together in this arena. The case material here comes from three of our forums concerned with linking citizenship and business strategy (Global Leadership Network), moving responsibility from functional silos into the operations of the enterprise (Executive Forum), and connecting business to the community (Community Involvement Leadership Roundtable).

Social and environmental issues are business drivers.
Many big companies take a periodic look at societal issues that are most relevant to their business and growing numbers have begun to engage in stakeholder consultations and to use cross-functional teams to update policies and devise responses to the issues identified. Too often, however, this proves to be a piecemeal approach to setting a citizenship agenda and one that is largely disconnected from business strategy. Accordingly, select companies that we have studied have begun to scan the landscape with the same intensity and thoroughness they apply to other competitive, commercial matters and to calibrate strategically the *risks* and *opportunities* posed in the interaction of their business and society. In Chapter 6 we will see, for example, how Nike (in its supply chain), Diageo (in marketing and sales), Pfizer (in advertising and global outreach), and Levi Strauss & Co. (in its overall value proposition) are devising proactive strategies to deal with sociopolitical and environmental issues that confront them.

Next generation citizenship takes an integrative, strategic approach.
Only twenty years ago it was possible for most senior executives to do their jobs blissfully unaware of issues pertaining to community welfare, the natural environment, the healthcare and work-life concerns of employees, and human rights in nascent global supply chains, among numerous others. And they were largely unaffected by activist NGOs and shareholder resolutions, the threat of boycotts

and protests, not to mention calls for greater transparency and the dramatic increase in exposure provided by the Internet. No more. As one executive put it, "One of the main things that is different today, and will be different tomorrow . . . is that you have to make citizenship far more integral to what you're doing."

There are two different sets of ideas in play on how to take a more integrative, strategic approach to the relationship of business and society. One model stresses corporate responsibility, accountability, and reporting. This has firms take an accounting of their social and environmental impact in the form of metrics and criteria, such as those advanced by the Global Reporting Initiative (GRI) or the International Organization of Standardization (ISO 14000), and manage the business mindful of the triple bottom line (considering economic, social, and environmental performance). Another less regimented version has companies monitor their activities through the full value chain, from raw materials and sourcing through to the consumer, manage the key negative impacts, at minimum, and add value to society through corporate social innovation among visionary companies. In Chapter 7 we explore the intent in companies like Advanced Micro Devices (AMD) and IBM to marshal corporate assets—financial, human, and social capital—to add value to both the business and society.

From Ben & Jerry to Ray Anderson: Leadership matters.
Visible, active, top-level leadership appears on every survey as the number one factor driving citizenship in a corporation. But what does it mean to lead the next generation of corporate citizenship? Our interviews with the fifty top executives in our study yielded mixed reviews on this point. Many, to be candid, had neither an interest in nor appetite for innovating in the social and environmental frontier. Their main emphasis was on minimizing harms, contributing through philanthropy, and otherwise pursuing their traditional business lines. Others, such as GE's Jeffrey Immelt, Jeff Swartz of Timberland, Hector Ruiz of AMD, and Phil Marineau and John Anderson of Levi Strauss talked of the tremendous opportunity to influence social change that comes with positions of corporate leadership.

To garner more perspective on the positive power of leadership, one of our students, Keith Cox, also interviewed the founders or CEOs in twenty smaller, historically progressive companies, including ShoreBank, the Body Shop, Green Mountain Coffee Roasters, Seventh Generation, and the like. In Chapter 8, we look at lessons from these trailblazers alongside the insights of contemporary leaders who are moving their firms forward. A comparative look at the transformational leadership of Ben & Jerry (twenty-five years ago) and Ray Anderson (today) details what it takes to succeed.

Citizenship matters to today's employees.
It is well documented that both managers and workers suffer from change fatigue in most firms and are deeply suspicious of "flavor-of-the-month" business ideas, no matter how uplifting they might seem. At the same time, surveys find that employees, as well as consumers and prospective employees, are

gravitating toward companies that are committed to citizenship.[7] In Chapter 9, we look at this research and see what it means to engage employees as citizens— as workers, to be sure, but also as members of their families, communities, countries, and the planet.

The Center has longstanding experience working with companies on their community service and volunteer programs. On the practice side, we will look at how IBM, with its "on demand" community, and Timberland, with its customer oriented "serv-a-palooza" program, are engaging employees, customers, and consumers in serving society. We will also see how select firms are moving from "best practice" to "next practice" in management and organization development by, among other things, taking their people to the heart of the world's problems through journeys to communities- and environments-in-need.

Part III: Putting Citizenship to Work

Part III considers how next generation citizenship is shaping companies in three arenas: (1) internal operations and management, including social reporting to stakeholders and the public; (2) innovative new products, services, and other socio-commercial activities; and (3) new forms of strategic philanthropy and partnerships between companies and NGOs that are changing the relationship between business and society. The research is based on the Center's corporate citizenship management framework; here we drill down to specific practices and results.

Business faces a new operating environment.
One of the Center's multicompany bodies, the Executive Forum, brought together ten or so companies, including Abbott, AMD, Levi Strauss & Co., Petro-Canada, and Verizon, to understand and address integration of citizenship into each company's operations. In Chapter 10 we describe how these firms adapted to the new operating environment through top-to-bottom moves such as creating Board-level committees and cross-functional staff groups to coordinate citizenship efforts, adopting social-environmental metrics and balanced scorecards to control operations, and setting performance goals to align managers behind their firm's citizenship agenda. 3M illustrates this top-to-bottom model. Interestingly, leadership in many of these efforts came not from the CEO but from citizenship professionals leading change from the middle of their organizations.

Companies are taking citizenship to market.
Top- and mid-level executives in AccountAbility's and the Center's Global Leadership Network, including Nokia, GE, and IBM, have told us emphatically that citizenship means a lot more to them than completing checklists, minimizing their environmental footprint, or even managing the various "social impacts" of their everyday business. For them it's a means to innovate in products and services. In Chapter 11 we see how CEMEX prospects its markets and prospers by helping low-income families add to their homes, how Starbucks and

Green Mountain Coffee have created end-to-end value with free trade coffee, and how Bono's Red campaign has changed the business model at the Gap.

What is important to recognize is that these socio-commercial innovations are not driven solely by strategic calculations or market necessities. Companies in our GLN forum considered how corporate citizenship might open up business opportunities and translate into strategies that could add value to both their business *and* to society. In so doing, these innovators often spoke about their personal passions to make a difference in the world and about how their innovative ideas expressed the most deep-rooted, important, and vitalizing values of their companies.

The next challenge is to co-create value for business and society.
Already, a next generation of partnerships between business and NGOs has been launched that aims at social needs, environmental sustainability, and reducing the gap between haves and have-nots. Chapter 12 covers the globalization of strategic philanthropy in the social strategies of SK Corporation based in Korea and multinationals entering and growing in China. Here we will also see how leading companies and their partners are promoting democracy and combating corruption through philanthropic and commercial efforts. All of this hints at new contours in the relationship between business and society. In addition, there are multicompany and multi-interest partnerships forming around subjects ranging from organic produce and high-tech product standards to carbon emissions and conflict diamonds. Finally, we will also profile multisector groups, such as the UN Global Compact, that are redefining the playing field for citizenship.

Will business step up?
There is a substantial body of public opinion buttressed by scholarship that casts big business as a primary cause of the world's social and environmental, not to mention economic, problems. This is amply evident in polls on attitudes about business in society and borne out sadly in examples of corporate profiteering, environmental degradation, and exploitation of people. This story is well known and all too familiar. The upshot is captured aptly by a CEO we interviewed: "My view is that left unchecked, capitalism will eat us alive."

Yet even as people worry over the power and excesses of big business they also admire its efficiency, productive capacities, and can-do spirit. This is, after all, the era of business, and corporations the world over are being asked to address society's ills. The reasons are very much on the minds of today's CEOs. Said one, "Twenty years ago, the most sophisticated technology and processes were government controlled. Today they are in business hands, and in multiple businesses' hands, not one company."

The relationship between business and society is often framed in a Venn-type diagram with three circles representing business, government, and NGOs or community groups, each with distinct responsibilities and only modest overlap. But many whom we interviewed complained that governments in the United States and elsewhere were either shirking their responsibilities or simply not up to the task of addressing significant national, let alone global, problems. And more than a few complained that NGOs are mostly "single-issue" advocates unable to see the big picture or not in a position to broker tradeoffs. At the same time, select business leaders have a new vision of these roles where they increasingly overlap, and business exerts leadership on selected issues by working hand in hand with government and NGOs to address the challenges of twenty-first-century life. To close this book, we look at the positive possibilities—and challenges posed—should business assume a more active and courageous leadership role in society.

1

Next Generation
Corporate Citizenship

Jack Welch, dubbed "Manager of the Century" by *Fortune* magazine in its review of twentieth-century business, multiplied General Electric's market value from $14 to $400 billion during his twenty-year tenure and he continues to be a role model for business leaders and certainly many of our M.B.A.s.[1] But one of his final acts, according to insiders, "left GE looking like a bunch of slugs."

The presenting problem, not nearly as dramatic or mediagenic as, say, the Exxon *Valdez* oil tanker accident in Alaska or the Greenpeace occupation of Shell's Brent Spar oil rig slated for demolition in the North Sea, was that GE's business units had discharged tons of the toxic chemical PCB into the Hudson River in the 1960s and '70s.[2] In 1976, Welch, then heading GE's chemical businesses, negotiated a settlement with the state of New York that involved payment of some $3 million to clean up the river. Over the next two decades, the Hudson became the Environmental Protection Agency's largest Superfund site but the PCB contamination persisted.

When challenged in 2000 to pony up $460 million to dredge the river bottom, Welch went on the defensive, pointed out that GE had fully complied with then existing environmental protection laws, and then spent a substantial sum—estimated from $15 million (according to Welch) to $60 million (outside experts)—on a public relations campaign. Sixteen different television commercials, a half-hour infomercial, radio blurbs, and full-page newspaper ads argued variously that the dredging wouldn't work, that PCBs really aren't so bad, and that the river would "clean itself."

Behind the PCB problem is a larger question of corporate citizenship or what many term *corporate social responsibility* (CSR). In the classic form, this field asks broadly, "What are a company's responsibilities to society?" and urges managers to consider what they can and should do in this kind of situation.[3] It is easy enough to question GE's tactics—PR campaigns, although commonplace in cases like this, seldom work very well. A McKinsey & Co. survey of over four thousand global business executives asked: "When large companies in your industry try to manage sociopolitical issues, which three tactics do they rely on most frequently?" The top three tactics cited were: (1) using media and public relations; (2) lobbying regulators and governments; and (3) speeches and public actions taken by the CEO.[4] This was in essence GE's script. A follow-up question in the McKinsey survey asked about the effectiveness of such tactics. Just 35 percent cited media and public relations as an effective tactic; 25 percent cited lobbying; and only 14 percent cited speeches and actions by the CEO. No wonder GE's PR efforts foundered.

There are also questions of judgment to consider. Certainly GE's reputation took a hit during this period. The costs of such damage can be substantial. One study for example concluded that, depending on the industry, reputation accounts for between 6 and 10 percent of the total market value of a company.[5] Certainly a clearer-headed calculation of cost and benefits in this case would have opened GE's wallet, limited the reputational harm, and at least saved its Hudson Valley managers and employees considerable embarrassment.

We do not know what specifically was behind GE's decisions in this case. In some firms we still find executives who bristle at having to deal with government officials on compliance issues and who denigrate environmental groups as "tree huggers" or, as one put it more generally, "the wackos." More often we meet managers who regard CSR primarily as a cost to their companies and fail to see or calibrate many benefits from it. Now to be fair, Welch had a solid record on legal compliance, supported GE's charitable work, and led his executives in periodic community service days. But he is also an exemplar of the major reason why big businesses lag in citizenship: It is a secondary corporate priority. In his view, "A CEO's primary social responsibility is to assure the financial success of the company. Only a healthy, winning company has the resources and capability to do the right thing."[6] Welch's priorities vis-à-vis the Hudson River were plainly out of touch with public expectations of corporate responsibilities, and the contradiction between GE's success at wealth creation and its failure to fund the cleanup was palpable.

So what's a company to do? Welch's successor, Jeffrey Immelt, took a different view of GE's role. As one manager told us, "Welch challenged the government on health effects. Immelt came in and said, 'Tell us what you want us to do and we'll do it.'" In the end, GE committed $111 million to reimburse the EPA for current and future costs associated with the dredging and paid many millions more to federal and several state governments to resolve claims. When queried as to why he took a different stand than Welch, Immelt was circumspect and simply noted that he was of a different generation than Jack and that these were different times.

Since 2002, GE has moved its citizenship agenda forward aggressively. The company has, for example, established a "Spirit and Letter" compliance policy that reminds employees that they must not only adhere to the letter of the law, but also its spirit or intent. This has been published in thirty-one languages and distributed in over a hundred countries to over three hundred thousand employees who must sign it. GE issued its first comprehensive citizenship report in 2003 and, in the spirit of greater transparency, its Web site today features facts and figures on environmental performance, governance, employee relations, supply-chain practices, community involvement, and the like. And the company has begun a formal stakeholder consultation process that includes, among others, its shareholders, socially-responsible investment firms, community groups, and GE employees. (These are the kinds of actions, incidentally, that the executives surveyed by McKinsey found to be most effective in dealing with sociopolitical issues.)

We will look in more depth at these practices at other points in this book. However, GE's turnaround on its corporate responsibilities is hardly unique. It has parallels to those of Nike (when taken to task over treatment of workers in its Asian supply chain), Shell (over environmental and social justice issues), and various lumber and building supply companies (over virgin timber and rights of indigenous peoples). The scenario is familiar: it occurs whenever a sociopolitical issue or crisis stimulates responsive rather than defensive action and when enlightened leaders, sometimes in the form of a new CEO, take citizenship seriously and begin to innovate in this arena. Indeed, even absent a crisis, it is evident that many companies today are making positive moves on social and environmental issues, talking to multiple stakeholders, and issuing social reports.

What we find notable about GE are not its socially responsive initiatives per se. This book is about how GE and other leading companies are taking society's needs and expectations deep into the heart of their business strategy and in so doing, defining the next generation of corporate citizenship.

Bringing Citizenship into the Heart of the Business

In remarks to the Center's Annual International Corporate Citizenship conference in March 2004, Immelt stated his reasons for GE's new stance: "If you want to be a great company today ... you also have to be a good company." In our face-to-face interview at GE headquarters, he elaborated on his aspirations:

> One of my passions was to see if you could really build a great and a good company. That has just been a pervasive thought I've had for most of my working life. I know that's the way I want to do this job. I think people who run companies have to have their own kind of inner core belief about what they want to see done. I want to see if you can be an ultra-competitive company and still one that has compassion. I may be wrong, but we're going to find out.

GE's efforts to be a good company include a new value statement that stresses "unyielding integrity." The intent, according to former GE EVP Ben Heineman, is "to create a culture where people act not just because they're afraid of sanctions, but because it is their ideal of what the company should be." How about the ultra-competitive dimension? Here GE wants to go beyond traditional definitions of a "good company" and is positioning itself to, as its value statement proclaims, "help solve some of the world's biggest problems."

Ecomagination

GE's aspirations are most visible in its ecomagination investments that involve, as of this writing, a doubling of research-and-development spending on environmentally friendly technologies (to 25 percent of GE's $3.7 billion 2007 research budget), the hiring of thousands of Ph.D.s, new research projects in the fields of nanotechnology, hydrogen power, photo batteries and such, plus creation of new laboratories in Munich, Shanghai, and Bangalore. This strategy aims to transform GE from a Welch-era finance-based firm to an innovation-driven company. The original expectation was that revenue from ecomagination products would increase from $10 billion in 2005 to at least $20 billion by 2010. But with many new energy efficient products moving into the commercial space, ranging from redesigned jet and train engines to more eco-friendly light bulbs, GE could achieve that goal far ahead of expectations.

What's behind this move? Immelt offered the audience of our conference his views on the future: "The last twenty-five years were really about the development of information technology. . . . My belief is that the next twenty or twenty-five years are going to be about technology around the economics of scarcity. It's going to be about how you get more healthcare into people's hands. It's going to be about how you get more energy into the system."

Healthcare and energy are not new business lines for GE, but what is new is that Immelt is basing his company's growth strategy on, as *The Economist* put it, "saving the planet."[7] Before embarking on this strategy, GE invited its big customers to two-day "dreaming sessions" where they envisioned life in 2015 and what they would want from GE. The combination of higher energy prices and impending limits on greenhouse gas emissions, plus booming demand from Asian economies and consumer preferences for cleaner technology, translated, in Immelt's eyes, into a spectacular business opportunity.

Innovation That Matters

GE's not the only one looking for opportunities in the evolving relationship between business and society. Lou Gerstner turned IBM around in the 1990s by transforming it from a technology hardware company to a service-and-solutions provider.[8] Even as he restructured the corporation, Gerstner also decided to restructure its approach to philanthropy and community involvement with three major moves: (1) to concentrate on systemic changes in K–12 education, a longstanding interest of the firm and high priority of its employees; (2) to globally centralize the IBM community function that had historically been defined and managed differently in its many country organizations and in local markets in the United States; and (3) to apply the company's tools and talents to innovation in education rather than just "write a check." Stanley S. Litow, formerly Deputy Chancellor of Schools in New York City, was hired to focus the effort.

Problem 1: Did IBM have anything to offer to educators? Litow spent months visiting IBM's research labs and querying R&D teams: Could we find a way to teach children how to read using voice recognition technology? Could we use automatic tools to translate from Spanish to English and vice versa? Could we help teachers do a better job, get parents more connected to classrooms, engage more IBMers in service to education, and improve administration in school districts? These challenges had parallels to problems that business teams were tackling with their commercial clients; could their business experiences and insights be used to create value for education?

Problem 2: Would educators work with IBM? Education in the United States is a local operation and there's no way to effect national reform unless you play on the policy front. At that time, state governors were under attack for the poor performance of public schools. Gerstner issued a bold invitation to the National Governors Association: Give us twenty-four hours, come to IBM, let's work together to find solutions. A group of CEOs and state governors, Democrat and Republican, joined together with the president of the United States in 1996 in an Education Summit managed by IBM.

IBM launched twenty-five demonstration projects in U.S. school districts during this period through its signature social campaign "Reinventing Education," which applied the company's technology and know-how to education. Innovations included KidSmart, a computer learning center and software targeted to preschool children, their teachers, and parents; TryScience, an interactive program supported by hundreds of science centers and museums to stimulate children's interest in science; MentorPlace, an online system where IBMers could mentor K–12 students; and a variety of other programs.

Certainly IBM's interest in this field was more than philanthropic. It gave the firm a leadership position in the public debate over education in the United States and helped to forge corporate relationships not only with school systems, but also with state and local governments and with other corporate partners. Moreover, like many new-economy companies dependent on brains rather than brawn, IBM was naturally concerned with the current quality of K–12 education and the implications this would have for IBM's future workforce and customer base in the United States and abroad.

This kind of business-relevant corporate-community involvement is termed "strategic philanthropy." Its leading practitioners undertake social investments where they apply their industry-specific knowledge, skills, and technology to social problems rather than just donate equipment or cash. An early innovator, high-tech Cisco, has in the past decade established ten thousand Network Academies that have reached nearly half a million poor and undereducated students in over 150 countries with IT training. This transfer of knowledge from business to society not only helps to reduce the digital divide, it also gains the company word-of-mouth acclaim, access to an untapped market of highly-trained employees, and strong relationships with a confederation of nonprofit and business partners.

Today IBM and a select set of firms are moving into new territory by looking to corporate citizenship as a source of business innovation and market creation. As an example, IBM has over the past several years hosted Education Summits in Latin America, Europe, China, and elsewhere in the Asia-Pacific region, and its reinventing education technologies have likewise spread to dozens of countries, including India, China, and Vietnam. All of this provides substantial benefits to societies and introduces IBM to new markets through high-level relationships.

How about innovation? Under the leadership of new CEO Sam Palmisano in 2003, IBM's social strategy took a significant new turn. Even as the company launched its "e-on-demand" business strategy and a new generation of interactive tools, Litow recalls, "our social strategy 'morphed.'" Building on its experience applying innovative technology to education, the company expanded its attention to other societal challenges, like healthcare and the environment, and committed itself broadly to "innovation that matters"—for the world.

In so doing, new opportunities for cross-fertilization between its commercial and social efforts emerged. To illustrate: A team of IBMers in Bosnia after the Balkan conflict found that relief workers from the International Rescue Committee, CARE, Doctors Without Borders, and other NGOs couldn't communicate across one another's computing systems without open sourcing tools. Meanwhile, its commercial teams were facing similar problems with inter-connectivity in business. R&D specialists, engineers, and business process consultants, operating in these two different spheres found that they could trade in ideas and solutions. An insight was birthed: perhaps IBM's on-demand community and commercial efforts were part and parcel of an overall business strategy. Making the point, Palmisano told Litow that, in his eyes, citizenship was not something unique or special, or just to apply to "crown jewels" like education; on the contrary, he said: "It's who we are; it's how we do business; it's part of our values; it's in our cultural DNA."

In the past several years, IBM has combined its social and commercial interests into what we call a *socio-commercial* strategy that applies innovative technologies like grid computing, social networking, and virtual worlds into problems faced in healthcare, transportation, the environment, and urban life. It has also created an on-demand volunteer community engaging its employees. But all of this, as we shall see, hinged on making citizenship part and parcel of IBM's business model and, critically, connecting it to IBM's values and culture.

Trailblazers

The idea that business models can incorporate or be built on socially-responsible criteria was not discovered by GE or IBM. Firms like Ben & Jerry's, the Body Shop, Smith & Hawken, Patagonia, and others like them—labeled "caring capitalists" or "companies with a conscience" by the CSR community—had strategic foresight in establishing their business models.[9] These firms capitalized, variously, on growing interest in all-natural ingredients, eco-friendly products, and cause-related consuming; and while these may have been countercultural views in the 1960s and '70s, they have since been carried forward by baby boomers into the marketplace and passed on to their children. These socio-commercial pioneers also had a clear vision on how to use their companies to best effect social change. Ben Cohen remarks, "I think philanthropy is great. But there is a limit to how much you can just give away. If you integrate social concerns into day-to-day profitmaking, there's no limit to how much you can do."[10]

Once at the margins of the marketplace and frankly ridiculed in many managerial circles, commercial practices aimed at promoting human welfare and environmental sustainability are making their way into larger, more traditional corporations. Jeffrey Hollender, CEO of Seventh Generation, made this argument in his 2003 book *What Matters Most: How a Small Group of Pioneers Is Teaching Social Responsibility to Big Business, and Why Big Business Is Listening*.[11] One telling indicator has been the recent acquisitions of CSR-driven businesses like the Body Shop by L'Oreal, Tom's of Maine by Colgate, Stonyfield Farm by Groupe Danone, confectioner Green & Black's by Cadbury Schweppes, and Ben & Jerry's by Unilever.

Other Players

Even as these early innovators are being bought up, there is a new generation of socio-commercial entrepreneurs coming to the fore all around the globe, leading what some term hybrid enterprises—profitmaking firms with an explicit social mission. Examples:

- Greyston Bakery, in Yonkers, New York, provides "great desserts by great people doing great deeds." Combining an economic and social mission, it sells brownies to food purveyors and the public made by the "chronically unemployed"—ex-convicts, former drug abusers, and disadvantaged youth—whom it hires and trains in business and social skills.
- Natura, in Sao Paolo, Brazil, is helping to preserve Brazilian rainforests by using indigenous plants in its personal care and ambience products. Its products are all biodegradable and refills are provided to reduce the environmental impact of bottling and packaging.
- Hemisphere Development, an Ohio real estate developer, specializes in turning "brownfield" industrial properties into viable residential or commercial sites. It evaluates the ecological problems, helps secure funding, and works with government and community groups to clean up the sites and redevelop them.
- The Orchid, an eco-hotel in Mumbai, India, is the first five-star hotel in Asia certified as ISO 14001 for its environmental sustainability. Guests are frequently enlisted in environmental campaigns and cleanup efforts in the city.
- Salesforce.com offers a variety of on-demand computing services to assist companies in managing their sales force. It also donates its products to hundreds of nonprofits, has over 85 percent of its workforce engaged in community service projects, and enlists its business partners and customers in, as its chairman puts it, "changing the world."[12]

In addition, a growing legion of NGOs that represent varied social and environmental issues and interests is operating at the nexus of business and society. Over two hundred thousand new citizen groups have been formed around the world since the mid-1980s and global NGOs have been rising in numbers, scale, and scope.[13] Amnesty International, for example, has nearly two million members in every country where multinational corporations do business and the World Wildlife Fund has over five million. Both of these groups, as well as Oxfam, Greenpeace, and thousands more have historically acted as corporate "watchdogs" and forced companies to account for their social and environmental inaction or misdeeds. Now they are beginning to join with industry in multisector partnerships concerned with human rights, natural resource stocks, climate change, world hunger, and the like, and are working with individual companies to address specific concerns.[14] A sampling:

- TransFair certifies that coffee beans, loose leaf tea, cocoa, bulk sugar, and a range of fruits are acquired under "fair trade" principles that concern direct trade with local farmers, rather than through middlemen, and ensure fair prices, fair labor practices, and sustainable farming methods. TransFair works with six hundred thousand agricultural producers and companies ranging from Costco to Sam's Club to McDonald's. Fair trade coffee sales have grown an average of 72 percent per year since 1999.
- EcoLogic helps to support fair trade through microlending to local farm cooperatives. Through its partnerships with Green Mountain Coffee Roasters and Starbucks, this small NGO has made 270 loans totaling nearly $50 million to co-ops throughout Latin America, East Africa, and Southeast Asia.
- Grameen Foundation, taking this to scale, has built a bridge between large banks, fifty-two microfinance partners, and 2.2 million people living in poverty hoping to start small businesses. Its founder, Muhammad Yunus, won the 2006 Nobel Peace Prize.
- Hands On Network, based in Atlanta, Georgia, helps to enlist and organize corporate community service. Its partnership with Home Depot saw forty thousand employees complete one thousand projects in the corporation's "month of service."
- City Year, an NGO that promotes national service for youth, helped bootmaker Timberland link its employees with over eight thousand consumers and partners in an annual "serv-a-palooza."

The relevance of these NGOs as both overseers and service providers for next generation corporate citizenship cannot be understated. The *Stanford Innovation Review*, a journal on management for social entrepreneurs, features articles on corporate social responsibility—pro and con. Among the latter are papers on the many "myths" of CSR and cautions that former watchdogs have become corporate "lapdogs."[15] Ashoka, an organization set up originally with the assistance of McKinsey & Co., has elected over eighteen hundred social entrepreneurs as fellows and provides them with living stipends, professional support, and access to a global network of peers in more than sixty countries. And the popular business magazine *Fast Company* now features its annual "social capitalist" awards for NGOs that contribute most creatively to society and the marketplace.

What Is Corporate Citizenship?

In our studies and work with executives, we constantly hear this refrain: What exactly is corporate citizenship? There is a lot of misunderstanding about what is meant by corporate citizenship and its namesakes, corporate responsibility, CSR, and so on. Many tend to see it as employee volunteering and charity. Perhaps this shouldn't surprise—not too long ago, corporate citizenship was equated with philanthropy and handled mainly by the community affairs function in companies. The field is still in what scholars call a "pre-paradigmatic" phase, where there is scant agreement on definitions and terms and no consensus has been reached about what it includes and does not include in its boundaries.[16]

What are the common features of most views of corporate citizenship? To begin, the field has its roots in ethics. This stresses the importance of moral conduct and associated ideals, very much in the spotlight post-Enron, that a corporation be a responsible employer, neighbor, and contributor to the common good. At a minimum, this translates into *compliance*: behaving in line with current law, accepted business principles, and codes of conduct. But this is an elastic standard because companies can choose to comply not only with the letter but also with the spirit of regulations (à la the new GE); to exceed the law in select areas, say, product safety, environmental protection, or employee relations or to apply the most demanding global standards to their dealings in emerging markets where these may not be required; and some law-abiding firms may choose not to.

Beyond compliance, philanthropy is an important part of the business-society equation. Firms, in the United States in particular, are more or less expected to "give back" a portion of their profits to help the disadvantaged, support community life, and, when necessary, provide disaster relief. This translates into a voluntary *contribution* to society in exchange for societal benefits like market infrastructure, property rights, and a general license to operate. Of course, corporate giving and employee volunteerism can also yield commercially relevant benefits in an improved reputation and stronger community relationships.

Still, business has its biggest impact on society through (1) its own operations and (2) its interactions with myriad suppliers, distributors, and partners through the entire value chain to end users (business customers and consumers). For a big corporation, roughly two-thirds of its sales revenue might be used to pay for raw materials, goods, and services from suppliers, and an even larger percentage of the wealth it generates through its operations goes to pay wages to employees, taxes to governments, and dividends to shareholders.[17] In this context, the charitable funds donated and their economic impact on society are comparatively modest. Most would agree then that corporate citizenship and CSR also encompass the harms and benefits of a company's commercial activities on society. This translates into two criteria:

- *Minimize Harm.* This means taking account of and minimizing the negative impact of a firm's footprint in society. The main injunction is "do no harm."
- *Maximize Benefit.* This means creating *shared value* in the form of economic wealth *and* social welfare, including reduction of poverty, improved health and well-being, development of people, and care of the natural environment. Here the message is "do good."

Advances in Corporate Citizenship

After studying centuries of scientific discoveries and practical inventions, philosopher Gunther Stent observed, "many ideas are premature, but few are unique."[18] This aphorism also applies to the field where the foundational ideas of CSR and newer ideas concerning stakeholders and sustainability were developed, advanced, and extended in different pockets of scholarship and practice and in different places around the globe.

Certainly one generally accepted advance in the field is the idea that corporations not only have responsibilities to their *shareholders* but also to multiple *stakeholders*. Stakeholder theory, developed by Edward Freeman of the University of Virginia in 1984, proposed that companies need to take an account of, and respond simultaneously to, the interests of investors, employees, customers, the supply chain, business partners, communities, and others who are touched by corporate behavior.[19] Studies show that the term has gained traction in the popular press as evidenced by its increasing use by newspapers and periodicals such as the *Wall Street Journal, New York Times*, and *Business Week* to the point that it is now part of everyday business vocabulary.[20] Furthermore, as we shall see, most business leaders acknowledge responsibilities to multiple stakeholders and their firms increasingly undertake some form of stakeholder consultation. This includes meeting with a growing voice in society: the NGOs who act as stakeholder representatives.

More recently, the idea has been advanced that business is responsible for and needs to take an *accounting* of the full range of its social, economic, and environmental outputs—what England's John Elkington terms the *triple bottom line* (TBL).[21] Interest in social and environmental accounting developed mainly in Europe, and even today many more European than American firms issue social reports. Ben & Jerry's was certainly ahead of its time in the 1980s when it devised its three-part financial, social, and product (quality and environment) mission and later issued, with Elkington's help, its first public accountings of same. But the idea of the triple bottom line did not gain much of a following until the mid-1990s with Shell's publication of its felicitously phrased "People, Profits & Planet" campaign and annual public report. It has taken hold now—a search on Google shows that from 2002 to early 2005 there was an increase in "hits" on the term "triple bottom line" from 15,600 to 187,000. Today: 2,700,000.

Concurrently, there has been growing interest in notions of *sustainability* that turns attention to how the natural environment and society fare under the force of commerce. The main ideas and models of sustainability were developed in the arena of environmental studies but the concept has been expanded to include social sustainability or the welfare of people on the planet. If you really want to see an idea diffusing through business and society, search on line for the key word "sustainability," you will be invited to surf some fifty million sites.

Category	Term	Company
Figure 1.1 **What are Companies Calling It?**		
Responsibility	Corporate Social Responsibility Corporate Responsibility	Starbucks, Norsk Hydro Nike, IBM, Chiquita
Accountability	Corporate Accountability	SAB Miller
Sustainability	Sustainable Development/ Sustainability	Johnson & Johnson, BP, Rio Tinto, Novo Nordisk, Procter & Gamble
Corporate Citizenship	Corporate Citizenship/ Global Citizenship	Ford Motor Co., Novartis, GE, Hewlett Packard, Intel

What Do Firms Call It?

In the last decade, there has been rapid adoption, in parallel, of the concepts of stakeholder management, social accounting, and sustainability in companies, sometimes included within a redefinition of their citizenship or CSR. We did a scan of what different companies are calling their activities in this arena. They cluster under the themes of responsibility, accountability, sustainability (social and environmental), and corporate citizenship (Figure 1.1).

Confusion over definitions and a proliferation of terms are common in any field where the territory is changing rapidly and new ideas and entrants from many disciplines are, in some sense, competing for space. Managers are familiar with how ideas emerge, develop, and enlarge in their own spheres. The quality movement, for example, went through periods demarked by quality circles, then total quality management, and then Six Sigma. Managers have also operated through eras of equal opportunity, affirmative action, and valuing diversity as regards women, ethnic minorities, and nowadays people's sexual orientation.

Naturally, scholars have tracked how ideas and concepts in this field have evolved. As an example, Henri de Bettignies of INSEAD traces the history of the field from its origins in ethics and philanthropy to CSR to what he describes as the more encompassing and integrative logic of sustainability and corporate citizenship.[22] It is in this inclusive sense that we use the term *corporate citizenship* throughout this book.

Beyond "Good Company"

Not long ago, the gold standard for citizenship was to be a "good company." This meant taking serious steps to minimize the harms of business activity and maximize the benefits not only to shareholders but also to a broader set of stakeholders. It also meant being responsive to the needs of society and being accountable to stakeholders and the public about corporate conduct.

Frankly, many companies today are not playing the good company game. In the Center's 2005 and 2007 surveys of American business, we asked a random sample of over a thousand executives to rate "how important" a variety of business practices were to their company's role in society. Roughly four in ten adopted a minimalist view: maximize profits, report finances accurately, obey the law, ensure safety and health, provide basic employee benefits, and the like. Slightly more than six in ten, however, had a more expansive view and saw it as very important that their company treat workers fairly and well, protect consumers and the environment, improve conditions in communities, and, in larger companies, attend to ethical operation of their supply chain.

Within this latter group, businesses and their leaders are in different places about what they must, should, and can responsibly do as corporate citizens and about how to enact their overall role in the society. We have framed the development of citizenship in companies in a series of stages that shows how a firm progresses from compliance and contribution to engaging stakeholders to devising a more sophisticated, organization-wide approach to managing the business-society relationship. Movement into these advanced stages takes a firm—and the field—beyond contemporary definitions of "good company" and the turf staked out traditionally as CSR. What then characterizes the next generation of corporate citizenship?

One feature is a more expansive and inclusive view of corporate responsibility and accountability. Companies that are moving forward on this front develop a more holistic view of their role in society and assume greater responsibility for their economic, social, and environmental impact on society. This helps to propel them into regular stakeholder engagement and toward more thoroughgoing measurement and management of their triple bottom line.

The operating challenge for companies that embrace a more extensive set of responsibilities is to *integrate* the efforts and dealings of the different corporate staff groups that handle human resources, government relations, public affairs, health and safety, and environmental and legal matters and to get "everybody on the same page" when it comes to responsible conduct. This requires a deeper understanding of citizenship in a company, a shared perspective on potential harms and benefits produced, and higher levels of transparency about corporate behavior through disclosure and public reporting.

At this point, the evidence suggests that corporations based in Europe seem to be ahead of the United States when it comes to integration and reporting. Many European countries, for example, regulate corporate conduct more so than in the United States and set guidelines for firms in several citizenship arenas. Moreover, the European Union has hosted multiple convenings on CSR and sustainability, established working groups between leaders in business, government, and NGOs on select issues, and issued position papers aimed at companies. One impact is evident: European firms are far more likely than American ones to issue social-and-environmental reports and to have them verified by external auditors.

Now many of our academic colleagues see this as offering the field the best of both worlds: American-style free market activity leavened by European-based standards and criteria for corporate conduct.[23] Not surprisingly, many American managers reject the idea of external guidelines out of hand and chafe at the notion that corporate conduct be further regulated à la the Sarbanes-Oxley legislation that, post-Enron, has required firms to improve their governance and financial reporting. But others we talk to have a different concern and worry that putting a primary emphasis on accountability and responsibility leads only to more third-party surveys, as well as audits, committees, and reviews—in effect, a super-sized version of citizenship based on compliance. Some contend that stressing social accountability narrows their firm's potential contribution to society. Framing this sentiment, Ian Davis, worldwide managing director of McKinsey & Co., points out, "CSR is limited as an agenda for corporate action because it fails to capture the importance of social issues for corporate strategy."[24]

Another feature of next generation citizenship, just beginning to emerge in select corporations, connects it to the very purpose and operating strategies of a business. In several of the next generation companies that we profile in the book, the strategic intent of the firm is not simply to go about its business responsibly and sustainably, it is to make a responsible and sustainable business out of addressing the world's social and environmental needs.

In firms like GE, IBM, and others, large and small, the aim is to *change the game by making a business out of citizenship*. The operating challenge for such companies is to *align* marketing, manufacturing, finance, R&D, and other operational and commercial functions with a strategy that *connects* them to the needs and issues of society. This implicates the whole value chain of the company, moves citizenship onto senior management's agenda, and shifts it from the margins to the mainstream of a business.[25]

Certainly there is a social x commercial calculus to this next generation of corporate citizenship. Firms on this frontier seek to create *shared value for business and society* through a combination of their philanthropy, operations, innovations, and products and services. And even as these firms strive to minimize harm and maximize benefits to society, so also do they seek to minimize their risks and maximize their opportunities.

Business for What and for Whom?

Charles Handy raised this provocative question in his thoughtful volume, *The Elephant and the Flea*.[26] Next generation companies are repurposing themselves for a socio-commercial role—often by revisiting corporate values and by learning from other innovators and pioneers. In so doing, they are creating a new social contract that positions them alongside, rather than in opposition to, NGOs and governments as co-protectors of the environment and co-creators of value for society—a big step beyond the traditional role of the firm as a corporate citizen.

There is a cadre of business leaders, academics, and activists who postulate that business can make a dramatic contribution to positive social change through its socio-commercial know-how and capabilities. A group of scholars at Case Western Reserve have taken the Center's studies on stages of corporate citizenship and identified a frontier where firms move beyond traditional standards of CSR and sustainability to what they call "revolutionary renewal," where companies actively contribute to the repair of the environment and rebuilding of societies.[27] This highlights the arc of corporate citizenship from yesterday and today to tomorrow (see Figure 1.2). This is what we mean by "a movement afoot" covered in Part I of this volume.

All of this sounds fine in theory, you might say, but what do the leaders of big profitmaking businesses say about citizenship and the role of their firms in society? To find out, we interviewed fifty of them and found that some were rather skeptical about the import of citizenship, many of the mind that it was relevant to their company's reputation and interests, and a select few, like Immelt and Palmisano, who saw it, to use their terminology, as a main business driver.

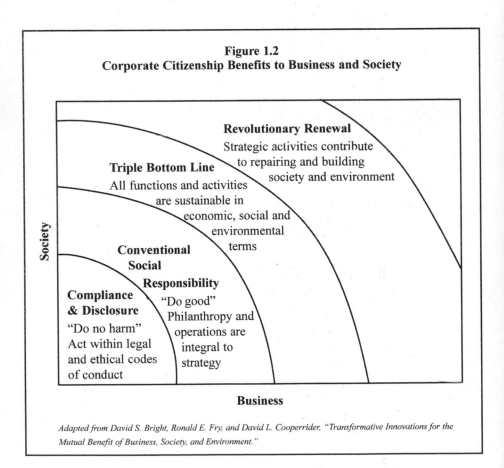

Figure 1.2
Corporate Citizenship Benefits to Business and Society

Revolutionary Renewal
Strategic activities contribute to repairing and building society and environment

Triple Bottom Line
All functions and activities are sustainable in economic, social and environmental terms

Conventional Social Responsibility
"Do good" Philanthropy and operations are integral to strategy

Compliance & Disclosure
"Do no harm" Act within legal and ethical codes of conduct

Society

Business

Adapted from David S. Bright, Ronald E. Fry, and David L. Cooperrider, "Transformative Innovations for the Mutual Benefit of Business, Society, and Environment."

Part I

A Movement Afoot

"Taco Bell Tomato Pickers on Slave Pay"
"Starbucks to Boost Fair Trade Image"
"Missed Hunger Targets Costs Lives and Growth"
"Nestlé to Move into Healthier Foods"
"Climate Panel Confident Warming Is Underway"
"GE Chief: All Engines Go for Alternative Energy"

These are just a sampling of headlines gleaned from the daily newspaper. Those who seek a steady diet of this kind of news can subscribe to CSRwire, a clipping service run by Meadowbrook Lane Capital, LLC, a socially-responsible investment bank that provides what it calls a "raw and unfiltered" picture of media coverage of the field. Or for a more specialized look, subscribe to GreenBiz.com's news service or to the feeds of *Fortune* magazine's Marc Gunther, one among two million others who blog regularly in this section of cyberspace.

Want to see media coverage of your company's citizenship? Most of the public relations outfits slice data this way for corporations and scan Web sites for postings from dissatisfied customers, ex-employees, and anyone else with an ax to grind can post their raw information. Does it surprise you that, on recent count, there are over fifteen thousand Internet "hate sites" that rail against specific companies and brands? Have you seen alternative media that tout "Starsucks coffee," "Calvin Klone jeans," and the "Killsbury" doughboy among other ad-busters?

The research team at the Center tracks these diverse kinds of data and meets regularly with member companies to understand what they are up to and to hear their take on trends. Three points stand out:

• Public perception of the role of business has changed substantially since the 1970s;
• New expectations and responsibilities are being thrust on companies; and
• The current business model is on a collision course with society unless companies recognize that society's issues are affecting—positively and negatively—their long-term business success.

One CEO of a Fortune 100 company succinctly stated one of the paradoxes facing business: "There's both a higher expectation, and a higher cynicism, among the general public." Executives admit business has brought much of this upon itself; for example, after years of advocating for greater labor market flexibility that fractured the employer-employee bond, some companies find themselves in a war for talent where employees hold the upper hand and feel little or no loyalty to their employer. Likewise, companies lobbied aggressively for less government interference and a diminished role for unions, but are now expected to fill the holes that this has created in the social fabric.

Just as expectations regarding product safety and workforce were once contested, new expectations coming to the fore about environmental stewardship and human rights in supply chains have become accepted as part of business's responsibilities. What emerges from this dynamic and at times confusing picture is a real shift in public expectations: Today's company can no longer be a passive bystander in society, but rather is expected to engage directly in addressing societal issues, including greenhouse gas reduction, healthcare provision, product and workplace safety, and responsible global development. What do company CEOs say about these responsibilities? What are companies actually doing about them?

Part I surveys this changing landscape, considering first the views on the role of business in society from a sample of CEOs and company leaders we interviewed face to face (Chapter 2). Next we describe what this means for corporate citizenship through a detailed look at Unilever, a home, personal care, and foods company that has adopted a forward-looking citizenship agenda that addresses risks and seeks out opportunities at the intersection of the firm and society (Chapter 3). Then we drill down into the makeover of Wal-Mart, where some envision a new eco-consciousness emerging and others think it all smacks of clever PR or "greenwashing." This yields a set of new rules for business success (Chapter 4). This first section concludes by pulling things together via a model of the stages of corporate citizenship in companies and a data-based look at where American business stands today (Chapter 5).

2

Business and Society:
A View from the Top

"The Social Responsibility of Business is to increase its profits."

In a now infamous 1970 article in the *New York Times Magazine*, the late University of Chicago and Nobel laureate economist Milton Friedman spelled out this fundamental precept of the free enterprise system.[1] "There is one and only one social responsibility of business—to use its resources and engage in activities designed to increase its profits so long as it stays within the rules of the game, which is to say, engages in open and free competition without deception or fraud," he explained. "In a free-enterprise, private-property system, a corporate executive is an employee of the owners of the business." Actions such as "providing amenities for a community . . . or reducing pollution . . . or hiring the 'hardcore' unemployed," he decried as window dressing and, should these come at the expense of corporate profits, as tantamount to fraud.

This has been the orthodox view of business management since that time. It is the received wisdom passed on to M.B.A.s and undergraduate business students throughout the United States and increasingly, the rest of the world. It's the logic behind agency theory, which contends, among other things, that managers' interests and incentives must be aligned wholly with those of shareholders and that executives must be monitored and controlled to prevent any "opportunism" that takes monies away from shareholders.[2] This theory was the intellectual fuel behind the shareholder rights movement that began in the 1980s that has led to higher shareholder returns but also to widespread and repeated waves of corporate restructuring, downsizing, hostile takeovers, cheap labor outsourcing, and the like. Managers' fixations on quarterly returns and short-term profit taking seem to be its enduring legacy.

Here's the hitch: *The vast majority of senior executives in business in the United States and abroad don't buy Friedman's views on corporate social responsibility.*

In the first study in which a large group of top executives have spoken out on the role of business in the twenty-first century, researchers from the Center interviewed the CEO and another top executive in twenty-five major multinational companies (see interview roster in Appendix 1). Without minimizing the fact that business's relationship with society ebbs and flows, over 70 percent of the forty-eight executives interviewed felt that a fundamental transformation was taking place and that this would have a long-term effect on business. The interviews, face to face and on the record, included, among others, Jeffrey Immelt of GE, Bob Parkinson of Baxter, Hector Ruiz of AMD, Chuck Prince of Citigroup, Mike Rake of KPMG, and Susan Rice of Lloyds TSB. What did they have to say about business and its role in society?

Only three of the executives we talked to embraced Friedman's stand full on. One stated this emphatically when asked about the role of business: "Make money for your shareholders; next question?" A second had a similar view but more sanguine attitude: "Our main enterprise, which is to make money honestly, is a pretty damn important thing." A third argued that the pressure to meet new social and environmental standards was hampering performance: "The fact that the [European] economy is slowing down," he opined, "is directly related to the amount of attention which business is giving to complying with things like this, instead of thinking about innovation and renovation."

Does it surprise that, by comparison, so few top executives, whose job security hinges on investor satisfaction, validated the conventional view of the responsibilities of business? Could either our selective sample or the PR aspects of a personal interview be sources of bias? Interestingly, as we began our interviews, McKinsey & Co. released the results of its survey of more than four thousand executives in 116 countries.[3] In that anonymous, Web-based survey, just 16 percent adopted the view that business should "focus solely on providing highest possible returns to investors while obeying all laws and regulations." The other 84 percent agreed with the statement that business should "generate high returns to investors but balance that with contributing to the broader public good."

The rest of the CEOs and other top executives we talked to espoused a balanced view but for a variety of different reasons. As one put it, "I used to be a proponent of the idea that our job is to generate shareholder value. But I came to believe that that is a naïve proposition. It is intellectually correct, but it is naïve." We can classify the CEOs' views into several broad and overlapping categories— from those referencing ethical and social obligations to those advancing a value proposition for corporate citizenship to those taking it to the global stage.

A Moral Dimension

Nearly one-fifth of the executives we spoke to talked about the role of business in terms of a company's ethical and social obligations. Perhaps this shouldn't surprise readers familiar with modern corporate history and emerging acceptance of social responsibility. The term "social responsibility" was proposed by Frank Abrams, Chairman of the Board of Standard Oil of New Jersey in 1951, in a statement about the duties of executives to society.[4] It gained something of a following with the publication two years later of the "Social Responsibilities of the Businessman" by economist Howard Bowen who, having surveyed the consequences of laissez-faire economics in the 1920s through to the Great Depression, concluded that business had obligations "to pursue those policies, make those decisions, or . . . follow those lines of action which are desirable in terms of objectives and values to society."[5]

CSR, as it was popularized as an acronym, gained a lot of visibility with Friedman's riposte and was spread to business leaders as a more humane view of business life through a 1971 publication by the Committee for Economic Development, an association of big business chieftains. For the next twenty or so years, the idea waxed (under Carter) and waned (under Reagan) in the United States. Otherwise, it was more or less consigned to academic study and addressed conventionally in companies through traditional pursuits like volunteerism and philanthropy. It did, however, get fresh impetus, though not yet under the social responsibility mantle, in companies' attention to the employment and advancement of women and racial minorities, in improvements in working conditions and employee relations, and in pollution prevention, recycling, and other environmental programs.

Some argue that, at least in the United States, these thrusts were chiefly a function of regulation in the areas of occupational health and safety, workplace practices, civil rights, environmental protection, and, as regards banking, community reinvestment legislation.[6] That said, it is indisputable that select business owners and companies have engaged in socially responsible practices since at least the start of the industrial revolution. As one CEO reminded: "The beginning of industrialization was characterized by a high level of social commitment. If you went to the United Kingdom, there were whole company villages being built." This sense of noblesse oblige carried over to New England and the East Coast of the United States where company founders helped to build roads, canals, and other public infrastructure, set up company towns for workers, and even provided for their moral education. Wealthy industrialists, like Rockefeller and Carnegie, turned to philanthropy and endowed the arts, museums, universities, libraries, and parks. As this philosophy spread, Midwestern firms such as Case Tractors and Herman Miller incorporated moral precepts into their management practices and involvement in local communities. On the national front, all of this presaged an era of "welfare capitalism" wherein American companies assumed responsibilities to provide health insurance and pension programs for their employees and were expected to invest in local communities—activities handled by the state in Europe.

Indeed, it is debatable how far Friedman's viewpoint was ever representative of the corporate community as a whole, as reflected in this definition of a company's purpose offered by Apache founder Raymond Plank: "I believe that responsible corporations, if they choose to embark on anything other than self-aggrandizement, have both the opportunity, but principally the responsibility, to use the progress that they're making on the monetary side to enhance their outreach for the benefit of other segments of the human race."

This notion that business ought to "give back to the community" is a moral precept. It is based on the philosophy that business has a contract with society and gets access to resources, gains protection under the law, and receives societal approval in exchange for good behavior. Edward Ludwig, CEO of medical technology company BD, generalized the idea when he said to us: "You know, there's only so much of this world here. . . . It's not just to be consumed without conse-quences. We have a moral obligation, almost like a fiduciary obligation, to take care of what we've got. I think it's beyond Judeo-Christian ethics. Any organized religion would argue that we are somehow accountable to each other for out-comes."

A License to Operate

While this kind of philosophizing was hardly universal, everyone we spoke with acknowledged that the traditional social contract between business and society today is in tatters and in need of repair. It began to break with employees twenty to thirty years ago when cradle-to-grave job security gave way to massive job dis-location, and the idea of a having a lifetime career in one company went away too. In addition, organized labor ceased being a powerful counterforce to indus-try and employees were obliged to assume a greater share of responsibility for their healthcare costs and retirement savings. To many eyes, this was the death knell of welfare capitalism in the workplace.

The recent wave of corporate scandals and the dot-com bust broke the social contract with investors. Billions of dollars of shareholder value were lost in accounting scandals, leading to a number of high-profile criminal cases in the United States and elsewhere centering on large-scale malfeasance. In the United States especially, the response has been tighter regulation and greater trans-parency and accountability, notably the 2002 Sarbanes-Oxley Act. "There's been a big loss in confidence in companies, boards, management teams, and the audit profession as a result of scandals over the last four or five years. And what's clear is that while that confidence is coming back, investors have long memories," said one CEO. If some executives still feel the cure was disproportionate to the dis-ease, nonetheless most seem to agree with this comment from another CEO: "Public trust was violated, and this is the price of restoring public trust."

A commitment to corporate citizenship is one practical way of dealing with the lack of trust in business. As has been widely reported, business executives rank very low in public opinion in terms of their "honesty and ethical stan-dards." In a recent survey of the professions, the polling firm Gallup reports that nurses are rated as having high or very high ethical standards by 84 percent of the American public and college teachers get good marks by 58 percent. Business executives, by comparison, are rated highly by only 18 percent—a score equiva-lent to ratings for lawyers, but somewhat ahead of politicians and car dealers.[7]

To be sure, mistrust of business leaders has been consistently documented in the United States since the early 1960s and typically peaks whenever misdeeds come to light—such as exposés on the safety flaws of the Chevrolet Corvair in the 1960s, hazards of the Dalkon Shield birth control device in the 1970s, the Exxon *Valdez* environmental mess in the 1980s, and so on. Now seems to be no exception: Another poll, asking about reactions to the financial misdeeds of high-profile companies, found a substantial segment of the U.S. public to be "much less trusting" (22 percent) or "somewhat less trusting" (another 22 per-cent) of major corporations in the aftermath.[8]

Public relations firm GolinHarris provides a glimpse of U.S. public opinion today. Its 2006 poll asked, "How would you rate American business today for its corporate citizenship?" Some 40 percent gave business average or fair marks and 37 percent said below average or poor. Thus just one in four said good or excellent. In addition, over 40 percent opined that business is "headed in the *wrong direction* on corporate citizenship."

Is this all strictly a U.S. phenomenon? While some of the complaints about business leaders, particularly about excessive executive compensation, are more pronounced in the United States, disappointment with business's social role is widespread. Recent data from the Reputation Institute documents that in twenty-five countries studied, an average of just one in five people agree that "most companies are socially responsible." Roughly 16 percent of Americans see it this way—less than in Mexico (35 percent) and Canada (26 percent) but more than in the United Kingdom (11 percent) and Japan (9 percent).[9]

"When the wheels start to come off because of lack of trust, the cost to the shareholder is astronomical," said one CEO. A key reason why, according to surveys by Boston-based PR firm Cone, Inc., is that the public—as consumers, investors, and employees—takes a punitive view of "bad corporate behavior."[10] When asked how they would respond if they were to find out about corporate misdoing, here is a sample of what the public reports:

- 90 percent would consider switching to another company's products or services;
- 81 percent would speak out against that company among family and friends;
- 80 percent would refuse to invest in that company's stock; and
- 75 percent would refuse to work at that company.

We will look more closely at the reliability of these kinds of data and any associated costs throughout this volume. At this point, suffice it to say that an agreeable social contract, based on a modicum of trust, is essential to what companies characterize as their "license to operate."

Doing Good and Doing Well

Another one-fourth of the executives we interviewed took a pragmatic view on their firm's role in society, contending in effect that corporate citizenship was primarily a matter of good business sense. As Ernst & Young's Jim Turley explained, "I believe very strongly in the private sector, but I think an executive's duty is to do more than create wealth for investors. If you don't think about anything but that, you get short-term thinking versus long-term thinking." Echoing this view, several noted that if firms only sought profit for profit's sake, they would make decisions that would short-shrift customers, exploit employees, and damage the environment. "It may be profit maximizing in the short term, but it doesn't add to shareholder value in the long term," one said. Or as a peer phrased it, "A company's responsibility is to create value for shareholders in a way in which all of the various constituencies involved are seriously considered. And the challenge that business has today is to figure out how those relative responsibilities to constituencies are best served."

This argument, phrased in different ways by several interviewees, makes the base case that companies should not *harm* their stakeholders because it will, in the longer term, harm the firm and the interests of shareholders. Many also spoke to the upside: the advantages that come to a company from doing *good*. Mike Harrison of Timberland explained: "Business leaders should look for ways to make positive contributions to society because not only is it a good thing to do but ultimately it's a way to create the passion and affiliation to the business that you want employees, customers, and consumers to have." These he pointed out "can be a source of competitive advantage and strength over time."

Several executives referenced the importance of citizenship in winning the "war for talent," especially in light of the aspirations of the twenty- to thirty-year-old Millennial Generation workforce. Baxter's Bob Parkinson explained, "I'm finding that when a lot of our new recruits come in to interview, they aren't asking about our share price, they want to see our social report!" Recently retired Levi Strauss CEO Phil Marineau said, "I call it the brand employment proposition. Being proud, and saying to your next door neighbor, 'I work for Levi Strauss.' Or 'You know we had volunteer day.' And the neighbor says, 'What a great company.' There's a pride of association. A commitment to community enhances the employee/brand proposition in an immeasurable way and allows you to attract the best people."

In different ways, executives made a business case for "doing good" for the purposes of attracting employees and customers, differentiating themselves from competitors, and adding to their image and reputation. Bob Catell, CEO of KeySpan, a natural gas and electricity supplier, used the "Cinderella Project" as an example. His company funded and worked with community groups to renovate brownstone buildings in Brooklyn, New York. "I always use the term 'enlightened self-interest,'" he explained. "The investment in the community was tied to a business reason, because if we don't get new customers, or have customers paying their bills, the company is not going to survive."

What is the evidence that companies can do good and do well? The Center has done a comprehensive review of the business case for corporate citizenship. Combing hundreds of academic studies, we identified a roster of documented benefits for business in the form of cost reduction and value creation (see Figure 2.1 and Appendix 2 for details). These benefits include not only goodwill, but also the relevance for customers, employees, reputation, social investors, and, in select cases, innovation and market development. No wonder, then, that many business executives see value in corporate citizenship. Our biennial survey of U.S. companies finds, on this count, that two of every three company leaders today believe that citizenship makes a tangible contribution to the bottom line.

How does it contribute? Many researchers are documenting a link between CSR and reputation. Research by the Reputation Institute, a consortium of researchers throughout the world, examines annually the reputations of over six hundred companies based on thirty thousand online interviews with consumers in twenty-five countries. In response to a general question, it finds that between

---

Figure 2.1
Corporate Citizenship Business Case

Generate Revenue
Sales
- ○ Customer retention and acquisition
- ○ Product development
- ○ Market development

Equity (enhance market valuation)

Enhance Asset Vale
Reputation
Innovation (product & process)
Trust account
- ○ Social capital
- ○ Reduce transaction costs
- ○ Reduce information costs

Employee satisfaction
- ○ Recruitment and retention
- ○ Productivity

Reduce Costs
Reduce risks/license to operate
Reduce waste
Employee recruiting costs
Customer acquisition costs
Leverage investments in R&D, market development, etc.

---

50 to 80 percent of the public (depending on the country) agree that citizenship programs have a strong effect on the reputations of companies.[11]

This relationship is strongest in countries like South Africa, Brazil, China, and Mexico where, the researchers argue, companies play a more important role in societal development. Still, over 53 percent of the public in the United States see a strong link between citizenship and reputation.

Digging deeper into the database, the Reputation Institute's researchers have analyzed the relationship between different aspects of a firm and its overall reputation. The top predictor of corporate reputation is what they term the "heartbeat" factor—the public's overall respect for and trust in a company. What is the next most significant predictor? In its 2007 global survey, ratings of a company's social and environmental responsibility was the next most significant predictor of its reputation overall. This means, at least in the public's eyes, that citizenship is a bigger factor in reputation than perceptions of a company's products and services, innovativeness, financial performance, workplace practices, governance, and leadership.

It is not just the public that makes this connection. Hill and Knowlton's Corporate Reputation Watch finds that 80 percent of CEOs believe that corporate social responsibility contributes to their company's reputation to some extent, with three in ten holding the belief that it has a very significant effect.[12] This same survey reports that the majority of CEOs also believe that reputational benefits can significantly increase their company's ability to recruit and retain employees, generate additional sales, and achieve many of the other business benefits we have identified. The upshot, according to our interview with John Kennedy, EVP at Johnson Controls, is that "the ability to capture the social good as part of the business gives your company a tremendous value."

Interestingly, several companies are beginning to test these relationships for themselves. Research by British Telecom found that its citizenship activities account for 25 percent of its reputation among three thousand customers sampled.[13] Mirvis' studies at Ben & Jerry's ice cream, in turn, found that the company's social mission was a stronger factor in employee commitment than wages and benefits and even job content.[14]

Another area of research examines the relationship between citizenship and corporate profitability. We have noted the Goldman Sachs research that showed that firms with the strongest environmental, social, and governance records outperformed the market and their peers from 2005 to 2007. Here is just a sampling of other studies:

- A comparison of total returns for firms listed on the Dow Jones Sustainability Index (DJGSI), which includes only those companies that pass economic, social, and environmental screens, shows that from 1999 to 2005 the DJGSI outperformed the traditional Dow Jones Group Index by over 33 percent.[15]
- A compilation of studies, highlighted in the UN Global Compact's "Who Cares Wins" report, demonstrates that environment, health, and safety performance accounts for a substantial portion of the market value of companies in select industries.[16]
- A meta-analysis covering fifty-two major academic studies, over thirty years of research, shows a statistically significant positive association between corporate social performance and corporate financial performance.[17]

Such findings have been a comfort to those who preach citizenship on a business case— Marjorie Kelly, former editor of *Business Ethics* magazine, even headlined them under the theme "Holy Grail Found."[18]

Nevertheless, two points should be mentioned about this kind of research. First, several of the academic studies found a negligible relationship between social and financial performance. The results seem to depend on the industry studied and trends in its sectoral market. Second, it is not clear what causes what. Companies with good financial performance, for example, also have more monies—and perhaps mindshare—to invest in CSR-type activities. Hence it can be argued that good financial performance leads to social responsibility, rather than the other way around. Sorting through all of this, most researchers now see corporate social and financial performance as part of a "virtuous cycle" whereby each reinforces the other. Both kinds of performance, they contend, are a function of good management.

It's Who We Are

Even as they acknowledged their business case for citizenship and the bene-fits of being seen as socially responsible, another one-quarter of the execu-tives we interviewed pointed to a different reason for connecting to society. As Manpower's Jeff Joerres explained: "How you manage your relationship with society strengthens a company. It's not the nice thing to do. It creates who you are." In our research, two chief concerns emerge about building corporate social responsibility on the back of a business case.

First, treating citizenship as a means to ensure a license to operate or to enhance reputation focuses a company on external audiences. When this becomes a sole or even primary motivation, choices about where and how to invest in society, or what steps to take to prevent harms, can center on image-burnishing and turn into a public relations campaign. Considerations of corpo-rate identity, culture, and competencies—the inner essence of a company—can be lost in an effort to "look good." Second, we have found that the business case methodology can turn a company's relationship with society into a fragmented series of initiatives and programs—each cost and benefit calibrated but without a sense of how they hang together and what a firm is trying to accomplish over-all. The alternative, as one executive put it, is living the "full life."

Tom McCoy, EVP at computer chipmaker AMD, expressed it this way: "There is something in our DNA about pushing frontiers, about taking risks, about liv-ing a life and growing, something within us and in our communities that is beyond money." What does this mean for a business leader? Here's Timberland CEO Jeff Swartz: "We didn't set out to say, 'How do we get to be the best manu-facturer? Ah, the tactic is, let's treat workers right.' We started from 'This is what we believe in. Now, how do we make that pay off?'"

IBM has taken this values-oriented, inside-out approach to redefining its overall relationship to society under the leadership of Sam Palmisano. This thrust began in 2001 with an "online jam" that had tens of thousands of IBM employees participate in brainstorming, debate, and follow-up planning on var-ious efforts in the company. Two years later the company held a "values jam" that consisted of seventy-two hours of brainstorming that established three IBM core values: dedication to every client's success; innovation that matters—for the company and the world; and trust and personal responsibility in all relation-ships. Since then, the company has created a site called ThinkPlace for ongoing e-conversations and has hosted online jams with customers, suppliers, myriad other stakeholders, and the public at large centered on innovations—some of which we'll look into later in this book. All of this, Palmisano says, is "a matter of living by your values and winning with your values."

Howard Schultz, founder of Starbucks, expresses a value proposition for citi-zenship this way: "A company should lead with its heart and nurture its soul as it makes money. It should inspire other companies to aim high. It should do more than simply avoid doing harm; it should consciously seek to do good." In dis-cussing this affirmative view with other CEOs, a surprising number had similar sentiments. Ernst & Young's Jim Turley found the statement "flowery" but agreed with its intent. "We've got 107,000 people spread around 140 countries, living in different cultures," he told us. "They all operate under different regulatory systems. What binds us together are global company values." Bob Parkinson of Baxter added: "Companies are like people. They have value systems. I think great companies have a soul that employees can put their own words on. It's a sense of purpose."

Interestingly, company traditions and values are the primary motivator of citizenship in companies throughout the United States. Our 2007 biennial survey of American business leaders finds that although laws and political pressures, the expectations of customers and community, gains in recruiting and retention, and the benefits to reputation all exert an influence on a company's embrace of citizenship, the most important driver seems to be "who we are"—the company's traditions and values (see Figure 2.2).

Globalization and Citizenship

Naturally the CEOs also spoke about an array of forces in their environments that impinge on the corporate role. One major theme was globalization and what it means for firms. "For the first time we're having to compete with countries that not only have equivalent natural resources," said one, "but countries that have equivalent or potentially better human resources." This, to his eyes, has implications for corporate involvement in education in the United States and to business decisions about where to locate, whom to hire, and corporate

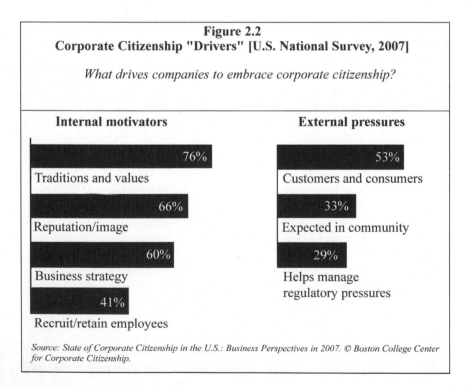

Figure 2.2
Corporate Citizenship "Drivers" [U.S. National Survey, 2007]

What drives companies to embrace corporate citizenship?

Internal motivators	External pressures
76% Traditions and values	53% Customers and consumers
66% Reputation/image	33% Expected in community
60% Business strategy	29% Helps manage regulatory pressures
41% Recruit/retain employees	

Source: State of Corporate Citizenship in the U.S.: Business Perspectives in 2007. © Boston College Center for Corporate Citizenship.

responsibilities on a global scale. As another executive expressed it, "I'm an American, but I'm a CEO. If I take a call center out of the U.S. and I put it in India, is that bad? Am I more obligated to people in the U.S. or to the 350 people I already employ in India who will now get advancement and create more for society in India?"

The opening up of global markets for trade and investment has altered business practices, fostered rapid corporate growth, and affected expectations about what responsibilities a company has to the communities it is impacting for the first time and to the communities it leaves behind. Several we spoke to were concerned that antiglobalization rallies in Seattle, Genoa, and elsewhere had stirred segments of public opinion even more against big corporations, and that critics ranging from Canadian journalist Naomi Klein (author of *No Logo*) to CNN's Lou Dobbs were sounding popular anticorporate notes.[19] What are the facts about globalization? What is the substance of critics' complaints?

Globalization and Business

Although the term was coined in the 1980s, globalization is not a new phenomenon. Global connections have been building over past centuries, the result of powerful forces such as exploration, migration, trade, and innovations such as the telephone, radio, and internal combustion engine. The first great wave was brought down by the explosion of conflict in the First World War, and remained on hold until a new political world stage emerged following the Second World War. The second wave of globalization, the post-war period through the 1970s, was characterized by a gradual process of trade liberalization to break down the protectionist policies limiting the free movement of goods from one country to another. This process was facilitated by the introduction of the General Agreement on Tariffs and Trade (GATT), now the World Trade Organization (WTO).

Today's globalization is more integrated than in the past, having unleashed the unlimited mobility of technology, capital, and people. This is known as the "third wave"—a period that has experienced the introduction of the Internet, cellular phones, and the fall of communism in Eastern Europe. It has created an unprecedented development of knowledge and relationships and unparalleled economic growth. The mobility of capital, technology, and methods of production has allowed multinational firms to grow and thrive. Companies today can locate most anywhere and many are doing so.

The increased scale and scope of corporate activity worldwide can be mind-boggling. For example, of the world's top one hundred economies, fifty-three are corporations and forty-seven are countries (based on a comparison of corporate sales and country GDPs). The number of multinational corporations has doubled in the past fifteen years (from roughly 36,000 in 1990 to over 72,000 in 2006). And the number of their foreign operations and affiliates has nearly tripled in the same period (from about 240,000 to over 700,000). Multinationals directly employ over 90 million people and produce 25 percent of the world's gross product. And the top one thousand firms account for 80 percent of the world's industrial output.[20]

Globalization that lowers barriers to economic activity, lowers costs of communication and transportation, and opens new international business opportunities sounds positive. Indeed, standards of living have risen in many parts of the globe, consumers have benefited from lower prices and a greater variety of products, and innovations in technology have eased life and work burdens of millions. Yet this is not the whole story of globalization. Is globalization good or bad? It depends on who you ask.

New manufacturing and technology workers in China or India mostly say it is good. Globalization has brought them capital, access to lucrative international markets and buyers, and a wireless connection to the world. Their nations are more prosperous as a result. Multinational corporations, their shareholders, and many of those who work for them in the United States and globally have also gained. New markets and cheaper inputs create impressive profit margins and greater return on capital and skilled knowledge.

Yet the same benefits have not accrued to many of the world's poorer nations. They were not prepared with sufficient governance, infrastructure, or human capital and have not found their niche in the competitive global system. Poor farmers in developing regions have been pitted against one another in export markets and must compete with cheaper (often subsidized) imports from richer nations, and many have been driven out of business. Groups all over the world have been disenfranchised by the rapid pace of change, creating an atmosphere of instability and discontent that affects everyone. Consider some of the issues globalization raises:[21]

- *The inequality gap is widening.* In 1960 the average per-capita GDP in the richest twenty countries in the world was fifteen times that of the poorest twenty. Today this gap has widened to thirty times.
- *Outsourcing has displaced workers in the United States.* Although estimates vary widely, Forrester Research predicts that over 250,000 American jobs will be outsourced annually from 2007 to 2015. Manufacturing has already been decimated; these numbers represent white-collar communication, banking, and IT jobs.
- *Western monoculture is spreading throughout the world.* The percentage of countries that hold multiparty elections has grown from less than 30 percent in 1974 to over 60 percent today. But in addition to exporting ideals of democracy, the United States also spreads less sanguine aspects of its culture. A popular and sometimes violent backlash has grown in reaction to the feeling that Western-led globalization is aimed at destroying cultures, particularly Islam.
- *Insecurity in the world is intensifying and widespread.* The world's worst problems, including health pandemics, organized crime, violent terrorist attacks, and natural disasters, are often international in scale and more difficult to contain in what Thomas Friedman aptly describes as a "flat" world.[22]

• *Increasing demand for energy drains the earth's supply of raw materials and exacerbates environmental destruction.* According to United Nations Development Program estimates, it would require the resources of 5.5 planet Earths to provide an American-type lifestyle to the entire population on Earth.

These contradictory implications for business and society display the two faces of globalization. In other times, a national government or coalition of nations has been able to take control of challenges and respond with new policies and remedial programs. Today governments have their hands tied by the forces of globalization, and it is uncertain who will respond to the new challenges. In the absence of a global governance structure, the greatest responsibility to manage the effects of globalization may fall on its greatest benefactor: business.

Business Challenges

The integration of a global marketplace, the internationalization of labor markets, and the retraction of the public sector in the United States and abroad have together changed the business environment as we know it. This has largely been a boon for the private sector. Increased productivity due to innovation and specialization has improved competitiveness and efficiency; greater market opportunities worldwide have raised revenues and expanded the scope of business opportunity; and access to cheaper sources of labor and raw materials continually lowers costs. These advantages have raised the power position of business, often beyond national governments. The private sector is now the power leader of today, but it has a role that is not without complexity and challenge.[23] Consider:

• *Increasing competitive pressures on a global scale are forcing companies to drastically cut costs.* This often means outsourcing non-critical business functions to business partners overseas. Even domestically focused companies cannot remain competitive by operating in a single country dimension.
• *Globally integrated production requires complex management and monitoring.* The sourcing of raw or finished goods from developing countries, the transfer of service operations to off-shore call centers, and international human resource recruiting all expose a company to new risks. Given the weakness of international law, NGOs are growing in numbers and influence and promulgating their own expectations of corporate conduct.
• *Globalizing increases the number and variety of stakeholders to manage.* Doing business in multiple countries increases the number of stakeholders that are affected by business and that expect consideration and buy-in. Each group's interests, priorities, and needs vary and are becoming more complex to manage.
• *U.S. firms risk losing competitiveness to new global powerhouses.* China, India, and others are beginning to rival the United States as centers of innovation, technology, and knowledge. As the public sector pulls away from the provision

of effective services, primarily education, the United States will slowly lose its competitive advantage unless business steps in.

- *Increased competition is depleting stocks of natural resources.* As more and more countries grow as a result of global opportunities, they will demand more of the resources that have been primarily funneled to the rich and industrialized nations. Demand for oil is projected to increase by 50 percent in the next twenty years, pushing costs higher for everyone.
- *Standards of conduct are unclear absent a coherent regulatory environment.* Firms doing business globally must function within a web of varying regulations and standards. As a result, companies must largely manage their own actions according to a mix of multiple stakeholder expectations and their own sense of what's the right thing to do.

Social Issues and Business

What does all this mean for today's big-company CEOs? The litany of societal issues on the executive horizon is notable. The CEOs we talked to spoke variously of climate change; rising inequality; problems with public education, healthcare, and social security; an aging population; immigration, security, and privacy concerns; governance reform; and drives toward more corporate transparency and accountability—and that's with a U.S. domestic focus. Globally, their attention turns to developing and emerging markets and such issues as human rights in supply chains, extreme and persistent poverty, an exploding youth population, environmental degradation affecting water, marine life, and eco-productivity, as well as corruption, terrorism, wars and conflict, and so on.

A subset of CEOs seems to want to look the other way in the midst of these issues. But the great many others, as we shall see throughout this book, see these issues in terms of corporate risks and opportunities and are obliged to respond accordingly. In so doing, they find themselves in a complex new environment where, according to one CEO, commercial success is no longer a matter of company-to-customer relationships; it also involves the success of relationships with governments, NGOs, academic institutions, and other companies.

The CEOs feel at the very least that their companies cannot be absent from debates about the consequences of globalization and the new social contract; and they feel the pressure to do more than show up: "To simply say it's not my job [to take on societal challenges], or that I don't have time for that, reflects a complete lack of understanding of where the corporation is today," says Booz Allen's Chairman and CEO, Ralph Shrader.

Meanwhile, trust and confidence in the nation-state is in decline worldwide. One CEO we talked to lamented that he could not see any national leaders, save for Nelson Mandela, with a compelling vision of the future. In the United States, fewer than four in ten believe that government serves the common good, and cynicism about political leadership is widespread.[24] Indeed, at the very moment society needs leadership to navigate the turbulence of significant social challenge and change, many executives agreed with Jack Connors, former chairman and

CEO of Hill Holliday, who remarked that "government no longer does a particularly good job of running the government."

At the same time, the CEOs acknowledged that they resist regulation of corporate affairs and strongly favor free market activity. Putting this into context, Ernst & Young's Turley remarked: "Companies have, in general, wanted a freer hand, in terms of government regulation and restrictions on their business activities. But with that freer hand comes an obligation. You can't ask for one and not deliver the other."

Toward Next Generation Citizenship

"When I started here, we used to laugh and say we were good environmental stewards. We paid our fines on time," joked one CEO. The situation has surely changed and many executives are rethinking their whole approach to society. Certainly compliance remains front and center on their agenda along with the recognition that transparency, social reporting, and constant attention to governance are "must-dos." But select CEOs described a next generation view of corporate citizenship. Several spoke of citizenship as essential to the viability and prosperity of their companies. A few saw it as an integral part of business growth. This was best expressed by GE's Immelt who repeated his mantra "you can run good businesses, but also solve big problems," and reminded us, "typically profits are created by businesses that are doing things that ultimately have real societal benefits." Others, like Swartz at Timberland and Ruiz at AMD, believe that to be successful, companies need to align and integrate their social and economic missions.

Finally, a number of executives are coming to the view that serious action, in the face of daunting challenges, requires collaboration between business, government, and civil society.[25] Turley at Ernst & Young noted: "The focus for the last couple of years at The World Economic Forum at Davos has been around poverty, AIDS in Africa, and other things that the business community, government, NGOs, and others working together can help to address." Said another: "We need partnering with the NGOs. We don't need antagonism. If we're going to get something done in the communities we work in, we need a consortium." There also seems to be agreement that intercompany partnerships have promise. John Anderson, now CEO of Levi Strauss & Co., put it this way: "Leaders should be sitting down with their peers in the industry and finding the common ground, rather than trying to beat each other to be first in everything."

Pat Shrader, an SVP for BD, sees this kind of multisector activity as essential to global economic development. She describes its impact in stages: getting the entire tide to rise, and then getting it to rise at a higher rate. This is not about competition. It's about businesses working together with society to get "the whole level of discourse and economic environment raised to a higher level." This is the work of global corporate citizens.

The interviews also highlighted reasons why public firms don't make stronger moves on citizenship: short-term profit pressures, short tenure for CEOs, a lack of interest among financial analysts and some institutional investors, and, in a few cases, the notion that it is simply not the company's job. Baxter's Bob Parkinson offered another reason and then explained why at least one aspect of citizenship is fast becoming part of mainstream business thinking: "The natural environment today is like quality management in the past," he said. "Managers used to say if we want quality we have to pay for it, and it will increase our costs. They said it was a tradeoff, you have to find the balance. Well, we learned from the Japanese that it's a symbiotic relationship. You can have both. Today you have the same thing with the environment. It's no different from the cost and quality paradigm, and I think in a few years we'll look back and ask how could we have been so shortsighted?"

That, of course, speaks to the environmental agenda which, as of this writing, business seems to be picking up and advancing rapidly, albeit belatedly.[26] How about the broader set of social issues raised in the relationship between business and society? Let's next see how one global company is tackling them.

From Good to "Best of the Good"

B y almost any criterion or measure, Unilever is a "good" company. Its consumers, roughly 150 million a day worldwide, know the $50 billion global company, with operations in 150 countries, through its home-and-personal care brands such as Dove, Lifebuoy, Sunsilk, and Vaseline, or when sipping Lipton teas, preparing Knorr foods, pigging out with Ben & Jerry's ice cream, or trimming down through Slim-Fast. In the world of corporate citizenship, Unilever is well known for its historic concern for employees and communities, for its environmental practices, and for its efforts to promote human welfare in developing countries.

The basics: Unilever employs over two hundred thousand employees and typically pays them, as well as its contracted employees, well above national market rates. In 2006, out of € 39.6 billion in sales, the company spent € 28.2 billion with suppliers, and it paid € 5.4 billion in wages to employees, € 3.1 billion in dividends to investors, and € 1.1 billion in taxes to governments around the world. It has substantially increased its profits and dividends the past two years. Activists consistently praise the firm for its sustainable sourcing of raw materials from farms and fisheries and for its partnerships with groups ranging from UNICEF to the World Wildlife Fund. Unilever has been the "food industry" category leader for seven years running in the DJSI, is part of the FTSE4Good Index, and was listed among the 100 Most Sustainable Corporations at the World Economic Forum in Davos, Switzerland. *So, with things going well, why did this top-tier company see a need to make wholesale changes in its approach to CSR?*

Unilever wants to be among the "best of the good." So far, we have seen how the view from the top is shifting about the role of business as a corporate citizen. This chapter takes a look at how this view works its way into the minds of executives as they run their business and into a company's management processes and brands.

Unilever's Heritage

Unilever's corporate history begins in the 1880s with William Hesketh Lever who, along with his brother James, launched the world's first branded and packaged laundry soap, called Sunlight.[1] The Lever brothers had a firm sense of justice about inequities in Britain and had been schooled in Disraeli's writings that described the difference between rich and poor in England as "two nations between whom there is no contact and no sympathy; we are as ignorant of each other's feelings as if we were dwellers in different zones or different planets." William was determined, early in his business career, to make washing soap available and affordable to the working class who had never had access to quality hygiene products. Lifebuoy was its name.

Like other leading Victorian industrialists, William was also committed to "prosperity sharing" with his workers. Biographers report that the squalor of the slums in which most workers lived appalled him.[2] Thus he decided to buy a site on the banks of the Mersey River, opposite Liverpool, construct a factory, build twenty-eight cottages, and create Port Sunlight, a company village offering housing at reasonable rents. This was followed by more cottages, houses, shops and the first public building, Gladstone Hall, completed in 1891. The company village included a school for workers' children and special lodging and education in cooking, sewing, and shorthand for the large number of women he employed.

Lever Brothers introduced the then-unheard-of eight-hour workday at the factory and gave sickness benefits, holiday pay, and pensions for both male and female employees. The company also extended its paternalistic policies to workers in India and South Africa in the first decades of the twentieth century. In 1929, the company merged with the Margarine Unie, headquartered in the Netherlands, to become Unilever. Over the next decades, it expanded its scale through a series of acquisitions and introduced hundreds of new brands. The challenge confronting the company at the time of our study was, as one executive put it, "to take Lever's heritage and move it into the new world."

Assessing Citizenship at Unilever

In mid-2004, when we launched our research, Unilever, like other companies based in the United Kingdom and continental Europe, had been under the full lash of shareholder capitalism for just over a decade. The company had undergone several restructurings and extensive de-layering and downsizing, and was "cutting the tail" by slimming its product portfolio to select global brands and a few national gems. A global player in the home-and-personal care markets, it was ready to reach this scale in the foods-and-beverage business with the acquisition of U.S.-based Best Foods (home to brands like Wishbone salad dressings and Hellmann's mayonnaise), Slim-Fast, and Ben & Jerry's. In an effort to placate institutional investors and refit the firm to global standards, the company abandoned its historic division into English and Dutch operating companies, consolidated governance into one Board of Directors, and appointed a single CEO: Patrick Cescau. Now this formerly Anglo-Dutch firm would be led by a Frenchman!

Cescau, who rose through the ranks through several businesses and a stint as chief financial officer, had a mandate to improve the balance sheet and move Unilever forward on a path of profitable growth. Frankly, CSR, a longstanding interest of his twin predecessors, was not a big item on his agenda. Nevertheless, Cescau knew that Unilever was under pressure, like other European companies, to expand and integrate its social and environmental reporting. He was also aware that Proctor & Gamble, a major American competitor, had regained its competitive edge and was becoming more innovative in CSR around the world. Nestlé, long a bête noire for pushing infant formula as an alternative to far healthier breast feeding in developing countries, had also begun to make sensible moves in this arena. It seemed timely, then, for the new CEO to sponsor a full-scale assessment of CSR in Unilever that would look at "current reality," review competitors' efforts and global best practices, and then consider what, if any, changes in approach might be needed. He got more than he asked for.

Louis "Tex" Gunning, then a Unilever business group president in Asia, headed the study team. Our Center for Corporate Citizenship joined as a "research arm" to Unilever CSR specialists Santiago Gowland, Lettemieke Mulder, Paulus Verschuren, and assorted other social and environmental specialists around the company. Over the course of one month, this team, racing from executive offices to videoconferences, interviewed nearly all of Unilever's top executives, many of its business leaders and marketers around the world, and staff specialists in finance, human resources, logistics, and such, plus a bevy of outside experts advising the company and several members of the Board of Directors. The Center also benchmarked the citizenship practices of other firms in Unilever's industries, offered our views on best practices, and added findings from national surveys we have done with business leaders in the United States along with results from other multinational and global polls. A brief look at the Unilever story shows what's behind the change in its approach to CSR. As one executive explained it: "We have no choice given our business."

Outside In: Unilever's World

The quotes in Figure 3.1, from interviewees in the company, depict a slice of Unilever's world. Many of the themes—increased scrutiny of corporations, more NGO activism, emerging social and environmental issues, new consumer trends, and myriad threats to a firm's "license to operate"—are familiar to business. Still, their scale and significance is notable.

Public scrutiny of companies, for instance, has increased dramatically over the past decades—and with good reason. The dirty doings of Enron and others touched legions of employees, shareholders, customers, and suppliers and stimulated sweeping legislation on and greater attention to corporate transparency. But the critical media and public eye are reaching beyond financial finagling to business practices. Witness Michael Moore's documentaries eviscerating GM (on mass layoffs and swollen executive bonuses), Nike (on labor exploitation overseas), gun manufacturers (post-Columbine), and healthcare; industry critiques like *Fast Food Nation*; and the antiglobalization movie shown regularly in college classrooms, *The Corporation*.[3]

We have noted the vast number of anti-company Internet "hate sites." Have you heard about the anticorporate film festival sponsored by the San Francisco group CounterCorps? In this wired-up world, where cell phone cameras can record corporate misconduct, a firm can feature cinematically (and badly) on

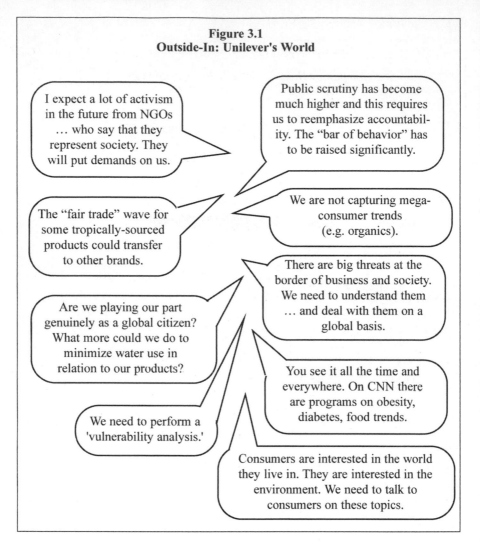

Figure 3.1
Outside-In: Unilever's World

I expect a lot of activism in the future from NGOs … who say that they represent society. They will put demands on us.

Public scrutiny has become much higher and this requires us to reemphasize accountability. The "bar of behavior" has to be raised significantly.

The "fair trade" wave for some tropically-sourced products could transfer to other brands.

We are not capturing mega-consumer trends (e.g. organics).

Are we playing our part genuinely as a global citizen? What more could we do to minimize water use in relation to our products?

There are big threats at the border of business and society. We need to understand them … and deal with them on a global basis.

You see it all the time and everywhere. On CNN there are programs on obesity, diabetes, food trends.

We need to perform a 'vulnerability analysis.'

Consumers are interested in the world they live in. They are interested in the environment. We need to talk to consumers on these topics.

YouTube, myriad hate sites, and a film festival—and of course be "outed" in countless blogs.

Even as people know more about what companies are up to through increases in corporate communication and activists' counter-programming, they also expect better behavior of them. For many reasons, ranging from their massive wealth to their capacities to do great good and great harm, corporations are being held accountable by the public on many counts. A 2005 GlobeScan poll asked the public whether or not companies were "not at all," "somewhat," or "completely" responsible for various aspects of business operations and their impact on society. The pollsters found that large majorities in twenty-one countries hold companies *completely* responsible for the safety of their products, fair treatment of employees, responsible use of raw materials, and for not harming the environment. These are, of course, operational aspects of firms and well

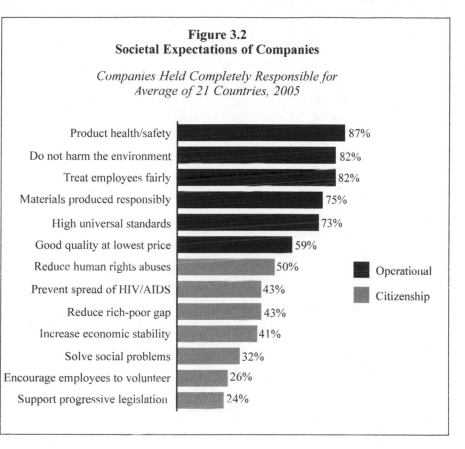

Figure 3.2
Societal Expectations of Companies

Companies Held Completely Responsible for
Average of 21 Countries, 2005

Category	Percentage
Product health/safety	87%
Do not harm the environment	82%
Treat employees fairly	82%
Materials produced responsibly	75%
High universal standards	73%
Good quality at lowest price	59%
Reduce human rights abuses	50%
Prevent spread of HIV/AIDS	43%
Reduce rich-poor gap	43%
Increase economic stability	41%
Solve social problems	32%
Encourage employees to volunteer	26%
Support progressive legislation	24%

■ Operational
■ Citizenship

within their control. But in addition, a significant segment of the public holds companies *completely* responsible for reducing human rights abuses, preventing the spread of HIV/AIDS, and reducing the rich–poor gap (see Figure 3.2). Add in the category of *partially* responsible, and business is responsible, in the public's eye, not only for minding its own store but also for addressing the world's ills.

Who in business would have imagined, say, twenty years ago that a corporation would be held responsible for how employees are treated in a poor, faraway land working in a factory the company doesn't even own? Kathie Lee Gifford learned this lesson the hard way when her clothing line was boycotted by groups holding her responsible for the child labor used in its manufacture. Nike got an even bigger dose of this when reports of physical and sexual abuse of workers, salaries below minimum wage, and an exploitative quota system surfaced from its Vietnamese and Indonesian suppliers. Its sales dropped precipitously for months thereafter, as did its reputation.

How is business doing overall on its responsibility scorecard? A multiyear look at public opinion by GlobeScan shows that public expectations of companies are rising and ratings of their performance are dropping (see Figure 3.3).

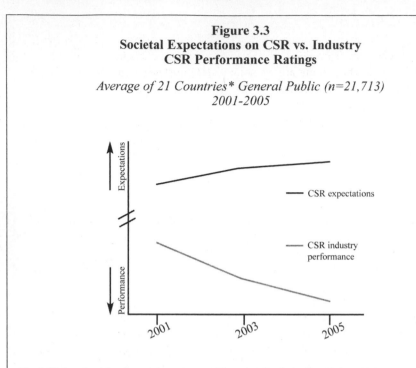

Figure 3.3
Societal Expectations on CSR vs. Industry
CSR Performance Ratings

Average of 21 Countries* General Public (n=21,713)
2001-2005

*In 2005, asked in Argentina, Australia, Brazil, Canada, Chile, China, France, Germany, Great Britain, India, Indonesia, Italy, Mexico, Nigeria, Philippines, Russia, South Africa, South Korea, Switzerland, Turkey and USA

Source: GlobeScan 2005 Corporate Social Responsibility Monitor survey. Reproduced with permission of GlobeScan Incorporated (Toronto).

What are the threats on the border between business and society cited by Unilever's managers and professionals? They echo many of the ones reported by the sample of CEOs we interviewed, including global warming, rich–poor gaps, and so on. But given the company's global reach, some additional ones appear: illnesses ranging from bird flu to E. coli outbreaks; massive migration to mega-cities and across national borders; the threat of nationalization of industry in parts of Latin America; concern over corruption in parts of Africa, Russia, and elsewhere; instability and war in the Middle East; and fears over Islamic fundamentalism. Tally these up and you see why firms, not to mention governments and academics, seek to track social issues and perform their own "vulnerability analysis."

Two threats were particularly notable at Unilever. The first concerns its access to and use of natural resources.[4] As an example, over two-thirds of the company's raw materials come from agriculture. At a 4 percent growth rate, that would mean the company would use, over five years, 20 percent more raw material. That would translate, in turn, into 20 percent more pesticides on farms, 20 percent more packaging and associated waste and litter, 20 percent more water needed to grow crops, and 20 percent more water used by consumers to cook, wash, or clean with company products. The issues? Most of the company's growth is expected from developing and emerging markets in Asia, Africa, and South America where there are growing water shortages and serious concerns over water contamination, plus the environmental costs associated with transport, waste, and the like. And then there's fish. We'll get to those issues later.

A second set of threats involves consumption.[5] Obesity, as one example, is widespread in the United States and Europe and growing in India, China, and elsewhere. As a result, type II diabetes is projected to reach pandemic proportions—from roughly 180 million cases today to 370 million by 2030. At the same time, public attitudes have shifted dramatically about the "causes" of obesity. An analysis of *New York Times* articles on obesity found that in 1990 some 84 percent of the stories stressed that obesity was caused by individual eating-and-exercise habits and only 14 percent attributed causation to the environment. Some thirteen years later, by comparison, personal causes were emphasized in 54 percent of the articles while 46 percent cited environmental causes—a threefold increase.

The chief culprits—fast-food companies and soft-drink makers- -have been targeted as proffering what some term the "new tobacco." Needless to say, this technically termed problem of "over-nutrition" is very relevant for a food purveyor like Unilever. It applies to everything from ingredients and their processing to advertising and promotions. And then there are the problems of "under-nutrition" in poor parts of India, Southeast Asia, and Africa, where fortified foods could be a godsend.

But these also provide opportunities for Unilever. Particularly in the West, but growing worldwide, there is a move toward healthy and sustainable consumption.[6] This is reflected in trends as varied as preferences for organic foods and clothing (a market growing 20 percent annually), for fair trade coffee and chocolate (over 70 percent annually), and for local sourcing of agricultural produce (a requisite on many campuses and a signature of Whole Foods grocers). There is also interest in "ethical" consumerism, as evidenced by an increase in cause-related products and marketing, as well as interest, among at least half of the world's consumers, in a brand's connection to social responsibility.

There is, not surprisingly, considerable debate about the gap between people's expressed interest and actual buying behavior in these regards, and certainly as to whether consumers will pay a premium for such goods and services from socially responsible firms.[7] For example, the UN's environmental program describes a 40/4 gap where 40 percent of consumers say they want to buy green product but only 4 percent regularly do, at least as of 2004 when the report was issued. And claims that consumers will pay 5 percent more for brands from "visionary" corporate citizens versus those of comparable quality from "non-visionaries" simply don't bear out, except in the case of a few well-known icons like Ben & Jerry's and the Body Shop.

It is well documented, however, that a firm's social credentials can help differentiate its brands, that consumers will switch brands due to CSR issues, and that when they know about a firm's bona fides in this area, it is a factor in purchasing decisions. Indeed, evidence is that when a product's social content aligns with consumers' personal interests, it can be decisive in building brand loyalty.[8] This helps to explain broadly an estimated 13.4 percent per annum growth in cause marketing from 2004 to 2007 and specifically why Unilever bought Ben & Jerry's. Now sourcing and marketing are critical parts of the citizenship equation, but the larger challenge for a company that seeks to be the best of the good is to develop a deep, holistic understanding of citizenship and align its operational and commercial functions with a strategy connected to the needs and issues of society. This was the focus of the study at Unilever.

Inside Out: Unilever's Social Agenda

The research team found that the company had a plethora of citizenship initiatives but no consistent strategic thrust behind them. "Too many unaligned programs and messages," reported one leader. "CSR has not been 'interiorized' in the company," said another. We see this in many companies, including those that rate highly on citizenship rankings and scorecards. They may have many "islands of excellence" throughout the firm but not much pulls them together.

In many respects, this is the natural order of things within companies. Each of the corporate staff units has its own issues, constituencies, and agenda, and its unique and specialized knowledge is its greatest strength. Companies want their human resources (HR) departments to be expert in matters of, say, recruiting, developing, and retaining a diverse workforce and expect community relations (CR) to know a lot about community needs and know whom to talk to when concerns arise. But specialization can also be a weakness when it comes to corporate citizenship.

The problem is that social and environmental issues don't come bundled in staff-sized packages. Are concerns raised about the wages, working, and living conditions of contract employees on a tea plantation an HR or CR matter? Shouldn't the health, safety, and environmental people be involved, too, because questions have been raised about water use and about the cleanliness of water in the nearby community? And what about the legal department? Surely this is a "local" problem that can be handled by the site or, if necessary, country managers. But who should deal with the global NGO that has taken an interest in the situation? And what about the global media? And, an executive might reasonably ask: Does what is happening here have any relevance and implications for, say, sourcing tomatoes or soybeans in other parts of the world or even for a packaging plant two states over?

Companies like Unilever face these kinds of issues and questions daily. They also use tools like social issue scans and scenarios and sponsor training programs to prepare their people to handle the challenges. But in most cases these efforts to integrate activity are not sufficient for three interrelated reasons:

1. Corporate staff units don't see the necessity or value of working together, particularly as they are stretched by their own agendas and competing for scarce resources;

Figure 3.4
Inside-Out: Unilever's Social Initiatives

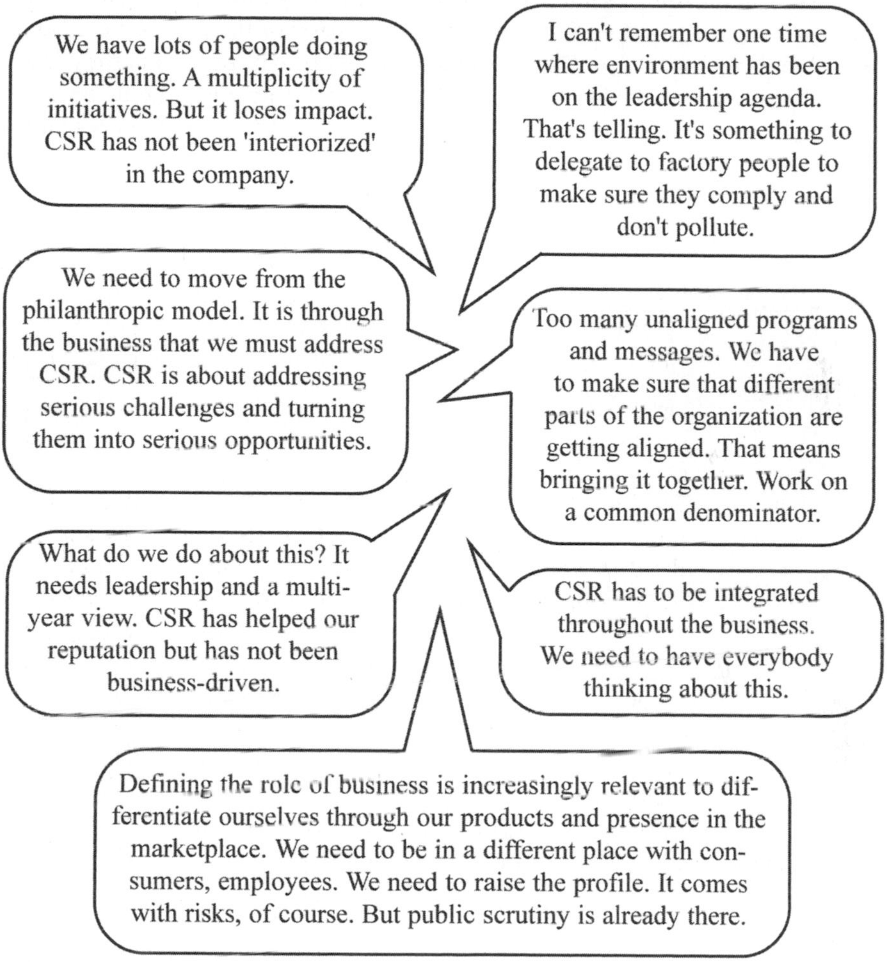

> We have lots of people doing something. A multiplicity of initiatives. But it loses impact. CSR has not been 'interiorized' in the company.

> I can't remember one time where environment has been on the leadership agenda. That's telling. It's something to delegate to factory people to make sure they comply and don't pollute.

> We need to move from the philanthropic model. It is through the business that we must address CSR. CSR is about addressing serious challenges and turning them into serious opportunities.

> Too many unaligned programs and messages. We have to make sure that different parts of the organization are getting aligned. That means bringing it together. Work on a common denominator.

> What do we do about this? It needs leadership and a multi-year view. CSR has helped our reputation but has not been business-driven.

> CSR has to be integrated throughout the business. We need to have everybody thinking about this.

> Defining the role of business is increasingly relevant to differentiate ourselves through our products and presence in the marketplace. We need to be in a different place with consumers, employees. We need to raise the profile. It comes with risks, of course. But public scrutiny is already there.

2. Many line managers don't see the relevance either, particularly as they face other competing short-term priorities; and
3. Most importantly, a comprehensive view of citizenship has not been articulated and embraced throughout the organization.

The quotes in Figure 3.4 show how Unilever suffered on all three counts. Many we talked to spoke of the need for a "common denominator" or a "framework" to integrate things, and urged: "We need everybody thinking about this." Ironically, the company is to some extent a victim of its own success in reaching out to society. It has so many different social and community programs, launched in so many different countries, by so many different people that, according to one interviewee, they have simply let "a thousand flowers bloom."

When it comes to some of the biggest risks facing the company—and societies—Unilever has been a recognized leader. In the areas of sustainable agriculture, water, and fishing, for example, Unilever is either the founding force or a leading member of global, multicompany forums that develop policies, share best practices, or monitor results in these natural resource areas. Jan Kees Vis, a member of our study team, chairs Unilever's Sustainable Agriculture Programme and participates in these forums and other groups on palm oil, soy, and commodity sourcing. In addition, the company participates in countless other roundtables and partnerships, alongside other firms, government agencies, and NGOs concerned with social issues involving nutrition, health, hygiene, dental care, and the plight of the poor.

As important as these efforts are, they were not connected to the commercial side of the business at the time of our study. No one had set goals on sustainable sourcing for major brands, and business leaders had not considered carefully whether their social and environmental interests had any marketing relevance or might differentiate products for consumers. After all, Wal-Mart, its number one grocery customer, was at this point interested in only one thing: lower prices. At the same time, marketing-minded executives were learning that brands that have social in addition to functional benefits were gaining broader and preferential appeal in select markets. Questions arose: Could Unilever add social benefits to more of its brands? Should it?

We heard a consistent message during our interviews at Unilever: "We need a change from 'corporate initiatives' to 'business initiatives.'" Here's where leadership can help. But in many companies, including this one at the time, CSR is not regularly on top management's agenda. Furthermore, there are often naysayers in the business and financial managers who contend, for one reason or another, that collective attention to such matters can be a distraction from more pressing business priorities and, in any case, is largely irrelevant to the fiduciary responsibilities of corporate leaders.

Suffice it to say that Unilever's top leaders saw it as their responsibility to address the company's stance on society. They recognized that there were serious challenges to face and big opportunities to consider, and agreed that "now was the time" to focus on corporate citizenship. Many noted, too, how competitors like P&G, Danone, and Nestlé were doing a better job of managing CSR internally and getting more external visibility for their efforts. They added that employees, worn out from constant restructuring, were hungry for more meaning and inspiration in their work—something that a fresh social agenda might provide.

Strategic Intent: Unilever's Vitality Mission

Many companies move forward on their citizenship agenda by building a "business case" for their efforts, calibrating the potential impact of initiatives on, say, company reputation, or employee recruiting and retention, and other potential benefits to their business. To direct and calibrate their efforts, in turn they may point toward criteria advanced by socially responsible investment groups, ranking bodies, or one or another of the growing number of CSR rating forms. The problem in any case is that firms who do often take a fragmented look at their overall corporate strategy and often miss the real benefits and impact that comes from first asking more fundamental questions, such as: "Who are we?" "What are our values?" "How do we want to do business in society?"

An alternative to the business case is to build citizenship on a platform of a company's identity and values. This translates into a "value proposition" for citizenship that aligns actions and mobilizes employees and managers behind them. Unilever, like Johnson & Johnson in the United States, Novo Nordisk in Denmark, and Omron in Japan, has had a values-based platform since its founding over 120 years ago.

Under the stewardship of executive Clive Butler, Unilever had developed a new corporate brand identity that would integrate its home-and-personal-care and food-and-beverage businesses beneath a corporate umbrella. Butler and his team proposed the unifying theme of "vitality"—and the new corporate mission would be: "To add vitality to life by meeting everyday needs for nutrition,

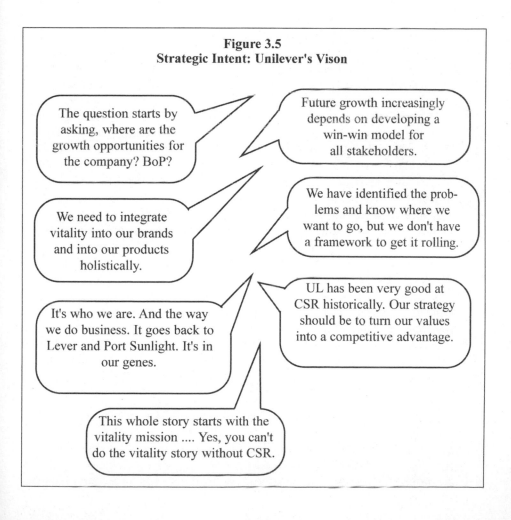

Figure 3.5
Strategic Intent: Unilever's Vison

The question starts by asking, where are the growth opportunities for the company? BoP?

Future growth increasingly depends on developing a win-win model for all stakeholders.

We need to integrate vitality into our brands and into our products holistically.

We have identified the problems and know where we want to go, but we don't have a framework to get it rolling.

It's who we are. And the way we do business. It goes back to Lever and Port Sunlight. It's in our genes.

UL has been very good at CSR historically. Our strategy should be to turn our values into a competitive advantage.

This whole story starts with the vitality mission .... Yes, you can't do the vitality story without CSR.

hygiene, and personal care brands that help people feel good, look good, and get more out of life." In a contentious move, the decision was made to put Unilever's new logo on product packaging, and let consumers know the corporation behind the brands they selected in the marketplace. Recognizing Unilever's historic commitment to and contemporary strengths in its relationships to society, Butler proposed that the company vigorously express its vitality—in messaging and deeds—in its community and environmental thrust.

The study team found great interest throughout Unilever in the new brand identity but a lot of uncertainty about what it actually meant for corporate conduct. "It's like a bar of soap," said one. "Difficult to grasp." Yet several we talked to argued that citizenship was integral to the company's Vitality mission. As one put it, "CSR becomes relevant through the vitality mission; and vitality becomes more exciting with the CSR thrust." Still others saw new possibilities from linking citizenship to the new mission: "We have many relevant themes under the vitality umbrella: children's health and nutrition, women's health and self-esteem, building families," said one. Another opined: "We are living the vitality paradox. Vitality touches us everywhere but we cannot find it in a holistic manner. How can it relate to our consumers in a more holistic way?"

Building on these themes, the study team made two major proposals: (1) Integrate citizenship into the company under the Vitality mission and (2) Align business strategies and brands with a more expansive corporate commitment to add vitality to society. As leader of the study team, Gunning delivered these proposals in a brief, passionate presentation to Cescau who greeted it with a combination of skepticism and interest. Following a series of charged executive meetings, Cescau and his team determined that Vitality would be the theme to integrate citizenship into the company, and that "values-led" brands would help drive business strategy.

Internally, this would mean creating a unified CSR reporting structure, appointing Gavin Neath, a senior business executive, to head the function, and then staffing it with top talent. The corporate function would be connected to community affairs and environmental experts in Unilever's country organizations and, significantly, to brand managers and marketers in its businesses. All of this was designed to give the diverse functions and groups keyed to Unilever's relationship to society a common identity and some sense of shared mission and responsibility. That Cescau and the top executives were stepping out in front of this integrated thrust added some oomph and got the attention of business managers. One of the key undertakings was to introduce social and environmental criteria to Unilever's brand development keys and thus, in effect, develop a value proposition for bringing Unilever's new generation model of citizenship to the marketplace.

Bringing Vitality to the Marketplace

One of the first orders of business was to be more proactive on issues around nutrition. The company had previously introduced a margarine aimed at reducing cholesterol. But with its Vitality mission, nearly twenty thousand recipes were put through a nutrition profile model and subsequently reformulated to reduce trans fat, saturated fats, sugar, and salts—amounting to over thirty thousand tons worth in three years, according to the latest company reports. In addition, Unilever began to put a "Healthy Choices" logo on products to help consumers identify foods that have limited amounts of these ingredients. On the market face of sustainability, Unilever's fish products began to display a certification from the Marine Stewardship Council, co-founded by Unilever and the World Wildlife Fund, which assures consumers that the fish comes from sustainable fisheries, and the company asked the Rainforest Alliance to certify the sustainability of its tea plantations and products.

On the growth side, Unilever, like nearly all consumer goods companies, has found its markets saturated in the United States and Europe. The lion's share of its future growth comes from developing and emerging (D&E) markets. Indeed, Unilever projects that sales in the D&E world will overtake developed markets by 2010. Unilever's prior citizenship in those markets had given it what might be called a "license to grow." The question at hand was whether its new approach could help to both unlock markets and serve pressing human needs in D&E markets—a "win-win" value proposition.

C. K. Prahalad, whose case studies and book *The Fortune at the Bottom of the Pyramid* drew extensively on Unilever's "BoP" efforts, had been nagged for years by the question of why business, with its technology, know-how, and monies wasn't doing much for the poorest people of the world, whose desperate needs were being reached primarily by aid programs and charity.[9] "Why can't we create inclusive capitalism?" he asked. He opened business leaders' eyes when he sketched the economic pyramid: at the top, some 800 million consumers, with twenty thousand dollars or more of purchasing power per household; in the middle tiers, between 1.5 and 2 billion consumers able to spend between fifteen hundred and twenty thousand dollars; and at the bottom, over 4 billion consumers spending less than fifteen hundred dollars a year. Do the math: If these consumers could be reached, it would redress poverty, promote inclusiveness, and add a fortune to the bottom line of companies that could take a radical approach to business strategy.

You may be aware of Unilever's unique steps to reach the world's poor with innovative product designs and business models. Its strategies include the sale of iodized salt in India and parts of Africa, which addresses a dietary deficiency common among the poor, and a campaign for hand washing in India, where its Lifebuoy soap aims to reduce diarrheal disease. In each instance, the company devised new local supply chains to make products more affordable and developed distribution channels that turned underprivileged women into village-level entrepreneurs. In the case of hand washing, Unilever launched its *Swashya Chetna*, or Health Awakening, campaign that has sent health education teams to thousands of schools and communities, many in remote areas, to teach children about germs and the importance of hand washing. The health teams also give every child a height and weight checkup and invite mothers to health education workshops. This overall socio-commercial thrust, pioneered in the Indian operating company, has spread to water purification (where P&G is also a player) and to clothes washing (where local competitors have initiatives too). Now under the corporate-wide Vitality mission, many of these heretofore local innovations are migrating regionally through Asia and globally to Africa, Latin America, and the Middle East.

Meanwhile, Unilever began looking to add social and health content to growing numbers of global brands. On the beverage side, the company introduced new tea products that feature their antioxidant benefits and at the same time dramatically reduced the sugar content of iced tea. It also has on offer a new smoothie beverage made from concentrated vegetables and fruit juices. And on the food side, in partnership with UNICEF, Gunning helped to launch a "kid's nutrition" campaign that includes research into the impact of saturated fats on children's physical and mental performance, conferences on improving youth eating patterns and preferences, and development of healthy breakfast foods aimed at fortifying the diet of poor kids. A first high-nutrition, low-cost product hit the market in Turkey in early 2007.

Another manager raised a provocative question about Unilever's ambitions: "We undertook vitality as our corporate mission for the right reason. Now the question is: Is it bigger than we thought? Shall we be involved in vitality in society?" Perhaps the most visible of the Vitality initiatives of this type has been the Dove soap "inner beauty" campaign that is, according to one Unilever leader, a "dislocating idea." Company research found that just 12 percent of women are very satisfied with their physical attractiveness; 68 percent strongly agree that the media sets an unrealistic standard of beauty; and 75 percent wish the media did a better job of portraying the diversity of women's physical attractiveness, including size and shape, across all ages. Dove's public message about inner beauty has been conveyed through advertisements showing "real women have curves" and a film that shows how fashion model images are distorted to conform to an idealized but unattainable type. It is carried to schools around the world in a complementary program to promote young women's self-esteem.

CEO Cescau summed up the global business logic for Unilever concisely: "Companies that succeed will serve the whole pyramid—with consumers at every economic level . . . Social responsibility is not just about sustainable development and building reputation. It's also about growing markets and fueling innovation."

Business and World Benefit

We next saw Cescau in October 2006 at an unlikely venue, a sports hall at Case Western Reserve University in Cleveland, Ohio at an even more unlikely gathering, a multisector conference on "business-as-an-agent-for-world-benefit" (BAWB). The purpose might seem a utopian aspiration given that, according to our evidence, the great many firms are either defending against global trends or running hard just to keep up with them. Yet there is, among a select set of next generation corporate citizens in business, NGO, philanthropic, and governmental circles, and in a slice of academia, a growing movement to imagine and push for the idea of BAWB—an admittedly odd-sounding acronym.

Many of the leaders shaping the themes of BAWB gathered in Cleveland to meet five hundred fellow travelers, connect virtually to thousands more in over forty countries, and share knowledge, take stock of progress, and consider how to further spread these ideas through practice, research, and education. The Center was represented by Mirvis and by Michele Kahane who, along with Rochlin, has studied how business can grow by reaching untapped markets of lower-income and racial and ethnic minority populations in the United States and abroad—a key subject at the conference and one of Unilever's key strategies.[10]

Who sponsored this meeting? One sponsor was Case's Weatherhead School of Management, namely Professor David Cooperrider whose pioneering work on what is called "appreciative inquiry" is a practical example of a wave of fresh thinking about how people might approach situations and take positive action in many aspects of life.[11] The broader field of positive psychology, with its emphasis on building on strengths rather than countering weaknesses, on seeing difficult situations as opportunities rather than as problems, and on stressing the power of positive thinking, has gained ground in medicine, mental health counseling, athletic performance, and personal development. It also has a following in business where concepts like the "psychology of abundance" buttress GE's efforts to counter the "economics of scarcity." The methodology has gained adherents among organization change practitioners and was used throughout the BAWB meeting in small group discussions and in the gathering as a whole.

A second sponsor was the United Nations' Global Compact. This is an international initiative, launched by then-UN Secretary-General Kofi Annan in January 1999, that brings companies together with UN agencies, labor, and civil society to support universal environmental and social principles relevant to business. The Compact has promulgated standards for business concerning human rights, labor, environmental responsibility, and anti-corruption. Many of its member companies have also keyed their philanthropy and CSR investments to the corollary UN Millennium Development Goals that include, by 2015, laudatory aims such as halving extreme poverty and hunger around the globe, reducing infant mortality by two-thirds, achieving universal primary education, empowering women, and creating global partnerships for development.

Several business leaders in attendance at BAWB had met in June 2004 at the Compact's summit meeting at UN headquarters in New York. The private sector was represented by the leaders of over two hundred fifty companies and heard from John Browne, then-CEO of British Petroleum, Bertrand Collomb, Chairman of Lafarge, and the heads of Goldman Sachs and Pfizer (from the United States), Eskom (an innovative electric company in South Africa), and Talal Abu-Ghazeleh (a conglomerate in India), plus luminaries the likes of the president of Brazil, the executive director of Oxfam, and the Secretary-General. They had assembled in the employee cafeteria of the UN because it was the only space large and flexible enough to accommodate roundtable discussions. These sessions used the appreciative methodology and were facilitated by Cooperrider.

A third sponsor was the Academy of Management. This is an association of over sixteen thousand business school faculty and graduate students from more than one hundred nations. Over the years the Academy has defined itself as a member-service organization with its academic mission being the refereed publication of theory and research that fits the traditions of what it terms "normal science." Its strategy, organization behavior, and human resource management subspecialties account for the lion's share of the members, though a modest number are in divisions concerned with social issues and the natural environment. One not-so-subtle agenda of the meeting was to get the Academy activated around corporate citizenship and BAWB.

Citizenship via "Smart Mobs"

One student in attendance, commenting on the network of diverse interests connected to citizenship personally and virtually at the conference, characterized it as a "smart mob." A brief look at some of the actors present gives a sense of the scale and contour of this mob and illustrates how indeed movement is afoot around citizenship today.

Socially Responsible Investors

Barbara Krumsiek, president and CEO of the Calvert Group, gave a profile of the field of socially responsible investing, which includes research about companies, shareholder advocacy, community investing, and social venture capital. According to recent figures, socially responsible investing in the United States grew from $639 billion to nearly $2.3 trillion the past ten years, an increase of 249 percent. This accounts for roughly 10 percent of total assets under professional management.[12] Companies like Calvert evaluate firms along several dimensions, including governance and ethics, product safety and impact, the workplace and environment, and human rights, along with the typical financial screens; they advocate for shareholders and are involved in community investing and provide social venture capital.

Think Tanks and Policy Institutes

There are today many think tanks, policy institutes, and NGOs that study, support programs, and advocate for nearly every social and environmental issue that companies face. Increasing numbers take a more integrative view and focus on corporate citizenship. At the BAWB meeting, Judy Samuelson, Executive Director of the Aspen Institute's Business and Society Program, gave an update on her group's doings. These include, since its startup in 1998, the convening of several CEO roundtables to address the role of business in society; the gathering of corporate directors of executive development and business school deans and faculty to discuss curricula, case material, and faculty preparation in this fast moving field; and the funding of several major research studies. One, reported by Professor James Walsh at the meeting, is a meta-analysis of hundreds of academic studies that affirms the generally positive relationship between CSR and a company's financial performance.[13] Samuelson's group also publishes *Beyond*

Grey Pinstripes, a biennial survey and ranking of business schools in the areas of CSR, another push for change in business education.

Student Groups

There are, in addition, innumerable student groups that organize around one or another social issue. Now they are populating the corporate citizenship space. Martin Smith, for example, co-founded in 2002 a group for students interested in a sustainable economy called StartingBloc. It now has fellows on more than three hundred campuses, runs training institutes on social innovation and related subjects, and is rapidly globalizing. At the BAWB meeting, a group representing M.B.A. students and recent graduates took center stage. Liz Maw, executive director of Net Impact, reported on a survey of her group's members. Started in 1993 by a handful of business students who wanted to promote responsible business practices, Net Impact today is a network of over ten thousand with 125 student and professional chapters on four continents in seventy-five cities and eighty graduate schools. The group's most recent survey of business students, over two thousand members and nonmembers in M.B.A. programs, found the great majority of students hungry to learn more about CSR and sustainability in their studies and committed to finding a job that is socially responsible.[14] How many students believe that business should work toward the betterment of society? Over 80 percent of the members (and 66 percent of nonmembers). How many agree business is currently working for the betterment of society? Some 18 percent of members (and 24 percent of nonmembers). The key message from her profile of students: Let me introduce what matters to tomorrow's business leaders.

Educators

Nancy Adler, professor of international management from McGill University, spoke about changes in the business school M.B.A. curricula and how corporate executives are learning about CSR and sustainability in executive development programs. Anders Aspling, of the European Foundation for Management Development (EFMD), gave an update on European trends. During both talks, faculty from several Eastern European business schools, and a new one being constructed in Moscow, were feverishly taking notes. Today business school faculty have access to case studies, instructional materials, and research reports at Web sites hosted by BAWB, the Aspen Institute, and many other groups, and can get profiles of companies on the Socrates database managed by KLD Research & Analytics, Inc. and from other research shops. Academic programs of teaching and research are multiplying on every continent.

A Tipping Point?

One of the young enthusiasts in attendance, Nadya Zhexembayeva, recorded on her blog that "a tipping point emerged for me at exactly 3:11 p.m., October 25, 2006." This was the closing ceremony of the BAWB gathering where it was announced that the Academy of Management would take up the gauntlet in its 2007 international conference theme "Doing Well by Doing Good."

That conference has, as of this writing, come and gone—successfully. But what is the evidence that the movement carries on? Certainly the Global Compact has grown. As of 2007, it had enlisted over three thousand signatory firms from all regions of the world. Its second leaders' summit, held in Geneva in July 2007 and hosted by new UN Secretary-General Ban Ki-moon, drew one thousand chief executives, government ministers, labor leaders, and civil society members and featured research presentations by Goldman Sachs and McKinsey & Co. that documented significant movement on corporate citizenship in the finance and business communities. Among the achievements of the Compact was to announce "Principles of Responsible Management Education" drafted by a global group of academics and business school deans.

Scholars who study the development of social issues note that they move through phases from an initial emergence, to expansion, to embedding themselves into public consciousness and ultimately policy.[15] We see corporate citizenship in an expanding phase and the many stakeholders behind it as a growing social movement. The BAWB gathering, its successor meetings, and now countless academic, corporate, and multisector conferences, workshops, and forums are bringing together, in tipping point terms, the mavericks, mavens, and connectors who might embed citizenship further into public consciousness.

This takes salesmen and women, too. On this count, *CRO* (Corporate Responsibility Officer) magazine estimates that in 2006 big firms in the United States spent over $30 billion on corporate responsibility services. Interestingly, over two-thirds of these monies were spent on auditing and financial reporting, business protection, and compliance—a sign of the prime emphasis on risk management in companies and an indicator of what currently "sells."

It is premature, then, to see next generation citizenship as nearing a tipping point on the world benefit or opportunity side. Research on the diffusion of new ideas shows, however, that at the leading edge of practice, innovators turn to the new because of the power of ideas and the appeal to their worldview and values, rather than because of airtight evidence or the tested example of others.[16] In testimony to this, BAWB conferees heard not only from the CSR mob, but also from business visionaries like Cescau and Collomb, thought leaders like Prahalad, Stuart Hart (green strategy), and Amory Lovins (green technology), and tough minded, honey-voiced businessman cum evangelist Ray Anderson, who, along with journalist Marc Gunther, had recently visited the bane of corporate citizenship: Wal-Mart—who, at this point, is to some extent buying in.

4

New Rules for Business Success

We had our first inkling that something was up at Wal-Mart in May 2005 when a Unilever manager, responsible for its fish business, said that he was astonished by what happened during his just-completed visit to Bentonville, Arkansas, to "take orders"—in both senses of the term. The normal routine, as he described it, was to travel to Wal-Mart headquarters, struggle to get a parking spot, go through security, get a badge, and then wait on a bench to be "called." Then you meet in a Spartan cubicle with a Wal-Mart rep, make your pitch, and more or less get told how much the world's largest retailer and grocer will buy from you—and always at a lower price than last year—all in thirty minutes or less.

This visit, by comparison, he was asked if he could spare some time to meet with several vice presidents and a corporate strategist to talk about the Marine Stewardship Council, an independent nonprofit formed originally by Unilever and the World Wildlife Federation, after the unregulated North Atlantic cod fishery collapsed in the early 1990s. The Council developed standards for sustainable fishing to avoid another collapse and today certifies fisheries that meet them. Wal-Mart, he surmised, was interested in getting into the "sustainability game." What's more, he told us in a subsequent conversation, this seemed to have something to do with Hurricane Katrina.

A Katrina Moment

In October 2005 Lee Scott, Wal-Mart's CEO, issued his vision of Twenty-First Century Leadership and wrapped it in what he described as his personal "Katrina moment":

> When Katrina hit last month, the world saw a picture of great suffering and misery. At Wal-Mart, we didn't watch it, we experienced it. Some of our stores and clubs were under water. Associates lost their savings, their homes, and, in a few cases, their lives. I spent time with a few of them in the Houston Astrodome. I saw the pain, the difficulty, and the tears. But I saw something else. I saw a company utilize its people resources and scale to make a big and positive difference in people's lives. This was Wal-Mart at its best. . . .
> Katrina asked this critical question, and I want to ask it of you: What would it take for Wal-Mart to be at its best all the time? What if we used our size and

resources to make this country and this earth an even better place for all us: customers, associates, our children, and generations unborn? What could that mean? Could we do it? Is this consistent with our business model? What if the very things that many people criticize us for—our size and reach—became a trusted friend and ally to all, just as it did in Katrina?[1]

This was a new vision for a company that is loved by many consumers but reviled by main street merchants, social activists, labor unions, and a broad spectrum of the public in the United States and around the world. A survey by GlobeScan illustrates the paradox. For seven years running, this survey house has asked people around the globe to "name a company that you believe is fulfilling its responsibilities to society better than others." Who gets the most (unprompted) citations in the United States? Wal-Mart. Then the pollsters ask who the least socially responsible company is? Wal-Mart again![2]

Mindful of this, not to mention a flat stock price and slow domestic growth, Wal-Mart preceded its visioning with a year of "fact-finding"—meetings with customers, government leaders, NGOs, academics, environmental experts, and even critics who, according to Scott, "feel business needs to change, not just our company, but all companies." "After a year of listening," he went on to say, "the time has come to speak, to better define who we are in the world, and what leadership means for Wal-Mart in the twenty-first century. Nothing brought this home more clearly than Hurricane Katrina. Katrina was a personal moment for me."

Scott spoke of many "issues" facing the company: wages, healthcare, diversity, product sourcing, and so on, and noted one of particular concern to him—the natural environment. In a clarifying statement, he made the case for change in this way: "We should view the environment as Katrina in slow motion." The environmental challenges he cited—"just to name a few"—included increasing greenhouse gases, air pollution, water pollution, and destruction of critical habitat. Then he went on to say, "I believe that being a good steward of the environment and in our communities, and being an efficient and profitable business are not mutually exclusive. In fact, they are one and the same." The sustainability goals he set out for Wal-Mart at that time were three: (1) to be supplied 100 percent by renewable energy, (2) to create zero waste, and (3) to sell products that sustain our resources and environment. And he put cash behind these commitments: $500 million as a first step and more to follow.

A Revival Meeting in Bentonville

We've seen how Unilever, with its historic and sustained commitment to social responsibility, moved into the next generation of citizenship by bringing people together who were eager to move forward with the leading trends. Wal-Mart's heritage is quite different. Sam Walton, the founder, even after becoming a billionaire, continued to travel with his gun dogs in the back of his pickup truck in the single-minded pursuit of people who would sell to him at rock bottom prices.[3] And, its attitudes are different, too. While Wal-Mart has a reputable record of giving monies to charity and promoting employee volunteerism, until Scott's change of heart it had maintained a bunker mentality in the face of complaints over its role in society. How do you open up a company of this scale? GE, IBM, and Unilever are big companies, but Wal-Mart is a behemoth with 1.9 million "associates" worldwide, over 6,700 facilities, and 176 million weekly customers and counting. Add to this over sixty thousand U.S. suppliers, another twenty thousand in China, and you can picture the challenge of getting everyone aligned. Nike, Shell, and Home Depot had tangible and urgent crises to activate their people. Wal-Mart's crisis in the CEO's eyes was moving in "slow motion." As Scott himself said it: "You won't find any case studies at the Harvard Business School highlighting answers for companies of our size and scope."

Julie Manga, a researcher and consultant from our Center, was one of fifty "guests" who joined two hundred or so specialists from sustainability groups with expertise in farming, energy use, packaging, organic cotton, seafood, and the like, and roughly five hundred Wal-Mart associates for a day of analysis, discussion, and action planning at company headquarters in March 2006. After a warm welcome by the head of Wal-Mart's People Division, an introduction to the 21st Century Leadership vision, and remarks by Jib Ellison, a strategic management consultant hired to support Wal-Mart's outreach and initiatives, the "target" for the day was established: Expand the base of support for sustainability and accelerate the pace of activities.

Then Ray Anderson, CEO of Interface, along with his associate Jim Hartsfield, led the attendees in what they call a "global village" exercise. This began with a look at the history of the earth and its ecology, covered the emergence of *Homo sapiens* and agrarian capitalism, and carried through to the Industrial Revolution and the ecological harm done by modern industry up to the present. Ray then asked the attendees what the earth would be like if industry adopted the principle to "do no harm." Citing figures on world hunger and malnutrition, he noted that Wal-Mart, as the world's leading expert in distribution, might have a role to play in these matters, too.

Anderson is a credible corporate spokesman on sustainability for several reasons.[4] One is that he is a "student" of ecology—in the best sense of the term. The story he tells is that up to age sixty, as CEO of the world's largest commercial carpet maker, "I never gave one thought to what we took from or did to the earth, except to be sure we obeyed all laws and regulations." When pressed by his research division to provide interested customers with Interface's environmental vision, he found he had nothing to say. Then a saleswoman in the company sent him Paul Hawken's 1993 book, *The Ecology of Commerce*, and he had an epiphany: "Hawken's message was a spear in my chest that remains to this day."[5]

Anderson has a gift for taking complex but important ideas and making them clear and sensible for business people. This day he talked about Hawken's critique of the "take-make-waste" logic of modern industry and its alternative, which he calls a "restorative economy." He also spoke of Hawken's writings, with Amory Lovins and Hunter Lovings, in the book *Natural Capitalism* that addresses, among other subjects, the possibility of zero industrial waste, the potential for radically increased resource productivity, and the promise of biologically inspired production processes.[6] It is worth noting that Anderson and fellow executives at Interface actually do read such books, talk over the ideas together, and share the information with their employees and even the public. The Interface Web site, for instance, has an informative section on the company's relationship to society and the environment, replete with graphic models and data-based charts. To be a credible spokesman on such matters, you simply have to know your stuff.

In addition, and especially important to the audience in Bentonville, Anderson has a success story to tell. Plus there is Ray's personal story and manner. He calls himself a "recovering plunderer." His awakening by a powerful message, his acknowledged ignorance about environmentalism and sense of shame over the take-make-waste ways of his business, and his high hopes for natural capitalism are the ingredients in the modern-day recovery-from-addiction mantra. They are also integral to the biblical message of salvation. It should not surprise, therefore, that Anderson talks about this as a journey to "Mount Sustainability." With a sunny, seasoned, southern drawl and a closing poem that speaks to "Tomorrow's Child," he transforms a business gathering, by turns, into a seminar, pep rally, and revival meeting.

From Quick Wins to Accelerating Change

We leave Anderson here but will revisit him again at later points in the book. Meanwhile, Julie Manga reports, the Wal-Mart meeting segued into an "open space" learning format where participants grouped around sixteen topics according to their interests. Subjects ranged from how to get the marketing people involved, to educating suppliers on sustainability, to stimulating store participation, reaching recycling markets, creating product scorecards, and so on. Next, the participants joined a "standing in the future" exercise and prepared to welcome Wal-Mart's top executives with a presentation or skit on the company's sustainability results circa 2015. These methodologies—breaking into small groups to discuss issues, using large group dialogue to come to a common view, and employing creative exercises to envision the future—are staples in companies looking to engage people in change.[7] They open up lines of communication about hard subjects and can stimulate imagination about otherwise technical matters. We'll see them at use, in different ways and shapes, in many companies profiled in this book. Suffice it to say here that they generated a buzz at this Wal-Mart meeting.

Five sustainability groups then presented updates on developments in global logistics, sustainable buildings, packaging, and so on. A series of "quick wins" in the works were updated: saving 5,000 trees and 1,300 barrels of oil by reducing the size of cardboard packaging on a Wal-Mart brand toy; saving $26 million a year in fuel costs by installing units in trucks to keep the driver's cabin heated or cooled without running the engine; and saving $28 million by recycling and selling plastics that used to be thrown away in the stores.[8]

The meeting ended on a high note. But here's the topper: Four months later former U.S. Vice President Al Gore brought his film *An Inconvenient Truth* to Bentonville and received a standing ovation. Gore responded to the cheers: "Doesn't it feel good to have this kind of commitment? Don't you feel proud?" Now, you might ask, what is the *real* story here?

Story 1: Reactive and Defensive

One story about this, a familiar one when a business faces bad publicity, is that Wal-Mart has been on the defensive and countered with a public relations campaign. Certainly, the company has been under attack by community groups for many years for driving small retailers and main street merchants out of business with its superstores, buying power, and discount prices. But since the mid-1990s the criticism has escalated, focused on skinflint wage rates that keep many associates' earnings below the poverty line in the United States, meager healthcare coverage, and cases of gender discrimination in pay and promotions. On the Q.T., you also hear tales of the company's heavy-handed dealings with suppliers and secrecy bordering on paranoia.

In addition, there have been countless critical academic studies of the company, public television features that ask "Is Wal-Mart Good for America?" and scathing documentaries such as "Wal-Mart: The High Cost of Low Price."[9] Want to tap into some of this? Just type in "anti Wal-Mart" in your Web browser and millions of hits appear that range from the encyclopedic wal-martwatch.com to corporate hate sites like hel-mart.com. Hate Wal-Mart? That entry gets you to a cornucopia of personal stories, songs, YouTube videos, and blogs plus some poetry.

Needless to say, there has been a lot of counter-communication from Wal-Mart that touts its founding mission of bringing whole categories of urban, middleclass goods to rural and poor America, its positive impact on retail prices and the national economy, its many charitable efforts, and now its early successes with sustainability. A company that hitherto "hit the sandbags" in the face of criticism decided to "come out fighting" with a political-style PR campaign, pitched as "Candidate Wal-Mart" by operatives of The Edelman Group, that stresses the company's commitment to "working families" and, among other things, arranged for Gore to visit and set up the revival meeting that we attended.[10]

Critics of the PR point out, however, that Wal-Mart slants findings from academic studies—chiefly on its economic and ecological impact—to present a rosy rather than realistic picture of its operations and has disguised its financial support and involvement in pro–Wal-Mart documentaries, Internet blogs, media events, and consumer campaigns.[11] Many recall, too, how Wal-Mart's "Buy American" campaign during the recession in the mid-1980s was short-lived and, according to several domestic suppliers, was used as a "negotiating club" to reduce their prices and, in a cruel twist, force them to exit from manufacturing and source their goods from overseas. Given this track record, it is not surprising that they view Wal-Mart's new agenda as an example of greenwashing.

Should the defensiveness and public relations efforts surprise? Not at all. We earlier noted GE's similar response to PCB pollution and to the primacy given to PR whenever corporations are under criticism and pressed to do better on the environmental and social front. Has Wal-Mart got something more going on than this?

Story 2: Responsive and Innovative

A second story is that Wal-Mart gets it. Poll after poll shows that the public expects corporations to "exceed the law" when it comes to the natural environment—not only in the United States, Europe, and Japan but also throughout Asia, Latin America, and even Africa.[12] Very few support economic development at the expense of the environment, and big companies especially are expected to apply the same environmental standards to their operations in the developing world as they do at home. What is more, our national surveys show North American managers understand these public expectations and subscribe to them. Wal-Mart, too, seems to understand the message. It came home to them directly when a McKinsey Global study found "that up to 8 percent of shoppers had stopped patronizing the chain because of its reputation."

In the year before Scott's call for Twenty-First-Century Leadership, Wal-Mart studied up on what we see as a new set of rules for doing business. 3M, a company we have worked with in the Global Leadership Network, understood these new rules for the environment over thirty years ago when it launched its 3P— Pollution Prevention Pays—program with nineteen projects under the guidance of Dr. Joseph Ling. Today it uses life cycle tools to track, manage, and reduce its use of natural resources, chemicals, energy, and manufactured materials at every step of its manufacturing process through to the end use by businesses and consumers. DuPont had its awakening in 1989 when a new CEO, Edgar Woolard, declared that the company would move from simply complying with environmental laws toward winning the public's trust. This put the company on the path to sustainability some fifteen years ago. Wal-Mart, by comparison, is a latecomer.

But Wal-Mart is following a familiar script. Companies at this stage wake up to the idea that they are responsible to stakeholders, not just shareholders, and reach out to them as Wal-Mart did in its listening campaign and continues to do in meetings throughout the world. They often go outside normal channels to bring in new voices and subject matter experts to educate themselves on new dynamics and how to respond to them. Wal-Mart brought in Peter Seligman, co-founder and CEO of Conservation International, along with his partner Glenn Pritchett, as well as Jib Ellison at Blu Skye Sustainability Consulting and Chris Laszlo of Sustainable Value Partners. They educated Scott and others in Wal-Mart about the innovations of Starbucks on Fair Trade coffee and those of Unilever on sustainable agriculture and fishing. It helped, no doubt, that Rob Walton, son of founder Sam, was a friend of Seligman and had a strong owner's interest in the company's environmental record.

Story 3: Transformative?

As of this writing, Wal-Mart is expanding its action projects and has achieved some quick wins. The company has, for example, conducted experiments using LED lighting in its freezer cases, burning used cooking and motor oil for fuel, and watering its landscape plants with drip irrigation. In early 2007, in Kansas City, it opened its first energy-efficient and environmentally-designed super-store. On the retail side, Wal-Mart committed to sell one hundred million energy-saving light bulbs (from GE), signed deals to use corn-based plastic in its food wrapping (saving an estimated eight hundred thousand gallons of gasoline and preventing eleven million pounds of greenhouse gas), and pledged to reduce its packaging by 5 percent in 2008 through adoption of a "packaging scorecard" by its suppliers. It also announced its Sustainability 360 strategy—Doing Good, Better, Together—that has it also exploring ethical consumerism, fair trade, and cause marketing. Meanwhile eco-innovations continue to emerge from what are now fourteen sustainability networks in the company.[13]

Arguably, Wal-Mart continues to make a substantial contribution to the world economy and consumers' lives with its founding business mission. Its $4-per-prescription program in the United States, with caveats about the number and kinds of drugs it covers, is significant. Recent commitments to source organic cotton and sustainable seafood will also reverberate through global supply chains, affect international economies and ecologies, and likely resonate with consumers. As important as these efforts might be for the company and for the planet—given Wal-Mart's scale—they do not address the many other issues, like employee wages and healthcare coverage, or the much larger questions of global social and environmental sustainability that intersect in Wal-Mart's world.

For example, Wal-Mart, like many global companies, has pledged not to pur-chase goods produced from "sweatshop" labor. This means that the suppliers must at least comply with the host country's minimum wage, work hours, and work conditions standards. Yet a late-2006 *Business Week* survey of factory prac-tices in China revealed widespread cheating and fraud.[14] Several suppliers kept two sets of employment records—one neat-and-tidy set for inspection by Wal-Mart and another set used internally for payroll purposes that revealed countless violations. There is even a mini-industry in China of what are called "corporate responsibility management and consulting companies" that will, for a hand-some fee, falsify the books and coach managers and employees on how to lie about workplace practices should they be queried by multinational's compli-ance auditors.

How about the move toward sustainable seafood? In a compelling account in *The Wal-Mart Effect*, journalist Charles Fishman tells the story of how the com-pany can sell Atlantic salmon fillets at $4.84 a pound, one-quarter the price twenty years ago.[15] His story leads to the Chilean coastline where industrial fish farming has been an economic boon and threatens environmental calamity. The problem, Fishman told us in a recent conversation, is "fish feces." Tens of mil-lions of salmon living in pens and producing tons and tons of waste are creating dead zones along the coastline where ocean plants are dying along with other aquatic life. Meanwhile, workers in the fish factories earn meager wages and operate in miserable and unsafe working conditions.

Now Wal-Mart, sourcing $750 million in seafood in 2006, has pledged to purchase wild-caught fish for its North American markets through Marine Stewardship Council-certified fisheries. As for farmed fish, like that coming from Chile, nothing much has been said. But imagine if Wal-Mart, perhaps in partnership with national governments, took a leadership role in tackling the problem of fish stocks in the world. Or applied its newfound commitment to sustainability to the full range of agricultural produce and products it sells. Or applied the same eco-efficiency and sustainable sourcing standards to its non-North American stores. As of now, Wal-Mart is only taking baby steps in this long march.

What about Katrina?

Katrina was not only a symbolic wake-up call for Wal-Mart, but maybe for the United States as a whole. On the one hand, it showed the comparative ineffectiveness of government—at the local, state, and national level—to protect its citizens from natural disasters and care for them in the aftermath. Newspapers told us of repeated warnings that the levees of New Orleans were at risk and described how monies made available to fix them were diverted by politicians to river navigation rather than flood protection. The utter incompetence of Federal Emergency Management Agency leaders before, during, and after the hurricane is well known as is the continuing inability of state, local, and national leaders to figure out what to do about rebuilding the city. [16] Many see this as a message of our times: Government hasn't got the capability to solve the nation's problems.

Meanwhile, big business was at its best: opening its wallets, using its expertise in logistics, transport, communications, and human resource management to provide relief, and not only taking care of its own employees in the delta but enlisting them from around the country in voluntary service to the region. This was the largest response to a disaster by the U.S. business community in history. And it followed its unprecedented generosity after the Asian tsunami and 9/11 devastation.[17]

Big as this contribution to society is, it is but a footnote in the larger business success story. The past twenty-five years have been a business era in the United States. The best and brightest college graduates head into business. Today it is the top college major by far. And M.B.A. enrollment has skyrocketed. What is more, U.S.-style business is seen as the model for the world. India, after forty years of state-industry and protectionism, has turned to Western capitalism, and China, while not open to democracy, has certainly adopted the U.S. business model. Whole industries—electricity, oil and gas, healthcare, even education—are being privatized in other parts of the D&E world. Suffice it to say, business is increasingly the lead sector throughout the world and certainly the role model for how to get things done.

Now Katrina was, according to many scientists, an environmental phenomenon. The storm, to some expert eyes, as well as Al Gore's, was part of the "weird weather" pattern observed around the world the past decade that is indicative of global warming. It was also a social phenomenon. Recall that after Katrina *Time* magazine did a cover story on the sordid problems of poverty in New Orleans and a longer, more detailed one on poverty around the world.[18] Jeffrey Sachs's book, *The End of Poverty*, was also a cover story and best seller.[19] Now many in business will say that business is the solution to poverty: jobs, goods, profits, and taxes. But the evidence is that income distribution gaps are widening—domestically and globally—and poverty is getting worse.[20] And, as you likely know, four billion people earn less than two dollars a day around the world and one billion children go to sleep hungry. What does all this have to do with business?

A growing set of interests—leaders in business, government and NGOs, journalists, growing numbers of business students and their faculty, and many, many others—have a view on this. It may be wrapped in aspirations of business for world benefit, the logic of social and environmental sustainability, or expressed simply as next generation corporate citizenship. The message is in either case straightforward: business cannot succeed if society fails.

The Global Context and Commerce

We have listed some of the benefits and costs of business globalizing, seen glimpses of the new business landscape through CEOs' eyes, and sampled the worlds of Unilever and Wal-Mart. The many issues at the intersection of business and society can be subsumed under four larger mega-trends:

- The spread of democratic market capitalism throughout the world based in the expectation that it will accelerate the delivery of prosperity, health, and security;
- The globalization of commerce that has enabled giant multinationals to emerge and prosper;
- The gap between rich and poor—in the United States and on a global scale—growing; and
- The emergence of climate change and environmental sustainability as two of the most significant challenges facing humankind.

These trends are inarguably consequential for business: market liberalization has also allowed national government oversight and services to decline, leaving many to expect business to answer to the public's interest. Global economic growth, for all of its touted benefits, isn't working for the good of all and risks creating a backlash against global businesses. Conflicts, wars, disease, and environmental damage all follow from and contribute to mass poverty in a vicious cycle. The resulting global instability, in turn, depresses economic growth. And, when it comes to the health of the natural world, the public is blaming business for our collective folly and is also looking for its leadership to save the planet.

New Rules for Twenty-first-century Business

There is a set of "old rules" for companies for dealing with society, rules that are clear, simple, but antiquated. They say don't get distracted by societal considerations because they could harm the business and destroy shareholder value. They tell companies to identify what they need from governments and communities in order to compete and to lobby hard to get the legislation, tax breaks, and other support they want. They tell companies to keep a stable of high-priced PR pros and lawyers close by in case something goes awry and the company is tried in the courts of law, public opinion, or the press. And finally the old rules say that companies should continuously show their soft side by writing checks for charity and sending volunteers to demonstrate how much they care for communities—and leave it at that.

Meanwhile, a parallel set of old rules for running the business by, say, cutting costs to the bone, growing with scant attention to the environmental and societal consequences, and running the firm solely for the benefit of its shareholders has gone unquestioned.

Many of the business-and-society trends identified by the CEOs we studied—and experienced by Unilever and Wal-Mart—are neither transitory nor escapable. The mega-trends pressure all companies to do business differently. Visionary leaders realize that sitting on the sidelines or playing the role of skeptic diverts attention from engaging with possible threats and opportunities. Demanding that someone give them a "business case" for each and every

---

Figure 4.1
Ten Precepts for 21st Century Business

1. Compliance is not enough

2. Size invites scrutiny

3. Transparency is a requirement

4. Cutting costs can raise risks

5. Reducing risks means engaging society

6. Stakeholders are a link to society

7. Society's needs are growth opportunities

8. Global growth requires global gains

9. Sustainable corporations need sustainable societies

10. Society needs business, NGOs, and government

initiative that their companies take is unresponsive and unproductive. Instead, these kinds of leaders are educating themselves on the issues, getting their people informed en masse, and refashioning their businesses for the twenty-first century to adopt new rules about doing business *in relationship* to society. These new rules include the following ten precepts (see Figure 4.1):

1. Compliance is not enough.

The wake of the corporate scandals in the United States has left business there with new regulations and externally mandated controls and governance requirements. But merely complying with national laws is not enough for twenty-first-century companies. GE's "spirit and letter" code of conduct addresses everything from fair employment practices and environment, health, and safety matters to financial dealings and supplier relationships. GE CEO Jeffrey Immelt sums up its impact: "We export the highest standards in the world any time we globalize." To back this up, GE has made compliance a core operating process.

2. Size invites scrutiny.

Look at how Wal-Mart's market power invites worldwide scrutiny and widespread activism. The bigger you get, the more market dominance you achieve, the more attention and demands you face for exemplary performance in ethical behavior, good governance, environmental management, employee practices, product enhancement, honest marketing, support for communities, and the like. Indeed, Nike was targeted by critical NGOs over supply-chain lapses largely because it was the market leader. Size also calls for more responsibility. As one CEO we interviewed said, "If you're the big kid in the room and you don't act like the big kid, you're going to break something."

3. Transparency is a requirement.

Today, a section of the company's Web site on "Wal-Mart facts" provides at least some measure of transparency from a company that hitherto never responded to requests for information and prided itself on its secrecy. This is all part of the transition, also observed by Shell amidst its social and environmental crises, from a "tell me" to "show me" world where skepticism is the norm and cynicism is to be expected. Social reporting is only one example of transparency in action. Don Tapscott and David Ticoll have documented how companies, NGOs, government officials, academics, and other interested parties keep an eye on one another through their "many-to-many" transparency networks.[21] The lesson is simply: Business can no longer operate in the shadows; assume you are in sunlight.

4. Cutting costs can raise risks.

It is well established that CEOs can build the confidence of Wall Street by aggressively cutting costs. However, the more companies rely on traditional means to cut costs—using low-wage producers in less developed countries, keeping health benefits to a minimum, squeezing suppliers, laying off higher paid older workers, and cutting corners in raw materials, ingredients, handling, transport, and such—they do so at increasing risk. Two dozen U.S. states are contemplating legislation that would force Wal-Mart to provide better health benefits and the retailer has been denied access to several urban markets. Experts say that cost-cutting was behind the refinery accident and pipeline breakdown that has robbed British Petroleum of its responsible reputation.[22] What savings companies gain from shortsighted cost cutting can pale in comparison to the expense of reputational damage, litigation, boycotts, market closures, and legislation. Cost cutting in the twenty-first century needs to be considered in relationship to society's changing expectations for employee welfare, product safety, the natural environment, and ethical dealings with stakeholders of all types.

5. Reducing risks means engaging society.

It's conventional wisdom that citizenship can help a company's "license to operate." It builds goodwill and helps to counter opposition that might constrain a company's ability to do business. But firms are well advised to follow the example of Wal-Mart and crawl out of the bunker when facing opposition, conduct a broad scan of trends in society, and not only talk to but learn from critics.

6. Stakeholders are a link to society.

There is a corollary new rule: In the long run, the company that pays attention to the business-society relationship ultimately serves its investors' interests because (1) its antennae are better tuned to identifying risk; (2) it is better positioned to build trust with its stakeholders; and (3) it just might learn about new kinds of new goods and services society will value.

7. Society's needs are growth opportunities.

For forward-thinking companies, social and environmental problems represent the growth opportunities of the future. Consider how GE is looking to solve challenges related to the scarcity of global natural resources and how Unilever is dealing with the threat of obesity and the preference for healthier eating and lifestyles. There are countless other examples of firms tapping underserved markets in U.S. inner cities and among racial and ethnic groups and new business models being developed to reach the bottom of the pyramid in the developing world. In addition, there are in the United States an estimated fifty million people, representing over $225 billion a year in purchasing power, in the growing "lifestyles of health and sustainability" (LOHAS) consumer base. That market is expected to increase to $420 billion by 2010 and to $845 billion by 2015 [23]

8. Global growth requires global gains.

At its root, growth requires strong communities to supply infrastructure, maintain stable business climates, attract investment capital, supply healthy, educated workers, and generate consumers with greater purchasing power. Leaders in the twenty-first century will be at the forefront of finding innovative ways to promote equitable growth. Unilever, testing its own commitment to corporate responsibility, partnered with its longtime critic, the NGO Oxfam, to assess the socioeconomic impact of its business in Indonesia.[24] The report showed that a significant majority of the cash value generated by the company remains in Indonesia in the form of taxes, wages, contract payments, and contributions. At the same time, it highlighted the vulnerability of small farmers and shopkeepers at the farthest ends of the value chain. The movement toward fair trade is one step toward including them in global commerce. There are plenty of other ideas in motion, ranging from microlending to efforts to bridge the digital divide.

9. Sustainable corporations need sustainable societies.

Coke, Pepsi, and even P&G have, in recent years, been forced to cease operations in India over water use. Their growth in arid China is constrained for the same reason. No wonder environmental sustainability is moving to the top of the corporate and societal agenda. Within five years, it is estimated that phone and calling costs will drop enough to permit another three billion people to have access to a mobile phone.[25] Visionaries like Nokia realize that they need to prepare themselves and first-time consumers in their markets for a new era of connectivity. Auto safety is another social issue worthy of attention. The World Health Organization predicts that by 2020 more people will die from auto accidents than from HIV.[26] To continue to grow sustainably, automakers such as General Motors and Toyota, and oil companies like Shell are taking leadership in enhancing road safety around the world.

10. Society needs business, NGOs, and government.

No one is suggesting that business alone can solve the world's problems or should even take a leadership role in addressing many of them. Rather, the twenty-first-century model is for business, government, and civil society, including NGOs and communities, to partner together. Business–NGO partnerships are the "best practice" model for delivering real value through corporate philanthropy. The "next practice" is for them to partner together in socio-commercial ventures. At Unilever, for instance, we identified nearly twenty global and over one thousand country-based or local partnerships. There will also be new multi-business associations and multisectoral forums to address issues of global scale and import. The World Economic Forum, the World Business Council for Sustainable Development, and the UN Global Compact are harbingers of alliances to come.

Companies that understand and embrace these principles, or variations of them, will constitute the next generation corporate citizens. This could put a new spin on a timeworn slogan: Tomorrow the business of business will be global citizenship.

Stages of Corporate Citizenship

Unilever is ahead of the curve with its citizenship agenda and Wal-Mart has finally gotten into the action. What's happening in a broad sampling of companies? Our biennial surveys of U.S. business leaders find that some 80 percent believe that citizenship needs to be a priority for companies and a large majority (69 percent) agree that the public has a right to expect it. So what are they doing about it?

Some are revising their codes of conduct, adopting sustainable environmental practices, and updating their community programs; others are forming citizenship steering committees, measuring their environmental and social performance, and issuing public reports. Select firms are striving to integrate staff functions responsible for different CSR-type issues and are moving responsibility—and accountability—into lines of business. And a vanguard is trying to create a broader market for citizenship and offer products and services that aim explicitly to both make money and make a better world.

What accounts for these differences? The Center's studies suggest that how a company configures its relationship with society depends on what stage the firm is in relative to its development of citizenship. Comparative neophytes often lack an understanding of their many different connections to society and have neither the expertise nor the machinery to respond to the diverse interests and demands they encounter. Their chief challenges are to put citizenship firmly on the corporate agenda, get better informed about stakeholders' concerns, and take some sensible initial steps. At the other extreme are companies that have already made a significant investment in this area. Their CEO is typically leading the firm's stand on social issues, and their board is fully informed about and oversees company practices. Should these firms want to move forward, they might next try to connect citizenship to corporate branding and everyday employees through a "live the brand" campaign like those at IBM and Novo Nordisk, or establish citizenship objectives for line managers, as DuPont and UBS have done.

To understand the differences in the way companies view and activate citizenship, you have to look at what a firm has accomplished to date and how far it wants to (and has to) go. The Center's surveys of a random sample of American businesses find that a handful of companies don't seem to have a clue as to what citizenship is all about. On the other end of the spectrum, another handful of them are fully integrating citizenship into their businesses and setting new standards of performance. Among the great majority in between, there is a wide range of firms in transition whose knowledge, approach, and practices represent different degrees of understanding and sophistication about corporate citizenship.

Stages of Development

What does it mean that a company is at a "stage" of corporate citizenship development? The general idea, found in the study of children, groups, and social systems of all types, is that there are distinct patterns of activity at different points of development. Typically, these activities become more complex and elaborate as development progresses.[1] In his groundbreaking study, University of Southern California professor Larry Greiner found that companies also develop more complex ways of doing things at different stages of their growth.[2] In his framework, the development of an enterprise is punctuated by a series of predictable challenges that demand ever more sophisticated responses that enable a company to move forward. The triggering mechanisms are tensions between current practices and the problems they produce that demand a new response from a firm. For instance, creativity—the entrepreneurial fire in companies—also generates confusion and a loss of focus that can stall growth. This confusion poses a "crisis of leadership" that requires more direction, often through formal structure and new leadership, for a new stage of orderly growth to emerge. In time, however, formal structure can produce bureaucratic silos and prompt cross-functional conflicts. These, in turn, produce a "crisis of control" and generate moves toward more coordination—and so on as firms grow. In development terminology, companies in effect "master" these challenges by devising progressively "smarter" responses to them.

Development of Citizenship

There are a number of models of stages of corporate citizenship.[3] On a macro scale, for example, scholars have tracked changing conceptions of the role of business in society and have documented how more elaborate and inclusive definitions of social responsibility, environmental protection, and corporate ethics and governance have developed over recent decades. In a pioneering study some years ago, James Post and Barbara Altman showed how environmental policies progressively broaden and deepen as companies encounter more demanding expectations and build their capability to meet them. More recently, Simon Zadek's case study of Nike's response to challenges in its supply chain highlights a series of stages in the development of citizenship attitudes and practices in companies.

Our research has considered the generative logic and mechanisms that drive the development of citizenship within companies. We consider the development of citizenship as a stage-by-stage process in which a combination of internal capabilities applied to social and environmental challenges propels development forward in a more or less normal or normative path. Here, too, the triggers for movement are internal and external challenges that call for a fresh response.

These challenges, as we shall see, initially center on a firm's *credibility* as a corporate citizen, then on its *capacities* to meet expectations, followed by the *coherence* of its many subsequent efforts, and finally, its *commitment* to institutionalize citizenship in its business strategies and culture.

There are, naturally, many dimensions to development. In the case of people, for instance, there are different physical, intellectual, emotional, and social dimensions to consider. In our field, key dimensions include (1) a company's concept of citizenship and what it encompasses; (2) what a firm wants to accomplish with citizenship or its strategic intent; (3) to what extent top executives are

---

Figure 5.1
Dimensions of Citizenship

1. Citizenship Concept: How is citizenship defined? How comprehensive?
Definitions of corporate citizenship are many and varied. From a developmental perspective, our interest is in to what extent a company has a broad and inclusive picture of its role in society, not what it calls its overall citizenship thrust.

2. Strategic Intent: What is the purpose of citizenship in a company?
Few companies have a strictly moral commitment to citizenship; many see it also as a part of their corporate strategy. Regardless of the terms or frameworks used, we focus on to what extent citizenship is embedded in a company's business plans, products and services, and culture and ways of doing business.

3. Leadership: Do top leaders support citizenship? Do they lead the effort?
Visible, active, top level leadership appears on every industry and executives survey as the top factor driving citizenship in a corporation. This third dimension addresses how well informed top leaders are about citizenship, how much leadership they exercise, and to what extent they "walk the talk."

4. Structure: How are responsibilities for citizenship managed?
This dimension concerns the management of citizenship throughout an enterprise. We look at this in developmental terms as movement of citizenship from a marginal position to its management as a mainstream business activity.

5. Issues Management: How does a company deal with issues that arise?
There are myriad social, ethical, and environmental issues that impinge on businesses. Here we consider how pro-active a company is when engaging these issues and how responsive it is in terms of policies, programs, and performance.

6. Stakeholder Relationships: How does a company engage its stakeholders?
A wide range of trends, from increased social activism by shareholders to an exponential increase in the number of NGOs, has driven wholesale changes in the ways companies communicate with and engage their stakeholders. Here we look at this development in terms of the increasing openness and depth of such relationships.

7. Transparency: How open is a company about its financial, social, and environmental performance?
From a developmental perspective, our interest is in when and how companies adopt transparent practices and how much information they disclose.

showing leadership in this area; (4) how a firm is organized to manage citizenship; (5) how it deals with social and environmental issues; (6) how it relates to stakeholders; and (7) how open and transparent the company is in these regards (Figure 5.1).

The stages of development we posit—from elementary to engaged, innovative, integrated, and then to transformative—emphasize continuous organizational learning (Figure 5.2). At each stage, the way companies think about their responsibilities and understand citizenship becomes more complex, the action requirements are more demanding, and the organizational structures, processes, and systems used to manage citizenship are more elaborate and comprehensive. It is important to acknowledge, however, that in models of this type, as opposed to biological or life-cycle frameworks, movement along a single development path is not fixed nor is attaining a penultimate "end state" a logical conclusion. This means that the arc of citizenship within any particular firm is shaped by the specific socioeconomic, competitive, and institutional forces impinging on the enterprise. Nevertheless, companies have choices on how they enact this environment and thus traditions, values, and leaders' outlooks all inform decisions about how citizenship develops in a firm. That's the theory anyway. What does it look like in practice?

	Stage 1: Elementary	Stage 2: Engaged	Stage 3: Innovative	Stage 4: Integrated	Stage 5: Transforming
Citizenship Concept	Jobs, Profits & Taxes	Philanthropy, Environmental Protection	Stakeholder Management	Sustainability or Triple Bottom Line	Change the Game
Strategic Intent	Legal Compliance	License to Operate	Business Case	Value Proposition	Market Creation or Social Change
Leadership	Lip Service, Out of Touch	Supporter, In the Loop	Steward, On Top of It	Champion, In Front of It	Visionary, Ahead of the Pack
Structure	Marginal: Staff Driven	Functional Ownership	Cross-Functional Coordination	Organizational Alignment	Mainstream, Business Driven
Issues Management	Defensive	Reactive, Policies	Responsive, Programs	Pro-Active, Systems	Defining
Stakeholder Relationships	Unilateral	Interactive	Mutual Influence	Partnership, Alliances	Multi-Organization
Transparency	Flank Protection	Public Relations	Public Reporting	Assurance	Full Disclosure

Figure 5.2
Stages of Corporate of Citizenship

Stage 1: Elementary

Citizenship Concept: Jobs, profits, and taxes
Strategic Intent: Compliance
Leadership: Lip service; out of touch
Structure: Marginal; staff driven
Issues Management: Defensiveness
Stakeholder Relationships: Unilateral
Transparency: Flank protection

In this base stage, attention to citizenship is episodic and a company's social and environmental programs are undeveloped. The reasons are straightforward: scant awareness of what corporate citizenship is all about, uninterested or indifferent top management, and limited or one-way interactions with external stakeholders, particularly in the social and environmental sectors.

The mindset in these companies, reflected in policies and practices, often centers narrowly on compliance with laws and industry standards. Responsibilities for handling matters of compliance are usually assigned to the functional heads of departments such as legal, human resources, investor relations, public relations, and community affairs. The job of these functional managers is to make sure that the company obeys the law and to keep problems that arise from harming the firm's reputation. In many cases, they take a defensive stance toward outside pressures. In the early 1990s, Nike exemplified this stage in its dealings with labor activists.

Still, it is not fair to label leaders of companies at this stage as backward or to see their citizenship efforts as necessarily suspect. Some corporate leaders, for example, have taken a stand—à la economist Milton Friedman—that their company's obligations to society are solely to "make a profit, pay taxes, and provide jobs." In a provocative interpretation of Friedman's message, Cypress Semiconductor's CEO T. J. Rodgers argues that firms contribute far more to society by maximizing long-term shareholder value than by catering to stakeholders—a term he notes is "often used by collectivists to justify unreasonable demands." He goes on to argue that CSR-type programs reflect the philosophy of Karl Marx rather than free market capitalism.[4]

Needless to say, many other business leaders don't have as strong an ideological position but nevertheless stick to the conventional business-of-business-is-business thinking. Our surveys find this attitude most prevalent in small to midsize firms that seem to equate citizenship with complying with employment and health, safety, and environmental regulations and making some charitable contributions but have neither the resources nor the wherewithal to do much more for their employees, communities, or society writ large.

We used former GE CEO Jack Welch to illustrate why some big businesses lag in citizenship: It is simply not a corporate priority. But things changed dramatically at GE when Jeffrey Immelt took over. As an industry peer CEO described the makeover to us, "I think Immelt has done a remarkable job in a short period of time of turning GE's perception ... from the polluter of the Hudson River ...

to one which is in the lead on the environment." As a result of this and other measures, GE has gained credibility as a corporate citizen.

Challenge: Gain Credibility

It's clear that society expects more from companies today—particularly larger businesses. A survey of public opinion found that just one in ten adults subscribes to Friedman's narrow view of corporate responsibilities. Contrariwise, a follow-up poll found over 80 percent agrees that "larger companies should do more than give money to solve social problems."[5]

These prevailing expectations challenge a firm at this basic stage of citizenship. The cases of Nike and Shell in the 1990s illustrate how mere compliance with legal and industry standards threatens the credibility of a company when it proves unable or unwilling to respond to new expectations and do more than regulations or norms require. Such challenges are most potent when, as in these cases, they take the form of a crisis and threaten a firm's reputation or competitive status.

Interestingly, most U.S. business leaders today understand these changing expectations and have taken steps to further develop a citizenship agenda. The Center's survey of business leaders, for example, finds that 75 percent believe that the public expects them to exceed laws to make sure products are reliable and safe, and 58 percent believe that the public expects them to exceed laws to protect the environment. More broadly, over half agree that the public expects them to be involved in solving problems in society. Such awareness, inside of a company, evidences a developmental "readiness" to make the transition from a basic law-abiding stance to initial engagement with broader realms of corporate citizenship.

Stage 2: Engaged

Citizenship Concept: Philanthropy, environmental protection
Strategic Intent: License to operate
Leadership: Supporter, in the loop
Structure: Functional ownership
Issues Management: Reactive, policies
Stakeholder Relationships: Interactive
Transparency: Public relations

At this second stage, top managers often wake up to what is involved and adopt a new outlook on their company's role in society. We have noted how DuPont had this awakening in 1989 when the company declared it would move beyond complying with environmental laws to setting new standards. Chiquita, a late riser by comparison, got its wakeup call in 1998 from outside the firm when it was attacked by the media and NGOs protesting the firm's woeful employment practices in Central and South America. The company subsequently interviewed hundreds of employees, revised its statement of core values, and adopted a new code of conduct that articulated the firm's social responsibilities.

There are a number of signs that mark a company's transition to engagement with corporate citizenship. Zadek points out that companies at this stage often adopt a "policy-based approach" to mitigate the likelihood of litigation and risks to reputation. We have observed that policies are typically drafted that call on the firm to exceed the law with respect to employment and health, safety, and environmental practices. Furthermore, social issues begin to be studied and gain more visibility and attention within the firm. Top leaders, who may have been out of touch with these matters, also begin to take an interest and monitor what is going on. Staff units, formerly left to their own devices, are typically tasked with owning corporate-wide policies and performing to higher standards. The leaders of these functions are expected to become better informed about developments in their industry and among their competitors.

Still, companies at this developmental stage tend to be reactive to emerging social and environmental issues—as was the case with Chiquita, Nestlé (regarding infant formula), and certainly Wal-Mart. A firsthand account of the Shell Group's response to such issues in the mid-1990s illustrates what can happen when companies don't anticipate the full range of risks in their environment.

One member of our team began working with Royal Dutch Shell in 1995 when a crisis erupted over the proposed sinking of an obsolete—and contaminated—oil storage platform, the Brent Spar, in the North Sea.[6] Greenpeace, the environmental activist NGO, opposed the plan, sailed to the rig, and briefly occupied it. The media had scant interest in Shell's nuanced position papers on the economic and environmental tradeoffs behind the dumping plan. Video of Shell repelling the Greenpeace ship, the *Moby Dick*, and its sailors with water canons was the lead story. The uproar over the Spar was a loud and urgent wakeup call for the Shell Group, made doubly so by the arrest, only days afterward, of Nigerian author and environmental activist Ken Saro-Wiwe. In this instance, Shell had asked the host government to protect its facilities in the Niger Delta and so the police arrested Saro-Wiwe, a strong voice of resistance among the Ogoni people to Shell's pollution and colonial-like exploitation of the region. His subsequent conviction in a show trial and grim execution are stark reminders of what can happen when companies get it wrong.

The Group's scenario-planning process had not anticipated such threats; and its then-current Business Principles were woefully inadequate to guide a response to the issues. In the midst of the turmoil, Shell therefore created a crisis management group of all relevant interests in the company to address the immediate issues. Later, a cross-functional, multibusiness team was formed to study the larger questions of Shell's role in society, engage external stakeholders, and set new socially and environmentally responsible business principles. The strategic intent of their efforts, characteristic of this early stage of citizenship, was to protect Shell's reputation and preserve the company's license to operate around the globe.

Shell relied on its capable internal staff and select outside experts to build its citizenship capacities. In most other companies at this stage of early engagement, an army of outside professionals or consultants with specialized knowledge and experience must be brought in to upgrade functional know-how and get things moving. These experts might introduce new concepts and performance standards that enable a firm to better protect human rights in overseas operations, gain ISO 14000 certification for eco-friendly technologies, ensure transparency in financial disclosures, or become a more family-friendly employer.

Throughout this evolutionary stage, many companies begin to undertake more extended, two-way communication with stakeholders—talking with, rather than just at, community groups, socially responsible investment bodies, and a variety of NGOs. Employees may gain input on human resource practices overall or on special issues involving, say, the needs of working parents, ethnic minorities, or gays.

Challenge: Build Capacity

Throughout this stage, however, staff units are often overwhelmed by engagements with stakeholders and seldom equipped to respond to new issues, opportunities, and threats. This gap, in turn, is a trigger for a period of innovation where senior executives become more deeply involved, corporate staff launches more programs, and firms reach out to stakeholders and become more open about their doings. A company simply needs more capacity to address the spectrum of new and varied interests.

In the years following its twin crises, for instance, Shell began to gain traction. In 1998, it devised a sustainable development-management framework that addressed four key subjects: economic development, wealth creation, climate change, and engagement with society. It also established a council of key staff and line executives to oversee its implementation. Shell was also one of the first large, public companies to issue a report on its social and environmental performance.

It is when companies broaden their knowledge of and capacities to manage citizenship that they are poised to move into a stage of innovation. But there's a cautionary note here, too. Shell's efforts to strengthen its social and environmental capabilities were not matched by developments in transparency and ethics. Knowing misstatements of its oil reserves and failings in environmental reparation in Nigeria have since harmed Shell's reputation and license to operate. This echoes a theme throughout this book that expectations of transparency and accountability from corporations are expanding dramatically and thus, that it takes vigilance and diligence on many fronts to operate responsibly. As of this writing, both British Petroleum and Chiquita, excelling in some aspects of corporate citizenship, have fallen down badly in others.

Stage 3: Innovative

Citizenship Concept: Stakeholder management
Strategic Intent: Business case
Leadership: Steward, on top of it

Structure: Cross-functional coordination
Issues Management: Responsive, programs
Stakeholder Relationships: Mutual influence
Transparency: Public reporting

One company that progressed into an innovative stage of citizenship early on is Baxter, a pharmaceutical company. The company piloted what would become the Global Reporting Initiative in the early 1990s and began to measure and report on its economic, environmental, and social performance. In 1997, it became one of the first adopters of the CERES (Coalition for Environmentally Responsible Economies) principles to report on and improve its environmental performance. In the process, the company embraced the still controversial idea that it was responsible to both stockholders and stakeholders and would be held accountable for its performance. Interestingly, this commitment would be tested in Spain in 2001 when six patients died during dialysis treatment—potentially because of problems with filters manufactured by a subsidiary. Baxter responded by recalling the filters, apologizing publicly, taking a $189 million hit, and reducing, at his own request, the CEO's bonus.[7]

The Baxter story illustrates two ways that a company moves forward in this stage: (1) by broadening its agenda by embracing a more comprehensive concept of citizenship and (2) by deepening its involvement as top leaders assume more of a stewardship role. Most firms seem to get a more mature sense of what citizenship involves as they progress through this stage. One spark is increased consultation with a diversity of stakeholders that involves more open, two-way communication. This serves to educate people about the many issues, interests, and needs in society. In many cases, citizenship chiefly involves stakeholder management at this stage.

As companies move further into this stage, stakeholder dialogues often shift from bilateral conversations to multiparty investigations of issues of common concern. Several compelling examples of this come from the natural resource arena. For instance, two of the Center's workshop leaders, Ann Svendsen and Myriam Laberge, helped to facilitate what they called a "whole system engagement" involving the forester Macmillan Bloedel (later acquired by Weyerhaeuser), environmental groups, First Nation tribes, and local communities on British Columbia's west coast for over eight years.[8] Here there were marked conflicts between and even within the several parties, attempts by the B.C. government to legislate compromises that suited no one, local protest rallies and an international boycott engineered by Greenpeace, and repeated breakdowns in communication. Over time, however, areas of common interest were identified and ultimately an agreement on land use was reached. What led to the success? According to one of the corporate members of the dialogue, the secret was to get beyond conventional "stakeholder negotiations on social license issues" and to move toward "the next generation model where we ask, 'How do we learn together? How do we innovate together despite the fact that occasionally we hate each other and we can't get along?'"

As companies evolve through this innovative stage, they typically grapple with the business case for their citizenship programs. Research among the eight companies in the Center's Executive Forum suggests, however, that the criteria and metrics tend to be functionalized at this stage. Those responsible for social agendas, for example, refer to specific benefits to recruiting, retention, and reputation; those on the environmental front are concerned with factors of risk and life-cycle costs; and those on the financial side stress matters of exposure and access to capital. Meanwhile, senior leaders, taking an enterprise perspective, point to the strength and value of the corporate brand.

Not surprisingly, a businesslike approach carries over into CSR program management during this phase. Programs typically include internal and external input, an analysis of needs and opportunities, a plan of action, and proposals on budget and staff, all buttressed by a business case to sell the benefits to senior management. And what would have been more ad hoc or reactive at an earlier stage is now more programmatic and responsive to stakeholder needs.

Furthermore, companies at this stage also begin to monitor their social and environmental performance and issue public reports on the results. Again, our experience is that most firms at this stage are simply compiling data prepared by operating units and presenting it with a corporate overlay. And much of the motivation behind it comes from outside pressure from socially responsible investors, the supply chain, and religious, social action, and environmental interests. Still, reporting raises awareness of citizenship throughout a company and, according to Gene Endicott, who was responsible for Agilent's initial social reports, "brings a lot of people out of the woodwork."

Challenge: Create Coherence

Ironically, the launch of so many new programs, the increased requests for information and the exposure, and the dialogues with stakeholders often mean that, as in the case of Unilever's social thrust, "a thousand flowers bloom." This seeds a new developmental crisis: coping with a variety of seemingly unrelated activities. As their companies are knee-deep in initiatives, surveys, reports, and programs, many executives wonder what's going on and worry whether or not their citizenship initiatives make sense. Is there any connection between, say, corporate efforts in risk management, corporate branding, stakeholder engagement, supplier certification, cause-related marketing, and employee diversity? Should there be?

The case of Petro-Canada illustrates the phenomenon. An inventory of existing programs in the company revealed that activity was widespread but based in silos and without alignment or strategic purpose. Says Hazel Gillespie, community investment manager, "We all realized that we were contributing to the company's reputation, but we weren't doing it in a coordinated, concentrated, focused, and strategic way."

Asea Brown Boveri (ABB) was a pioneer in addressing this kind of chaos in an orderly fashion. The Swiss maker of power and automation technologies established a sustainability management program in 1992 and today has a stakeholder advisory board composed of the CEO, a sustainability department head, and seven ad hoc advisors. ABB distributes responsibilities among different groups in its global operation. Business ethics, for example, fall under the company's legal department while the human resources department is responsible for upholding labor principles. In total, nearly 500 people in more than fifty countries have specific responsibilities for sustainability programs and coordinate through work groups and committees. The system reflects ABB's viewpoint that citizenship should be, according to Michael Robertson, former sustainability affairs officer, "set from the top and driven down through the organization by example, leadership, and top management support."

Such efforts to systematize, coordinate, and manage this flurry of activity illustrate again the developmental tensions between differentiation and integration. These are attempts to pull together a response to the increasing lack of coherence in the citizenship agenda in many companies. Cross-functional coordination and top-down oversight are a start. But a change in mindset and strong executive leadership are needed to really get people thinking and working together.

Stage 4: Integrated

Citizenship Concept: Sustainability or triple bottom line
Strategic Intent: Value proposition
Leadership: Champion, in front of it
Structure: Organizational alignment
Issues Management: Proactive, systems
Stakeholder Relationships: Partnership, alliances
Transparency: Assurance

One of the developmental challenges for companies moving into this stage is to progress, in Griener's terms, from coordination to collaboration in driving citizenship into the business. Select firms are making moves in this direction. Boards of Directors are increasingly setting standards and monitoring corporate social and environmental performance. An analysis of firms that are members of the DJSI estimates that roughly two in five member companies have board-level committees overseeing CSR, a proportion that is growing annually.[9] Examples of other corporate-wide efforts to integrate citizenship into the fabric of companies are multiplying. These include risk management systems, sustainability training for managers and employees, "issues" management frameworks, balanced scorecards, and the like—which we will explore in more depth throughout this volume.

British Petroleum has been a leader in attempting to integrate citizenship from top to bottom and throughout its businesses.[10] BP's integrated agenda begins with a commitment to multi-stakeholder responsibilities but integrates its efforts under the theme of sustainability. This means to BP, among other things, "the capacity to endure as a group by renewing assets, meeting the evolving needs of society, attracting successive generations of employees, contributing to a flourishing environment, and retaining the trust and support of customers, shareholders, and communities." BP's particular emphasis is on energy and its efforts include leading the policy debate within its industry on climate change, supporting research on alternative energy, developing cleaner technologies, and keeping its own house in order. Other firms have expressed a more integrative and holistic conception of business in society in the form of the triple bottom line.

BP has put into place an integrated governance system that includes a board-level ethics and environmental assurance committee, corporate directors of social policy and business ethics, group-level oversight bodies, corporate and regional coordinators, and business unit measurements and audits. Heading these moves toward integration, until recently, was Lord John Browne, CEO, a champion of sustainability and global spokesman for all of industry. BP exemplifies three keys to development in this phase: (1) vocal, out-in-front leadership; (2) an inclusive vision of its role in society; and (3) integrative structures, processes, and systems.

Where BP failed was is in driving accountability deep into its lines of business, evidenced most visibly and harmfully by the shocking neglect of maintenance on pipelines under its control in the Alaskan oil fields, a deadly accident at a Texas refinery, and allegations of financial chicanery in energy markets. The important message in this is that achievements in the upper strata of citizenship have to build on a solid record of compliance and an ethical culture. Lord Browne's early departure as CEO from BP only reinforces this message.

A stronger example in this area comes from 3M, which has adopted a health, safety, and environment management system with representatives in every business. The company applies life-cycle management policies to its product development functions and requires that all of its manufacturing facilities obtain ISO 14001 certification. Another organization-wide model is Diageo, the British beverage company, where CEO Paul Walsh created an executive-level corporate citizenship committee and several tiers of multi-functional committees to support and oversee citizenship in the company's lines of business. In operational terms, this involves setting targets, establishing key performance indicators, and monitoring performance through balanced scorecards. Both 3M and Diageo also have corporate citizenship teams of internal consultants and business managers who offer advice and conduct audits in work units.

Social and environmental reporting, another integrative force, is no longer exceptional for big companies. However, as of 2007, estimates are that only 15 percent are subject to any external verification.[11] This may be the next big step in embedding accountability into the business. A related characteristic of companies at this stage is more openness and disclosure of its failings as a corporate citizen. Both BP and Shell, for instance, have disclosed social and environmental problems and conducted "warts-and-all" assessments of questioned practices.

Interestingly, we are finding that many of the companies that move into this integrative phase premise their citizenship efforts less on a specific business case and more on their core corporate values. Exemplifying this "inside out" logic, Groupe Danone, the French multinational, frames its code of conduct with a value proposition known as the Danone Way. Its origins date to the protest movements of the late 1960s when Antoine Riboud, then Chairman and CEO of a predecessor company, vowed to meet new expectations of workers and society. This was expressed formally in 1974 with a statement setting out a "dual commitment" to business success and social responsibility. Today, this dual commitment is reflected in myriad criteria of citizenship used by Groupe companies in self-assessments that are, in turn, reviewed by a Groupe-level steering committee.

Challenge: Deepen Commitment

The truest expression of the value proposition for corporate citizenship is when it is expressed in a company's business strategy. BP, despite its reputational setback, still stands out for its strategic commitment and large-scale investments in environmentally sustainable technologies, products, and services. Another leader we have noted, Interface, the largest commercial carpet manufacturer in the world, has translated its commitment to sustainability into a commercial strategy. Its innovations include inventively easy things, like using plastics and polymers, rather than petroleum-based materials, for carpet backing; that way, carpets can be fully recycled and produce zero waste. It also makes ingenious use of the principles of "biomimicry" in carpet design. These inspired Interface to manufacture carpet tiles with natural leaf patterns that could be laid out on the floor in any order—just like leaves falling in the forest—with no time wasted lining the carpet tiles up and matching seams. And, with nature in mind, the company invented a way to tape the tiles together, like a spider web, rather than glue them to the floor surface.

All of these environmental innovations have translated into over $335 million in cost savings since 1995, as well as big reductions in greenhouse gas emissions, and have contributed to gains in sales, despite a massive turndown in the overall market. Ray Anderson, the CEO of Interface, says: "We have found a new way to win in the marketplace . . . one that doesn't come at the expense of our grandchildren or the earth, but at the expense of the inefficient competitor."[12] This "green is gold" environmentalism makes a lot of sense to businesses who can see market opportunities in citizenship.

The key question a company at this stage has to confront is how deep is its commitment to citizenship? Such a question is raised when a company seriously considers its values and contribution to sustainability versus the social, economic, and environmental situations it encounters in the world. A select few firms identify opportunities in this and find partners willing to co-create new models of sustainable commerce. Confronting this question moves a company into a transformative stage that moves citizenship into its business model. New organizational structures for managing and delivering real value for society have to be created.

Stage 5: Transforming

Citizenship Concept: Change the game
Strategic Intent: Market creation or social change
Leadership: Visionary, ahead of the pack
Structure: Mainstream, business driven
Issues Management: Defining
Stakeholder Relationships: Multi-organizational
Transparency: Full disclosure

The central problem facing U.S. and European companies today is how to grow their businesses in often saturated, hyper-competitive markets. The book *Untapped*, by social entrepreneur John Weiser, the Center's Steve Rochlin and Michele Kahane, and researcher Jessica Landis, offers scores of examples on how companies can grow by tapping into underserved markets.[13] These lower-income and racial-and-ethnic minority populations are at the nexus of citizenship and business strategy. The authors show how managers and their companies have to: (1) develop the capacity to access and translate local market information; (2) adapt business models to radically reduce costs or build on scale; (3) change their internal incentives and cultural assumptions; (4) create and work through community partnerships; and (5) make at least some investments in community infrastructure and what they broadly term the "enabling environment." None of this is easy. But neither is eking out a marginal share increase from a competitor in an over-served market. And the rewards, financial and emotional, are especially appealing.

As we have seen, Unilever has been progressively expanding its commitment to this socio-commercial frontier the past several years. There is more to this, however, than the immediate bottom line. While C. K. Prahalad makes the case that there is a fortune at the bottom of the pyramid, the experience of Unilever (and others) is that these are long-term investments to unlock markets. Few BoP investments achieve accustomed hurdle rates of return on capital in the short term. Our interviews with sixty or so marketers, top executives, and citizenship specialists in Unilever revealed broader, strategic motivations to "change the game."

We have already noted, and will explore in more depth later on, the game changing represented by the entrepreneurship of Ben & Jerry's, the marketing campaigns of the Body Shop, the eco-innovations of Patagonia, and the fair trade supported by Green Mountain Coffee. Add to these the socially responsible investing of Trillium, the community involvement of ShoreBank, and the efforts of increasing numbers of micro-credit bankers. But we have also made the case that select big blue-chip firms are embracing these kinds of ideas. Some examples:

- Leading pharmaceuticals are giving to the developing world free or discounted drugs to treat river blindness (Abbott), HIV/AIDS (Merck), leprosy (Novartis), and diabetes (Novo Nordisk). Many are going beyond donations to assist developing countries build their healthcare infrastructure, train doctors and nurses, and work with local companies to manufacture generic versions of their drugs.

- Hewlett-Packard has invested in digital communities in Sao Paulo, Brazil, in villages in India and South Africa, and in inner-city Baltimore to create market opportunities and promote community economic development. On the citizenship side, this is all part of HP's "e-inclusion" strategy to reduce the digital divide.
- HP has fellow travelers heading in this direction. Chipmaker AMD has a 50x15 strategy whereby it aims to have 50 percent of the world's population connected to the Internet by 2015. Finnish phone manufacturer Nokia has reached a hundred thousand young people around the world with e-learning curricula developed by its business partner, the publisher Pearson. Both companies premise these investments on social benefit and future sales.
- Campaigns by Diageo on responsible drinking, by Timberland and its partner City Year to promote principles of democracy, and by Working Assets to transform consumers into social activists all exemplify business aimed at social change.

It's easy enough to pigeonhole these initiatives under the labels of strategic philanthropy, cause-related marketing, or community relations. But those companies moving into this transformative phase of citizenship have bigger aspiration to, in effect, change the game of business. Their strategic intent is to create new markets and ensure social sustainability by fusing their citizenship and business agenda.

Characteristics of Transformers

We cannot, at this point, specify all of the characteristics of this stage of development. However, some features of this stage seem clear. First, firms that innovate, rather than imitate, at this stage seem to have a vision of being global citizens and are often led by visible, visionary leaders. Indeed, some of them become global spokespeople for industry in this arena: As an example, Interface's Ray Anderson, along with Mark Moody-Stewart, formerly of Shell and later Anglo American mining and natural resources, put a positive face on the corporate role in the otherwise antibusiness film *The Corporation*.

Second, these firms seem to take stated corporate values seriously. A recent study of CEOs in twenty companies at this transformative stage found them to be deeply troubled by social and environmental conditions in the world and motivated by a higher sense of corporate purpose. Accordingly, a stated value expressed in many of their companies was the aspiration to make the world a better place.

Finally, firms at this stage seldom operate solo in the social and environmental realm. They partner extensively with other businesses, community groups, and NGOs to address problems, reach new markets, and develop local economies. At Unilever, for instance, we identified nearly twenty global and over one thousand country-based or local partnerships. Not surprisingly, Zadek terms this a "civil" stage in the growth of corporate responsibility as it involves cross-industry and multisector cooperation in addressing societal ills.

A schematic of these five stages of citizenship and their developmental triggers might seem to imply that transformation and multisector partnering is the final stage of development (see Figure 5.3). But in our view it is only a place-marker because scholars have not as yet mapped what a shared role for business, government, and civil society in commerce could look like.

What Stage Are Corporations in Today?

Many citizenship practitioners have rated their companies along the dimensions of this stage model in the Center's Web-based survey (see Figure 5.4 and the stages survey in Appendix 3). After considering the options, most find that their businesses are not at any single stage of citizenship: in some aspects their firms are integrated, in others innovative, and in still others just getting started. This means that the dimensions we have outlined are not invariant. Companies are apt to be ahead in some dimensions and behind on others. One observer pointed out, for instance, that there are companies that win citizenship awards based on their social reports but have seemingly mastered citizenship only in the reporting aspects. Others, by comparison, may be proactive in their programs but lagging in transparency.

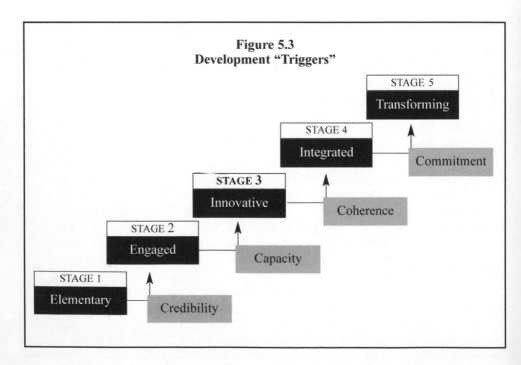

Figure 5.3
Development "Triggers"

STAGE 5
Transforming

STAGE 4
Integrated

Commitment

STAGE 3
Innovative

Coherence

STAGE 2
Engaged

Capacity

STAGE 1
Elementary

Credibility

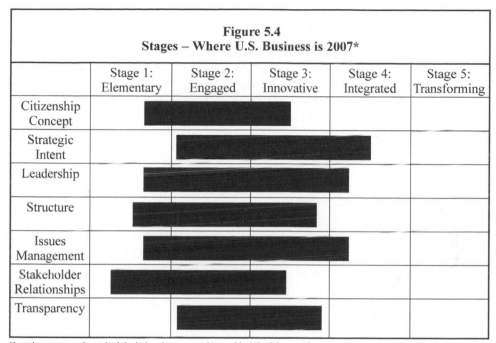

Figure 5.4
Stages – Where U.S. Business is 2007*

	Stage 1: Elementary	Stage 2: Engaged	Stage 3: Innovative	Stage 4: Integrated	Stage 5: Transforming
Citizenship Concept	███	███			
Strategic Intent		███	███		
Leadership	███	███			
Structure	███	███			
Issues Management	███	███			
Stakeholder Relationships	███	███			
Transparency		███			

*based on mean and standard deviation; boxes contain roughly 2/3 of the sample

This should not be a surprise. These kinds of variation are found in developmental models of all types. After all, the pace of a child's physical, mental, and emotional development is seldom uniform. One facet typically develops faster than another. What shapes the profile of citizenship in companies is a distinctive mix of stakeholders, industry dynamics, and other external influences, plus a leadership, traditions, and company culture. Nevertheless, the normative pattern of activity at each stage has an internal consistency that many practitioners have found useful in gauging where their company is in the development of its citizenship thrust and where it might choose to develop further.

If we look at the ratings of a hundred or so companies, mostly big businesses, we find the "average" has the majority of U.S. companies progressing from Stage 2 to Stage 3. Now this is hardly a representative sample of big business as the survey was completed by citizenship professionals from companies who are Center members. Overall, about 10 percent of the companies are at the first stages and slightly fewer show themselves as transformative. On the individual components, it is notable that very few of the U.S. firms surveyed have an integrative conception of citizenship, associated with sustainability or the triple bottom line, or have structures and processes that coordinate the ways that they manage their citizenship agenda. Our impression is that Europeans may be ahead of U.S. corporations in these regards. The same is true with social reporting. At the same time, a number of U.S. firms have made strong value-based commitments to

CSR. And, as we shall see, this is the very basis of their movement into next generation corporate citizenship.

Our interest is with the frontier, Stages 4 and 5, where "next practice" companies or those that might be termed "positive deviants" are producing the next generation of citizenship innovations and practices.[14] Granted few companies are there today but the ones we profile are moving in that direction. Part II of the book examines how these companies are redefining corporate citizenship, how they are activating and leading it, and how they are creating the infrastructure to bring it into being.

Part II

Repurposing the Enterprise

B y many measures corporate citizenship, as it is currently understood and practiced by mainstream corporations in the United States (and for that matter in most of the world), is high on aspiration but comparatively low on priority, design, and payoff—for society and for business. In the majority of firms, it is not based in a clear vision or linked credibly to corporate values or even well understood by line managers, many of whom see it as a "nice thing to do" or just another initiative from HQ. Citizenship responsibilities and programs are typically managed by myriad corporate groups operating in silos. Valuable work is often done by these professionals but, absent cross-communication and a common sense of purpose, an enterprise-wide perspective on the company's engagement with society is lost.

In these respects, today's citizenship resembles the early stages of the quality movement, where slogans about quality as job one and initiatives from the quality control function proved to be relatively weak, particularly in the face of corporate attitudes that would not motivate and systems that could not ensure continuous and consistent levels of quality. The citizenship movement is learning the same lessons as the quality movement: Unless and until the business "owns it" and drives citizenship into strategy, develops structures and processes to operationalize it, and ties it to measurement and everyday performance, the results will be modest and citizenship will remain on a tactical footing.

Creating a more advanced citizenship profile in the midst of stakeholder pressures poses challenges and opportunities for companies who see the value of adopting a more integrated, strategic approach. For the past several years, the Center has hosted three action-learning forums involving companies that aim to move toward next generation citizenship. In the Executive Forum, firms such as Advanced Micro Devices (AMD), Levi Strauss & Co., Abbott, and several others met for over two years to share knowledge and mark progress on developing a more integrated approach to managing corporate citizenship. In the Global Leadership Network, composed of IBM, GE, 3M, and other corporate giants, we witnessed these firms move toward more business-linked citizenship. In the Community Involvement Leadership Roundtable, companies are reshaping their social and philanthropic engagement with society.

In Part II, we see how these and other next generation companies are repurposing their business by analyzing social issues and defining what matters (Chapter 6) and by developing an integrated, strategic approach to their role in society (Chapter 7). Then we turn to what it takes to lead a company to the fron-tiers of citizenship, drawing on the lessons of trailblazers like Ben Cohen and Jerry Greenfield of Ben & Jerry's and today's exemplars like Ray Anderson of Interface (Chapter 8). This part concludes with a profile of how next generation companies are beginning to engage their employees as citizens and deploy them in service to the business and society (Chapter 9).

Defining What Matters

Wal-Mart brought Ray Anderson in to open its associates' eyes to the contours of the global village and has been talking regularly with "outsiders" ever since. IBM conducts electronic "jams" on broad trends and business-relevant sociopolitical issues with thousands of people and key stakeholder groups around the globe. GE holds biennial "Energy 2015" and "Healthcare 2015" convenings with a cross-functional group of government officials, industry leaders, key suppliers, NGOs, and academics that feed back into the company's strategy.

What's this all about?—gathering intelligence on social, political, cultural, and environmental issues that bear on the business. Once consigned to the public affairs function in companies and consumed as background reading by strategic planners, the scanning and calibration of this kind of data is today the work of top executives, board members, and operating managers. The reasons for their sharpened focus on the many issues at the intersection of business and society are twofold: These issues pose potential risks and portend significant opportunities.

Companies moving into advanced stages of corporate citizenship actively engage their many stakeholders not only to build relationships but also to gain a better understanding of what's going on in the world surrounding the firm. We've seen how Unilever was a first mover in its industry on issues related to water, fish, and sustainable agriculture in concert with leading NGOs and select peers. It is now moving from a somewhat reactive to more proactive stance in light of health concerns and leading consumer trends through organic sourcing, all-natural ingredients, and fortified foods and beverages. We've also seen how Wal-Mart has finally caught the green wave even as it is still on the defensive on the employment front. The key steps in moving from a reactive to proactive position on citizenship are to understand the issues facing the business and to address them with vigor and imagination.

Nike and Human Rights

Nike is an example of a company that moved from reactivity to proactivity in its dealings with unhappy stakeholders over wages, production quotas, and the working conditions of laborers in its supplier plants in Asia. Recall that the company was positioned, from its founding, as marketer of high-end athletic shoes and equipment while its manufacturing was outsourced first to Japan, then to South Korea and Taiwan, and then to Vietnam and Indonesia, wherever the cheapest labor could be found. The company's genius as a marketer is studied by business students and competitors. Through a series of celebrity jock endorsements, from runner Steve Prefontaine, to basketball's Michael Jordan, to golfer Tiger Woods, combined with changes in consumer tastes and lifestyles, Nike became an iconic fashion brand that extended into sportswear and casual apparel. Its missteps as a corporate citizen are being studied as well.

Throughout the 1990s, as Nike's fortunes grew its sociopolitical troubles began to mount.[1] A 1992 article in *Harper's* magazine by labor activist Jeff Ballinger contrasted the piddling pay of an Indonesian contract laborer (19 cents per hour) with Jordan's mega-million dollar endorsement contract. The broader story of exploitation of overseas labor began to gain attention in left-of-center political and collegiate circles. The comic strip *Doonesbury* lampooned the company and documentary filmmaker Michael Moore caught Phil Knight flatfooted justifying the employment of fourteen-year-olds. In 1998, the story hit the mainstream with a *Time* magazine article on the "Sneaker Gulag." It contained the account of Nguyen Thi Thu, a twenty-three-year-old girl who was trimming shoe soles in a Nike supplier plant in Vietnam when a co-worker's machine broke, spraying metal parts across the factory and into her heart. Over the next years, Nike's reputation, sales, and market value plummeted.

Simon Zadek, founder of the think tank AccountAbility and adviser to Nike, gives a neat accounting of its transition in handling supply-chain issues through defensive, compliant, managerial, and strategic phases.[2] In the first transition, for example, the firm moved from denying any responsibility ("We don't make the shoes.") to establishing basic labor codes and employing outside firms to audit compliance. In the next transition, it beefed up its own compliance function and created a team of senior managers to assess why the labor problems persisted. This team not only looked at the overall supply chain but also at Nike's own business practices. It documented how just-in-time procurement methods, internal cost allocation rules, and production incentive schemes encouraged suppliers to pressure their workers and require overtime. These were practices that Nike fixed—at some cost and amidst grumbling.

In its strategic phase, Nike has been going after an industry-wide fix that evens the competitive playing field. The company has joined with other shoe and apparel makers, NGOs, and select retailers in groups such as the Fair Labor Association (in the United States) and Ethical Trading Initiative (in the United Kingdom) to ensure broader-based buy-in to, and compliance with, labor and trading codes. In another move on the CSR front, Nike became the first in its industry to voluntarily disclose the names and locations of the more than seven hundred active contract factories that currently make Nike-branded products worldwide.

From Defense to Offense

But this only tells half of the Nike story. According to Mike McBreen, director of global apparel operations and corporate responsibility for Nike, the company had a two-pronged strategy to manage the business issues in its supply chain.[3] One thrust was to minimize risk and protect the brand. Here Nike had to understand and address the many environmental, health, and safety issues extending backward from the company to its suppliers. Then it had to establish new codes of conduct and improve its compliance models, structures, and methods. This was framed as simply a cost of doing business. The second thrust was to enhance the brand. Here Nike chose to connect the whole value chain and promote responsible practices through to the retailer. In addition, the company took steps to improve conditions in its contracted supplier plants and the communities that surround them. This strategy aimed to "maximize differentiation" and was based on what the company characterizes as ROI decisions. This second track, according to McBreen, shifted the "game plan" from defense to offense.

So what are the plays? We've noted Nike's involvement in global, multisector initiatives to set standards for industry supply chains. In addition, it has supported the Global Alliance for Workers and Communities that offers education and health programs for workers in Southeast Asian plants, launched its own education program in factories in China, and helped to improve factories in Vietnam, including ones that are not currently its suppliers in order to improve its supplier base. On the charitable front, Nike has significantly increased its giving overseas, developed a signature program (NikeGO) that promotes physical fitness among young people ages eight to fifteen, and supported programs targeted at women and girls. And then there is the Reuse-A-Shoe program where the company recycles materials from its shoes and sports balls into court surfaces for playgrounds abroad and in the United States.

Naturally, the company still has many critics who raise legitimate questions about the effectiveness of efforts in its supply chain and the motivations behind its strategic philanthropy. But this much is agreed upon: First, many consumers like what the company is doing. After learning of Nike's charitable events and programs, one Nike-funded study found that 69 percent had more favorable opinions of Nike and 38 percent felt more inclined to purchase Nike products. Second, its broader CSR agenda, which includes involvement of a committee of the Board of Directors, an annual cycle of strategic CSR planning and reviews, and use of a balanced scorecard to track results, has gained plaudits. Finally, its CSR thrust has delivered on the bottom line. Assigning only a fraction of Nike's improvement in share price and market capital to its CSR efforts, McBreen estimates that the social-return-on-investment or SROI is $182 million and counting.

Social Issues and Business

Many polling and consulting shops profile the issues that keep executives awake at night. PricewaterhouseCoopers's (PwC) 2006 survey of nearly eleven hundred

CEOs in 2006, for example, found that concerns about overregulation, the availability of key skills, low-cost competition, and energy and commodity prices were uppermost on the minds of top executives. Issues around scarcities in natural resources, global warming, and potential pandemics, such as obesity and bird flu, were further down the list of *immediate* concerns for most company heads.

McKinsey & Co.'s 2007 global survey of over 3500 top executives, by comparison, asked how important select issues would be for business in the *next five years*. Looking forward, business leaders cite social issues such as the growing number of consumers in emerging economies, a faster pace of technological innovation, constraints on supply or usage of natural resources, and an aging population in developed countries.[4]

Interestingly, McKinsey has also asked about the relative balance of risks and opportunities posed by certain issues.[5] Pensions, privacy, and political influence are primarily seen as risks to companies. By comparison, most executives put an equal balance between risk and opportunity in the clamor for more investment in developing countries, for ethical standards in advertising and marketing, and for attention to human rights. And while climate change and affordability of products for poor consumers are viewed chiefly as risks by most executives, a minority see opportunity in addressing these issues. That sense of opportunity is what is behind GE's ecomagination and Unilever's bottom of the pyramid investments.

Public relations firm GolinHarris looks at corporate citizenship from the outside in—asking what the public thinks of the citizenship of companies. Its 2006 poll asked people to rate the most important social issues for a business to address as a good corporate citizen. The U.S. public rates attention to the environment (ranked 1, 2, or 3 by 47 percent), education and literacy (40 percent), and human, civil, and animal rights (35 percent) as the key issues in good corporate citizenship.[6] GlobeScan, in turn, has asked the public around the world what it expects from companies. One poll asked the world: "What is the most important thing a company can do to be seen as socially responsible?" That study found significant differences in priorities around the globe: The United States, Canada, and Brazil put prime emphasis on community involvement; Australia on protecting the environment; and Mexico and China on the quality and safety of products. The most important criterion globally: treating employees well.[7] Finally, there are studies about which issues are of most concern to different industries. PwC, from the standpoint of corporate chiefs, and GlobeScan, based on public polls, provide industry breakouts. We have looked at these data, other such studies, and our own polls to glean a roster of business challenges for various industries (see Figure 6.1). While these kinds of lists can be instructive, the real benefit comes when companies delve into the issues and internalize the implications.

Figure 6.1
Business Challenges from Society

- **Energy**
  - energy security
  - climate change
  - political risk

- **Retail**
  - supply chain practices
  - consumerism

- **Pharmaceutical & Health**
  - access
  - HIV/AIDS
  - low income
  - IP and trade

- **Finance**
  - low-income
  - financial scandals
  - responsible lending/investing

- **High Tech & ICT**
  - off-shoring
  - IP and trade
  - digital divide

- **Agriculture + Food & Beverage**
  - trade & globalization
  - health & nutrition

- **Manufacturing**
  - China & offshoring
  - job protection
  - supply chain
  - climate change

- **Shipping & Logistics**
  - climate change
  - security
  - low income market

Issues in a Global Context

"Globalization has been a catalyst, and a positive catalyst, to help U.S. execs expand their horizons and open their minds to this interconnectedness of business to society," Bob Parkinson, CEO of Baxter told us. "Outside the U.S. business people understand that they are not on an island. They have a broader construct to operate with. They see the social, political, and cultural dimensions." In this light, leading companies are today scanning issues in their global context to see what it means for their business fortunes and for their role as corporate citizens.

The main facts, if not specific figures, about the state of the world are familiar to many executives.[8] For instance, despite recent gains, roughly one-fifth of the world's population (1.2 billion) live on less than $1 per day and another 2.8 billion people live on less than $2 per day. Some 2.4 billion people lack adequate sanitation facilities, even simple latrines, and 1.1 billion lack access to clean water. This combination has dire consequences for the world's poor. It is estimated that close to half of all people in developing countries suffer at any given time from health problems caused by water and sanitation deficits. Two million die annually from infectious diarrhea, 90 percent of them children.

This context of poverty and disease frames Unilever's campaign to promote hand washing in developing countries, its water purification product, and its socio-commercial investments. It motivates Baxter, and so many of the pharmaceutical companies, to donate medicines or sell them at cost in poor, disease-ridden regions. And it is what's behind the community economic development efforts of IBM, who, in partnership with the International Finance Corporation of the World Bank, makes its small- and medium-size company "toolkit" available free to enterprises in developing countries and, it should be noted, to women- and minority-owned businesses in the United States.

More than 800 million people go to bed hungry every night, 300 million of whom are children. Of this number, only 8 percent are victims of famine, floods, or other emergencies. More than 90 percent suffer from long-term malnourishment and micronutrient deficiency. This is why leading food companies are partnering in the World Economic Forum's Business Alliance Against Chronic Hunger, in the Global Alliance for Improved Nutrition and its business group involved in food fortification, and with community groups and NGOs around children's nutrition.

People in Africa and Southeast Asia, many of whom lack access to clean water, adequate nutrition, or proper healthcare, account for 75 percent of global deaths from infectious diseases, but make up just 36 percent of the world's population. Europeans and Americans constitute just 28 percent of world population, but account for 42 percent of deaths from cardiovascular diseases and cancers—diseases often triggered by lifestyle factors such as smoking, being sedentary, and eating foods rich in salt, sugar, and fat. This is why food companies are cutting back on trans fats, conducting research on cholesterol-reducing foods, and promoting healthy choices in the marketplace. NikeGO fits into this space, too.

On the environmental side you are surely aware of the evidence of global warming. Note as well that one in four mammal species is in serious decline, mainly due to human activity; fish stocks are eroding; half of the world's wetlands have been lost since 1900; forest cover is declining markedly; and desertification puts some 135 million people worldwide at risk of being driven from their lands. The UN's Environment Programme projects 50 million environmental refugees worldwide by 2010. Is it any wonder why companies are working on sustainable agriculture, water use, and fisheries?—or, more broadly, why so many more corporations are going green?

A further look at the state of the world reveals that nearly a billion people entered the twenty-first century unable to read a book or sign their names, fifteen million children have been orphaned due to HIV/AIDS, and women and children experience a disproportionate share of the suffering. This helps to explain why the number one area of social investment by companies is education; why firms that aren't even in healthcare nevertheless get involved in AIDS; and why leading companies are targeting especially the needs of women and children in their philanthropy and community economic development efforts.

The statistics paint a worrying picture of the growing gap between haves and have-nots. Even as the spread of free market capitalism has promised to "lift all boats," the gaps between the richest and poorest countries in GDP, income, health, and life expectancy have increased substantially the past twenty-five years. And progress in bridging the gaps in literacy and infant mortality has slowed. On these counts it should also be noted, the gap in income, education, and health has grown between the richest and poorest segments in the United States as well.

Finally, the future portends significant demographic changes. For instance, the world's population continues to grow dramatically; even with China in neutral, the planet is expected to host another one billion persons in the next decade. The trends pose distinct issues. The population, in the United States and especially in Western Europe and Japan, is aging, which will further unravel the welfare state and could pit young against old when it comes to social spending and entitlements. On the other hand, the youth population is exploding in the D&E world. Rick Little, president and CEO of ImagineNations, an alliance of businesses, NGOs, and investors taking action on youth employment globally, projects that 500 million young people, aged eighteen to twenty-seven today, will never have a paid job in their lives. They are flocking into the world's mega-cities in record numbers; the result could be destabilizing at best, a global catastrophe at worst.

When the Center meets with executive groups about the state of the world, the cumulative effect of seeing, discussing, and digesting these statistics is by turns shaming, sobering, informative, and motivating. There is typically, in some quarters, heated debate about the moral responsibilities of corporations versus the moral hazard posed by using shareholders' monies to address the world's problems. In light of these statistics, most business people gain a deeper understanding of the public's antipathy toward swollen CEO pay and the riches of big business and better appreciate the passion of NGOs for their causes. But others rise to the defense of business and counter that NGOs should not define the corporate social and environmental agenda. Then executives do what they are best equipped to do: apply the mindset and tools of their craft to the world as they encounter it.

This means considering carefully the relative risks and opportunities posed by the issues in their business environment. It means defining a select set of issues that are most material to the firm and relevant for attention through either its charitable arms or commercial capabilities. And, ultimately, it means asking the most fundamental question—"who are we?"—and making value-based decisions about how to operate in society.

Assessing Risk and Opportunity

How do companies identify the risks and opportunities posed by the interaction of business and society? While there are many models and formats, several of the companies in the Center's action learning forums have scanned their environments from at least two perspectives: What are the risks and opportunities for our business? And what are they for society? This yields a two-by-two matrix of the type familiar to business people (Figure 6.2).

In the upper left quadrant, business and society are at both at risk. Social issues like the education gap, the digital divide, the scourge of HIV/AIDS, and other infectious diseases all fit here. These not only threaten the well-being and economic futures of peoples and societies, they also limit the growth potential of businesses that cannot get access to skilled labor, commercial infrastructure, and paying consumers. Widespread youth unemployment, mass migrations to

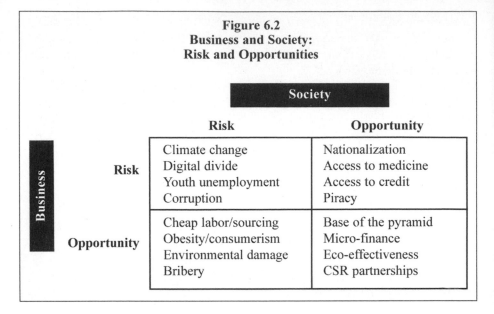

Figure 6.2
Business and Society:
Risk and Opportunities

		Society	
		Risk	**Opportunity**
Business	**Risk**	Climate change Digital divide Youth unemployment Corruption	Nationalization Access to medicine Access to credit Piracy
	Opportunity	Cheap labor/sourcing Obesity/consumerism Environmental damage Bribery	Base of the pyramid Micro-finance Eco-effectiveness CSR partnerships

mega-cities, and corruption fit here, too. Beyond the obvious costs to society, these create an unstable business climate. IBM's global programs to reinvent education and high-tech AMD, HP, Cisco, Intel, Nokia, and others' efforts to bridge the digital divide, alongside the widespread corporate involvement in the AIDS pandemic, all illustrate how business and society benefit if they work together to reduce their mutual risks.

The lower left quadrant shines a spotlight on how business creates risk for societies. The constant quest for cheap labor, the production of pollution and waste, the sale of junk food and shoddy goods: This is the legacy of business capitalizing on opportunities at the expense of the common good. The rationale for greater transparency from companies operating in this quadrant is straightforward: Access to information about their activities is a deterrent to misbehavior. But there is also an opportunity for business to align itself with aggrieved stakeholders' interests and public welfare. Supply-chain reform by Nike and Reebok in shoes, by Levi Strauss & Co. and the GAP in apparel, and by many high-tech companies in microelectronics is an example. The move into healthier eating-and-drinking categories by Kraft, PepsiCo, Coca-Cola, and McDonald's is another. The broad-based environmental cleanup by businesses of all types and their moves toward greater sustainability is a third.

In the upper right quadrant, society in its many forms avails itself of opportunities to protect its interests, but at the expense of business. Nationalization of industries, erection of trade barriers, and the elimination of agricultural subsidies, patent protection, and intellectual property rights are among the threats to business here. Traditionally business has countered these through lobbying and political contributions. But companies that continue to swim against the tide of shared societal values and good public policy will ultimately create costs for themselves and risk losing their license to operate. Misalignment in this quadrant calls out for an innovative response. Moves by the pharmaceutical industry to make therapies more affordable, and moves by energy users and banks to create a carbon trading market are means to forestall regulation and make risks manageable.

In the lower right quadrant, an opportunity for business is an opportunity for society. This is evident in the movement by business toward microfinance, eco-effectiveness, and creating a market at the bottom of the pyramid. This quadrant, more so than the others, is where companies can play offense, rather than defense, and transition from a philanthropic response to society to a socio-commercial venture. And this quadrant is also increasingly populated by NGOs and even government agencies that are redefining their own roles and working as partners with business.

Taking Responsible Action

Big, global companies find themselves facing issues in each of these quadrants. In cases where business and society both are at risk or see opportunities, conditions are ripe for them to work together. But how about instances where there are conflicting interests? Many companies in the Center's learning forums regularly bring these issues to the table. The cases of Pfizer and Diageo illustrate complementary approaches to handling them.

Self-Regulation

A big global pharmaceutical like Pfizer is the target of many interests around the world that see it as taking advantage of consumers for profitable gain. How does it craft a response? It starts with talking to relevant stakeholders. "We had a reputation for debating stakeholders more than learning from them," said Nancy Nielsen, the firm's senior director for corporate citizenship. In the past few years, however, the company has reached out and solicited the opinions of a wide range of stakeholders including patient groups, physicians, pharmacists, regulators, business partners, and an assortment of NGOs. It also garnered input from 250 healthcare opinion leaders around the world. The feedback, not surprising, was that although Pfizer shared many of the same healthcare goals as its critics, it had different ideas on how to achieve them and had been unresponsive to calls to assume more responsibility for healthcare in society.

One burning issue in the industry concerns marketing practices. There is controversy over what constitutes ethical marketing of prescription drugs directly to consumers. On the one hand, evidence suggests that advertising leads to early diagnosis and treatment of some diseases. On the other hand, critics contend that pharma-marketing tactics promote overuse of medicines. To address these concerns, Pfizer engaged its stakeholders and conducted research on direct-to-consumer advertising.

This research and stakeholder feedback led Pfizer to develop a set of global policies to self-regulate its interactions with healthcare professionals and the public. The policies dictate that physician meetings and customer events be purely educational, that medical communications be accurate and scientifically rigorous, and that marketing materials convey full information on side effects. Sales representatives cannot offer incentives to doctors to recommend or prescribe drugs or to influence clinical trials. As for advertising, new guidelines have the company partner with the FDA to educate the public about health and disease without reference to specific products and to talk with doctors for at least six months about new therapies before beginning any TV and print advertising. These guidelines are supported by an array of compliance machinery—a chief compliance officer with liaisons in every country, regular reviews, hotlines, penalties, and such—as well as high levels of transparency. Pfizer now discloses, among other subjects, information about customer complaints and the company's political contributions.

Like Pfizer, Diageo operates in a space where its marketing can create opportunities for business, but risks for society. Alcohol misuse and underage drinking are strategic issues for this brewer of Guinness and distiller of Johnny Walker, J&B, Smirnoff, and other brands. Groups such as the National Center on Addiction and Substance Abuse and the Center for Science in the Public Interest have criticized Diageo and others for promoting alcohol at venues and events that are frequented by children and teenagers. Recognizing its responsibilities, the firm established a stronger Code of Marketing Practice and guidelines on advertising content.

Even though operating in 140 countries that have vastly different laws, norms, and preferences on alcohol consumption, Diageo's global policies dictate that all of its marketing and advertising be targeted at adults over the legal purchase age; that it not associate alcohol consumption with sexual attractiveness and success; and that there be no use of images, music, or cartoon characters, à la Joe Camel, that appeal primarily to young people. As Chris Britton, global marketing director for Diageo, sees it, it is in Diageo's best interest to ensure that consumers are aware of the risks involved in alcohol consumption.

Engaging Society

We have described how lobbying and public relations campaigns, the traditional responses by business to the threats of regulation and public disapproval, are increasingly suspect and simply not delivering in today's world. Besides self-regulation and becoming more transparent on, say, ingredients, the risks of using its products, and the various social and environmental impacts of the business, what else can companies facing risks from society do to ensure their license to operate?

"Responsible consumer marketing should not be a constraint but a positive driver linked to company performance," says Britton of Diageo. Thus, the company has developed a broad-based strategy to educate the public and specifically its value chain on responsible alcohol consumption. Global brand teams work with its in-market companies to develop campaigns that educate retailers on underage drinking and over-consumption, train bar and tavern servers on how to identify fake id's and deal with problem drinkers, and raise public awareness of the threats of drinking and driving.

In the United States, the industry overall uses many media channels to promote responsible drinking; organized groups such as Mothers Against Drunk Driving (MADD) educate the public on risks; and industry norms promote self-regulation in this arena. In other parts of the world, however, this infrastructure is not present or runs counter to public norms. So what is Diageo doing around the world? In Australia, a Web site (think-b4u-drink.com) informs young people about responsible drinking and a video game reinforces key messages; in South Africa, Latin America, and the Caribbean, the company is promoting the designated-driver concept; in India, bus and truck drivers are educated on the risks of drinking and driving; and so on.

On the more affirmative side of citizenship, Pfizer adopted an innovative strategy of international corporate volunteerism that serves the needs of the business and society in the treatment of HIV/AIDS, TB, malaria, and other devastating diseases by helping to expand and improve healthcare infrastructure. To address the world's largest health calamity, Pfizer undertook a massive donation program for N. B. Diflucan, a medicine that treats HIV/AIDS-related opportunistic infections, and created the Infectious Diseases Institute in Uganda to train healthcare workers from throughout Africa. But given the company's position as world's largest drug maker, its leadership team was urged by activists and employees alike to take further action. In consultation with longstanding NGO partners, the company decided to beyond traditional industry aid responses of cash and drug donations and began sending its volunteer medical and managerial professionals to work with local nonprofit healthcare service providers in the developing world.

The assignments were designed based upon locally identified needs and contained specific objectives for each Fellow, including training local counterparts. The pilot phase of the Pfizer Global Health Fellows program was launched in late 2003 with eighteen Pfizer colleagues working with seven organizations in nine countries for a period of three to six months. The strategic intent was that Pfizer could help build local capacity while evolving its in-house expertise in developing world healthcare challenges. This would enable Pfizer to speak more credibly to key opinion leaders and stakeholders and help ensure its license to operate.

One of the Center's key contributors, Jonathan Levine, undertook a case study of this program. Obviously, he found limits in the scale of Pfizer's efforts. Well aware that a few dozen volunteers per year do not make much impact in the intractable pandemic, the company points to its multiplier effects: as of Spring 2007, Pfizer had sent 128 Fellows to over thirty countries through thirty-one partner organizations and graduated its one thousandth AIDS African healthcare provider through its partnership with the Infectious Diseases Institute (IDI) at Makerere University in Uganda.

Pfizer's efforts underscore the importance of and the difficulties with offering professionals' time and talent to address the needs of society. On the human scale, Sandy Logue, a Seattle-based Pfizer Inc. sales representative who worked in a neonatal care clinic in Kampala, Uganda, noted how local nurses worked barefoot in wards strewn with blood and used needles because the public hospital couldn't afford Western-style booties for them. "For take-charge corporate types who are used to being control freaks, it's really hard to accept the facts of life here," Logue says, "but you have to." Like many other volunteers, Logue has become a passionate advocate for patients, caregivers, and nonprofit aid organizations whose voice is being heard as the company develops R&D and marketing policies.

On the business side, taking talented people out of their daily jobs in an extremely competitive industry has raised concerns, particularly because Pfizer's fortunes have flagged of late. But its commitment on this sector of the social front has not. "Pfizer could never have predicted the value of this program at the outset or the degree to which it would put a human face on the company," reports Lisa Foster, director of global philanthropy. "We listened to our partners, responded to a critical need in a meaningful way, and it resonated with our employees and those who influence our operating environment, from regulators to activists." Despite recent business challenges and a new CEO, Pfizer has reaffirmed its commitment to this program and is working with other corporations to expand international corporate volunteering in partnership with the Brookings Institution and others.

Defining Issues that Matter

There are many tools and frameworks leading companies might use today to identify issues that matter to the enterprise. For example, Michael Porter and Mark Kramer, of the Harvard Business School and Kennedy School of Government respectively, have mapped how a firm's value chain impinges on society through its operations, marketing, technology, human resource management, and so on. This full body scan framework can help companies to identify the source of problems they create in society and where their vulnerabilities to social problems might be. McKinsey & Co., in turn, has devised a "heat map" that prioritizes social issues in terms of their impact on a company and on the public. In 2005, for instance, the consultancy asked 4,063 consumers in the United States, France, Germany, Japan, India, and China for their views on the most pressing social issues. Consumers ranked the environment, pensions (or retirement), and health benefits as their top three concerns. A comparison between consumer and executive worries is striking, particularly when it comes to the natural environment and retirement—top concerns of consumers and secondary worries of business leaders. No wonder McKinsey labels these as two key risks facing business in the years ahead.[9]

Leading firms also typically scan their environment to identify the interests and actors who might influence their fortunes. This involves preparing a stakeholder map that identifies parties within the company, through its value chain, and on its borders, including the media, NGOs, and communities that have an interest in the company and its practices. Typically, this kind of outside-in mapping stimulates further analysis: a charting of the issues of concern to stakeholders, ratings of their degree of support for or against the company's interests, their ability to influence the course of events, and so on. Sustainability specialist Andrew Savitz describes how such methods can help companies to identify risks and opportunities in their environment and target what he calls the "sustainability sweet-spot."[10]

Identifying "Material" Issues

Business can't address all of society's ills, most every executive reminds us. How does a firm decide which issues are most relevant to its interest and to set its priorities? One criterion being adopted because of its familiarity in accounting and risk management concerns the "materiality" of issues. The concept of materiality is that companies must take an account of and disclose all information that is material to the financial decisions of its investors. In the field of social and ethical accounting, the materiality concept is being extended in two directions. First, firms are being called upon to take an accounting of not only quantifiable financial risks, but also nonfinancial risks that bear on, say, reputation, safety and health, and so on. This is not especially controversial because, as the argument goes, these have implications for the longer-term financial health of an enterprise. Second, companies are asked to consider not only what might be material to shareholders but also material to their many stakeholders. This factors society's risks and opportunities into the accounting.

Companies like Nike, Ford, BP, and others have been working with AccountAbility to incorporate business *and* society's interests not only into their social reports, but also into their operating agendas. AccountAbility's five-part materiality test asks companies to consider social issues as follows:

1. Does the issue pose substantial risk or opportunity to the *business*?
2. Does the issue pose substantial risk or opportunity to *stakeholders*?
3. Is the issue covered in your code of conduct or corporate values?
4. Is the issue being addressed by leaders in your industry?
5. Is the issue becoming judged to be material by the "court of public opinion"?

An affirmative answer to these questions moves a social issue higher up on a company's priority list and makes it a candidate for concerted action.

In the case of Nike, for example, labor issues in their supply chain were clearly identified as posing risks to the company and to workers in Southeast Asia. They also called into question corporate values. Obviously critical media coverage and student boycotts signaled that the issues were being judged as material by at least some influential segments of society. And, to add more urgency, its competitor Reebok adopted a strong code of conduct, called the "Human Rights Production Standards," and became the first mover in the industry to launch an aggressive compliance and supplier education campaign.

Putting Issues into Context

Issues come in complex packages and corporate response to them must come in the same form. On the broadest strategic scale, Shell famously develops scenarios about trends in society to stimulate and inform dialogue within the company.[11] Its most recent scenarios, for example, concern a "trilemma" facing business, pulled between competing forces of market incentives, community interests, and national cultures, including the possibilities of further regulation. One future scenario yields a path of "low trust globalization," where companies continue to maximize profits but have to deal with increased regulatory pressures from nation-states and pushback from NGOs. Another path is one of "open doors," where companies pursue their commercial agenda aligned with stakeholders and with a commitment to transparency. This is the one favoring what we see as next generation citizenship.

There is a third scenario, an anathema to global corporate citizenship, which companies must also consider. This path, where national and ethnic flags predominate, would put a brake on globalization and force companies to manage risks associated with religious and nation-state conflicts. All three of these scenarios, developed by Shell's strategic planning specialists, are discussed and digested by executives throughout the company and folded into contingency plans.

Many of the member companies in the Center's three learning forums have had to grapple with such complexities and resist simplification in understanding the many issues surrounding their businesses. For example, at Agilent, the high-tech measurement company spun off from HP, citizenship specialists from diverse functions used agreed-upon rules of engagement and a whiteboard to work as a group to analyze and amend models of the context surrounding their company's sustainability agenda. Nokia employs a team of experts and has enlisted six thousand of its employees to develop its "World Map." And IBM, as we will see in more detail in the next chapter, brings this to unprecedented scale in its global electronic jams.

Making Values Matter

Conversations with stakeholders, maps of social issues, analyses of complex interactions, ratings of relative priorities: While all of these inform decision making, ultimately executives have to make judgment calls about what to do. Here, interestingly, our research indicates that values guide the choices of leading corporate citizens. Ask, for example, what's behind 3M's strong moves toward environmental sustainability? Legal counsel Mike Nash answers: "Our company values drive what we do. We see it this way because it's in the culture. It's ingrained from top management. We always ask 'Are we doing the right thing here?' and not 'Are we doing the legal thing here?' We set the standard as going way beyond compliance . . . about doing the right thing. Legal doesn't drive it— the company drives it."

A Booz Allen Hamilton/Aspen Institute survey reports that nearly nine out of ten global companies have value statements that speak to ethics and integrity, and that a great majority of them profess a commitment to customers, employees, shareholders, and other stakeholders as well as to corporate citizenship or CSR.[12] Interestingly, the study found that companies that were top financial performers had a stronger belief than the rest of the sample in the value of values. They were also more likely to believe that environmental responsibility and corporate citizenship are drivers of business success.

There are, of course, plenty of companies that counterfeit their values in practice. These are the firms that say that people are their most important asset and then short-shrift them or exploit workers in their supply chain; those that pledge support for local communities and then move facilities to secure tax breaks; those that claim to care for the environment but lobby hard against protective measures and limit their emphasis to legal compliance. This is a prime source of cynicism about business and its leadership.

But how about the other side, where companies positively and actively express their values in the ways they do business? Johnson & Johnson, for example, is tackling the nursing shortage with its educational and recruitment campaign for nursing's future. General Motors, long committed to diversity, has a Supplier Diversity Council and spends billions with its minority suppliers. Ford is out in front on this, too. What is distinctive about these companies is that they have not only identified business-relevant issues and done their homework on how to address them; they have made public commitments to do so based on their corporate values.

A Value Proposition for Citizenship

The Booz Allen/Aspen study of corporate values found that the practice of linking values to strategy is, at this stage, an early work in progress. To speed this along, companies in the Center's forums have put values at the core of their relationship to society and built out their strategies in light of them. Diageo considered: How do we strengthen our business model by leading on responsible consumption of alcohol? Its marketing codes and education campaigns exemplify one answer. FedEx asked: "What leadership do we take to reduce the environmental footprint of a transportation-intensive business model?" The company has received extensive attention from its rollout of fuel-efficient hybrid electric delivery trucks. Along with saving energy and maintenance costs, the company received reputational benefits. As the company's Environmental Management Director Mitch Jackson notes, however: "We understand the business case for doing this. But what sold this inside our company wasn't the business case, but the appeal to our core values."

A value proposition for citizenship begins with a fresh look at corporate values: Do the values of the company align with the interests of employees, customers, suppliers, communities, environmental interests, human rights activists, and government? Asking these questions enables key stakeholders from both society and the marketplace to shape and influence values. Unilever, IBM, and

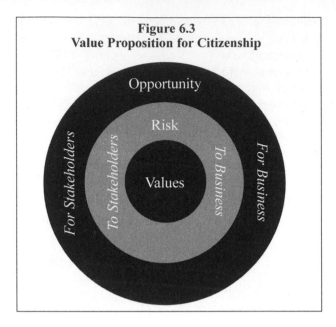

Figure 6.3
Value Proposition for Citizenship

GE all redefined their values in this light. Strategy, in turn, is informed by the risks to stakeholders and the business and by joint opportunities that might beckon (Figure 6.3).

Citizenship and the "LS&CO. Way"

Levi Strauss & Co. has exemplified a values-led business since founder Levi Strauss first set up his dry goods firm in San Francisco in 1853. A year after his arrival, Strauss gave $5.00 to a local orphanage (the current equivalent of about $110), beginning a tradition of philanthropy and community service that continues today. In the next century the company grew to iconic status with its jeanswear brand and recorded a significant citizenship profile: keeping its employees on payroll after the 1906 earthquake; cash bonuses to sewing machine workers based on company returns in the 1920s; split-shifts to keep people employed during the Depression; racial integration in its California factories in the 1940s and in the American South in 1960; minority supplier program in the 1970s; full medical benefits to unmarried partners of employees in the 1990s; as well as a first-in-industry supplier code of conduct for global sourcing.

Although the company was a pioneer in corporate citizenship, a business downturn beginning in 1997 affected some of its programs. With the executive team focused intensely on business needs, citizenship programs that were free-standing (e.g., the Levi Strauss Foundation) or nested within a business unit (e.g., supplier code of conduct within the Global Sourcing Organization) continued to operate. Citizenship efforts that were not connected to business imperatives (e.g., employee affinity groups and HIV/AIDS education) began to fall away. When the company joined the Executive Forum in 2002, its "profits through principles" philosophy was in place, but citizenship programs were not yet a part of the firm's management model. Theresa Fay-Bustillos, vice president of worldwide community affairs, took advantage of her position on the world-wide leadership team and the interest of Chairman Bob Haas to redesign the company's approach to corporate citizenship.

Having noted that the company's brands used value propositions as a tool to define their qualities and character for consumers, Fay-Bustillos worked with the company's worldwide leadership team to develop a value proposition for corpo-rate citizenship. Accordingly, and with the blessing of the CEO, she convened a cross-functional, multi-level working group around corporate citizenship, which included some top executives. Fay-Bustillos, a lawyer and community activist, focused the group on understanding the company's 150-year legacy of corporate citizenship; listening to employees, executives, and shareholders; and identifying current and potential future societal issues facing the apparel and textile industry. The group's work highlighted how citizenship was material to the company's strategic decisions. As Fay-Bustillos put it, "It is about listening to the business people talk, boiling it down, and then using their own language to sell it back to them."

Fay-Bustillos presented the findings of the cross-functional group to the worldwide leadership team, along with the following quote from Walter Haas Jr., the company's CEO from 1958 to 1970, to inspire the team and spur the discussion:

> Each of us has a capacity to make business not only a source of economic wealth, but also a force for economic and social justice. Each of us needs to recognize and use the power we have to define the character of our enterprises, so they nurture values important to our society. Only then will each of us know the full rewards that a career in business can yield. Only then will business achieve the true poten-tial of its leadership. Only then will business fulfill its obligation to help an econ-omy worthy of a free society and civilization worth celebrating.

Even as top executives struggled with the "fast fashion" trends in consumer behavior in the market, and launched a massive cost-cutting campaign, Robert Hanson, president of North America and of the U.S. Levi's brand, joined the working group's conversation and asked: "Who are we?" Out of the discussions, a corporate citizenship value proposition emerged aligned with the company's values—empathy, originality, integrity, and courage. The worldwide leadership team then pledged to educate employees on the new value proposition, incorpo-rate it into the strategic business planning process, and hold themselves accountable for making progress going forward. Key elements of the value proposition include:

- *Business Practices That Reflect the Diversity of the World We Serve.* The com-pany seeks to build on its record of diversity among employees, consumers, suppliers, and other stakeholders, as well as in its advertising and marketing efforts.

- *Supply Chain Practices That Respect the Workers Who Make Our Products*. The company seeks to build on its pioneering sourcing code, continuing to work at the factory, community, and public policy levels to improve working conditions for garment workers worldwide.
- *Environmental Initiatives That Support Sustainability*. The company aspires to build on its leadership supply-chain water-quality program and expand sustainability initiatives to other parts of its operations.
- *Societal Engagement That Contributes to Positive Social Change*. The company aims to build on its achievements in employee community involvement and social-change-focused grant making through deeper engagement with employees, consumers, and diverse stakeholders.
- *HIV/AIDS Initiatives That Protect Employees, Workers, and Consumers*. The company intends to build on its longstanding leadership in this area by activating employees, consumers, and workers to oppose HIV/AIDS stigma and discrimination and work with contractors to promote workers' access to prevention information, treatment, and care.

As of this writing, Levi Strauss & Co. is back on its feet commercially and has completed a pilot program integrating the value proposition into strategic planning in select business units in its North American operations. As an example, the company made a public commitment at the 2006 Clinton Global Initiative to provide a comprehensive HIV/AIDS therapy and treatment program for all Levi Strauss & Co. employees and their families, worldwide, that can serve as a model for other global apparel companies and is in the process of building the program. The company has begun to roll out the value proposition to all business units through the strategic planning process and to employees worldwide as part of an organizational development program entitled *The LS&CO. Way and You*.

On overall progress, Hanson says: "We're getting there." Then he adds, "Just as in the marketplace, we also need to innovate with citizenship if we want to remain relevant with our stakeholders. This is why we're working to deeply integrate citizenship into our business at every level in our organization."

None of this is to suggest that a value proposition, in and of itself, can drive a company toward next generation citizenship. Efforts to bring a company's values into balance with marketplace and societal interests inevitably involve trade-offs as there is no consensus in society and the marketplace about what really matters. It is simply unrealistic to expect that companies can find and operate in a sweet spot where every decision delivers a win for the business and a win for society. What next generation citizens are doing, therefore, is devising strategies that best apply their assets to risks and opportunities at the border of business and society.

7

Taking an Integrated, Strategic Approach

Consider the distinctions between world-class performance for business versus world-class performance for corporate citizenship. In business, world-class performers design strategies that provide sustainable competitive advantage, and reinforce them with operating processes to deliver top-level execution with high levels of quality and productivity. Businesses use sophisticated management systems to gain efficiency, provide training and development for employees, and rely on clear performance metrics to guide continuous improvement. World-class performers also develop close connections with their customers, suppliers, and employees. And, in what might be the most distinguishing characteristic, world-class performers align and integrate every component from strategy to execution to performance feedback in a virtuous, self-reinforcing cycle that builds sustainable value.

Corporate citizenship, by comparison, has adopted a different performance model, typically associated with administration, which centers on policies, programs, and reports:

- Citizenship policies are often found in codes of corporate conduct and apply to everything from governance to ethical business practices to supplier relationships, and they are subject to enforcement;
- Citizenship programs range from environmental management and employee assistance to charitable giving and community volunteering; and
- Citizenship reports review company social and environmental practices and typically include some discussion of progress, setbacks, and goals for the future.

Now, good corporate citizens often have forward-looking policies, effective programs, and informative reports, but can you imagine a world-class business allocating discrete tasks to R&D, manufacturing, and marketing without an overall game plan or effective means to align interests, coordinate efforts, or drive to common, agreed-upon objectives? Yet, in so many companies, responsibilities for corporate citizenship are housed in and led by corporate staff functions known by their acronyms—EH&S, HR, PR, and CR—without a shared mission and absent coordination, let alone cross-functional teamwork.

Redressing this situation was the challenge taken up by the companies in the Center's Executive Forum. While the eight companies took different tacks, each adopted a "whole-system" approach to citizenship that engages a full range of internal and external stakeholders in identifying issues and devising a coherent and integrated citizenship agenda. AMD, one of the Forum companies we profile in this chapter, worked diligently to enlist every function in the business in a coordinated approach to corporate citizenship.

A second problem with the prevailing model of citizenship is that it is very difficult to know how it contributes to the success of the business. Would a manufacturing plant, sales office, or marketing group legitimately view world-class performance as a series of well-run, discrete programs that comply with standards, and then publish a report about the results? Odd as it might sound, this is how many companies gauge the success of their citizenship efforts, and they win awards from CSR ranking groups for doing so.

The challenge of embedding citizenship into the business was taken up by companies in the Global Leadership Network. As a business manager in one of the GLN companies said it bluntly: "A company like [ours] is not going to pursue corporate citizenship for its own sake. Ultimately it will be based on how corporate citizenship is perceived as a business driver." Later in this chapter, we will see how one GLN company, IBM, is driving its business with corporate citizenship.

Integrating Citizenship into a Company

In 1995, when computer chipmaker AMD produced its first annual Environmental, Health, and Safety (EHS) report, it was seen as cutting edge for a company to publicly report nonfinancial information.[1] In 2000, the company broadened the scope of the report to include social and economic data. Since then its approach has continued to evolve, yielding an integrated Corporate Responsibility Report and management framework. Leading this effort was Philip Trowbridge, then a member of the worldwide EHS technical staff, and other key people from the EHS and community affairs departments. Their progress illustrates how top companies tackle demands for transparency by devising more comprehensive measurement and reporting schemes. It also illustrates movement toward a more *integrated* approach to citizenship where different interests and functions within a company are brought together and *aligned* within a cohesive, company-wide framework that is commonly understood in different parts of the business.

AMD's movement on these fronts was influenced to some degree by pressure from various stakeholders for greater transparency and accountability. In 1998, as an example, its Board received a shareholder resolution "seeking assurances that their labor and environmental standards in facilities are adequate" from Mission Responsibility Through Investment (MRTI), an NGO-affiliated with the Presbyterian Church. "It was a real eye-opener for the company," reports Trowbridge. "It was a significant turning point when we brought MRTI in and discussed their concerns. They were surprised to find that we were a lot further ahead than they thought, because they hadn't seen much information on AMD.

We had an EHS report, but it didn't go into many of the other things that the company was doing."

"A couple of years later, we received the first Dow Jones Sustainability Index survey," he went on to say. "It asked a lot of hard questions we were not quite sure how to answer, and that made us look at how communications needed to change in order to address the difficult issues." Next came a flurry of queries from other socially responsible investing (SRI) organizations and from customers. Especially for business-to-business companies like AMD, the seriousness and regularity with which customers began to want data about social and environmental performance was a huge change. "More and more of our customers began to ask us specific questions about our management systems, our business continuity, our environmental, health, and safety codes of conduct, and our social responsibility conduct," says Trowbridge. "They're even incorporating these types of things into sales agreements."

As a result, AMD began to systematize its measurement and reporting strategy. An EHS team pored over the framework developed in 2000 by the Global Reporting Initiative (GRI), an association of social and environmental accounting professionals, NGOs, and corporate partners that issues reporting guidelines, recommends core indicators, and sets standards for disclosure. Some of the GRI criteria seemed very relevant for AMD. Others did not. Adapting the GRI guidelines, AMD issued its first integrated report in early 2001 with economic, social, and environmental data. Then Trowbridge and Allyson Peerman, vice president for public affairs, who had joined in the effort, took a step back and asked: Is this what corporate citizenship is really all about?

Their top-of-mind worry was that social reporting would become a "box checking" exercise, where information would be compiled from different parts of AMD, matched to the various reporting categories, and then published without any serious consideration of what it all meant and without much real benefit to the company. In their guts they were concerned that it would not have anything to do with how AMD designed its products, developed its strategy, did its business, or made its contribution to society.

Leading Integration from the Middle

These two middle managers, one on the environmental side and the other from community affairs, adopted an opportunistic and organic approach to organizing citizenship at AMD. Rather than develop a detailed business case for citizenship or seek direction from top management, they took it upon themselves "to integrate disparate efforts around the company."

Their first year or so was spent in what they term "awareness building." This meant knocking on electronic doors, collaring people face to face in the cafeteria, arranging meetings with peers in investor relations, human resources, and other corporate functions, and seeding interest throughout the organization. Compilations of CSR headlines were sent to managers, worldwide standards of business were issued, discussions were held with SRI funds and customers, and momentum began to build. "This work is all about relationships, that's how things move forward in the company," says Peerman. "It's through individuals understanding the importance of corporate citizenship, how it impacts the company and their particular business unit, and the role they can play in it."

Next the two created a Corporate Sustainability Advisory Team that brought together all the relevant corporate managers and, in time, representatives from different parts of the business. This marked the phase of coalition building. This group functioned as a coordinative body and think tank, talking equally about what was going on in various parts of the company and in the environment around each of their disciplines. To create a big-picture overview, Trowbridge prepared a matrix of the many criteria used to account for a company's triple bottom line performance (see Figure 7.1). He then had the Advisory Team assess where AMD stood on each of these dimensions and their relative priority.

"We went through a classic SWOT analysis, looking at our strengths, weaknesses, opportunities, and threats in each area," says Trowbridge. "But we also asked the fundamental question: Do we have a program that addresses this issue? And if not, do we need one? And how would people rank this issue in terms of importance to AMD?" Immediately, there were gaps identified: AMD had language about human rights in its value system and business contracts, for example, but human rights had not been considered fully in audits of its supply-chain operations or in the training of procurement managers and staff. The analysis also revealed that regulatory changes in the European Union were prompting their company's customers to accelerate their compliance schedules. The resulting speedup in this area gave AMD a brief spell of competitive advantage in dealing with them.

From Silos to a Common Agenda

In the past three years, AMD has moved citizenship into an integrative action phase. Trowbridge and Peerman's organic efforts are reaching the top and bottom of the company and citizenship has morphed from the fragmented work of functional silos into a more cooperative, comprehensive, corporate-wide agenda. For one, there has been a name change. Given its origins in EHS, the thrust was originally encapsulated under the name of "sustainability." With the active engagement of the relevant corporate functions, and the active involvement of senior management and the Board, it was decided to rebrand it "Corporate Responsibility." This, according to Peerman, "was a term that more aptly described our end goal and was consistent with the company's core values."

Second, the company has moved its overall agenda forward. On the environmental front, for instance, AMD has formulated a global climate protection plan that applies to all of its facilities and has yielded significant reductions in greenhouse gas emissions and improvements in eco-efficiency. It has also adopted new industry codes, such as the Electronics Industry Code of Conduct, that applies social and environmental standards to the supply chain of companies in the semiconductor industry, and joined The Green Grid, a consortium of manufacturers that aims to increase the energy efficiency of computer servers. And, on the community side, AMD's formerly localized and decentralized model has

Figure 7.1
AMD Issue Analysis

At AMD, Philip Trowbridge and his cross-functional advisory group used this matrix as a way to prioritize issues and strategize the road ahead for corporate citizenship.

	Programs		Priority		S.W.O.T. (Strengths, Weaknesses, Opportunities, Threats)			
	Do we have a program to address issue?	If not, do we need a program?	Importance Rating (1 = High; 3 = Low)	Priority Ranking	What are our strengths in this area?	What are our weaknesses in this area?	What opportunities are available to us in this area?	What threats do we face in this area?
ECONOMIC RESPONSIBILITY								
Corporate Governance								
Code of Ethics								
Socially Responsible Investing								
Risk Management/ Crisis Management								
Business Continuity Planning								
SOCIAL RESPONSIBILITY								
Supplier Diversity								
Supply Chain CSR								
Workplace Safety								
Employee Wellness								
Employee/Leadership Development								
Code of Conduct								
Community Involvement								
Corporate Philanthropy								
Employee Commitment								
Human Rights								
Workforce Diversity								
Talent Attraction/Retention								
Wages & Benefits								
Customer Satisfaction/ Relationship Management								
Knowledge Management/ Organizational Learning								
E-Readiness/E-Learning								
Stakeholder Engagement								
Product Stewardship								
ENVIRONMENTAL RESPONSIBILITY								
Environmental Policy/ Management								
Resource Conservation								
Design for EHS - Products								
Design for EHS - Manufacturing/R&D								
Climate Change								
Customer EHS Inquiries								
Environmental Preferred Purchasing								
COMMUNICATION								
CSR/Sustainability Questionnaires								
Sustainability Report								
Balanced Scorecard								
Corporate Strategy								

been complemented by a global framework that addresses practices ranging from stakeholder and community consultations to volunteerism and community service.

Third, the company is taking a more holistic approach to citizenship. An emphasis on financial, social, and environmental performance is not just a reporting practice at AMD. It is now an integral part of the design of the company's Experienced Manager Academy, a global immersion program that sends AMD's next generation leaders to India, China, and other emerging markets to gain a firsthand understanding of its next generation customers and their communities. It is also, as of this writing, making its way into key performance indicators and management performance reviews.

Citizenship and Strategy

What does it take to move further into the frontiers of citizenship toward a transformative landscape where companies "change the game" and align their citizenship to market creation and social change? This is the terrain being scouted by GE and the other companies that are members of the Center's Global Leadership Network. Its corporate founder and chair has been IBM.

The largest company in the $1.2 trillion IT world, "Big Blue," so-named because of its size and iconic logo, was built on a determination to apply high-level research and development to its marketplace.[2] Under the leadership of, first, Thomas Watson Sr. and later, Thomas Watson Jr., the company enacted the principle that "Thought has been the father of every advance since time began" and its offices and plants famously featured signs with the one-word slogan, in large block-letters, "THINK." Throughout the century past, IBM was at the forefront of information technology—tabulating machines, electro-mechanical punch card systems, mainframe computers, personal computers—until its near collapse in the early 1990s. When Lou Gerstner took charge in 1993, IBM shifted its identity as a producer of computer hardware to a provider of business solutions through software and consulting. This was manifest in the acquisition of Lotus Development Corporation in 1995 and the consulting arm of PricewaterhouseCoopers in 2002.

But the trouble in IBM was that its values went south along with its business fortunes in the late 1980s into the early '90s. Internal groups competed with one another. Commitments to career plans, program funding, and new ventures were routinely broken. The jape inside the company was that IBM stood for "I've Been Mislead." Gerstner set out a new strategic agenda and fixed some of the infighting. Sam Palmisano, Gerstner's successor in 2002, focusing on vision and values took it to the next level and in so doing opened a bold new chapter in IBM's relationship to society.

Technology lends itself to multiple applications, and IBM is today in dialogue within the company and with other businesses, academe, think tanks, NGOs, government agencies, and many other stakeholders to consider how it can apply its tools to a variety of social and environmental issues. We have described how IBM first forged a link between citizenship and commerce when it introduced its "reinventing education" program in the United States and then took it to global scale thereafter. Now, in research centers and product groups, IBMers look for other forms of cross-fertilization in the design and marketing of new products and services under its core value "innovation that matters for the world."

IBM is today applying its know-how in a range of socio-commercial ventures to find cures for disease, to provide disaster relief, and to ease the plight of urban slum dwellers in the world's mega-cities. This is how IBM intends to live its corollary mantra, "collaboration that matters." But to get there, the company had to take a deep look at itself and decide who it wanted to be.

Leading with Values

Research supports the proposition that companies with strong values perform better. In their well-known study *Built to Last*, Jim Collins and Jerry Porras document that successful, enduring companies are built on a foundation of values that establishes the purpose of an enterprise, dictates how it will operate, and guides decisions from the strategic to the everyday.[3] Research confirms the corollary: "Built to Last" companies are also ranked by respected third parties as top corporate citizens.[4] A complementary conclusion is reached by money manager Joseph Bragdon who has studied sixty firms whose credit ratings and growth rates far exceed those of their peers. He finds that these top performers do a better job of caring for their "living assets"—employees, customers, communities, and the environment—and as a result "profit for life."[5]

Over the course of IBM's history, we were told in our interviews, the company has been most successful when its values were strong and its employees were aligned with them. The alignment was still out of kilter when Palmisano took over in 2002. In the year prior, IBM introduced the first in a series of what it calls "online jams"—virtual conversations over the firm's Intranet that allowed its employees all over the world to talk about issues of concern to them. As they have evolved, these e-meetings last up to two or three days. Subject-matter experts offer input and perspectives, and moderators guide jammers to build on each other's ideas. Text-analysis tools from IBM research capture and play back key themes, striving for consensus.

In 2003, under Palmisano's lead, IBM held an important and focused conversation, its "ValuesJam," which involved almost the entire company in a redefinition of corporate values.[6] This jam lasted for seventy-two hours and has been described variously as "freewheeling," "passionate," and "brutally honest." The contributors debated whether or not company values existed and what was involved in establishing them. They talked about what values IBM needed to be successful and what unique contribution IBM could make to the world. In a virtual room dedicated to positive thinking, they also talked about what made them proud about IBM and what it was like when the company was at its best.

Ultimately this dialogue was text-analyzed, themed, and translated into three IBM core values: dedication to every client's success; innovation that matters, for the company and for the world; and trust and personal responsibility in all relationships. In a message that announced IBM's new values, Palmisano explained their genesis: "Given the realities of a smart, global, independent-minded, 21st-century workforce like ours, I don't believe that something as vital and personal as values can be dictated from the top."

In a follow-up "WorldJam" in 2004, more than fifty-seven thousand employees posted thirty-two thousand ideas and comments on how the new values could be applied to improve IBM's operations, workforce policies, and relationships. To date, thirty-five of the best ideas—as rated by IBMers themselves—are in various stages of implementation, with executive owners responsible to the chairman for their development. These include actions to align executive compensation to shareholder interests, to give first-line managers a discretionary $5,000 annually to spend on customer or employee needs, and a reinventing of the employee suggestion system, now operating under the name ThinkPlace.

IBM and Next Generation Citizenship

Each of the companies in the Global Leadership Network undergoes an assessment of the alignment of corporate citizenship with its core business priorities. The main priorities of IBM at the start of the GLN program were: (1) capitalizing on technological, business, and social trends and developing innovations in light of them; (2) maintaining market share in key business areas; (3) focusing investment in emerging growth areas and business lines; (4) continuing the global integration of the company; (5) furthering its leadership position in select technologies and business processes; and (6) acquisitions and divestitures that strengthen its portfolio.

Next, the research team mapped IBM's key citizenship drivers: (1) community innovation, (2) employee skills development, (3) responsible supply-chain management, (4) environmental management, and (5) transparency through reporting and audits. Comparing the two sets, it was apparent that these drivers were integral to company strategy. For instance, transparency and supply-chain management, matters of compliance in some companies, were core to what Palmisano defines as the next generation corporate form—the globally integrated enterprise. Employee skills development and environmental management naturally were integral to IBM's strategies, too. But the most distinctive of IBM's citizenship drivers was the emphasis it had given to community innovation.

This led the team to identify a series of corporate citizenship "winners" at IBM—where the company could apply its core competencies in innovation to build or reinforce strong and positive relationships with key stakeholders, including national governments, industry, and professional bodies; perhaps open new markets, either through commercial activity or technology migration; and, most importantly, effect meaningful social change (see Figure 7.2). IBM's "jam" methodology and technology platforms were identified as ways to expand thinking, engage stakeholders, and open up a whole new relationship between the company and society.

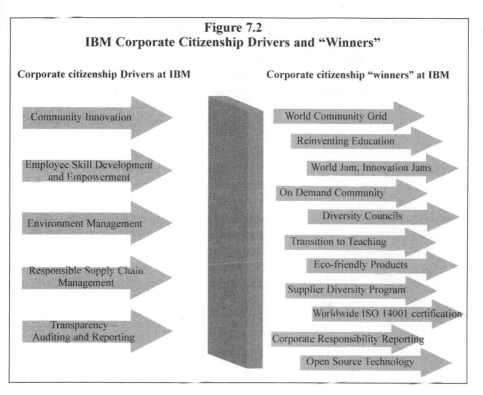

Figure 7.2
IBM Corporate Citizenship Drivers and "Winners"

Corporate citizenship Drivers at IBM

Corporate citizenship "winners" at IBM

- Community Innovation
- Employee Skill Development and Empowerment
- Environment Management
- Responsible Supply Chain Management
- Transparency – Auditing and Reporting

- World Community Grid
- Reinventing Education
- World Jam, Innovation Jams
- On Demand Community
- Diversity Councils
- Transition to Teaching
- Eco-friendly Products
- Supplier Diversity Program
- Worldwide ISO 14001 certification
- Corporate Responsibility Reporting
- Open Source Technology

Global Innovation and Corporate Responsibility

For IBM, the focus of what it terms Corporate Responsibility and its business are one and the same: using its technology to reach out to and connect people to find new and lasting solutions to the world's most vexing problems. In 2004, IBM connected its internal technical and forecasting professionals with external thought leaders to look into the most pressing issues facing the world and what role IBM might play in addressing them. The Global Innovation Outlook (GIO) has continued annually since then—adding new contributors from thirty-six countries and 178 organizations.

On the environmental front, GIO participants have suggested several innovations that apply to product life cycles. For example, firms might do "soft updates" to high-tech goods such as cameras, computers, recorders, and the like; this approach would replace outmoded components in lieu of scrapping the whole product. It would also reduce distribution costs, perhaps increase brand loyalty, certainly cut waste, and have an impact on energy use and emissions. Or firms might create "reverse supply chains" whereby they would trade used materials and goods with other firms. These and hundreds of other ideas are under review at IBM in terms of their technical feasibility and in light of possible resource shortages and an expected wave of environmental regulation.

In 2006, IBM went where no other firm has gone before: the company invited thousands of outsiders across multiple sectors of the economy into a virtual boardroom to learn about and discuss new product and service ideas with

Palmisano, his staff, and thousands of IBMers. Why would a business in its right mind open its intellectual property and patents to the world? The rationale, according to Nicholas Donofrio, IBM's executive vice president for innovation and technology, is this: "Open, multidisciplinary, global collaboration is the key to creating both a climate and a culture that enable innovation to thrive." He goes on: "Here we are, the quintessential proprietary operating system company in the IT world, and who is it that defends the open source movement? Why? Because we understand the power of the community. We understand what it's like on the other side when you stand alone. It's lonely; it's also not very wise. It's not a business strategy that will work in the end."[7]

That first "InnovationJam," held over an online platform, allowed visitors to tinker with existing IBM technologies and supply fresh ideas. Some visitors debated how to use RFID-tagged (Radio Frequency Identification) bracelets to improve the traveler's experience at the airport. Others focused on early warning systems for health pandemics. As a result of the process, IBM has committed to put up to $100 million behind the strongest ideas. According to Palmisano it was the first time "a technology company takes its most valued secrets, opens them up to the world and says, O.K., world, you tell us [what to do with them]."

Corporate Social Innovation

IBM is using its combination of technology, open sourcing, and collective jamming in myriad engagements with society. For instance, the company hosted "HabitatJam"—an online conference with nearly forty thousand people from 194 countries that included teachers, children, urban planners, and government leaders—to generate ideas on making urban areas more habitable. Meanwhile, UN-HABITAT partner organizations mobilized twenty-five thousand slum dwellers in urban centers in Kenya, India, Egypt, and elsewhere to offer their views on these matters at local Internet cafés. Their collective recommendations on access to water, environmental sustainability, finance and government, safety and security, improving life in slums, and the future of global cities were taken up by World Urban Forum delegates at their third annual conference in Vancouver, in June 2006.[8]

The World Community Grid is another significant social innovation cum collaboration. This has nearly four hundred thousand people—including IBM customers and business partners—donating the idle processing power from six hundred thousand computers to create, in effect, a virtual supercomputer devoted to humanitarian research. Its first application was the Human Proteome Folding Project, which, drawing on the massive computing capacity of the grid, enabled researchers to develop models of how protein structures might factor into cancer, Alzheimer's, SARS, and malaria. Dr. Richard Bonneau of the Institute for Systems Biology says the grid enabled his organization to complete in one year a project that otherwise would have taken an estimated one hundred thousand years with their existing computational power. Since then, IBM has seen the grid applied to AIDS, where a new FightAIDS@Home initiative, sponsored by Scripps Research, is keyed to the design of therapies that can be effective in the face of viral drug resistance, to cancer research, and most recently to the environmental sciences.[9]

How does all of this fit with IBM's commercial agenda? For one, some of IBM's business customers use grid technology to address their own particular business problems. Ideas and innovations from one space naturally spread to the other.

Second, as head of corporate affairs and corporate citizenship, Stan Litow points out that IBM's social innovations are relevant for marketing and branding its capabilities. When IBM salespeople meet with customers, for instance, they might show them the World Computing Grid, how it scales globally, how many calculations can be done, and how the whole thing was "set up from idea to action in four months." Customers can see how all of this, demonstrated in three minutes on a PC, "might be adapted to solve a business problem." At the same time, Litow is adamant that in IBM's socio-commercial efforts, the community comes first. Only when the company proves its value to society, whether by applying grid technology to climate study in South Africa or, in France, to the study of muscular dystrophy, does it use its efforts in society to leverage marketing or build commercial extensions.

Finally, IBM has enlisted its employees in a new form of business-relevant volunteerism by giving them technology targeted for nonprofit community organizations and schools. This program provides nearly eighty thousand employees worldwide with more than one hundred forty specially designed IBM technology assets and other resources, programs, and tutorials that they can access on line and share with the agencies where they volunteer. We'll look at some of the dimensions of this volunteer effort and its impact on IBMers later in this volume.

What all of these programs have in common is the commitment to share and co-create innovations that help the world. Some years ago Rosabeth Moss Kanter, observing this budding development, described IBM's approach as a move from giving "spare change" to promoting "real change" in the relationship between business and society.[10] Now it is gaining a following in citizenship circles under the moniker of CSI—Corporate Social Innovation. What IBM has done is bring it to a scale and level of credibility heretofore only imagined.

More broadly, IBM is demonstrating how citizenship can be integral to corporate strategy. In Sam Palmisano's eyes, and increasingly throughout IBM, citizenship is part and parcel of the business strategy. It is not something unique or special, or just to apply to "crown jewels" like education; on the contrary, he says: "It's who we are; it's how we do business; its part of our values; its in the DNA of our culture."

On Taking an Integrated, Strategic Approach

As businesses come to terms with new demands for corporate citizenship, fresh ideas are emerging about how to incorporate it into business strategy and operations. IBM has been one of the most adept in aligning its corporate values with its core business competency to move toward a new strategic approach to citizenship. We have also seen Unilever step firmly in this direction, GE make some bold moves, and Wal-Mart make what is figuratively and in a developmental sense a "step change." On the operational side, AMD has been a leader in integrating citizenship into its core processes.

What are some of the insights on taking an integrated, strategic approach that can be gleaned from their example?

A Strategic Framework

Managers seem to gravitate to frameworks when it comes to moving into new territory. This was certainly true in the quality movement and even more so in the field of social responsibility, where definitions and terminology are unclear and metrics are in an early stage of development. Criteria advanced by socially responsible investment houses, the guidelines promulgated by the GRI, the metrics used by the DJSI and FTSE4Good, and the comprehensive assessment methodology developed by Sandra Waddock and Sam Graves of Boston College's School of Management, and used by *CRO* (Corporate Responsibility Officer) magazine in its ratings of the top 100 Corporate Citizens, all provide useful ways for companies to conceptualize and to monitor their triple bottom line performance. These frameworks were helpful to AMD in pulling different functions together within the company and taking a more integrative approach to citizenship.

But these concepts, criteria, and indicators come primarily from the fields of social and environmental accounting and were designed to help firms to account for their performance through semi-standardized metrics, akin to the type used in financial accounting. Granted, leading companies have adapted these metrics into managerial accounting in the form of, say, a balanced scorecard. But accounting systems are not designed to shape business strategies.

The GLN assessment framework, in skeletal form, covers four domains (see Figure 7.3). In the area of business strategy, for instance, companies compare their business priorities and citizenship agenda, as IBM did, and consider that alignment of corporate citizenship with business strategy. This considers, as well, societal expectations of the company. A second domain is termed *engaged learning*. The questions here address how companies engage their multiple stakeholders directly and define their strategic position on corporate citizenship through a process of true consultation. A third area concerns a corporate commitment to take the lead on select social and environmental issues that are material to the business. Finally, the area of operational excellence covers how companies embed citizenship through appropriate governance structures, coordinative mechanisms, measures, and such, a subject we will consider in more detail later on in the volume.

The GLN assessment is itself evolving and is by no means unique. We have noted as well the value-chain model elaborated by Porter and Kramer and McKinsey & Co.'s heat map and Five R framing of strategic business-society considerations (e.g., Risk, Renewal, Regulation, Relationships, Reputation).

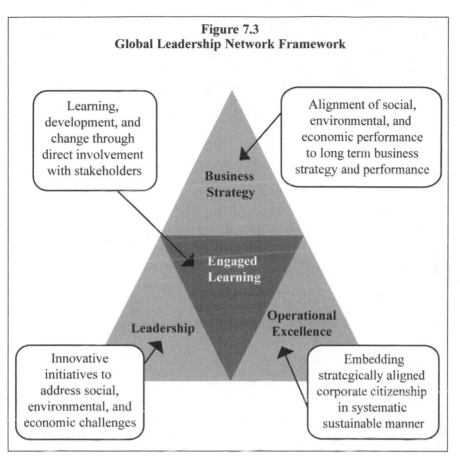

Figure 7.3
Global Leadership Network Framework

The key message is that frameworks can make the abstract seem more concrete and manageable.

Differentiation and *Integration*

A second insight, more theoretical but no less important, concerns the need to balance differentiation and integration in the development of a citizenship agenda. At issue is how organizations and subunits adapt to best deal with the demands of their complex, multidimensional environments.

Differentiation is a key feature in development and growth.[11] In organizations, this takes the form of dividing things up by job responsibility, geography, hierarchy, and function. We've described how this allows a firm to take a more professional approach to its work as a corporate citizen: developing distinct and advanced capabilities in community affairs, public affairs, investor relations, human resources, health, safety and environmental matters, not to mention expertise in how citizenship factors into traditional business functions like finance, marketing, manufacture, and so on.

Differentiation is also essential on the journey to next generation corporate citizenship. Demands placed on each of these functions will continue to escalate: Calls to form partnerships to address vital social issues, heightened community concerns over growth or outsourcing, increased shareholder or NGO activism, challenges posed by an aging workforce and the war for talent, cause-related marketing opportunities, new climate change-related regulations, and a socio-commercial frontier that beckons. Each of these will impinge on different people with different expertise and rightly need an informed and expert response. And, with the continued globalization of commerce and communication, the complexity of the sociopolitical and commercial environments companies face will continue to increase and so must their capacities for differentiation.

As companies develop their citizenship capabilities, however, some will find themselves in a situation like Unilever's where "a thousand flowers bloom." Ironically, as they engage a broader and more disparate range of stakeholders, and get a better perspective on needs and possibilities, literally millions of disconnected initiatives can be launched. This seeds a new developmental crisis: coping with extensive differentiated activity.

What pulls things together?—education, systems and processes, coordinative structures, measures and accountability schemes, and such. The capacities of a company to develop an integrative approach are crucial in the development of next generation citizenship. We'll see these mechanics in the case of other Executive Forum companies further on in the volume. But pay attention to the integrative option favored by IBM.

What was the intent of grassroots involvement in establishing new IBM values? As Palmisano puts it: "You have to empower people while ensuring that they're making the right calls the right way. And by 'right,' I'm not talking about ethics and legal compliance alone; those are table stakes. I'm talking about decisions that support and give life to IBM's strategy and brand, decisions that shape a culture. That's why values for us aren't soft. They're the basis of what we do, our mission as a company. They're a touchstone for decentralized decision making."[12]

Outside-In and Inside-Out

A third and related insight has to do with the importance of taking both an outside-in and inside-out approach to citizenship. There are many indisputable pressures driving corporations from the outside in to advance their citizenship agenda. One of the most significant has been the very idea that firms need to take account of the interests and concerns of multiple stakeholders, not just shareholders, in their business practices and decisions. We have noted throughout how leading firms are developing competencies in engaging their customers, suppliers, community groups, NGOs, and other external stakeholders.

Another outside pressure comes from the many reputation-ranking groups, the socially responsible investment community, and the various accounting and reporting bodies that specify social and environmental performance standards and metrics for companies. We have featured these pressures in the case of AMD but they are found in most every company we have studied.

At the same time, these cases also highlight the importance of building a citizenship agenda from the inside-out. This means engaging the most important of internal stakeholders, the employees of a company, and building citizenship on the basis of the vision, values, and very purpose of an enterprise. This is a matter of companies deciding "who we are" and making strategic choices accordingly. On this foundation of values rests the potential of next generation citizenship to effect social change through business. Here is where AMD seeks to "change the game" when it comes to business connecting to society.

AMD's 50x15 Campaign

You may have heard of AMD's 50x15 program, announced in 2004, that seeks to make the Internet accessible to 50 percent of the world's population by 2015.[13] AMD, like other firms in the computing industry, is confronting a digital divide. At present, only 18 percent of the world's population has access to the Internet. Naturally there is a business case for reaching out to this untapped market. More users mean more demand for computers and thus the sale of more AMD chips and technology. But if one applies purely business logic to this kind of socio-commercial venture, the opportunity needs to be compared against other possibilities and its rate of return weighed against other potential investments. Is there something that would lead a firm to adopt different criteria and standards?

Hector Ruiz, CEO of AMD, reflected on the company's strategic choice to launch the 50x15 campaign in two ways. First, he told us: "When we did 50x15 there was a question I kept asking myself: 'Is this the right thing to do?' And based on your values, your experience of who you are, and where you're living, if the answer keeps coming back 'Yes,' then by definition you're responsible, and on some level accountable, for taking action." Needless to say, these are not traditional legal definitions of corporate responsibility and accountability; they are instead moral convictions and expressions of personal and corporate values.

Then, he went on to say, "I started thinking of myself. I grew up in a little town in Mexico. What got me out of there? It was access to information, access to education—I was just one of the lucky kids in that little town in Mexico to have found that [access]. But it would be nice to make it not just a matter of luck, but actually institutionalized—as a method." This got him to reading about Unilever's innovations in India and led to a meeting with C. K. Prahalad who had begun writing about the bottom of the pyramid. "I began to look at all these things and said, 'Wow.' You know, there's an equivalent here for us in technology. We have this incredible challenge, an excess of three billion people in the world who have yet to make a phone call." These three billion, he understood, did not have access; there was no method to connect them to the information and education available on the Internet. "And so," he said, "we got a group of people together and asked, 'How do we create a project in technology that allows people to be able to do things in an affordable way?' We came up with a plan, decided to create this umbrella called 50 by 15, and began to work under it."

On the technology side, AMD introduced the Personal Internet Communicator, an affordable, low-power device that is now offered by a growing number of Internet providers around the world. To reach its market, the company has adopted an ecosystem approach that has it working with national and local governments, NGOs, educational institutions, manufacturers, distributors, microlenders, and content providers. Some 50x15 results gleaned from the Web site illustrate this ecosystem model and its impact to date:

- *China (Internet penetration: 8.5 percent).* Partnership between AMD, Lenovo, and Dawning. Millions of students have been connected with more than two hundred ten thousand PCs deployed.
- *Brazil (Internet penetration: 14.1 percent).* Partnership between AMD, Telefónica, and the State Government of São Paolo. An E-Poupatempo (time-saver) center that gives locals free access to Internet services.
- *South Africa (Internet penetration: 7.4 percent).* A learning lab with PCs installed that are designed to withstand rugged environments while providing reliable computing capabilities.
- *Uganda (Internet penetration: 0.7 percent).* AMD, Wyse, and NGOs Inveneo and ActionAid united to bring solar-powered thin-client computing capability and Internet access into several villages.

The 50x15 program is a significant corporate social innovation that draws on and helps to build AMD's technical prowess, partnering skills, and global reach. But in defining principles for this new socio-commercial form of citizenship, Ruiz noted its twin justification: "This has got to be both good for business and good for the world." Then he added this compelling message about the possibilities of this kind of effort: "We have a historic opportunity to take the remarkable influence business has in the world and leverage it not just to fatten our balance sheets, but to end poverty. Educate a new generation. Bring affordable healthcare to millions. Slow global warming. Prevent cancer or eradicate disease."

That, in our view, is the positive potential of next generation corporate citizenship. What then does it take to lead a company to this frontier? Next we will look at leadership lessons from Ruiz, Palmisano, Immelt, and others and from the example set for them by the first generation of modern leaders to take citizenship into the heart of their business.

Leading Next Generation Companies

The rapidly changing business environment of today requires chief executives to deal with challenges that business school and early career experiences did not prepare them to manage. Strategies to stay globally competitive and return dividends to shareholders consume a majority share of a top executive's time. But pressures from outside and inside the firm are forcing social and environmental issues onto the CEO's agenda. Based on our interviews with leading corporate exeßcutives, covered in Chapter 2, a great many CEOs believe that managing the business-society relationship is a vital part of their job. The majority say that they are now attentive to a wide range of stakeholders and a disparate set of issues.

We have noted how, in nearly every survey and field study, leadership stands out as the number one factor driving citizenship in companies—in forward, neutral, or even sometimes reverse. The evidence is equally clear that this applies not only to top executives, but also to C suite leaders, middle managers, heads of corporate citizenship and sustainability functions, plant managers, and even front-line supervisors. Still, most managers we talk to say that the CEO must be the one to set an example for the entire company if it is to continue moving on a sustainable and responsible path. "I don't think anyone else can do it," acknowledges Jeff Joerres, CEO of Manpower. "Others in the organization are involved, and can bring great things forward, but unless the CEO gets into that water, the company doesn't really go all of the way."

In our model of the stages of citizenship, we still see some top executives giving mostly lip service to CSR, but increasing numbers are moving from a benign, supportive role into one of enterprise-wide stewardship. They are many reasons why. For the most part, a CEO is a much more public figure today than he or she was twenty-five years ago. The faces of CEOs appear on magazine covers; they are interviewed on daily business and late-night talk shows; and their actions are closely scrutinized by the press. Moreover, just as mistrust of business has climbed in the preceding few decades, so has skepticism about the motives and mores of corporate leaders. As one top executive told us: "The bulls-eye on CEOs is getting bigger and brighter than it's ever been. Audit committees, Sarbanes-Oxley, these are fundamental changes that every CEO is feeling. The next big issue will be executive compensation." All of this compels CEOs to exercise oversight of their corporation's social and environmental activities, to report to the Board on associated risks and concerns, and to look out for their own and the firm's reputation.[1]

"My responsibility is to try and protect the reputation of the brand, protect the people, protect the values, operate within those, and keep a view, without being lost in the heat of the day to day, to make sure there's balance within the organization, and recognize if you do that over a period of time, you'll be successful." This is a clear example of the stewardship role as one top executive defined his job. But there are examples, aside from the high-profile cases of John Browne at BP or Howard Schultz at Starbucks, where executives have taken a stronger stand vis-à-vis society and assumed a more affirmative role. This takes different forms: GE's Jeff Immelt's insight that societal challenges can be turned into business opportunities; AMD's Hector Ruiz's pledge to get 50 percent of the world on the Internet in fifteen years; Timberland's Jeff Swartz's commitment to put social purpose at the center of his firm's business; and the leaders of Levi Strauss & Co.'s insistence that a company's values cannot be shed just because it is going through hard times. It is in these leadership roles—as *champions* of citizenship within their firms and as *visionaries* who set an example for or lead entire industries—that top executives move their companies and themselves into next generation citizenship.

Back to the Future: Trailblazing Corporate Citizens

Even as these CEOs get high marks and closer scrutiny for leading their companies to the frontiers of corporate citizenship, there is much to learn from their forebears, the trailblazers that came of age in the 1960s and '70s. Paul Hawken, for one, founded Erewhon, a natural-foods market, in the early 1960s, then cofounded Smith & Hawken, a garden tool purveyor, in the late 1970s, all the while gaining insights that would appear in his volume *The Ecology of Commerce*.[2] Ben Cohen and Jerry Greenfield, "two real guys" (there's "No Mr. Häagan, No Mr. Dazs" went the jingle), started their company in the late 1970s and twenty years later were touting how to turn "values into value" in their book on creating socially responsible businesses, *Double Dip*.[3] The Body Shop's Anita Roddick got started about the same time and fifteen years thereafter was on the lecture circuit challenging a business audience:

> We, as business leaders, can and must change our views and our values. Less than a century ago, visionary business leaders were hooted out of business associations for saying that businesses had a responsibility to support charity; they were told that the concept of "good corporate citizenship" was radical pap. . . . Depressions and world wars changed them; global poverty and environmental destruction must change us now.[4]

Recently, Jeffrey Hollender, CEO of Seventh Generation, a company that sells green home products, made the case that these trailblazers have much to teach big business and that big business is listening.[5] It was in search of these lessons that Keith Cox, an executive doctoral student at Benedictine University, embarked on an ambitious dissertation that one of us helped to advise.[6] Cox interviewed these trailblazers plus D. Wayne Silby, founder of the Calvert Group, Mary Houghton of ShoreBank, Gary Hirshberg of Stonyfield Farm, and several others (see roster in Appendix 4). We thought it worthwhile to consider the pioneers' lessons on leading socially responsible businesses alongside those of the big company leaders we interviewed. Are there commonalities in the two sets of stories? Are there some insights that big business is missing? And do small company leadership practices scale to global firms? Cox's study highlighted some of the personal motivators of the trailblazers and a series of leadership practices. Some of these same motivators seem to drive select big company CEOs today.

Leadership Is Autobiography

Biographical studies by psychologist Howard Gardner of key figures in politics, business, social movements, academe, and the arts show how formative experiences shape the beliefs and practices of leaders in almost every culture.[7] They make up a leader's identity. What are the roots of these first-generation corporate citizens? Many trace themselves to the cultural shifts of 1960s.[8] As baby boomers, they witnessed "silent springs" when pesticides silenced songbirds, saw the trauma of thalidomide babies, and learned of carcinogens in the air, water, land, and in food and tobacco. The Club of Rome forewarned of "limits to growth" owing to a projected worldwide population explosion, while the Vietnam War made concrete the destructive powers of modern technology. That first Earth Day in 1970 seemed to intermix messages about peace, black power, and women's rights with calls to clean up pollutants, scale back technology, and legislate environmental protection as well as affirmative action and workplace reform. In time, these merged into movements concerned with global ecology, sustainable development, and corporate social responsibility—of which these leaders were a part.

Other trailblazers we talked with spoke of eco-feminism, liberation theology, and inclusive capitalism to explain what had fired their commercial ventures. Listen to Judy Wicks, founder of the natural-food restaurant White Dog Café and promoter of locally grown produce (and "local living economy"), passionately describe her calling:

> I love nature and animals and the abuse of animals in the corporate farm system is just unbelievable. It's barbaric the way that pigs and cows and chickens are raised in the corporate system; to me it's a spiritual issue. I believe in my interconnectedness environmentally, spiritually, and economically with other people and with other forms of life. So I feel it's my moral duty, you know, to work on these issues.

We heard some mentions of morality from the big company CEOs and a few referenced a spiritual duty to corporate citizenship. But, by comparison to the pioneers, most lacked the socio-commercial entrepreneur's sense of "being called" to this kind of work and only a handful cited a "grand theory" to explain their aims in running a socially responsible business. These are not necessarily requirements for leading a big company into advanced stages of citizenship but, in our estimation, they help to ignite employees' passions and educate them as well. Nevertheless, select big company CEOs expressed a lifelong affinity to lead a good company and wanted to test their predilections in the crucible of free-market capitalism. Here they found themselves in good company with their fore-bears.

Core Life Purpose

Many of the trailblazers in this frontier had that maverick, counter-corporate bent characteristic of so many entrepreneurs, but also a strong bias against business-as-usual views of corporate purpose, profit, and the marketplace. Ben and Jerry, for example, were quintessential anti-establishment "kids of the '60s" and the popular press cast them as hippies. Anita Roddick of the Body Shop had working-class roots and missionary ambitions to prove that you can make money by being good. Yvon Chouinard, a mountaineer and founder of Patagonia, openly questioned conventional notions of material progress. What they shared in common was a deep desire to run a different kind of business that does right by people and the planet.

Interestingly, this sense of positive purpose, developed over the life course, was also noted by several of the big company CEOs who are leading the next generation of citizenship. Jeffrey Immelt of GE expressed it as a desire to run a great and good company. Hector Ruiz of AMD, raised in a small rural Mexican town, feels deep responsibilities to the place and the people of his origin. And Timberland's CEO Jeff Swartz says he was influenced by the way his father and grandfather ran the family business. In their time, the business was closely inter-twined with the community in which it operated, and according to Swartz, it is still that way today: "There's a tradition of who we are and what we stand for. It may change programmatically, but it doesn't change in its core as values."

Walk the Talk

Both sets of leaders spoke about the importance of living their values or, more colloquially, walking the talk. In her autobiography, *Body and Soul*, Roddick writes, "I am not rushing around the world as some kind of loony do-gooder; first and foremost I am a trader looking for trade."[9] But Roddick's definition of trade includes protection of markets and ways of life. Body Shop campaigns to "Stop the Burning" in the rain forests, to prevent the spread of AIDS, and to sup-port Amnesty International, Friends of the Earth, and other causes, all make her appear a do-gooder. When pressed on her motivations, she replied: "It's the only way I know how to behave. It was never just 'clothes to wear.' To me you've got to live every part of it."

Several big company leaders have similar views on what social responsibility means for their own leadership. "You had better understand why you want to be a CEO because it's a much more complex environment today than twenty years ago," remarked Bob Parkinson of Baxter. "Are you doing it for the ego gratification? Are you doing it for the money? Are you doing it to do good and make a difference? To be effective, I believe you have to be motivated by a broader sense of purpose." Tom McCoy of AMD expressed it this way: "What is the point of leadership, what do you do with your gain? The point is to invest it in life."

Continuous Learning

Finally, leaders in both camps stressed the importance of continually learning about the world around them and about themselves. The Body Shop, as an example, initially used refillable containers (purchased inexpensively from a local hospital that used them for urine samples) only because it could not afford to do otherwise. Roddick later thought an in-house recycling plant was the "be-all and end-all of environmentalism." "Now," she laughs, "I die of embarrassment at the thought." Her personal development plan calls for journeying—visiting markets and peoples all over the world.

This message seems even more relevant for big company leaders. One of the big company CEOs noted that he is like many leaders in big business today: "[We] all went to the same twenty graduate schools and learned the same ways to maximize cash flow and create value." There was precious little talk, he told us, about social responsibility, environmentalism, sitting on nonprofit boards, or giving back to the community. "That was just not part of the CEO's wiring," he added, "especially in the '80s." Indeed, many top CEOs came of age in an era that saw the rise in business power, embraced the tilt to shareholder capitalism, and sanctioned a dramatic increase in CEO pay and perks. Now, at least the majority agrees with Ralph Shrader of Booz Allen Hamilton, that "the idea of profit at any cost is something that's past its prime."

What do tomorrow's CEOs need to learn? Many big-company CEOs advised studying ethics and exploring values, for the sake of leader's personal development and to help them run their businesses better. One said that a critical skill needed in today's leaders was anthropology—to understand different cultures; another pointed to the need for a better grounding in sociology—to learn to work with stakeholders; and several talked about the importance of learning how to interact with different governments around the world.

Leadership Functions

When it comes to the leaderly work of running a socially responsible business, there are also similarities between the trailblazers and big company CEOs. Here are just a few examples.

Higher Standards

Both sets of CEOs spoke about the importance of raising the bar on corporate conduct in relation to society. "It's not enough to be a good environmental citizen who recycles waste but discriminates against women in the marketplace, or against people of color. In other words, the 'leave no stone unturned' part of this is crucial," or so says Gary Hirshberg, CEO of Stonyfield Farm, a dairy specializing in organic lines. "People have an obligation, I would call it an opportunity, to improve," he adds. "You know we're not going to address the problems that we're leaving to our children by just using less energy. We have to talk about real restoration. And organic, in essence, is about restoration."

Many big-company executives also talked about higher standards: Several pointed out that the CEO's job is to establish or reinforce an ethical grid, to walk away from opportunities that might compromise principles, and to be role models of integrity. But some, like Mike Harrison of Timberland, express higher aspirations: "There's been a shift in emphasis in terms of the way people describe the role of business in society from not doing wrong to positively doing right or doing good." This is what leadership in next generation companies is all about.

Dialogue and Engagement

The two sets of executives also concur on the importance of talking with and listening to employees, customers, and other stakeholders. Listen to this newcomer to socially responsible business leadership: "We try not to talk about ourselves as a socially responsible company. We try to talk about our approach being socially responsible which means we're asking questions," says Seth Goldman of Honest Tea, adding, "and we try to be honest with ourselves and our stakeholders, and then from there to answer with integrity." Then listen to this old hand, Jack Creighton, former head of Weyerhaeuser and United Airlines: "The key is to be good listeners—not only to employees, customers, and suppliers, but to listen to people wherever you do business."

There is also the matter of give-and-take and advocacy for what you believe in. In the field of socially responsible investing, D. Wayne Silby expresses it this way, "Corporate social responsibility to us is a process of engagement. It's not about people subscribing to our values. It's only about people taking responsibility for whatever values they espouse." He adds, however, that his group challenges firms on issues like waste, energy use, diversity and such, questions their logic and evidence when it's found wanting, and often points them to ways that other companies have found to reconcile financial and societal tradeoffs.

On the receiving end of this kind of engagement, John Kennedy of auto supplier Johnson Controls notes how it can be instructive for big business: "The car industry has taken a leadership position in terms of the diversity of their supply base. It only makes sense for them, because they're obviously selling their cars to a diverse universe of customers. And so if they don't do this, that diverse universe has every right in the world to look at them and say, 'Why should I buy a car from you if you don't engage people of my color and so forth in your product supply chain?' There's a lot of compelling reasons why areas defined by social activists and social good have come to be a part of the business." Kennedy sees this phenomenon not as an obstacle, but as a new source of value that can help a company compete.

Balancing Demands

Finally, both sets of CEOs spoke of the importance of balancing social and economic factors in their business calculus. Seventh Generation is named in honor of the Iroquois belief that "in every decision, we must consider the impact of our decisions on the next seven generations." CEO Jeffrey Hollender is clear on the implications for his business:

> Responsibility is about linking our company's financial success with its ability to effect the kind of societal change we want to see. It's our acknowledgment that if we don't make money (in an ethical and responsible way, of course), we won't be in business very long. And if we lose our business, we lose our power to effect change. So this principle is about keeping everyone focused on economics in addition to ecology and continually emphasizing the crucial balance that must be maintained between the two.

Frankly, many of the big company CEOs we talked to seemed to err on the cautious side of this balancing act. One expressed it this way: "You develop a level of trust with investors. They say, 'He's performed every quarter, eighteen quarters in a row.' As long as that trust is maintained, we have a little more latitude to do interesting things, including on the social dimension." Yet some others took a more balanced stance: "If I don't produce profits to my shareholders, then they'll find someone else who will. But, on the other hand, if I don't plan for the future that will also . . . catch up with you."

Development of Citizenship: Three Trajectories

Leading with vision, purpose, and values is a central theme in the corporate citizenship stories of the trailblazers and many of the bigger company CEOs who are taking their firms to the frontier today. But there are differences in what these mean to leaders in companies founded on a citizenship platform versus more traditional firms that have to gear up for the journey.

Born to Citizenship

Mirvis's hands-on studies of Ben & Jerry's through the 1980s, along with the Body Shop, Esprit, Smith & Hawken, Patagonia, and so on, suggest that firms founded on principles of citizenship seem to "hop over" stages marked by defensiveness and reactivity, and begin to innovate with CSR at birth or early on.[10] Interestingly, the same might be said of UK-based Cadbury and Unilever, and U.S.-based Hershey and Pullman in the 1880s. Does this mean that the stage model does not apply to such firms?

Yes and no. Plainly in terms of their founders' orientation, these kinds of firms are rather like child prodigies when it comes to citizenship: highly receptive to environmental signals and creatively entrepreneurial in response. To illustrate the point, note that these first-generation corporate citizens were founded as the environmental movement was born, when growing numbers of customers were interested in "all natural" and "green" products, and heretofore countercultural movements began to move into mainstream niches. The synchronistic fit between the founder's internal compass and external conditions certainly affected the overall trajectory and pace of the development of citizenship in these firms.

At the same time, there were gaps in the infrastructure and capabilities of these firms that raised stage-based tensions having to do with capacity, coherence, and commitment. Ben & Jerry's, for example, fed ice-cream overflow to pigs near its headquarters in its early days. A heavy fine and adverse publicity over untreated wastewater led the firm to redesign quality control and construct a treatment greenhouse. But it was not until Gail Mayville, secretary to the CEO, led a self-initiated program in recycling and voluntary green teams were formed in plants that top executives took up the mantle of environmentalism. Here environmental activism developed bottom up and moved to the top of the corporate agenda only when the founders had to "run to get in front of the parade." Meanwhile, critics took on the company's cause products, saying it was all just crafty eco-marketing aimed at well-heeled consumers who want to salve their consciences while savoring top-of-the-line cosmetics, ice cream, and other "yuppie porn."[11]

Accordingly, the company, in concert with fellow pioneers in a series of annual meetings, did its commercial and cultural homework and crafted a clear, logical connection between its products, processes, and corporate purpose. This involved an analysis of the green product and consumer market, careful consideration of cause products in light of public opinion and media attention, along with consideration of employee involvement in the effort and the implications for company culture. All of this translated into an integrated, comprehensive framework showing how healthy products, produced by healthy processes, could contribute to a healthy planet and, in so doing, produce healthy profits (see Figure 8.1). This is the intellectual side of leadership—devising what Peter Drucker calls a "business theory" that aligns a firm's vision and business model to its marketplace.[12]

How about the values component of leadership? Until the late-1980s, B&J's stated purpose was to "have fun" (Jerry) and "give back to the community" (Ben). This, however, provided scant guidance of how to respond to quality problems and financial pressures. Nor did it preclude conflict over the company image, product positioning, and decision making over commercial and social investments. To bring these into sharper focus, the company began to work on both personal vision and corporate purpose.

Through a series of retreats, first with members of the Board, and then top management, all B&J leaders spoke to their personal aspirations and hopes for the business. In open-circle discussions, each person shared his or her own vision and how it fit with his or her view of the company. Several were confronted with discrepancies in terms of their commitment to the business side of things, their willingness to compromise with others, and their overall competency going forward. Tough, sometimes emotional stuff, but it clarified what people really wanted in their work lives and what the company would need from them.

As for company purpose, there was a sharp divide over a communal versus commercial emphasis. One influential Board member, Henry Morgan, drafted a "three-part" statement that addressed the firm's economic, social, quality, and environmental missions—all to be considered equally. This was a harbinger of the triple bottom line. It was debated vigorously by Board members and top

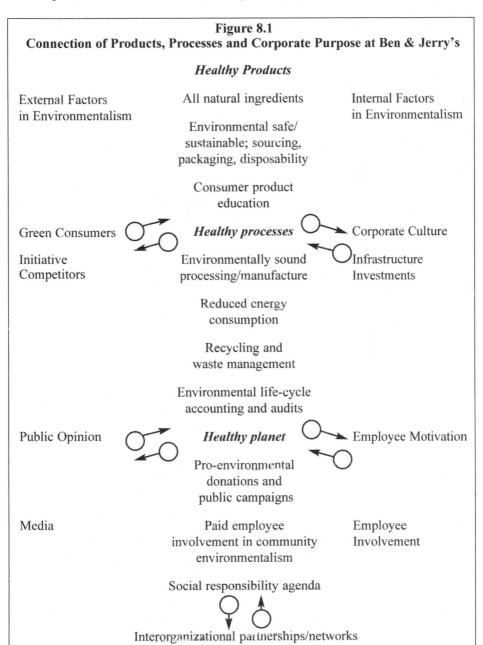

Figure 8.1
Connection of Products, Processes and Corporate Purpose at Ben & Jerry's

Healthy Products

External Factors
in Environmentalism

All natural ingredients

Internal Factors
in Environmentalism

Environmental safe/
sustainable; sourcing,
packaging, disposability

Consumer product
education

Green Consumers

Healthy processes

Corporate Culture

Initiative
Competitors

Environmentally sound
processing/manufacture

Infrastructure
Investments

Reduced energy
consumption

Recycling and
waste management

Environmental life-cycle
accounting and audits

Public Opinion

Healthy planet

Employee Motivation

Pro-environmental
donations and
public campaigns

Media

Paid employee
involvement in community
environmentalism

Employee
Involvement

Social responsibility agenda

Interorganizational partnerships/networks

Adapted from Philip H. Mirvis, "Environmentalism in Progressive Businesses."

managers and adopted as the company's mission statement. To communicate it to employees and the public, B&J launched a series of programs featuring a mix of education and fun. These included events covering the social mission (a talk by Anita Roddick), quality (a cleanliness campaign and a talk by Mr. Clean!), and finance (a visit to a company where every employee gets a P&L statement every day), plus homegrown skits, songs, and such. In turn, the mission statement began to appear on ice cream pints and was subject for dialogue at annual shareholder meetings—which included, in various years, Jerry wielding a sledgehammer to break a concrete brick over Ben's belly and then-CEO Chico Lager donning a skin-diving suit and diving into a pond of recycled ice cream to prove its safety and his own mettle.

Crisis-Driven Change

A second route to citizenship stems from crisis. Here firms seem to fast-cycle through the stages. We have described Nike's move from defense to offense in responding to crises in its supply chain. The Shell Group's response to socio-environmental calamities in the mid-'90s illustrates movement from crisis management to a complete makeover of policies and practices and ultimately of company values and culture. We gave you the bare-bones story in Chapter 5 and it is detailed in countless articles and books. But Shell is an instructive example of change for a couple of reasons.

First, many of its subsequent innovations in stakeholder consultation, in the use of societal scenarios in business planning, and in communicating to the public via social-and-environmental reporting are best-in-class. Second, its leaders at that eventful time, Cor Herkströtter and Mark Moody-Stuart, are role models for acknowledging grievous failings, getting to the root cause of crises, and pledging to transform what they called an "inward" and "arrogant" corporate giant into a global citizen. It was Moody-Stuart, in a heated meeting with Shell's top one hundred leaders, who drew the connection between Shell's flagging business results and its sociopolitical problems. Both, he argued, stemmed from an insular, technical, hyper-rational mindset. Shell, he argued, would simply have to reexamine its core purpose and get in touch with the world around it. On this external front, compare Shell's mea culpa and corrective actions to Exxon's foot-dragging in response to the *Valdez* tanker spill.

Transforming a Company

The third trajectory, the most common one, involves development of citizenship in a company through a process of change. Several big companies we have profiled have spent the past several years re-working visions of their business, developing a revised set of corporate values, and amping up both internal and external communications. IBM, GE, and others are well along the way. Wal-Mart is still very much a work in progress but shows many of the best practices in corporate transformation: internal and external engagement, action teams at work throughout the company, a series of quick wins, and a desire by CEO Lee Scott, if not yet much achieved, to transform the corporate culture. But if you want to see a traditional enterprise transformed into a next generation corporate citizen, there is no better story than Ray Anderson's at Interface.

Transformation at Interface

Anderson has told his story in his book *Mid-Course Correction*.[13] In addition, two other executive graduate students at Benedictine whom we advised have studied the Interface transformation more fully.[14] Mona Amodeo did a documentary study of the company and highlighted its transformation in terms of the five stages we present here. Guy Vaccaro drilled down on some of the technical features. We take up their version of the story with Anderson's awakening.

Awakening

Behind the social, environmental, and political shifts that began in the 1960s was a broader shift in thinking itself—what futurist Willis Harman calls a "global mind change."[15] Central questions about the nature of reality and the role of human power and purpose were thrown open to inquiry. Scientists found out that the forces of nature were far less predictable and controllable than imagined and that efforts to manage the natural world often yielded unintended and undesirable consequences. Lessons from the "new physics" showed that system dynamics were nonlinear and circular and that industrial models of growth and control ran counter to the natural course of life. A notion of living against, rather than with, nature seemed to sum up the feeling that something was terribly wrong with the path of development being followed by the world's most advanced nations and industries. But for Interface CEO Ray Anderson, "the idea that, while in compliance, we might be hurting the environment simply hadn't occurred to me." Then he read Hawken's work and experienced that "spear in the chest."

Afterward, Anderson began to "read voraciously." His literary journey traced the arc of ideas about sustainability in the latter half of the twentieth century.[16] He recalls: "To my mind, and I think many agree, Rachel Carson, with her landmark book, *Silent Spring*, started the next industrial revolution in 1962, by beginning the process of revealing that the first industrial revolution was ethically and intellectually heading for bankruptcy." Was there another path?

Aldo Leopold, author of *A Sand County Almanac*, offered the idea of a "land ethic"—a natural harmony between mankind and land—that would "preserve the integrity, stability, and beauty of the biotic community." Kenneth Boulding suggested a move from a "cowboy economy," where institutions roam recklessly and take what is desired from limitless plains, to a "spaceman economy" where they find their place in a cyclical ecological system. E. F. Schumacher made the point that "*small is beautiful*" and stressed the importance of appropriate technology in third-world development. More broadly, Wendell Berry argued for sustainable living where, rather than extract resources from the natural world and discard them, we would instead replenish resources out of concern for future generations. These high-minded ideas pepper Paul Hawken's writings and would soon make their way into Anderson's practice at Interface. Amodeo depicts this period of introspection as *cocooning*.

Cocooning

Committed to bringing this thinking into his company, Anderson assembled an advisory team including Hawken, Amory Lovins, and Hunter Lovins (co-authors of *Natural Capitalism*), plus Janine Benyus (author of *Biomimicry*), Bill Browning (Rocky Mountain Institute), Daniel Quinn (author of *Ishmael*), Jonathon Porritt (Forum for the Future—UK), John Picard (E2 Consulting), and Walter Stahel (Product-Life Institute—Geneva, Switzerland). Dubbed the "Dream Team," these advisors, plus a group of self-styled "cultural creatives" within the company, began to sketch out a practical and communicable agenda for action.[17]

Anderson told one of us, "I don't know the entire process of becoming more sustainable; you have to get lots of different points of view." The team understood the scale of the challenge. Said Anderson: "This is a mountain higher than Everest; we named it Mount Sustainability. It was probably a year or two before we had the seven faces defined and I can remember being in small groups of people at a blackboard drawing circles and linkages and this way of thinking about it and presenting it evolved." This brainstorming exercise among the Dream Team and key staff yielded seven macro-level models of the interconnection between the company, its supplier and consumer markets, communities, and the natural world. These complex models, accessible on the Interface Web site, show how in industrial ecology "everything connects to everything."[18]

The idea of Mount Sustainability was presented to company staff and work began on each of its seven faces: (1) eliminate waste; (2) benign emissions; (3) renewable energy; (4) closing the loop; (5) resource-efficient transportation; (6) sensitizing stakeholders, and (7) redesign commerce. Anderson was now ready to shed the cocoon and lead the metamorphosis of his company.

Metamorphosis

Anderson described his vision as follows: "I have challenged the people of Interface to make our company the first industrial company in the whole world to attain environmental sustainability, and then to become restorative. To me, to be restorative means to put back more than we take, and to do good to Earth, not just 'no harm.'" In a letter to employees he expressed a succinct vision for Interface: "To become the first name in . . . industrial ecology—worldwide."

His message was urgent and evocative. His readings and consultations gave him a new insight into the importance of industrial ecology. Drawing on the writings of Bill McDonough, Dean of the School of Architecture at the

University of Virginia—whose call for the "cradle to cradle" handling of natural resources redresses what he terms "intergenerational tyranny, the worst form of remote tyranny, a kind of taxation without representation across the generations, levied by us on those yet unborn"—Anderson spoke of this plainly to his people: "When Earth runs out of finite, exhaustible resources and ecosystems collapse, our descendents will be left holding an empty bag."

This began a company-wide campaign. Anderson's initial call to action was greeted with skepticism. One recalled, "Ray has been the visionary always. It's a big idea every month. After this one stuck a little while, I honestly heard people, with love and affection for their mythical hero, say that he at sixty years old had finally cracked. He had gone around the bend." On this point, Anderson remarked: "It took about fifty speeches by me before we really got a lot of buy-in from our people. The toughest challenge was really to be sure that we stayed on the drum beat, the consistent, persistent message. This is where we've been, this is where we're going, and we have got to do this."

It also took hands-on leadership. Anderson recalled the impact of his advisory team in the company: "Engineers would follow Amory Lovins around the factory. Amory would stop and get the nameplate date off of a motor and punch into his calculator and tell you what that motor was costing you." The ideas began to catch on: "When Browning (of the Rocky Mountain Institute) talks about Green Building our people listen. Those influences reach all down into and through the company," Anderson observed at one point.

Finally, in manufacturing locations on four continents, teams throughout the company began to work on hundreds of projects and technologies to take the company up those seven faces toward sustainability. This moved the company from its metamorphosis into its emergence as a sustainable enterprise.

Emergence

The Natural Step, a nonprofit founded in Sweden in 1989 by Swedish scientist Karl-Henrik Robèrt, has devised a model for creating a culture that integrates sustainability into its lifeblood.[19] The practice emphasizes the organic spread of sustainable principles through "islands" in organizations. Their job at Interface was to facilitate the "sensitivity hookup." As one internal change agent described it to us: "We went on to educate our employees and to build awareness. We also then went to sensitizing stakeholders. Okay, let's talk about what we're doing. Let's make sure that all of our stakeholders from our vendors to our customers to our community know what we're doing."

This wasn't always met with eagerness. One point of resistance was the industrial engineers. For those trained in environmental compliance, the ideas of developing closed-loop processes and sustainability-based commerce created a "culture gap." After all, they had not been trained in this approach nor had any experience with it. Said one: "We've surrounded ourselves with philosophical people, and I can tell you absolutely beyond a shadow of a doubt, sustainability is not necessarily intuitive." So how did he get on board? "I call it *applied sustainability*. Now the application is gonna be grounded with philosophy. But in order to improve you have to take the intuition out of it and make it a clearly defined and measured tool. And also with very, very well-defined system limit and constraint, and that's exactly what I've done." The result was a set of what Anderson terms eco-metrics that quantify "what we take, make, and waste."

Product development experts were also skeptical about the market prospects of "climate neutral carpet." This turned around when they dug into the subject matter, and realized that they were offering a full life-cycle value proposition that offsets the energy use of vendors and customers. In appropriate market-speak, they branded their new offer "Cool Carpet."

There were also challenges in developing needed technology. We have noted how principles of biomimicry led to the leaf-like layout of carpet tiles, the recyclable backing, and the use of spidery tape to connect tiles securely, instead of gluing them to the floor. All of these ideas bubbled up from project teams. During a visit to the city of LaGrange, Georgia, a team of Interface engineers had local politicians measure methane levels in city landfills. They found enough methane gas to run an Interface factory. The city was persuaded to invest $3 million to cap the landfill, capture the methane, and pipe it to the Interface factory nine miles away. The calculations show that because methane is a much more powerful heat-trapper than conventional energy sources, when a company burns it, it reduces its carbon dioxide emissions by a factor of twenty-three. In the carbon trading market, that is a triple win: good for the city because it has excess methane to sell to other businesses; good for Interface because methane is cheaper than conventional energy sources; and good for the earth.

Engagement

By 2005, the new products were out and new technologies were working. Results to date look promising. From 1995 through 2006, for instance, Interface has saved over $336 million in waste-elimination activities, total manufacturing waste sent to landfills decreased 70 percent, energy consumption at its carpet manufacturing facilities decreased 45 percent, and so on. Meanwhile revenues have climbed. Interface is today moving into its new phase: engagement as a voice for sustainability in industry.

Anderson described his ambitions: "We used to say that we are weaving a web of customer relationships. And now weaving the web has gone beyond customers to the whole network. So the 'doing well by doing good' web grows and customer relationships grow with that and the world gradually shifts direction."

This is the message that Anderson took to the Wal-Mart "revival" in Bentonville, to the BAWB meeting in Cleveland, and to many other venues. In so doing, he has become an industrial spokesman for the sustainability movement. Why don't other CEOs do the same? For the same reasons that most keep quiet about the role of their firms in society: They believe this is not what CEOs were chosen to do; executives living in glass houses should not throw stones; and there is more risk than advantage in becoming the poster child for particular causes. But justified though they might be, these beliefs ignore the reality that business is being held to account by multiple constituencies for myriad aspects of its behavior. Moreover, when business has a positive story to tell, it can be a source of inspiration for stakeholders and instruction for other firms.

On the self-aggrandizing side of this, Jim Hartzfeld, former vice president of sustainable strategies, recalls, "Ray was absolutely paranoid of greenwash. I remember sitting in a meeting when he threatened to fire on the spot anybody who tried to market (sustainability). He would always make the walk ahead of the talk. From the very beginning it was about deeds not words, deeds, and data. The only scorecard is the actual performance numbers at the end of the quarter."

When queried about the meaning of the Interface message, Hartzfeld cited a gathering of the 125-person leadership team where the team came to a near-unanimous conclusion that sustainability is "what our values are." He added, "It isn't just altruism and citizenship. This is the right strategy right now to be successful." Then, echoing the views of the pioneers and the relative newcomers like Immelt, Anderson, and others, he stated that one of the chief aims of this new phase is "to demonstrate to the world what sustainability is and why it works."

Lessons on Leading Citizenship

This brief description of Amodeo's phases of Interface's transformation could leave the impression that a move toward next generation citizenship is a linear, step-by-step, programmable model. On the contrary, she describes the journey as "incremental and recursive . . . the result of people being challenged to see things different, and seeing themselves differently, too." Many of the pioneers stress the idea that it is an act of will, more so than planning, that transforms companies. Ron Grzywinski of ShoreBank put it in a historical context: "I keep a quote somewhere on my desk from Sulzberger [when he took over at the *New York Times*]. He said, 'We had no great plan, we had no great scheme, we had a few good people.' Then there's a label off of a cheap brandy bottle that's stuck on my wall. It is a picture of Napoleon on a horse with a quotation, translated in English, 'Commit first, and then work it out.'" As testimony to the emergent nature of this kind of work, the pioneers confessed that, even though some had penned how-to books, there are really no "five easy steps" to sustainability or full-fledged corporate citizenship. Nevertheless, some lessons can be learned from their efforts and from those who followed them.

Planned and *Emergent*

Many models for advancing corporate citizenship advocate a planned approach whereby companies develop a comprehensive, long-term plan for citizenship. This is typically executed from the top down in a formal change program. There is much to recommend this counsel. First, top-level leadership can focus attention on and lessen resistance to needed changes in priorities, structures, and behavior. Second, a comprehensive and planned approach builds momentum for change and promotes coordinated movement on multiple fronts.

There are questions, however, as to whether a makeover of corporate citizenship can be effectively managed through a strategic program led from the top down. In many respects, CSR fits into the class of situations that organization theorists Fred Emery and Eric Trist call "meta-problems," where understandings of risks, cause-effects, and benefits are not agreed upon.[20] In such cases, practitioners have been advised to adopt a more gradual, incremental strategy that helps to clarify the situation even as "small wins" open possibilities for further movement.

Many of the pioneering companies progressed in a pattern of fits and starts. The same was true of those climbing Mount Sustainability. As one Interface engineer put it: "We were feeling our way every step of the way." The emergent process gradually yielded a series of small wins that helped to bring the overall effort into focus and built momentum for change. "We could start to see progress," recalled one manager. "The minute that you start to see progress you start to get enthusiastic. Then you realize these baby steps are taking you a long way."

To generalize the point, many executives in our learning forums operate with the pragmatic approach of identifying "low-hanging fruit" and capitalizing on opportunities that present themselves rather than adhering to a strategy of prescribed steps and activities. The process of finding and following what CSR executive Laurie Regelbrugge likens to a rock climber's "handholds" is shown, in contrast to the top-down model in Figure 8.2.

In the end, this approach is no less systemic or strategic than its top-down counterpart. Indeed, by building connections among more bounded and localized initiatives and leveraging experience gained, leaders create momentum behind a move toward company-wide corporate citizenship. Amodeo's account

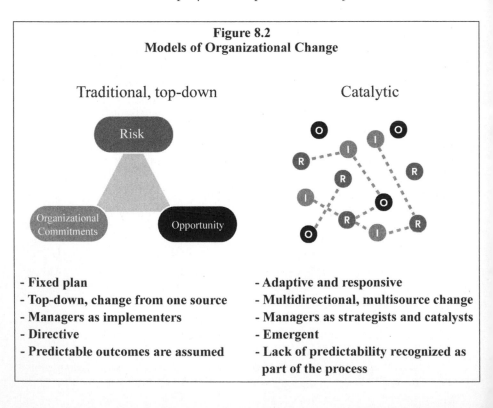

Figure 8.2
Models of Organizational Change

Traditional, top-down

Risk

Organizational Commitments

Opportunity

Catalytic

- **Fixed plan**
- **Top-down, change from one source**
- **Managers as implementers**
- **Directive**
- **Predictable outcomes are assumed**

- **Adaptive and responsive**
- **Multidirectional, multisource change**
- **Managers as strategists and catalysts**
- **Emergent**
- **Lack of predictability recognized as part of the process**

of the change process at Interface shows the eventual impact: "Changes in process created operational efficiencies, which translated to bottom-line success. This was proof that this approach was not only the right thing to do, but it was the smart thing to do. Furthermore, there seemed to be the realization this was also a better way to a bigger profit. Sustainability took on new meaning and organizational purpose; for many it emerged as a 'higher purpose'—something bigger than making carpet squares."

Heroic and *Shared Leadership*

The corporate leader-as-hero model, so prominent from the 1980s to the Enron fallout, has been widely criticized of late and has fallen out of fashion. But make no mistake, the success of the Interface story has been hugely dependent on the leadership of Anderson. The same, naturally, is true of the pioneering stories we've looked at and the big moves by big companies like GE, IBM, and AMD into next generation citizenship. All of this is a reminder of Peter Drucker's famous observation: "Management is doing things right; leadership is doing the right things."[21]

Nevertheless, just as it was crucial for Ben and Jerry to engage the board and managers throughout the company in developing and implementing their three-part mission, enlistment is even more crucial when a very traditional company embarks on a full-scale transformation. Listen to this Interface manager's typical reaction: "I think a lot of people in the trenches were waiting to see if their managers were going to be sold on the concept and whether they picked up and ran with the change. Would they get everyone to follow?" The subsequent reactions of an operator tell the story: "I was as cynical as anyone but I began to see that Ray was serious about this, that people who were close to him were serious about it, and that somehow we were going to make it happen."

A case can be made that shared leadership is integral to companies that speed their way to this frontier. Calvert Group's D. Wayne Silby describes it this way: "Leadership has a lot to do with creating a context, the ground for the people to do the work. And it's not that, 'Oh, our great leader did this.' No, it's like, the guy helped, did a few things, but actually the whole team did it. I think that is really the core of great leadership." This is especially important in his field where, he contends, "our leadership is really about a vision of a society that works for everyone."

Male and *Female Leadership*

Finally, pay attention to one obvious difference between the samples of trailblazing leaders and big-company chiefs: the numbers of women in their respective ranks. Roughly one-fourth of the pioneering executives that Cox interviewed were women. There were only two in our sample of big-company leaders. Is a female perspective and energy a factor in moving companies toward higher levels of citizenship?

It is speculative, but in our estimation some of the sensibilities historically and culturally expressed by women—about relationships to nature, care for others, and concern for the common good—are integral to the vision, purpose, and values of next generation corporate citizens.[22] Not surprisingly, the field of corporate community relations is disproportionately represented by women, in the ranks and in leadership positions. It is worth noting, too, that GE's ecomagination business is led by Lorraine Bolsinger. This is not to say that men or women are better suited to leading companies to this next frontier, but rather that leaders who are most effective in this transformation, singly and in concert with their teams, express both traditionally masculine and feminine qualities in their leadership. They are comfortable with and open to both the analytic and emotive sides of organizational change and recognize that you lead people by both the head and heart.

As if speaking to these points, Silby of Calvert says: "Leadership in this community is not 'here's the idea'; it's more of a nurturing, you might say maternal, midwifery kind of help. And that's really how the leadership of this industry [and CSR movement] is different. It's about making room and respecting others to play their role." Laurie Markham, board chair of alternative press Dragonfly Media, expresses a similar point about the importance of many voices in a company: "[Leadership is] helping get the blocks out of the way so that people can in fact contribute whatever their truth is, to help people to have a voice and to have every function to be valued for its contribution. I think that an organization like that is going to be more creative in what it produces and it will sing."

This "both–and" approach to leadership may be one of the defining characteristics of next generation citizenship where both the interests of business and society are merged as companies "change the game." But the test of this proposition is not in theory, it is in practice, and it is not in what CEOs say, but in what their companies do. This means getting employees engaged in corporate citizenship, and engaging them in their full selves, as citizens of the world.

Engaging Employees as Citizens

In the United States, three of four young people entering the workforce want to work for a company that "cares about how it impacts and contributes to society."[1] The Center has, for several years, characterized employees as the "missing link" in corporate citizenship. Now a case is being made to engage employees under the mantle of citizenship—and in progressively deeper and more meaningful ways. Here's why.

HR Is CSR

A great many companies recognize the importance of employee relations for their overall reputation and license to operate. It's well documented that the way employees are treated is the "litmus test" for how the American public evaluates its corporations. In GolinHarris surveys of the U.S. public, in each of the past five years, perceptions of whether or not a company "values and treats employees fairly and well" has been the number one factor in ratings of the citizenship of companies, more so than corporate philanthropy, community involvement, environmental performance, and other citizenship factors.[2]

Certainly there are more good reasons why companies should treat employees fairly and well, ranging from simple decency to advantages in recruiting and retention to effective human resource management. Connecting this to corporate citizenship, however, puts a public spotlight on employee relations and highlights its linkage to brand equity, consumer preferences, and even investor relations—as Wal-Mart has learned.

Nowadays, firms are seeing that HR issues are also citizenship issues and that they are expected to be accountable for their conduct. Safety and health, labor practices, and labor–management relationships are, of course, matters of law in many countries and thus fit into the compliance category for companies. But increasingly firms are being held to higher standards of human resource management. The latest version of the GRI, as an example, covers basic employment issues but also stipulates that companies report on the racial, ethnic, and gender composition of their workforce, management, and Board of Directors, the hours and monies spent on employee training, and details of their policies and plans to promote lifelong learning.

On a broader scale, Bradley Googins and Marcie Pitt-Catsouphes, who is co-director of the Center on Aging and Work at Boston College, contend that work–family support, like diversity, is a citizenship consideration because the way firms respond to the needs of working parents has implications for the children and elders they might care for and broad ramifications throughout society.[3] Of course, a case can also be made that job stress and even job satisfaction are also social issues. ABN Amro, the global Dutch bank, goes further on this HR/CSR front and publishes detailed results of its employee surveys in its annual report.

Citizenship Matters to Employees

The Reputation Institute finds that, on average, 75 to 80 percent of those polled in some twenty-five countries would "prefer to work for a company that is known for its social responsibility." [4] In the United States this seems especially true for the Generation Y or Millennials born 1978–1998 who are entering and moving up in companies today. Cone Communications finds that 65 percent say that their employer's social and environmental activities make them feel loyal to their company.[5] This is, of course, the central feature of the "good company" brand as it applies to employees. One study phrased its meaning succinctly: CSR minus HR = PR.

The appeal of corporate citizenship to employees is by no means limited to the United States or developed economies with their comparatively prosperous and well-educated workforces. On the contrary, while the Reputation Institute ranks social responsibility as a significant driver in attracting employees in the United States, it is even more important in India, South Africa, and China. Furthermore, GlobeScan finds that nine out of ten employees worldwide are interested in participating in the CSR initiatives of their companies.[6]

Not surprisingly, there is some evidence that companies moving into advanced stages of citizenship make citizenship a part of their value proposition for employees. We've seen how this is a central component of Levi's citizenship commitment. A recent Center Webinar with one hundred seventy of our corporate members focused on the role of employees as stakeholders within their firms. While this is hardly a representative sample, the conversation highlighted three features of the emerging HR/CSR connection.

First, leading companies regard employees as important stakeholders who express their voice not only in employment policies and practices, but also on social issues related to employment. These firms have diversity councils, work–family forums, and associations of minorities, women, and gay and lesbians where employees can share common interests and advocate for their concerns. These affinity groups not only provide input to and feedback on company policies and practices, they also influence public positions taken by their firm. Witness, as an example, the increasing number of companies in the United States taking an affirmative stand on gay rights or joining forces with other firms in the nonprofit coalition of businesses, Corporate Voices for Working Families, which advances bipartisan policies to promote work–family balance.

Second, leading companies actively engage their employees in citizenship. Typically this takes the form of volunteerism, especially relevant for American employees, but of increasing interest to working people around the world. We suspect that as companies progress through stages of citizenship, they tend to get more of their people involved and engaged in more significant volunteer service. Beyond this, leading firms work with outfits like The Natural Step to educate their people about social and environmental responsibilities; gain employees' hands-on participation in eco-friendly, cause-related, or fair trade marketing; and involve them in triple bottom line audits.

Finally, we see budding interest in companies (and certainly among employees) in what might best be called "socially responsible jobs." Long ago employers learned of the advantages of job enrichment—whether in the form of more variety, autonomy, and challenge or in opportunities for influence over how the job gets done. Today a new set of job design questions is coming to the fore: Is the operation green? Are materials or supplies being sourced ethically and sustainably? Are the products and services provided harmful, neutral, or helpful to the planet? Does my work contribute to human welfare and well-being? These are the kinds of questions that companies who treat employees as citizens are asking of themselves and are being asked by their people.

The Next Stage: Engaging Employees as Citizens

As far-reaching as this might sound, we hypothesize that as companies move forward into next generation citizenship, they will engage their people not simply as employees, but rather in their multiple identities as workers, parents, community members, consumers, investors, and co-inhabitants of the planet.

This idea took shape several years ago in identity theory when it was posited that people think of themselves and embody identity in the form of gender, race, ethnicity, and of course their life roles, whether as student, parent, plumber, and so on.[7] Some of these identities, such as gender, race, and sexual orientation, have been the subject of consciousness raising in society and in companies as well. In top companies today, for example, employee diversity is valued not only as an HR driver, but as a source of fresh ideas, as a means of mirroring and serving the multicultural marketplace, and as source of learning and effectiveness, as David Thomas and Robin Ely point out in their analysis of diversity in corporations.[8]

Why would a company concern itself with and seek to activate people's identities as citizens of a corporation, community, society, and planet? One reason is that when employees find that their company welcomes the full range of their interests and aspirations, including for instance a personal desire to serve society and protect the planet, they feel welcome to bring their "whole self" into the workplace. This yields more commitment to one's work, a deeper connection to a company, and a broader sense of meaning associated with one's job—providing, of course, that a firm attracts employees interested in these matters and can deliver on its value proposition to them. One study finds that 75 percent of employees who approve of their company's commitments to social responsibility are engaged by their jobs versus 37 percent of those who do not approve. Interestingly, they rate their company as more competitive, too.[9]

A second reason is that when employees feel free to bring these multiple identities into the workplace, they become a microcosm of the markets and societies in which a firm operates. Recognizing this, top companies like IBM in its InnovationJams and Nokia in its World Map exercise, regularly consult with employees on social trends and factor their ideas not only into employment policies, but also into corporate social investments, business innovations, and their overall socio-commercial agenda.

A third reason is that employees take these identities, whether enhanced or diminished by their companies, into society and the market. Studies find that the prime source of information about the citizenship of companies comes via word of mouth.[10] Employees whose aspirations to live and work responsibly are fulfilled through their companies thereby serve as effective brand ambassadors for their firms through their word-of-mouth commentary. They also produce social capital—a web of positive relevant relationships—that connects their companies to other stakeholders and the public at large. Finally, employees who feel empowered as citizens produce social value through their volunteer service, their jobs, products, and services, and the enriched understandings of corporate citizenship that are shared with friends, a subject of debate among colleagues and critics, and ultimately passed on to their children.

Employees Serving Society

IBM has embraced this employee-as-citizen philosophy in the development of its On Demand Community of volunteers.[11] In early 2000, as the company shifted its primary focus on reinventing education to serving society on many fronts, it also revamped its model of employee volunteerism. As CEO Sam Palmisano described it: "No company can mandate volunteerism. The decision and self-sacrifice comes from within the individual. What we can do is encourage and support this distinctive aspect of our culture by providing education, technology, funding, and recognition to tens of thousands of IBM colleagues who enrich their communities with their expertise and caring." Three aspects of this redesign are especially relevant here.

First, it unleashed IBMers to reach out to their communities or society more broadly and in personally relevant and meaningful ways. The message to employees was simple: Pursue your passions. This opened up service options that would range from volunteering in a social service agency to getting a team together to assist a nonprofit or community group to participate in MentorPlace where thousands of IBM employees mentor students on line.

Second, it encouraged IBMers to bring their whole selves to service. The message was clear: Serve not only with your own hands and heart, but in particular with your business know-how and the tools and resources of the company. As one executive described the impact: "Now when people volunteer for a soup kitchen, they're not just ladling soup, they're developing a strategic plan for the kitchen. When they work for a Lighthouse for the Blind, they are bringing them a software tool that can convert their Web site from text to voice."

Third, the aspiration was to bring this to a global scale. In prior years, there was no central thrust for volunteerism in IBM and operating companies around the world more or less did their own thing. In 2003, in ninety countries world-wide, IBM launched its On Demand Community program that would bring a new seriousness to the company's engagement with its employees and society. As Stanley Litow, head of corporate affairs and corporate citizenship, described it: "It's more inclusive. It's powerful. It's an identity for the company in the community. It's a way for our employees to live the IBM brand."

Diane Melley and Ann Cramer were key figures on the team launching On Demand Community. The program built on IBM's e-business on-demand initiative that included simple, automated, cost-effective software and hardware solutions that could integrate business processes and extend outward to customers and business partners. Drawing on all of this, the community team identified over 140 IBM tools, programs, and tutorials that employees could access on line and share with nonprofits and community groups with whom they volunteer. All of these are accessible through IBM's internal Web portal that contains the applicable tools as well as suggestions on how to get started, state-of-the art online presentations, videos, Web site reference links, software, and documents.

While the launch events in 2003 enlisted some ten thousand employees, the On Demand Community doubled in size in two years and scaled to over eighty thousand by mid-year 2007, including the addition of IBM's retirees. At last count, IBMers provide over five million hours worth of volunteer service.

Calling Consumers to Social Action

Timberland is another company stretching the boundaries of engagement by extending its service arms through its workforce and outward to retail stores and its consumer base.[12] In the early 1990s, City Year, a nonprofit "action tank for national service," asked Timberland to donate fifty pairs of work boots for its young adults working with youth in after-school programs, summer camps, and serving projects. That request sparked a long-term relationship based on a shared vision of revitalizing the "civic square" that set the boot and apparel maker on a trajectory of community service that would involve everyone from the CEO to corporate and store employees to customers.

The partnership began with a service day for Timberland employees arranged by City Year. Employees from corporate headquarters joined the City Year corps to renovate the Odyssey House, a local addiction-recovery home for adolescents. Based on the power of this experience, Jeffrey Swartz, CEO of Timberland, felt that a stronger connection could be forged between the two organizations. Timberland began annual company-wide service days in conjunction with City Year. It also established its Path of Service, a program that allows employees to take up to sixteen hours of paid leave to engage in volunteer service of their choice.

City Year, a community-based nonprofit founded by two Harvard Law graduates, recruits young adults (aged seventeen to twenty-four) who pledge themselves to a year-long commitment of community service in a selected city or community. Its aim is not only to provide support to communities, but also to develop young people's leadership skills and civic activism. Surveys find that young people of this age in the United States have an interest in volunteerism and a desire to address social issues such as education, poverty, the environment, and so on. Yet comparatively few have ever contacted a political official, voted in an election, or been actively involved in community-building efforts. City Year set out to change this and has succeeded: Its alumni are 45 percent more likely to vote and 65 percent more likely to volunteer than their peers are.

Swartz was Chairman of the Board of Trustees for City Year from 1994 to 2002. He saw the impact of service on his employees and on young people throughout the United States. Timberland thereupon decided to take its "boots, brand, and belief" directly into the market and call its consumers to action. Nowadays, Timberland, with City Year, activates ten thousand consumers and partners in over twenty-five countries in annual service days—one each spring on Earth Day and one each fall entitled "Serv-a-palooza." Its CSR report card details rates and annual increases in employee volunteerism and in its consumers' involvement in service. Timberland also houses its own City Year site, home base to twenty-four volunteers, in its corporate headquarters in New Hampshire.

This strategy has created a significant impact on the company's human resources. A Timberland marketing executive stated: "Many companies pay thousands of dollars for the type of team-building skills we learn through giving ourselves, together. So not only is Timberland furthering positive change and community betterment, we are making an investment in our infrastructure. This is not philanthropy. I firmly believe that the minds we turn here at Timberland explode our productivity and effectiveness."

Of course, Timberland is one of among many companies that engage their business partners and customers alongside employees in service to society. On a global scale, Nokia's Make a Connection campaign, in partnership with the International Youth Foundation, has reached over 330,000 young people in twenty-four countries.[13] An analysis of thirteen youth programs run by the partnership shows that the programs significantly increased young people's engagement with their communities as well as their self-confidence and optimism about the future. Indeed, the study, conducted by Brandeis University's Heller School, found that 72 percent of the youth continued serving in volunteer programs after their formal program was completed. During 2006, Nokia employees also volunteered twenty-five thousand hours in thirty-five countries. All of this information is tracked in Nokia through a measurement "dashboard" for each country that records rates of employee volunteering, number of youth in programs, the impact of the programs on youth involvement and social skills, plus ratings of Nokia's brand reputation over time.

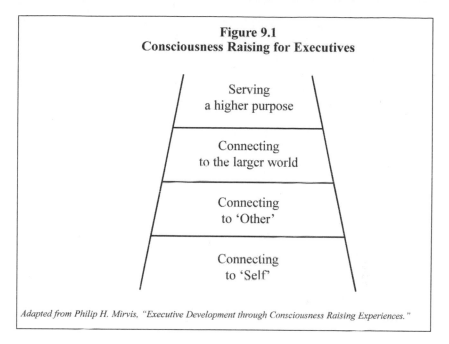

Figure 9.1
Consciousness Raising for Executives

Serving
a higher purpose

Connecting
to the larger world

Connecting
to 'Other'

Connecting
to 'Self'

Adapted from Philip H. Mirvis, "Executive Development through Consciousness Raising Experiences."

Developing Next Generation Management

In PricewaterhouseCoopers 10th Annual Global CEO Survey, covering over one thousand top executives in fifty countries, some 81 percent agreed: "My company's development program focuses increasingly on equipping leaders to take a role in creating a sustainable business environment."[14] This is certainly the trend in corporate education and in business schools the world over. In the executive education and M.B.A. programs at Boston College, as in many other schools, leaders learn about citizenship through readings, case studies, and class dialogue; corporate development programs typically offer the same with the added benefit of remarks from the ethics or compliance officer, and ideally provide for some interaction with the CEO or other top executives about dilemmas faced and resolved over the course of their business careers.

Meanwhile, high school and college students who seek to engage society participate in service learning in their communities, where they meet with the poor and disenfranchised, dive into complex sociopolitical issues, challenge and learn from community activists and frontline caregivers, and develop a personal point of view on their role in society. Recognizing the power of these kinds of consciousness-raising experiences, a number of next generation corporate citizens are re-doing their management development programs along these lines.[15] Consider:

> Thirty Ford Motor Company functional and business unit heads, participants in a global leadership program, talk with board members, managers, and staff at Homes for Black Children, an adoption service in inner-city Detroit. They share life stories, current challenges, and future aspirations with their nonprofit counterparts in

leader-to-leader dialogues. The two sides identify similarities and differences in their upbringing, values, and philosophies of leadership and talk shop about issues faced in, respectively, running a business and an orphanage. The day ends singing songs with the children and pledging to build ongoing relationships.

Thirty-two Novo Nordisk vice presidents, drawn from every continent, meet with leaders and staff in Sao Paulo, Brazil health centers that range from a world-class children's cancer clinic to an overcrowded hospital serving ten thousand patients a day to a makeshift clinic in a favela. The subject is "access to health" but the shared caregiving and conversation concerns the import of passion in health-care and the dilemmas faced in the allocation of costly medicines, technology, and other health resources. The next day the executives talk with officials and politicians in Brasilia about the role of government versus private initiatives in meeting health needs in the country.

Thirty or so young leaders join with senior executives from thirteen countries served by Unilever Asia travel to Sarawak, Malaysia to view environmental degradation and human displacement resulting from deforestation in teak rainforests. They meet with the Penan people, former hunter-gatherers who now live in tin huts in a village, their hunting grounds largely denuded of trees and game. A day-long walk and communal feast with the Penan opens their eyes to the spoils of industrialization and their hearts to the plight of indigenous peoples.

In each of these vignettes, executives move from the relative comfort of the corporate classroom into unfamiliar territory where they encounter people and problems seemingly far removed from the day-to-day scope and concerns of business life. Yet they come away with powerful and relevant lessons. "How can I complain about the size of my budget when I see how much they accomplish with so few resources?" observed one Ford executive. This led to an earnest discussion among peers about differences between corporate cultures based on a philosophy of scarcity versus abundance. A Novo Nordisk manager reflected on his Brazilian experiences: "Dr. Parelli of the cancer clinic said something that touched me deeply. 'We open our doors to all children, no matter their insurance or what their families can pay. We use state of the art technology and cure many of them. Still, some die. I want these children to know they are dying because of their disease, not because they are Brazilians.'" This raised questions for the executives about what kind of leadership was needed to transform their company from a Danish multinational to a global business with a significant presence in emerging markets. The encounters with the Penan tribe, in turn, led Unilever's young Asian leaders to debate the benefits and costs of economic growth in the region. Concluded one: "[This] reminds us that we have strong social responsibilities . . . to help protect the environment, to relieve poverty."

Consciousness Raising for Executives

On the surface, the practice of consciousness raising, rooted in empowerment movements and spiritual disciplines, would seem rather far afield for business executives. Yet the case can be made that it is applicable to the development of the "whole person."[16] Each of the programs featured above had elements to help leaders connect to themselves, to one another, to the larger world, and to a higher sense of purpose (see Figure 9.1).

Know Thyself

There is increased emphasis on self-awareness in leadership circles today. This is amply evident in the wide-ranging use of self-assessment tools, in the cultivation of emotional intelligence, and in experimentation with meditation, martial arts, and other forms of soul work among executives. All of this helps a leader to "know thyself."

The Ford program with Homes for Black Children (HBC) was designed with this in mind. Prior to meeting their counterparts in the orphanage, each of the Ford leaders prepared an "emotional lifeline." This technique has people chart their life's journey from childhood to present with careful consideration of emotional highs and lows. It is based on the psychodynamic notion that people re-experience their lives when they delve into emotionally charged aspects of their past. This helps to surface feelings about one's life course and to lift them up for fresh consideration. In this case, the leaders of HBC also prepared their lifelines and then met leader to leader with Ford executives to talk over their formative experiences.

The community meeting began with the president of HBC, a black woman in her late fifties, telling her story of growing up in Detroit guided by God-fearing parents, earning a college degree, and finding a calling in caring for underprivileged children and families. She then recounted a story of how her college roommate had married an employee of an auto company, who was subsequently laid off when his job was outsourced. The husband took employment at lower wages, received no benefits, and was laid off again. He went into debt and ultimately turned to drink, drugs, and adultery. In a very real and moving way, the director's story of her friend's sad fate was a story all too familiar to the Ford executives who had overseen outsourcing and layoffs and would be moving into senior decision-making roles in such matters. This sad story provoked considerable conversation and some hand wringing among the Ford executives present.

They, in turn, shared their own heartfelt stories of growing up, of having adopted children in some cases, and of trying to do the right things as parents, community members, and corporate leaders. Members of the two groups paired off to talk intimately of their lives, their leadership stories, and what might be done to strengthen families and safeguard children in the inner city. These kinds of conversations necessarily open up questions about personal identity, values, and priorities—Who am I?

Understand the "Other"

It is well established that human relations develop and deepen as people see themselves in another person and see another in themselves. The leader-to-leader dialogues between Ford and HBC illustrate how an introductory exchange can stimulate connections. A more sustained example comes from the young leaders from Unilever who were joined together in a leadership development community in Asia.[17]

Some thirty-five young Unilever leaders from fifteen Asian countries have been meeting biennially in a Young Leader's Forum (YLF), where they are being prepared to join their country managing boards. The YLF operates as a learning community where personal inquiry, small group dialogue, and communal reflection continuously broaden the curricula and deepen shared experiences. Reflections shared in this forum are not only *cognitive*; and the intent is not solely to help the group *think together* better. On the contrary, the expression of *emotions* and inclination to *feel together* are very much part of the communal dialogue with the young leaders.

Like the Ford managers, the Unilever young leaders initially prepared and shared life stories with one another. But they have continued to delve into their life scripts and reflect on leadership dilemmas over five years of meeting together. As they find comfort and courage in one another's stories, the young leaders are confronted with their sometimes hidden selves; said one: "Listening to other people's stories, you hear your own story. Other people's stories often clarify things in your own mind—what your past is and what drives you. I'm a thirty-three-year-old guy, and I'm still trying to get recognition from my parents. That's not necessarily a bad thing, but having that self-awareness at least allows you to acknowledge and deal with that issue."

Also, like the Ford executives, Unilever's young leaders dialogued with leaders in an orphanage. In Danang, Vietnam, the story of the director of an orphanage was a source of inspiration. Sitting on tiny chairs, the young leaders formed circles around the director and learned how the orphanage had formed after the ravages of the "American war." The director had been a primary school teacher who had a "big dream" to build the village; he had few resources but "an abundance of hope." When asked what drove him, he answered: "Faith and love. I have a dream that keeps me going, where I see each child is happy." And he added: "When you are fifty years old, you feel there is not much time left to do something worthwhile; one needs to share all he has."

When one of the young leaders questioned him: "What would happen to the children if something were to happen to you?" there was a moment of silence. Then his inscrutable face was overcome with emotion. He trembled and could not stop his tears. Seven or seventy years old, every person in the room cried with him. Howard Gardner, among others, documents the importance of such storytelling for leaders.[18] And he puts particular emphasis on "identity stories" as a means of connecting leaders and followers. The young leaders here were listening to such an identity story; one characterized the experience as "looking humanity in the face."

Connect to the World

Consciousness raising requires some degree of internalization of the problem at hand and placing one's self psychologically into the situation.[19] To illustrate, the development program for Novo Nordisk vice presidents led executives from around the globe to visit community health centers in Sao Paulo, Brazil to talk with doctors, care for patients, and get firsthand impressions on "access to health" in a large developing country. The leaders were formed into several teams and, while on site, each team conducted a community diagnosis that analyzed the setting and service process and considered how their company might be implicated in problems and potential solutions. Teams also prepared a roster of lessons from their community experiences that could apply to their company's operations and management. These findings were shared and discussed with fellow leaders and the chief executive who had also visited communities.

One executive spoke of a doctor's entrepreneurial spirit: "He built a diabetes clinic from nothing. How? Real passion and belief in what he's doing. There was no complaining about resources or roadblocks. Nothing got in the way of his vision and drive." Another spoke of the caring, as opposed to strictly clinical, approach to patients: "At the hospital, the nurses didn't feel sorry for the children. They held them, laughed with them, and treated their illnesses aggressively. They taught the children how to win."

Subsequent talk, late into the night, stressed the importance of vision, passion, and purpose in leading their own business and in achieving their company's commitment to "defeat diabetes." "We in Denmark could learn from the Brazilians," remarked one vice president. "Seeing how much people can do if they set their minds to it, how much can be accomplished and how many resources can be mobilized in a developing country."

The Danish-based pharmaceutical has a long tradition of community service whereby every employee spends one day a year with a diabetes patient, family, or physician and prepares a report for the company on how to serve them better. But their executive's stimulating service experiences and subsequent meetings with government officials in Brasilia, alongside the company CEO, led to calls for more community outreach in developing markets and lower hurdle rates on investments in therapies for the poor. The company has since adopted plans to open subsidized diabetes clinics in other countries to ensure greater access to health.

A Higher Purpose

Leaders are being urged to apply their business acumen to the fast-paced changes in the world around them and in particular, to come to grips with the social, moral, and environmental impact of their organizations. This means, among other things, becoming "global citizens" and developing a point of view about the role of business in society. At their annual meeting in Sarawak (once part of Borneo), Unilever's young Asian leaders joined with their full management teams to experience firsthand the terrible costs incurred in the clear-cutting of tropical rainforests.

They first learned about the state of the natural environment in Asia through a talk by the head of a global natural resources NGO. Then, to get closer to the scene and symbolically lend a hand, the young and mature executives cleaned a nearby beach of industrial flotsam and tourist trash. A trip upriver in hollowed-out wooden canoes took them to the village of the Penan. There they met villagers, in their tribal dress and loincloths, talked through translators to the chief, medicine man, and tribesmen, and took a long walk with them through their clear-cut forests.

Periodic group reflections along the way opened up hearts and led to earnest discussion of the benefits and costs of economic growth in Asia. "We started this knowing that it was about business, but somewhere along the way we instead learned about humanity," noted one leader. "It's really all about realizing that you want to make something out of your life and knowing what you want to make out of your life and that you want to touch other people's lives." This in turn led to calls to incorporate sustainability into strategic plans. The reflections of another leader: "The beauty of the nature and the majesty of the place helped deepen our insights about our roles as leaders and individuals on this earth. To be in the jungles of Borneo helped us feel and see the potential in this region, almost feel and touch the vision. We were able to move from discovering self to building a mental picture about the future with a clear direction of where you want to go and to be. And it is extremely powerful when you see around you a lot of people sharing the same picture."

In each of the three companies portrayed here, community service experiences were integral to but by no means the only element of leadership programs that also involved project-based learning, team exercises, and business-related inputs and deliberations. There are other notable models of consciousness raising of this type for business leaders. As an example, the United Kingdom's Business in the Community, a leading group promoting corporate citizenship, sponsors "seeing is believing" programs where business leaders can engage in community service in destitute areas in their home country or abroad.

On a more sustained basis, volunteers from Cisco help NGOs to develop their IT capacities and in so doing, the volunteers learn about technology challenges in underserved markets. Like Pfizer, Abbott and J&J also send volunteers to developing countries to train nurses. And consulting firms like Ernst & Young and Accenture have global fellows programs where their consultants provide business services to NGOs around the world. These programs, and others like them, enable young leaders to express their positive aspirations and in so doing, prepare them intellectually and emotionally to lead tomorrow's businesses.

Raising the Consciousness of a Company

Now picture 250 company leaders, ranging from top corporate officers to local brand managers, spending three days in India visiting ashrams, hospitals, schools, microenterprises, and charities. They tend to the needy, offer service and support, and ponder how spiritual leaders, caregivers, and community entrepreneurs can accomplish so much with so few resources. In a desert campsite for three days thereafter they reflect on the meaning of their experiences, talk over its relevance for them, and rediscover what a true mission is—and what a new form of leadership could mean.

Said one leader: "Looking at the Sikh community I cannot overstate the power of common values. People can simply work together in perfect harmony without a formal organization." Said another, after visiting the charity of Mother Teresa: "The sisters and volunteers really inspired me with their humility, self-lessness, courage, and mostly their faith. The energy they have to serve the poor, disabled, and left-over really touched me, and honestly I cried during the visit." While such experiences deepened understanding of the people and communities in India, there was more to this than benchmarking or lending a hand. Tex Gunning, then president of Unilever Foods Asia (UFA), had posed the challenge to the assembled leaders as they launched their foods business in Asia two years earlier: "We confront ourselves with the questions: What life do I want to live? Do I want to live my own dream? And, can we create a common dream, and take it into our hands and realize it?"

These questions provoked deeper considerations. An Indonesian recalled, "a new challenge arose for me: How could I be worried about my job and 'how much tea we sold last week' when thinking of all those who are giving their lives to care for people for whom life seems so unfair. This was a gap I could not bridge, and I struggled with the rest of the group to see the link between those communities and our business-driven environment."

Bringing Life to Mission

The idea that vision, mission, and values can guide a business and give meaning to its people is well established. Yet in so many cases (including Unilever's), company mission statements merely hang on the walls of offices or appear on mugs and plaques without carrying any real meaning for employees who don't—either individually or collectively—embody the mission. The results: empty rhetoric and uninspired people. To build a sustainable, profitable foods-and-beverage business in Asia, UFA leaders have been experimenting with a new way to create a genuine mission and infuse it with personal values. A starting point, in 2002, was to connect senior leaders of seventeen national companies in the Asia Pacific region—which operated independently—and to include the next layers of country marketers, supply-chain managers, and corporate staff in set-ting strategy and reviewing performance for the whole of the regional business. The next step was to create pan-Asian business models. The last link: to connect UFA leaders and employees in common cause.

To build a sense of community, leaders in the region have been asked to open up about their life experiences, values, and dreams, talk frankly about their own leadership, national culture, and business, and listen thoughtfully to one another in search of commonality and differences. In principle, this kind of sharing can take place in meeting rooms and in the course of everyday business. And it has. But UFA has created deeper bonds through a series of annual "learning jour-neys" where all of its leaders come together to see the region—and themselves—with fresh eyes. They have traveled together to locales of historic and cultural significance; hiked through mountains and deserts; met with schoolchildren, indigenous peoples, everyday consumers, and the poor; learned from leaders in business, government, and community organizations; and reflected with one another about personal and business lives.

An early journey in 2003 took them to rural China. Here they "got into the skin" of villagers by working alongside them as they swept streets, herded buffaloes, formed cement building blocks, and led schoolchildren in play. Still others repaired bicycles, built roads, cooked noodles. No matter what the task at hand, there were important lessons learned: "My experience living with the villagers was an eye opener. I was fortunate to be with a seventy-two-year-old who had the energy of a forty-year-old. In the late 1930s she made sandals out of dried grass straw for Chinese soldiers. She told us with enthusiasm how important these sandals were to protect the soldiers' feet when crossing marshlands or hiking mountains. Her understanding of the 'big picture' struck me . . . that no matter how small your role is, it is still part of the whole."

The business leaders met villagers in rural China whose income was less than US$125 per annum. "Seventy percent of the people in my country live like the family of the man I met today," said a Pakistani, "while only 5 percent has a lifestyle similar to mine. I need to respect them and to value them for who they are and what they deliver to all of us." An Indonesian added, "I am Asian, forty years old, living in a country that is 80 percent rural, but I have never planted a tree nor talked to rural people who buy our products every day. This is critical when we aim to improve their nutrition, their health, their happiness, life and future."

The 2004 meeting in India, where they studied community life and engaged community leaders, carried the consciousness raising deeper and the implications further. Through reflections on their experience and collective dialogue, the Unilever leaders came to a new vision of their business. Said one: "The communities we visited reminded me of an 'itch' that has been bugging me for the longest time, which is, to give my time and effort to a cause which is beyond myself (and even beyond my family). I have been blessed so much in this life that the least I can do is to help my fellow men. I need to act now."

In their 2005 journey to Sri Lanka, where leaders went to offer service following the devastating tsunami, the sense of collective consciousness raising was palpable. The executives spent several days cleaning up debris in schools and public buildings, helping local merchants to assess inventory and connect with suppliers, playing with children, and talking deeply with Sri Lankans, individually and in large gatherings. The report of a leader about his first encounter with a tsunami survivor illustrates the depth of the experience: "This man who had lost two of his family members told me how God has been kind to him—his neighbor had lost all of his five family members. He made me realize that there is such goodness in simple lives—where I have never bothered to look." What did this soulful work teach the leaders? "We listened to the fears and hopes of the mothers, fathers, and children left behind in this beautiful but devastated country. We shed tears of pain, hope, and love," recalled one leader. "We shed even more tears when we realized that by simply sharing our spirit with them we made an incredible difference not only to their lives but also to our own. It continues to surprise me how care and service for others helps me discover my own love."

Bringing Mission to Life

Beyond personal enrichment and communal bonding, these learning journeys stimulated fresh thinking about leadership and innovative action in building the business and bringing its mission to life. Gunning's reflections on lessons from the journeys illustrate: "The core insight about great leadership comes down to service. Somehow it humanizes us. One of our problems, especially as we advance in positions of leadership, is that our egos get bigger and bigger, we suppress our human sides, and we don't listen to people—employees, customers, and others—whose needs should shape our business agenda. Face to face with great need, a leader is compelled to listen to the one in need."

In their most recent journey, the Asian leaders trekked to northern Vietnam where they brought dentists and healthcare professionals, along with Unilever toothpaste and soap, to introduce the Hmong peoples to modern hygiene. In a report out on progress to date, the leaders described how they were activating their mission throughout their region. Consider some highlights:

- *Leadership Development.* Unilever China treks to Tibet; Indian managers and staff live in communities throughout their land; the Vietnamese lead volunteer efforts with customers. The emphasis is on shared leadership in UFA Asia and its country heads are today creating leadership communities in their home countries and leading their people on consciousness-raising journeys.
- *Organizational Development.* Their new collaborative structure has employees networking to build on global brand propositions and swap local insights. Thousands are engaged in community service. As one manager described it: "One of our most important responsibilities is to help our people to grow so that they can live meaningful lives as human beings as well as business beings. The better we grow our people, the better they will grow their business."
- *Business Development.* We've noted how Gunning was commissioned by CEO Patrick Cescau to help bring citizenship to Unilever's Vitality mission. Within the region, the UFA leaders have made collective commitments to emphasize the healthy, nourishing aspects of food. This meant dropping some profitable products in the Asian market because of their high sugar or fat content, investing in a variety of new tea-based beverages because of their healthy benefits, and the launch of a nutrition campaign for children to bring affordable foods to the bottom of the pyramid. Behind this is a shift in mindset: "This changes the paradigm of thinking that we are selling to consumers," said one. "Instead we are serving our communities."
- *Community Development.* Listen to Gunning on this count: "Caring for community needs to be in the heart of all our actions. Once we get this right, then the rest will come into place. The profits will be there because we are heading in the right direction. If our competitors start doing things similar to us, we should not be mad at them. In fact we should be happy, because they will also help people and grow the marketplace. With that in mind we will have a very strong foundation to bring value into to this world."

It is too early to judge whether or not shifting the business model from selling to customers to serving communities has commercial vitality or will promote better community development in Asia than the conventional business model. It's too early to tell, as well, how the personal development and engagement as citizens of Unilever's young Asian leaders (and their bosses) will translate into benefits for the company. But this is the value proposition that Unilever is offering to customers and employees on its path to next generation citizenship. This is one of many other compelling examples of how companies are translating good intentions into purposeful action as we see in Part III on next generation practices.

Part III

Putting Citizenship to Work

Nokia, a Finnish industrial that went from a wood pulp company to a conglomerate in its first hundred years of operation from 1865 to 1967, transformed itself over the next forty years into the world's leading mobile phone and multimedia device manufacturer. Today it is moving to the forefront of corporate citizenship. To scan the environment and map relevant trends in its global environment, the company supports a team of futurologists called Insight and Foresight. This team projects that four billion consumers worldwide could be mobile-ready in five years—a marketing and manufacturing stretch for a firm that in 2005 manufactured its first billionth mobile phone.

What's Nokia doing to prepare itself for this opportunity and for the risks involved? On the operational side, the company has set up modern ISO 14001 environmentally certified production sites in China, India, Brazil, Mexico, and Hungary; established a comprehensive supplier code and assessment system; and registered continuous improvements in its material and environmental management metrics. On the product side, it offers the latest technology in a fully recyclable phone that can be economically disassembled in less than a minute. It also has, as we shall see in Part III, a social strategy whereby, in partnership with the Grameen Foundation, it has created a mobile phone kit that includes a Nokia handset, SIM card, prepaid airtime, and an antenna set plus marketing materials, all made available through microcredit to small business owners and village-level entrepreneurs in developing countries.

Part III is about putting citizenship to work. It is based on the Center's corporate citizenship management framework (see Figure III.1) that differentiates three domains of citizenship activity: (1) an operational domain of governance, organization, and business practices; (2) a commercial domain of products and services; and (3) a community domain of social engagement and contributions to society. Linking these domains are the values, mission, and core management processes of a company.

In each of these three domains, there is evidence that companies are progressing from relatively simple but often not particularly effective practices toward more sophisticated and comprehensive "solutions." Chapter 10 describes developments in the corporate organization and operations of firms. Good companies today consult with key stakeholders, monitor their social and environmental performance, and report on the results. Next generation citizens

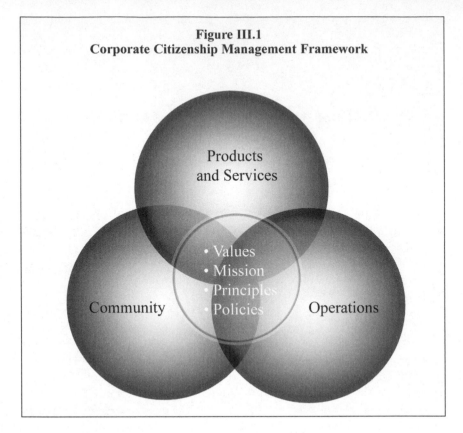

Figure III.1
Corporate Citizenship Management Framework

create integrated performance systems that provide regular "health checks" in these regards and engage the firm top to bottom in continuously improving performance. Chapter 11 scans how citizenship is showing up in products and services. Many firms today associate themselves with causes and are working toward more eco-friendly offerings in the marketplace. Here we will see how a select few are developing full business models based on fair trade, on reaching untapped low-income markets, and on connecting modern consumers to the emerging market producers through what is termed ethical consumption. Chapter 12 then traces how new models of strategic corporate philanthropy have spread from the United States to Asia and how new types of business, NGO, and even multibusiness partnerships are emerging where the parties co-create value for society.

Integrating Citizenship into the Business

When companies join the Global Leadership Network, they complete a self-assessment where they rank to what extent they engage stakeholders and define issues material to their business, how citizenship factors into their business strategies, and whether or not they are getting the kind of leadership needed to move their citizenship agenda forward. They also rate themselves along four, fundamental, blocking-and-tackling-type issues:

- Does the company employ its core management systems and processes to manage corporate citizenship?
- Are business units, managers, and employees responsible and accountable for economic, social, and environmental performance?
- Has the company built competencies and skill levels to manage citizenship effectively?
- Are there measures and evaluation processes to determine the effectiveness of citizenship in the company?

Faced with these kinds of questions, one manager pictured the way her company was handling the demands of corporate citizenship as a disintegrated array of programs, handled by corporate staff groups, and largely disconnected from one another (see Figure 10.1).

We have traced this all-too-common condition to the multiplicity of outside pressures on companies that require a cadre of internal specialists to understand and manage. This chaos is exacerbated as companies build their capacity to manage citizenship and issue new policies and launch new programs. Companies that move beyond this into an advanced stage create more coherence in their efforts and make moves to integrate citizenship into their business. Expressed more formally, the Center has found that companies with the most advanced citizenship profiles and practices have taken serious steps to *align* their citizenship efforts with their business strategies, *integrate* citizenship into their organization structure and processes, and *institutionalize* it into the mindsets, values, and culture of their organization:

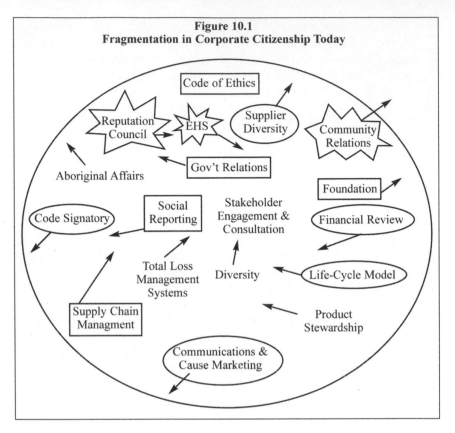

Figure 10.1
Fragmentation in Corporate Citizenship Today

- *Alignment.* To connect corporate citizenship to business objectives through a cohesive, company-wide framework that is commonly understood in different parts of the business and that guides responsible behavior. This creates a coherent context for citizenship and is expressed in codes of conduct, orienting models, and accountability measures.
- *Integration.* To embed shared corporate citizenship principles and responsibilities in business units and functional areas including corporate staff units, human resources, and supply chain. This often means creating cross-unit systems, processes, and structures
- *Institutionalization.* To ensure the sustainability of corporate citizenship by formalizing it in standard business practices and infusing into the mindsets of company personnel. This translates into statements of mission and values and efforts to make citizenship an integral part of a company's culture.

Aligning Citizenship with the Business

Five years ago, there was scant evidence that companies were aligning citizenship with their business strategies and operations. The Center's 2003 Citizenship survey, a first exploration of this subject in a national sample of U.S. business, found that while the majority of big firms in our sample addressed citizenship in their mission or vision statements, policies, and communications, far fewer incorporated it into the firm's strategic plans (41 percent), work-unit goals (36 percent), and manager performance appraisals (18 percent). Our 2007 survey of American business finds modest progress on these counts in that today nearly half of the larger companies (employing over one thousand persons) make citizenship an integral part of their business planning process. But the link between citizenship and business processes seems to be more prominent in leading edge corporations that are members of the Boston College Center, Conference Board, Businesses for Social Responsibility, and the UN Global Compact.[1]

There are several social, political, and commercial factors that to some extent influence how companies choose to align citizenship with their business. For instance, firms that extract natural resources, such as oil and timber companies, are monitored closely by NGOs and find themselves more exposed on their environmental performance. Risk management criteria naturally dictate that they give greater attention to environmental safeguards. Not surprisingly, the Center's industry scans find that the policies, structures, and metrics in companies like Rio Tinto (mining), DuPont (chemicals), and most oil and gas companies are stronger and more elaborate in the environmental arena than in, say, community affairs, where banks are stronger. Firms with a significant supply chain or labor force in developing countries—think apparel and shoe companies, or high-tech companies and even toy marketers—are more apt to have strong supplier codes and work with parties such as Social Accountability International or the Ethical Trading Initiative alliance on overseas working conditions and employment practices. In turn, companies like Petro-Canada or BP, whose business brings them into contact with indigenous peoples, tend to have sophisticated stakeholder and community consultation systems. A conglomerate like GE, by comparison, has to give across-the-board attention to citizenship.

GE Gets It Together

Recall how, when Jeff Immelt took over from Jack Welch at GE, he reversed course on the company's dealings with the government over PCB pollution, paid partially for the clean up of the Hudson, and devised a "Spirit and Letter" compliance policy to remind employees that they must not only attend to the letter of the law, but also its spirit or intent. This statement was revised again in 2005 and distributed in user-friendly format to all of GE's three hundred thousand employees. The larger intent, as Immelt puts it, has been to create a "culture of compliance" in the company and align the company with its core values around integrity.

What's involved? Apart from the policy, which covers everything from traditional code of conduct items to environmental safety and health, GE has made compliance a regular part of its fabled operating system. A corporate Policy Compliance Review Board (which consists of the CEO, CFO, General Counsel, and other senior executives) oversees regular "Session D" compliance reviews that review compliance risks and issues in every business and region. In addition, GE has an extensive "ombudsperson" process to monitor matters of ethics throughout the company. During 2006, for example, the company indicates that some fifteen hundred "integrity concerns" were reported through this process (38 percent anonymously), resulting in 395 disciplinary actions against managers, employees, and vendors. GE publishes an enumeration of these concerns in its annual Citizenship Report.[2]

Fallout over GE's handling of PCB pollution was not the only core citizenship issue facing Immelt when he took charge. In a 2002 public opinion poll, GE's corporate reputation slipped from twelfth to twentieth place, primarily because of concerns that the company was "treating executives like royalty."[3] In his severance package, Welch received a $9 million annual pension and an $80,000 per month stipend loaded with perks. Following Enron and the other scandals of its ilk, this all raised a stink. Troubled GE shareholders proposed that executive compensation be more clearly disclosed and more closely tied to performance. Further, they requested that the company's accounting practices in general become more transparent.

Shortly thereafter, Immelt facilitated numerous revisions to GE's corporate governance policies. First, GE increased the ratio of independent directors on its Board of Directors and required that its independent directors meet at least three times a year without management present, to encourage open debate. In addition, it determined that only independent directors would serve on its Management Development and Compensation and its Audit Committees.

Second, the Board consulted with Warren Buffett, a strong advocate of linking executives' pay to long-term performance. Thereafter it created a new form of stock-based incentive for the CEO that pays out based on shareholder returns and operating cash flow over a five-year period (and only if returns meet or exceed the S&P 500 total for that period and cash flow increases 10 percent or more). Additionally, to align directors' interests with the long-term interests of the company, 60 percent of director compensation comes through deferred stock units, which don't vest until one year after the director leaves the board.

Third, on the accounting side, Immelt unpacked GE Capital, which for years had increased or decreased its reserves to "balance" the company's profitability across businesses, and divided it into four distinct businesses, thereby giving shareholders a clearer understanding of the P&L of GE's main businesses. Additionally, rather than focus on earnings management, Immelt devoted his attention to boosting earnings the "old fashioned way" by selling off unprofitable businesses and investing in new labs and business lines associated with ecomagination.

Finally, GE created a Board-level committee to oversee the company's citizenship reporting, EH&S activities, and public policy activities. Robert Corcoran, in addition to heading the company's Crotonville training center, was named vice president for corporate citizenship and president of GE's foundation. Corcoran reports to the vice president of human resources in GE and directly to the Board's Public Responsibilities Committee. Interestingly, Corcoran insists that making money ethically is part of corporate citizenship. "Without a sustainable, thriving business model," he told an audience at the Conference Board's 2007 Leadership Conference on Global Corporate Citizenship, "your role as a corporate citizen is short-lived." Corcoran's "Top Ten Ways" to make it work reflect his and GE's no-nonsense approach.[4]

BT's Health Check

In the late 1990s, British Telecom (BT) obtained the international standard ISO14001 certification for its Environmental Management System, covering all of its operations in the United Kingdom.[5] As the company globalized and more holistic concepts of citizenship and sustainable development began to emerge, Chris Tuppen, head of sustainable development for BT, reports: "It was logical to ask ourselves if we should extend the scope of our management system to include all CSR activities, including human rights, ethical trading, community programs, managing diversity, and customer exclusion (digital divide for BT)." While some of these issues were quite new to the company, many were well established within existing management systems and processes.

"We decided that what was actually needed wasn't more control, but rather a means of ensuring these CSR 'aspects' were fully embedded in the management of the company," Tuppen told us. "Our response was to create a 'health check' to ensure that CSR is embedded into BT commercial operations."

BT's health check, a core business process, takes two forms. One part is semi-standardized and has each of the company's business units go through an annual cycle of goal setting, measurement, and feedback that covers traditional CSR criteria: integrity, employees, environment, health and safety, supply chain, digital inclusion, education, and charities. The company has set out key performance indicators in each area for monitoring. In terms of customer satisfaction, for example, BT reported a significant reduction in "dissatisfied" customers in 2004 and 2005 and an increase in the number who are "very satisfied" by 3 percent in 2006. On the environmental front, to take another example, BT has recorded significant reductions in CO_2 emissions the past few years and now aims at emissions 80 percent below 1996 levels by 2016. Each business contributes to corporate targets accordingly.

The other part of the system is concerned with "winning business." In this area, Tuppen and his team work with line executives to identify the "vital few" commercial initiatives for each business where social and environmental, alongside economic, factors could either aid or impede their success. They sit down at the table—"where you let the conversation flow in natural directions"—and come out with a sense of how CSR issues might factor into the business. The output of a health check is a one-page summary that contains a straightforward, triple bottom line analysis of the positive and negative impacts related to environmental, social, and economic factors. This is followed by a set of recommendations on addressing risks and opportunities.

How do health checks help to align the business behind corporate citizenship? Tuppen offers three examples:

- *Climate Change.* The 21st Century Network is a BT project to build a more efficient Internet protocol-based network. Through a health check, it was determined that some issues around climate change had not been built into its early design. For one, the company had not calibrated fully how "extreme weather" might put its huge investment in external infrastructure at risk. Second, it saw that it could offer products and services related to energy use and environmental health. Now BT has embedded these issues into its risk management and commercial plans.
- *Supply Chain.* During another health check, BT discovered that a product group was not following its Sourcing with Human Dignity standard on working conditions in its supply chain. This was corrected and in 2006, BT conducted four hundred thirteen risk assessments with its suppliers in this regard with 100 percent follow up on issues of concern.
- *Customer Interests in CSR.* BT conducts up to three thousand face-to-face interviews each month to assess customers' views and monitor their satisfaction. Statistical analysis of five to eight years of research revealed that, as a part of the overall customer satisfaction model, BT's CSR activities comprise 25 percent of the effect their reputation has on customer satisfaction figures. Its latest survey finds that customers who believe that BT takes its responsibility to society and the community seriously are 49 percent more likely than other customers to be very or extremely satisfied with the company.

Trends in Social Reporting

For nearly a decade BT has issued a social and environmental report and has been a thought leader in this arena among companies around the world. As an example, it published a provocative and prescient report in 2003, "Just Values," that made the case for business's active involvement in sustainable development and it continues to update its point of view in its annual social report.[6]

Overall, there has been a dramatic increase in voluntary non-financial reporting by corporations worldwide.[7] While a handful of global corporations issued annual CSR-type reports in 1990, this increased ten years later to roughly 750, and to nearly 2,000 in 2006. An analysis of these reports shows that ninety of the top one hundred companies in Europe issued reports, fifty-eight of the top one hundred in the United States, and sixty-one of the top one hundred in the rest of the world. Social reporting, while still taking hold in the United States and elsewhere will, in our view, become a standard practice for big, public companies in the next few years. Looking ahead, assurance will be the next step. On this count, European firms are far more likely to have their reports verified by external third parties.

On a broader scale, there are also general standards and guidelines for business conduct on all three aspects of the triple bottom line. The Organization for Economic Co-operation and Development (OECD), for example, has established a comprehensive set of guidelines for multinational companies that have been approved by thirty-nine countries, including the United States. We have noted how the UN Global Compact has promulgated standards for business concerning human rights, labor, environmental responsibility, and anti-corruption; and we have cited the GRI that sets guidelines for corporate reporting. As of this writing, over a thousand companies in sixty countries subscribe to GRI guidelines that have gone through their third revision; the G3 covers new territory on the social impact of business and stakeholder engagement. These kinds of metrics, and social reporting broadly, can produce a cohesive, company-wide framework that can be understood within a firm and helps to align its business with society.

Integrating Citizenship into the Company

A citizenship manager from Abbott told us a few years ago: "Most of our programs work in silos. We are trying to integrate them more throughout the company, but it has to be an effort by people, not just by systems and processes." Abbott was one of the companies in the Center's Executive Forum whose members, chiefly from their company's community affairs and environmental, health, and safety functions, shared ideas and best practices with one another in an effort to integrate citizenship more firmly in their respective firms. As one of the big pharmaceutical companies, Abbott faced heightened public scrutiny about issues such as access to medicine and product affordability. Yet, the company's senior management was focused on its therapy pipeline, competition, and ever-present pressures for profit. Reeta Roy, a divisional vice president for policy, sought to transform what had been a fragmented and decentralized approach into a unified model of managing citizenship. "I was hired for a job in 'issues management,' in the public affairs department, and different elements of citizenship were handled by different parts of the group," Roy explained. "When I took on the position, I did some internal research with senior executives about the issues confronting our business and our industry, and did some external benchmarking." Roy recognized that what Abbott really needed was not a stronger issues management unit but a unified policy function.

From Issues to a Unified Approach

We've described how AMD moved forward on its citizenship building with its social-and-environmental reporting. This was also a driver at Abbott where Kevin Callahan, who would become director of the function, explained: "The global citizenship report is a real catalyst for change, sometimes unbeknownst to us. The report has brought people forward from many different departments saying, 'We're going to try to do something different and we want to check with you and see if you think this would be a good idea.' The citizenship report has become a mechanism through which initiatives to integrate corporate citizenship can be recognized, supported, and brought into line with Abbott's broad citizenship vision."

Roy and Callahan devised a three-phase strategy to integrate citizenship into the company. In Phase I, Callahan recalls, they began to bring diverse interests together to move the agenda forward: "You have to pull together a group of people, externally and internally, whom you can use as a sounding board to start testing some initial strategies." Using the report as an entry point, he and Roy helped the purchasing group to conduct a supplier assessment and risk analysis. They also built bridges with the ethics and compliance function at Abbott. Later they would connect these separate and distinct functions into a working group that would consult with stakeholders and monitor societal expectations on a wide range of pharma-issues.

"We aren't here with any other agenda but to serve as a resource and a partner to help the business think through dilemmas, and figure out what needs to be done in a thoughtful way. It is part of our role to ensure that decisions are made bearing in mind the external context," Callahan observed. This kind of consultation, as Callahan describes it, would demark Phase II, where they would engage line managers on key social issues, including the affordability of medicines in general and therapies for HIV/AIDS in Africa in particular.

As of this writing, Abbott is entering Phase III, where citizenship is being factored more systematically into business decisions and has gained voice in the company's Board through its public policy committee. As a result, citizenship has become, in Roy's terms, "not only a reputation tool . . . it's a driver of performance."

From Programs to Formal Structure

The Center's 2007 survey of American business finds that 48 percent of large companies have an "individual or team" responsible for corporate citizenship issues. Meanwhile there are growing numbers of CROs (Corporate Responsibility Officers) and VPs of Citizenship or Sustainability who report directly to the CEO and join their firm's C-suite. Petro-Canada, the northern nation's largest oil company, illustrates how companies transition from having citizenship issues handled by myriad functions and programs to adopting a more coordinated and integrated approach.

Petro-Canada's approach to corporate responsibility when it joined the Forum included programs in aboriginal relations (in areas of drilling), community investment, and environment, health, safety, and security. Though each of these programs was successful in its own right, the company lacked a strategic perspective on citizenship and had limited engagement by top management. This programmatic approach was not consistent with the company's systems-oriented culture and was insufficient for dealing with the full range of issues raised in the acquisition of several international businesses.

Hazel Gillespie, a community investment manager, and David Stuart, of Environment, Health, Safety and Security, conducted an assessment of Petro-Canada's corporate responsibility initiatives and operations with the intention, says Gillespie, of making "a strong move forward on corporate responsibility in the company." The research process included: (1) benchmarking their company against best practices; (2) conducting in-depth conversations with counterparts at other oil and gas companies; and (3) meeting with internal stakeholders.

As a result of this research, the team favored creating a top-level corporate responsibility governance structure and management system. Anticipating that achieving buy-in from top executives would be difficult, however, Gillespie and Stuart decided to "piggy-back" on efforts already underway to strengthen the firm's reputation and update its total loss management system. This brought them into contact with groups concerned with communication and company values and business performance and control. Work in these separate projects helped Gillespie and Stuart to gain the credibility and traction needed to build a coalition supportive of their ideas. In particular, it suggested how the total loss management system, already geared to audit product quality and EH&S compliance, could be extended to cover the company's work on stakeholder relationships and monitor its social performance.

In due course, Petro-Canada added criteria of corporate responsibility into its total loss management system and created an executive-level Corporate Responsibility Steering Committee that would set policy, oversee citizenship in the company, and monitor compliance. Soon thereafter, the company created a director-level position in corporate responsibility. As one of the leadership team commented: "To have somebody who wakes up thinking about corporate responsibility every day is great—it brings all the pieces together."

Lessons on Taking an Integrated Approach

Decades of research into organizational change documents that the better informed and more knowledgeable people are about their current reality and details of a new course of action, the more facile they are at designing change and the more receptive they are to implementing it.[8] Forging and fostering relationships and alliances are also strong predictors of garnering political support and successfully launching organizational change. These were the central lessons of the citizenship managers in the Executive Forum. Indeed, because they typically operated with no formal authority and scant budget and staff, they had to leverage knowledge throughout their companies and build alliances with professional peers and business managers.

Build Knowledge

For the corporate citizenship manager, building knowledge about the business and the landscape in which it operates is crucial. Often the managers charged with advancing citizenship are from staff functions and may not have much experience in business management. Located typically in corporate communications, community affairs, public policy, the legal department, or EH&S, they need this business knowledge to establish their credibility and to understand how line managers view the world.

Abbott's use of select managers as a sounding board illustrates one way that practitioners gain a general understanding of their business's strategies and goals. Understanding strategic business drivers was also essential for corporate citizenship managers to gain traction for new ideas and initiatives. Petro-Canada's expansion into international markets for energy exploration motivated the company to take a fresh look at issues related to human rights, codes of conduct, contractors, and improper payments. Stepping into this business arena, the leaders in its corporate responsibility function assumed the role of identifying these issues and updating existing corporate policy, assurance, and monitoring that were not adequate for global operations. Equally important was the knowledge transfer from citizenship practitioners to line managers. Many of the corporate citizenship managers we studied said that a key aspect of their role was alerting and educating management on issues that were likely to develop into important industry-specific or general social debates.

Build Relationships

Many practitioners believe that a "bulletproof business case" is required before soliciting support for citizenship efforts from business units. In the forum, by comparison, we observed practitioners scouting for situations where managers had citizenship problems and building a business case with them. Several, for instance, found allies in their supply-chain areas—where a plethora of new supplier certification procedures and codes, as well as recognizable risks and threats, were all bearing on overburdened managers. Abbott's global citizenship group, as one example, sought out the purchasing department as a partner because of issues of drug affordability, counterfeiting, and the like that were racking the entire industry.

At Levi Strauss & Co., Fay-Bustillos recognized that employees are key drivers of incorporating Levi's citizenship into the business. "Employees play an important role in asking questions about our practices and in consistently reinforcing the perception by executives that one of the top reasons people come to LS&CO. is because they think we are a responsible company," she says, adding: "They can't articulate specifically why we are responsible, nor do they need to. It's the consistency of the message that keeps corporate citizenship near the top of a business-focused agenda."

Take Strategic Action

Our research found that in these companies, absent a sense of urgency or senior executive push for corporate citizenship, managers had to calibrate when and how much to push the envelope, take leadership, and be creative. While not always conscious of it, the corporate citizenship practitioners in our study adopted a dynamic and interactive approach to strategy—taking action on multiple fronts and operating as both strategists and catalysts for change.

Integrating citizenship requires connecting it with the corporate purpose and structure. While showing how citizenship encompasses a wide range of interests, actually "naming" the thrust and clarifying its scope gives it direction and authority. Reeta Roy and her colleagues had great success transforming "issues management" into a citizenship function. When she was named vice president for global citizenship and policy, however, both the title and change in name for the function gave the work a new identity in the company. She noted: "Our department's name more clearly reflects the end point we are seeking. We are not just managing issues but really trying to develop points of view and take action to address challenging issues facing our company and industry. It is more in keeping with our values and our mission and with how we support the business."

Rather than reinvent the wheel, managers in the forum often sought out opportunities to introduce citizenship into what already exists to lessen resistance, maximize efficiency, and avoid redundancy. The success of the team at Petro-Canada in bringing corporate responsibility to the fore through the company's total loss management system illustrates this. Creating a position and staff function for corporate responsibility, now filled by Fiona Jones, further solidified its importance in the company.

But nothing speaks louder than action. Certainly Abbott leveraged its social reporting as a means to regularly convene people and interests throughout the business. Its citizenship profile took on new dimensions when Roy's working group stimulated Abbott to expand its patient assistance program in the United States and its leadership position in AIDS treatment domestically and in the developing world. One citizenship-based innovation, creation of an HIV African American and Latino Treatment Council, provides the company regular feedback on how it is reaching a formerly disenfranchised group of stakeholders with its programs. More broadly, the company has more than two hundred scientists involved in antiviral R&D and provides access to its HIV medicines and tests at no profit in sixty-nine of the world's poorest countries.

Institutionalizing Citizenship: Top to Bottom

Companies that successfully move into higher levels of integration take a "top-to-bottom" approach. Googins and Rochlin conceptualize management of citizenship at three different levels of practice (Figure 10.2).[9] Citizenship at 50,000 feet is the province of corporate boards, managing directors, and senior executives of the company. They are, after all, the stewards of the enterprise and are charged with the vision and given the voice to define what citizenship means in a firm and what it aims to accomplish. IBM's innovative thrust, Unilever's Vitality mission, GE's ecomagination, and Wal-Mart's drive for sustainability were either birthed or affirmed at this level. The practical message is that work at the top is about vision, values, seeing the big picture, engaging people within and connected to the company about what it all means, and overseeing the citizenship agenda.

Citizenship at 30,000 feet is in the hands of senior corporate managers and business unit heads that enact it in policies and strategies, enlist their people, align organizational structures, and help to embed it in the company culture. Their work is to make the citizenship agenda concrete, develop value propositions, build political support, break down silos, and lead the effort in their areas of responsibility. The barriers to success can be daunting. McKinsey & Co.'s 2007 survey of UN Global Compact Companies found that four in ten firms were hampered from taking an integrated, strategic approach to citizenship by the "complexity of implementing strategy across various business functions."[10] CSR executives who break through these barriers operate within, across, and often maneuver around functional and business lines to raise consciousness, build coalitions, and solidify momentum as their firms move forward, typically step by step.

Citizenship at ground level, in turn, is all about execution. Here frontline managers and professionals are face to face with stakeholders, devising plans, juggling priorities, and, on the good days, delivering value for both business and society. These include the researchers, On Demand professionals, and frontline citizenship managers at IBM, the R&D teams and product designers at GE, the brand managers, marketers, and business partners at Unilever, and members of the fourteen sustainability teams at Wal-Mart, among many others.

What is important to note is that *unless and until citizenship is activated at these three levels, its potential value will never be realized.* On this point, John Anderson, CEO of LS&CO., stressed the importance of getting leadership behind it. "It starts from the top of companies," he told us. "Senior managers getting clear on what they stand for. Then getting aligned with the board to ensure that shareholders and stakeholders are comfortable with that point of view." But another CEO reminded us of the need for broader-based activation. "What is more important," he said, "is engaging employees with a sense of purpose."

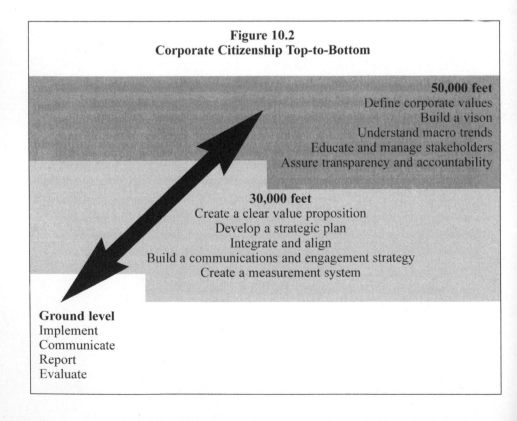

Figure 10.2
Corporate Citizenship Top-to-Bottom

50,000 feet
Define corporate values
Build a vison
Understand macro trends
Educate and manage stakeholders
Assure transparency and accountability

30,000 feet
Create a clear value proposition
Develop a strategic plan
Integrate and align
Build a communications and engagement strategy
Create a measurement system

Ground level
Implement
Communicate
Report
Evaluate

3M's Top-to-Bottom Model

"3M's founders built a corporate culture with strong values and a commitment to 'do the right thing,'" said one company staffer in the GLN forum. "Corporate citizenship serves as part of the business culture and is the means by which business gets done." The company's business units are highly diverse and historically decentralized, leaving them more or less free to focus on revenue, growth, and innovation in their particular markets. At the same time, 3M ensures consistency of performance on issues critical to risk management and reputation. In these regards, it has institutionalized a top-to-bottom approach to citizenship.

50,000 Feet at 3M

The tone for corporate conduct is set at the top through the 3M Board of Directors and its Public Issues Committee. This committee addresses sustainability issues by reviewing public policy and social trends affecting 3M; monitoring the company's corporate citizenship activities; and evaluating company policies and programs to enable 3M to respond appropriately to its social responsibilities and the public interest in the conduct of its businesses. Affirming values is also part of the work here. As Kathy Reed, 3M's vice president for environmental, health, and safety, notes: "Sometimes a company can buy its way out of a risk, but we don't do that. We walk away from good looking deals on paper because they aren't the right thing to do."

At a strategic level, the company uses a planning process called the business alignment framework. The first step in the process has top executives and corporate staff look at business, environmental, political, and social trends, as well as issues pertaining to employees. It then cascades the framework down through business units and across regions. In 2001, the company adopted defined climate change as a key business driver. It undertook aggressive measures to reduce greenhouse gases and volatile air emissions and to improve its energy efficiency. Since then, 3M has launched a series of environmentally-friendly products that range from a nontoxic, biodegradable paint and varnish remover that contains no methylene chloride, to roofing granules that keep a house cooler and sun control films that keep it warmer, each reducing home energy use and costs.

Finally, to foster an environment where ethical issues can be debated openly and intelligently, 3M has a program in which developing leaders are schooled in moral reasoning by their own senior executives and challenged to employ 3M values in action. Company executives introduce real case examples of tough decisions—where business gains do not necessarily align with the company's values. Participants discuss the competing issues, make recommendations, and then learn how 3M actually handled the matter. Executives, in the role of teacher-leader, also talk about how personal values factor into decisions. In addition, ethical topics are also subjects for lively debate at quarterly executive meetings. Together these efforts illustrate how, at 50,000 feet, top executives help to create an ethical grid for their companies.

30,000 Feet at 3M

Corporate citizenship at 3M focuses largely on the triad of core business practices, environment (along with health and safety), and support for communities.
The firm's signature emphasis, however, is on the environment, where the company has robust management systems to support its efforts. 3M's Corporate
Sustainability Committee includes representation from EHS, communications,
public relations and public affairs, investor relations, the legal department,
human resources, and community affairs. The committee evaluates the contribution of existing programs to 3M's social and environmental performance,
highlights gaps for attention, and keeps abreast of opportunities to innovate in
product and process design.

The Pollution Prevention Pays (PPP) program has created a company-wide
commitment to environmental protection, safety, and health in its thirty years of
operation and returned massive savings for the company. It provides governance, strategy, and oversight to environmental management both centrally and
at each of 3M facilities worldwide. A number of new processes have been developed to reduce business costs, such as moving to less expensive water-based
materials. Interestingly, many technologies resulting from PPP projects are
patented by 3M, such as solventless processes to reduce air emissions (hot-melt,
water-based coatings) for many products from tapes to sandpaper. Over the last
thirty years, more than half of the company's emissions reductions have resulted
from converting to solventless processes.

3M's Life Cycle Management (LCM) Process was developed in the late
nineties to examine how the full cycle of products, from raw materials to consumer use to disposal, were impacting the environment and has since become a
corporate standard. Multidisciplinary LCM teams guide the product development process from the onset and the company reports that, through this disciplined process, over two hundred products feature environmental or energy
attributes that help both 3M and its customers reduce their footprints.

As a result of establishing environmental performance as a strategic priority,
3M has created an EHS Performance Scorecard that monitors safety and the
company's eco-efficiency. Each 3M business unit and facility produces an EHS
plan. They set annual objectives on how to improve each year and progress is
tracked quarterly. EHS Scorecard results are reviewed through senior management. This ensures a strategic link between business objectives and EHS
priorities.

Ground Level at 3M

The process and product innovations just described are, of course, the work of
operating managers, staff, and some seventy-five thousand employees. The
Center has not looked closely in the GLN at how, specifically, 3M employees
operate within the company's PPP and LCM systems nor does the company
make public much information about wages, working conditions, or employee
engagement. It is well known, however, that 3M was one of the first companies

to offer "dual ladder" career paths to allow scientists and technically minded employees to advance without assuming management responsibilities, freeing them to personally pursue their research, and has an informal "15 Percent Rule" that allows employees time to explore ideas outside of their day-to-day job responsibilities.

Citizenship and Corporate Culture

Some companies, such as the aforementioned Ben & Jerry's or the Body Shop, have cultures born in the values of corporate citizenship. Others, like Johnson & Johnson, Herman Miller, and Timberland, seem to have citizenship "DNA" that keeps their values constant in the face of changing economic, social, and ecological pressures. J&J, for instance, doesn't use a plethora of committees or communications to align citizenship efforts throughout the enterprise. According to Owen Rankin, head of Brand Equity and J & J's Pediatric Institute, it instead relies on its corporate credo to ensure that its businesses and people are motivated to do the right thing.

One company that continues to infuse its culture, top to bottom, with corporate citizenship is the Danish-based pharmaceutical Novo Nordisk.[11] The company history dates to 1923 when Danish scientists visited Canadian researchers and together began a series of studies on treating people with diabetes with an insulin extract. The corporate story is complicated, involving its split into two companies, a subsequent merger, and then a de-merger, but the key point for our purposes, as expressed by the corporate branding team, is that values drive the business: "As Scandinavians we are value-driven. . . . We appreciate qualities such as being genuine, sincerity, authenticity, and originality. We are not materialistic, not driven by economic status." One indication of this is that the company, while publicly traded on the New York Stock Exchange, is controlled by the Novo Nordisk Foundation, a nonprofit.

In the mid-1990s, as competition increased and the company increasingly globalized, the company formulated its Novo Nordisk Way of Management (NNWoM). Beginning with a vision to defeat diabetes, the centerpiece was its charter that covered values, principles of management, and key commitments, including the ideas that products and services would make a "significant difference in improving the way people live and work" and that its "activities, practices and deliverables are perceived to be economically viable, environmentally sound and socially fair." Through its charter, the company was making a commitment to manage by the triple bottom line—a principle formally adopted in amendments in 2004 to its Articles of Association under Danish Law.

The company's leadership in responsible healthcare has taken the form of affordable medicines in developing countries and among the poor in developed nations, creation of the World Diabetes Foundation, extensive advocacy programs, and "changing diabetes" campaign. It's also been well recognized in *CNN*'s "Principal Voices" series and many awards. What's of interest here is how its philosophy is embedded in the corporate culture.

The NNWoM is an operating system that stretches from top to bottom. It's overseen by CEO Lars Rebien and the Board and directed by Lise Kingo, EVP and chief of staff, a member of the top executive team. Among its innovative practices, the company expects all employees to spend at least one day a year with someone connected to diabetes—a patient, a caretaker, or a healthcare professional—and then to suggest improvements for how the company does business. To ensure performance to the highest standards, it has built-in accountability that requires systematic and validated documentation of performance to the company's values-based management system. Each business unit, for example, has a balanced scorecard that cascades triple bottom line goals throughout the organization. The company's annual reporting accounts for performance in all three domains with an extensive analysis of results against targets and a detailed profile of its engagement with stakeholders.

In the spirit of leaving no stone unturned, the company continues to expand its definition of what it means to be a responsible company. As part of its commitment to support the United Nations Universal Declaration of Human Rights, and its signing of the UN Global Compact, Novo Nordisk has integrated human rights into business policies and practices, in the form of a Human Rights Management System. "A major challenge in implementing this system was getting decision makers in the global organization to understand and consider the aspects of human rights in every strategic decision they make—just as environmental considerations are already an integral part of the Novo Nordisk Way of Management," explains Elin Schmidt, a vice president of corporate responsibility management. Now it informs drug pricing and key decisions having to do with licensing local manufacture of generic therapies.

What is most notable at Novo Nordisk is its broad-based organizational audit. To continuously infuse the NNWoM into the culture, a group of thirty to forty non-executive "facilitators" meets with every work unit and every employee, over a three-year cycle, to ensure that actions and decisions live up to the promise of the company's values. Led by COO Kåre Schultz, this thrust reinforces the firm's commitment to accountability and helps to "secure and maintain eighty years of tradition and integrity." This company, like Unilever, was viewed by us as one of the select few "best of the good" in making citizenship a way a life in the business. We've seen it grow its next generation of leaders in the previous chapter; next consider how to profitably grow a business globally by taking citizenship to market.

Taking Citizenship to Market

"Jella Sujatamma is part entrepreneur, part healthcare advisor, part hygiene specialist and part mother in the many villages in India that she visits each week as Unilever India's most successful *Shakti Amma* [empowered mother]," writes Janet Roberts, one of the student reporters at the October 2006 Business and World Benefit Conference in Cleveland.[1] Sujatamma, a weaver who lost work when synthetic fabrics came into popularity, became the first Shakti entrepreneur on $200 in borrowed startup funds. Even though she is illiterate and needs the assistance of her husband and sons to perform inventory and accounting functions, her sales have made her the top-earning woman in Project Shakti (between Rs. 3,000 and 7,000 or U.S. $60 to $150 per month). "Sujatamma takes her unique knowledge about what the village needs and which products are in demand," adds Roberts, "and couples it with important lessons in sanitization and hand washing to prevent diarrhea and in the vital role that iodine, consumed through salt, can have in nurturing healthy children."

When members of the Center visited Project Shakti, we learned that a venture that started in fifty villages in 2000 had reached eighty-two thousand villages by 2007, involving nearly thirty thousand entrepreneurs serving consumers in fifteen states in India. Shakti women are equipped with Unilever products and are trained in matters of health, hygiene, and nutrition. They learn communication skills in seminars and connect to one another through iShakti, a communications portal with software that is enabled for illiterate users. And, interestingly, they help to train incoming Unilever managers, marketers, and salespeople in India, who spend four weeks living in villages as part of their orientation to the company and marketplace. Shakti, as of this point, earns $250 million in villages in India that would be uneconomic to reach with conventional business models.

This is one of many bottom-of-the-pyramid (BoP) business models that are at the nexus of corporate citizenship and commerce. But they are not only relevant to developing and emerging countries. For example, when Social Compact, a nonprofit that provides market information on inner cities in the United States, analyzed the Columbia Heights community in Washington, D.C., their research showed that this market is far larger and growing much faster than standard sources would suggest.[2] The Compact found that total population was 51 percent higher than the U.S. Census reported, and the market growth was 56 percent higher. The differences in market size and growth were a function of multiple families residing within one household and the huge influx of immigrants into the market, both of which are undercounted by standard approaches. Average household income, taking account of the cash economy, exceeded census figures by 33 percent. Big business and inner-city entrepreneurs alike are today capitalizing on this new found source of wealth.

In this chapter, we look at how companies are devising socio-commercial business models that reach consumers from the bottom of the pyramid to its top and that engage suppliers and labor from the beginnings of the corporate value chain—often in emerging market farms and factories—to the end user, sipping a latté at Starbucks or purchasing goods at the Gap. The principles and practice apply as well to business-to-business markets and value chains.

Citizenship, Market Creation, *and* Social Change

Are there business solutions to global poverty? The idea of business reaching to the BoP is being embraced by sustainable development experts as a powerful way to realize social goals. In a recent survey by GlobeScan of over three hundred experts in the field, just 30 percent rated strategic corporate philanthropy as effective in achieving the UN's millennium development goals. By comparison, nearly 75 percent credited new business models and innovations as either somewhat or very effective.[3] We see a set of next generation corporate citizens moving into this space where their efforts aim at *both* market creation *and* social change. What does it mean? On the commercial side, companies are prospecting in "untapped markets." On the social side, they are reaching out to "underserved communities." To effect this joint agenda, they adopt what we have called socio-commercial business models. It also takes corporate social innovation.

New business models and innovations take many forms and aim at different opportunities and needs; consider:

- *Bottom of the Pyramid.* With nearly four billion people in this income tier, companies need new business models to enable the poor to become consumers. These models include microcredit, village-level supply and distribution systems, and training for social entrepreneurs;
- *Workforce Development.* With the youth population exploding, and an aging workforce in Japan and the West, select companies are taking innovative steps to recruit, train, and employ disadvantaged youth and minorities and to activate older workers in new roles;
- *Supplier Development.* With strong corporate buy-in to the value of diversity and strong societal needs for inclusion of all persons in the economy, leading firms are working with minority, disadvantaged, and inexperienced suppliers to meet commercial and social needs;
- *Social R&D.* Engagement with untapped markets—whether of consumers, workers, or suppliers—requires rethinking old practices and experimenting with new ones. Some of these new ideas achieve scale or transfer to other products and processes.

- *Value Co-Creation.* Here customers, business partners, and stakeholders such as government and NGOs work together to create business and social value. Benefits are not only in products and processes, but also in forging more trusting and mutual relationships across sectors.

Needless to say, this business-based approach to citizenship is hardly limited to the lowest or even middle levels of the economic pyramid. We have noted how the ethical consumer market is growing at its upper end and that large numbers of young people in particular connect their brand preferences to companies that express social and environmental commitments. Here, too, corporate social innovation is needed, whether in constructing business models for fair trade coffee or in crafting ironic, post-modern advertising to awaken consumers, as Diesel has done with its "global warming ready" cause-related marketing of jeans. Now there are those who, like David Vogel of the University of California–Berkeley, contend: "The market has many virtues, but rewarding more responsible companies and punishing less responsible competitors is not among them."[4] Let's see what companies are doing to prove otherwise.

CEMEX's New Market

CEMEX is one of the world's largest building material companies with a global presence in cement and aggregates, and a leading position in ready-mix concrete. CEMEX, alongside GE, IBM, and other members of the GLN, has sought to tighten the link between corporate values, the marketplace, and the needs of society. Like other major players in the cement industry, CEMEX is facing issues having to do with climate change, water and energy consumption, integrating new markets, and expanding operations without losing efficiency. Founded in Mexico in 1906, the company has distinct challenges and opportunities in tapping the market of comparatively low-income consumers in Latin America.

As part of their GLN workup companies complete a self-assessment that compares their strategic business priorities with their citizenship agenda. In CEMEX, key business priorities today include: integrate recent acquisitions, create targeted solutions for different market segments, develop an additional focus or add-ons in construction services, create sustainable value for stakeholders, expand a core business line in concrete ready-mix, and standardize business processes. Such priorities are not unusual for a company seeking growth by expanding its position in current markets, extending its line of products and services, moving into new regions, and, in this case, prospecting BoP markets.

As for its social and environmental agenda, CEMEX identified four corporate citizenship drivers in addition to philanthropy and its management system, the CEMEX Way, which promotes standardization of processes and sharing of best practices. The four drivers and illustrative programs are:

1. *Promote environmental sustainability.* CEMEX has built an environmental management system based on sharing best practices across all units and certification through the ISO 14001 program. Externally, the company has a

number of education and training initiatives to promote good environmental management processes and is funding flagship initiatives to preserve the biodiversity of various key natural reserves.

2. *Ensure compliance.* CEMEX produces materials and services that are purchased by governments, large contractors, and individuals. Demonstrating compliance with formal and informal expectations is critical to the company's reputation and ability to do business globally. CEMEX has successfully certified 100 percent of its Mexican employees in its code of conduct. Certification includes classes and tests.

3. *Embed health and safety.* CEMEX makes a strong commitment to preserve employee and community health and safety. Its program of monitoring health and safety processes is one example of the CEMEX Way.

4. *Develop low-income construction markets.* CEMEX identifies low-income markets as a growing market segment especially in Mexico and other Latin American countries. Its efforts to reach this market include Piso Firme, Construmex, and Patrimonio Hoy.

Figure 11.1 compares the relationship between CEMEX's citizenship drivers and its key business priorities. First, note that the company's philanthropy includes support for education and community programs, and assistance to the disabled through the firm's purchasing, training, and employment practices. This is a

Figure 11.1
CEMEX Citizenship Agenda and Key Business Priorities

		Strategic Business Priorities					
		Successfully integrate recent acquisitions	Create targeted solutions for different market segments	Develop an additional focus on construction services	Create value for stakeholders in a sustainable manner	Expand concrete ready mix business	Standardized business processes
Corporate Citizenship "Drivers"	Promoting environmental sustainability	Indirect impact	Indirect impact	Indirect impact	Direct impact	Indirect impact	Indirect impact
	Ensuring compliance	Direct impact	Indirect impact	Indirect impact	Direct impact	Indirect impact	Direct impact
	Embedding health and safety	Direct impact	Low impact	Indirect impact	Direct impact	Indirect impact	Direct impact
	Developing low income construction markets	Low impact	Direct impact	Direct impact	Direct impact	Direct impact	Low impact
	Cemex Way	Direct impact	Low impact	Indirect impact	Direct impact	Indirect impact	Direct impact
	Philanthropy programs	Low impact	Low impact	Low impact	Direct impact	Low impact	Low impact

boost to reputation but is more a matter of tradition and values than strategic gain. Second, put the company's emphasis on compliance, health and safety, and environmentalism into context. The cement industry alone is responsible for 5 percent of all CO_2 emissions worldwide and is one of the major energy users in industry. The public perceives cement factories as "dirty" and in many developing countries they are placed in urban areas or nearby countryside. Thus attention to these citizenship drivers is essential to retaining CEMEX's license to operate.

Third, see how the strategic grid comes alive with "direct impacts" when it comes to developing low-income construction markets. With Piso Ferme, the company partners with the Mexican government to improve homes lacking basic amenities and replaces dirt floors with floors made of antibacterial concrete, which helps lower risk of disease. Through Construmex, Mexicans living in the United States can transfer money back to their families to help with their construction needs. Our main interest here is with its socio-commercial business model aimed at low-income consumers: Patrimonio Hoy.

Patrimonio Hoy

The development of CEMEX's Patrimonio Hoy ("Property Now") business provides a good example of how firms can profit by reaching untapped segments of the pyramid and serve society's interests as well. In the mid-1990s, CEMEX was hit hard by Mexico's crippling currency devaluation. The buying power of the peso was cut in half, dramatically reducing the market for its products. The company decided to pursue the do-it-yourself homebuilding market, which represents 80 percent of the families in Mexico. But to create a new product offering for this market, the company had to gather intelligence about these lower-income consumers.

In many Mexican communities, it is a struggle for families to obtain quality, affordable housing in which to shelter their children. Typical housing includes raw cinderblock or sheet-metal-based one- to two-room homes for families of six to ten people. It requires a significant investment of time, money, and resources for families to upgrade and expand their housing. Poorer people tend to build their homes incrementally, whenever these inputs become available.

To better understand this market, CEMEX organized a research team of eight managers and selected the town of Guadalajara to conduct a sociological study of family life for some two years. Living in neighborhoods and watching families construct homes one room at a time, the study team realized that financing was critical for the purchase of construction materials. In traditional Mexican communities, they noted, neighbors and families get together and form "tandas," whereby they pool a portion of their funds together and then draw on it for major projects or emergencies. Based on this tradition CEMEX targeted a bigger pool of community members, upwards of twenty thousand, and then enrolled customers in small "socio" groups of three to four persons in a tanda-like savings-and-credit program. In the new program, called Patrimonio Hoy, each member of a socio group contributes 138 pesos a week and after a second week receives a construction spending credit of 1,104 pesos to buy materials. CEMEX provides technical advice on materials and staff architects offer consultations and inspections on new self-construction projects. In addition, the company supports socio groups by providing storage warehousing and delivery services.

The results from the experience of the first thousand families in the program were dramatic: Whereas an average homebuilder had traditionally built one room every four to seven years, members of CEMEX's tanda clubs took an average of one and a half years, less than a third of the time. Not only was the speed of construction (and therefore the sale of building materials) accelerated but also, as a result of the program, 18 percent more families in the test region had begun building, and the average annual spending per family increased from $240 to almost $650. Families built two to three more rooms than they had originally planned and used materials more efficiently. Based on this initial success, CEMEX expanded the program and has benefited more than 168,000 low-income families, lending them more than $45 million to construct the equivalent of 83,000 new rooms of ten square meters.

Commenting on how CEMEX's citizenship creates value in the market, Edgar Rodriguez, head of the citizenship function, stresses the importance of a guiding strategy: "Every social initiative demands different resource allocations, skills, and knowledge. Once you take the first steps, almost everything becomes tactical, which means you have to take decisions in short periods of time in a constantly changing environment. There is one big advantage to having a long-term strategy: it gives you the opportunity to learn where your strengths and weaknesses are." One lesson learned by CEMEX concerns its comparatively quiet communications about Patrimonio Hoy. Rodriguez explains: "We have learned that people at the bottom of the pyramid are very sensitive and that you can undermine their trust with a corporate communications campaign. Our approach is to provide a natural channel through which people can talk about their own experiences. That way we keep intact their trust."

Untapped Segments in Developed Markets

In their book *Untapped*, social entrepreneur John Weiser, the Center's Rochlin and Kahane, and researcher Jessica Landis summarize their work on how companies are growing their businesses by reaching underserved markets.[5] Based in part on the Center's Ford Foundation-funded research into the markets of lower-income and racial and ethnic minority populations in the United States, this book features cases of companies capitalizing on untapped consumer and labor segments.

It begins, naturally enough, with some statistics about this market in the United States compiled by the Initiative for a Competitive Inner City[6]:

• The purchasing power of African Americans in the United States alone, if aggregated, would be an economy bigger than Canada's. Recent estimates show that the total purchasing power of all ethnic minorities in the United States will top $1.5 trillion in 2008.

- The hundred fastest-growing companies located in inner-city untapped markets in the United States have, from 1999 to 2006, averaged 709 percent growth in sales, for an average compound annual growth rate of 54 percent. They have also been responsible for the creation of almost fifty-three thousand new jobs and have an average ethnic minority representation on staff of 31 percent versus a national average of 11 percent.
- America's inner cities represent $122 billion in retail spending per year, approximately 7 percent of U.S. retail spending. One study found that Latinos in the United States spend 46 percent more than the general population on groceries, despite having lower incomes. According to the Initiative's study of inner-city grocers, this sector is the nation's retail frontier.

Consumer Markets

It is appropriate, then, to begin with inner-city grocers.[7] Shaw's and Pathmark, for example, have designed new inner-city stores to reach an economically and demographically diverse clientele. These feature a dizzying variety of racially and ethnically targeted brands, at multiple price points, and locally originated store layouts and displays. Like CEMEX, Shaw's had to do its own sociological study of the marketplace. The Shaw's market team identified forty-two different ethnic and religious affiliations within its inner-city New Haven, Connecticut trade area. To develop the right product mix, Shaw's management collaborated with community groups and organized meetings with the ethnic leadership to discuss product offerings. Held in a former YWCA, Shaw's buyers and category managers, sitting at tables identified by category (e.g., produce, seafood, etc.), met one on one with the community representatives and solicited ideas on what products to carry. From this input, the company customized its merchandising approach to fit the community's ethnic mix. As an example, the New Haven store chose to stock fresh goat meat to satisfy the needs of consumers from some Caribbean countries.

Safeco, a leading insurance company based in Seattle, wanted to expand sales in low income neighborhoods across the United States.[8] Pressed like so many financial institutions on issues of redlining that exclude consumers from certain neighborhoods or lower socioeconomic strata, the company vowed to do something positive on this front. Gordon Hamilton, vice president of public relations, emphasized, however, that this was a business decision: "It was more of a resolve to come up with a business strategy, as opposed to a PR strategy, to address the redlining accusations. We couldn't continue to deal with the issue from just a public relations standpoint."

Safeco recognized that successfully marketing its insurance products in inner-city neighborhoods would require coordinating activities across a broad span of business units, including public relations, claims, underwriting, administration, human resources, legal, marketing, regional management, and small business insurance. To accomplish this coordination, it created the Diversity Marketing Committee, which meets seven times a year to identify how the functions of each department can work to leverage the others. The company also launched a series of experiments in reaching underserved markets: a reduction in rates in St. Louis, agent education in Atlanta, and active recruiting of agents in minority and low-income areas of Portland, Oregon. In Portland, it set up its own equivalent of a street-level one-stop insurance market. It registered success on all fronts and has cross-pollinated these models across the country.

Also from the financial side, JPMorgan Chase has found a way to address cultural challenges that not only improves relationships within communities, but also embeds a cultural awareness within the business itself.[9] The company created the position of StreetBanker, staffed by former community-relations officers. Their jobs include assessing community needs, responding to concerns about banking services, and making connections between community groups and Chase business units. The amount of money involved in banking relationships with underserved communities is substantial: The monies lent via mortgages to underserved communities exceed total corporate philanthropy in the United States thirty-two times over.[10]

Minority Employment

Manpower Inc. is a world leader in the staffing industry, providing workforce management services and solutions to customers through thirty-nine hundred offices in sixty-three countries.[11] TechReach is Manpower's strategic, global initiative to provide technical skills training, work-readiness preparation, job placement, and career-advancement opportunities for the unemployed and underemployed. The objective of the program is to provide today's businesses with a new source of work-ready skilled technical workers while offering a gateway to high-wage technical careers to the unemployed and underemployed.

Implemented through community–business partnerships, TechReach brings together the expertise of employers, community-based organizations, educational institutions, government agencies, and business associations, offering trainees marketable skills and industry-standard certifications. For example, in Chicago Manpower has partnered with two community-based organizations, Instituto del Progresso Latino and Shorebank Neighborhood Institute. Both organizations conduct outreach and initial screening for program candidates and provide social services support for program participants. In May 2003 Manpower formed a National Business Partnership with the U.S. Department of Labor, which dramatically expands the level of activity and impact of Manpower's work.

On a smaller scale, DreamWorks is another innovator in this space. This company, a leader in the entertainment industry, has helped to create and develop industry-wide support for Workplace Hollywood, a nonprofit whose mission is to train and prepare people from historically underrepresented and economically disadvantaged communities in Los Angeles to effectively compete for, and gain access to, jobs and business opportunities in the entertainment industry.

Jeffrey Katzenberg and his partners Steven Spielberg and David Geffen each contributed $1 million to start the nonprofit, which has grown to significant scale in a short time.

Perhaps the best example of partnering in this space begins with Focus HOPE, a nonprofit started in Detroit by Father William Cunningham following the race riots in the late 1960s and now headed by co-founder Eleanor M. Josaitis. Originally started as a food bank providing for inner-city Detroiters, its mission moved upstream to provide job training and then downstream to connect its trainees to area employers in the auto industry. Today, Focus HOPE's training runs the gamut from basic math, reading, and communication skills to training institutes in advanced IT and manufacturing technology. The company also operates a state of the art manufacturing facility where its students and graduates make high-end auto parts for all of the auto companies, including Toyota. Visit this facility and you will find volunteers from Ford Motor Company providing mentoring, purchasing agents from industry looking for business, and likely as not Noel Tichy, Professor from the University of Michigan, leading M.B.A. students and Focus HOPE teams into community service in the area. Ford's partnership with Focus HOPE exemplifies next generation citizenship: It is about commerce, social change, and developing its own and society's future leaders.

Minority- and Women-Owned Suppliers

For over thirty years, Turner Construction has offered a Construction Management Training Program that provides a competitive strategy for the company while benefiting hundreds of minority- and women-owned construction businesses and building valuable relationships within local communities.[12] The program was first initiated in Cleveland in 1968 to level the playing field for minority- and women-owned construction companies and has since expanded to Chicago, Kansas City, Los Angeles, Miami, New York, and Philadelphia. An eight-week course is taught by professional staff volunteers and includes such topics as risk management, construction estimating, safety, and effective marketing. To date, more than fifteen thousand people have successfully graduated from this program.

Turner quickly met its original goals of increasing the viability of minority- and women-owned businesses and now has a database of over two thousand potential bidding partners. This has increased from a 10 to a 20 percent proportion of work coming from women- and minority-owned companies. In addition to the business benefits, the Construction Management Training Program provides a wealth of community benefits as well, according to Hilton Smith, Turner's vice president of community affairs. The program improves the visibility, economic viability, and opportunities of minority- and women-owned businesses; strengthens the subcontracting community; and creates an opportunity for small businesses to interact and network with each other, potentially leading to even more partnerships. According to one participant in the program: "We walked away not only with the knowledge of how we should conduct a business," he said, "but also with the knowledge of individuals we could call if we ran into a problem, had a question, or needed additional expertise."

Corporate Involvement in Low-Income Communities

The Center's biennial survey of corporate citizenship queries businesses on their involvement in low-income communities in the United States. Beyond their philanthropic giving, the most recent survey found that more than half of all businesses (51 percent) report that they are economically engaged in a significant way in at least one of these activities: providing training and development opportunities for lower-wage employees, hiring, improving conditions in the community, locating facilities and jobs, and offering job training programs. Select firms, roughly 25 percent, are specifically keying their purchasing on minority- and women-owned suppliers (see Figure 11.2).

As for trends, the Center's survey indicates that the number of firms hiring from low-income communities nearly doubled from 12 per cent in 2003 to 23 percent in 2007, an increase registered in small, medium-sized, and large firms. And while American companies overall reported that their investments in low-income communities remained pretty much the same from 2003 to 2007, these increased significantly in larger-sized firms.

These are glass half-empty and half-full data. On the one hand, it seems to us that U.S. business involvement in low-income markets is modest given the urgent need and profitable opportunities tapped by the retail grocers, bankers, and insurers, and by the many employers profiled here. On the other, the companies profiled here and others are finding their involvement in America's lower-income and ethnic- and racial-minority markets a source of first-mover competitive advantage in a society that is changing its demographic makeup and will have increasing numbers of Latinos and African Americans to serve in most communities and at every price point.

On Reaching Untapped Markets

John Weiser and his team of Center researchers have abstracted five lessons from their studies about how firms reach untapped consumer and labor market segments. Consider:

1. *Mine and translate local market information.* Unilever and CEMEX sent their managers to live in villages in India and Mexico respectively to inform their BoP business lines. Pathmark and Shaw's talked with inner-city community leaders and consumers about everything from store siting to shelf stocking. Safeco and Manpower hired employees from underserved communities to better mirror their marketplace and to teach their companies how to do business with lower-income and minority-group customer segments. These exemplify how companies need to take special steps to understand untapped markets before taking action to serve them.

Figure 11.2
2007 U.S. Business' Involvement With Low-income Communities

Question asked: "To what extent is your company involved in any of the following?"
The 5-point scale ranked from "not at all" to "very great."

	Large	Very Great	Total*	Small	Medium	Large
Providing training and development opportunities for your lower-wage employees	20%	11%	**30%**	23%	38%	43%
Hiring people from economically distressed communities	14%	9%	**23%**	18%	28%	29%
Improving conditions in economically distressed communities	13%	7%	**19%**	14%	25%	29%
Locating your company's facilities or jobs in economically distressed communities	10%	5%	**16%**	11%	17%	28%
Offering job training programs to people in economically distressed communities	12%	6%	**18%**	13%	21%	29%
Purchasing from minority-owned suppliers	15%	7%	**22%**	19%	18%	33%
Purchasing from women-owned suppliers	14%	10%	**25%**	25%	20%	28%

Small, medium, large columns represent "large" and "very great" responses for each category of company.
* Total may not equal sum exactly due to rounding.
Source: State of Corporate Citizenship in the U.S.: Business Perspectives in 2007. © Boston College Center for Corporate Citizenship.

2. *Adapt business models to radically reduce costs or build on scale.* Recall how Unilever offers a single-use sachet of soap powder to bring poor consumers into the market and reaches them through a village-level sales force and how CEMEX's savings-and-credit systems expanded access to construction materials. This is what it takes to build BoP business models. In the U.S. financial services market, there are more than 25 million individuals with no banking relationship, in part because the costs of providing financial services to them exceed potential revenues.[13] SunGard Bank is working in partnership with the nonprofit D2D Fund (Doorways to Dreams) to develop a Web-based record keeping, financial transaction, and product delivery system to serve this market profitably. This system significantly reduces the costs of promoting, administering, and managing individual deposit accounts.

3. *Change internal incentives and challenge cultural assumptions.* Microlending isn't reliable? Lessons from Citibank, Grameen Bank, and CEMEX prove otherwise. CEMEX has recorded 99 percent repayment of loans in its Patrimonio Hoy program. New ventures don't match accustomed hurdle rates? Probably not in the short-term calculus, but in many companies moves to lower-income and underserved segments are for market creation. These call for patient capital and might be best budgeted and evaluated in terms of social R&D.

4. *Create partnerships and strategic alliances.* Now imagine you work for an insurance company. Pressures against redlining have encouraged your company to serve low-income markets where residents have often been forced to purchase insurance from suspect providers at high costs. How can you successfully sell insurance to this market? Companies such as State Farm and Travelers have learned, like Safeco, that forming joint ventures with nonprofits is the best way to get started. These groups have the familiarity, skills, and credibility with community groups needed to open up the doors.

5. *Improve the enabling environment.* Codes and principles only go so far in improving the environment needed to do business successfully in BoP markets. Here is where the example of coffee companies Starbucks and Green Mountain is instructive. Each has built business models that have them assisting poor farmers in developing countries while serving the tastes of growing numbers of consumers in the most developed markets.

Citizenship and Markets: Sustainable Sourcing and Ethical Consuming

Coffee purveyors Starbucks and Green Mountain illustrate how next generation corporate citizens are creating socially innovative business models that stretch from sustainable sourcing through to ethical consuming. The model building started in the mid-1990s when, even as Nike was under pressure for practices in its supply chain, Starbucks was being criticized for sourcing its coffee beans from growers that did not provide decent working conditions, livable wages, or basic rights for their workers. David Olsen, then a VP in the company, admits that Starbucks was "prodded into" taking steps in the human rights arena.

But recall the philosophy of Starbucks founder Howard Schultz: "A company should lead with its heart and nurture its soul as it makes money. It should inspire other companies to aim high. It should do more than simply avoid doing harm; it should consciously seek to do good." Once awakened to the call, Starbucks accepted a mantle of leadership in the industry. In 2001, the company created its own coffee-sourcing guidelines in collaboration with Conservation International and the growers themselves. It agreed to pay higher prices to growers that met a long list of social, environmental, and quality standards. Then in 2000, Starbucks entered into an agreement with TransFair USA (an NGO providing independent, third-party certification of Fair Trade products) to market and promote Fair Trade coffee in its more than two thousand retail stores and on its Web site. Today the market for fair trade coffee is booming and has become a profitable business niche for a company consciously seeking to do good.

Supply Side

The Center's affiliate Jonathan Levine conducted an assessment of the Starbucks supply-chain program and found that it brings together a panoply of support elements and policies.[14] Foremost, it pays considerable premiums for top quality—ranging from 15 to 87 percent above local market rates depending on the crop year. The program also selectively offers long-term contracts of one to three years, which give suppliers unusual stability to invest in quality and production capacity, and feature access to affordable farm credit through underwriting an $8.5 million loan portfolio to three nonprofit lenders. Those loans provide a financial lifeline to small farms and their cooperatives during lean preharvest periods.

Through field staff and partners, Starbucks offers agronomic, quality, and environmental technical assistance; invests in schools, clinics, and other community development projects; and purchases targeted quantities of fair trade, organic, and shade-grown coffees for the financial and environmental advantages they provide. Ultimately, the centerpiece of the supplier initiative is an incentive-purchasing program launched in late 2004 of C.A.F.E. practices (for "coffee and farmer equity"), which rewards producers for meeting dozens of sustainability criteria. Verified by third-party evaluators, C.A.F.E. is designed to drive producers to continually improve their environmental, social, and economic performance; Starbucks, in turn, will increasingly favor verified suppliers over the coming years.

While each element is valuable, what makes the program work at the farm level is its cumulative effect. Starbucks' high prices do a farmer little good if he has no technical guidance to meet the company's tough quality requirements, no access to credit to pay for vital crop cultivation, and no fresh water and other basic services to care for his family and workers. Levine writes this about the human story:

A three-hour hike up Peru's cavernous Tambopata River valley to Faustino Quispe's farm tells the story. At the farm, which is perched on a lush mountainside of one of the world's most biodiverse, and endangered, ecosystems, Quispe shows me the lessons he's learned from a six-year partnership between Starbucks and Washington, D.C.-based Conservation International (CI). With counsel from CI agronomists, he and twenty-one hundred neighbor farms have put an end to such destructive practices as slashing and burning large tracts of virgin forest and dumping farm wastes into local rivers. Instead, the farmers now compost production pulp for fertilizer and build natural barriers to halt erosion. These and other techniques have boosted once-declining yields by 30 to 50 percent and raised quality significantly over just a few years. Some $600,000 of Starbucks-backed loans to the farmers' local co-ops, collateralized by Starbucks purchase contracts, has funded crop improvements and basic family needs.

As higher prices on fatter yields and better-quality coffee bring in more income than ever—$5,300 in the previous year, he tells me—Quispe's family has seen momentous improvements in their lives, even as world markets have cratered around them. Galvanized aluminum now crowns his newly renovated house, replacing a roof of leaky palm fronds. For the first time the family enjoys electricity from a gas generator and running water from a gravity-fed pipe, saving them arduous daily trips to a stream up the hill. Most gratifying, Quispe says, is that his oldest son—the first in his family's history—now attends university in the state capital, while three younger children go to high school nearby. "I could never have afforded to send them all to school only a few years ago," he beams.

As compelling as this and many other such stories might be, clearly not all have benefited evenly from the company's initiatives. Great numbers of small-farm families are still mired in poverty. And the company's rigorous demand for quality poses a heavy burden on many supply chains at the same time as it expects them to improve their social and environmental performance—a source of frequent irritation. Critics on the right argue that the fair trade movement further stimulates an industry marked by overproduction; a criticism on the left is that only 10 percent of the premium paid in a coffee shop reaches the individual grower. Mindful of these points, Levine draws some key lessons on the supply side.

First, Starbucks' supplier initiatives are not a case of feel-good or "add-on" corporate citizenship. The company has committed to responsible coffee-sourcing practices because sustainable suppliers are central to its core business, pure and simple. Second, as much as public debate over responsible coffee buying centers on paying high prices, no single element of assistance is enough to achieve supplier sustainability; a comprehensive series of supports and incentives is essential. Third, the company also faces some risks going forward. As apparel and footwear companies can attest from over a decade of trying to correct unacceptable practices of developing-world manufacturing vendors, effecting change takes many years of investment and a commitment to continual improvement. Finally, everyone in the industry recognizes that efforts by Starbucks and others cannot expect to single-handedly break the cycle of poverty plaguing coffee farmers. Fully realizing that goal will take a broader cast of government, civil society, and industry players.

Demand Side

Green Mountain Coffee, with its own value-based commitments to fair trade, is growing even faster than Starbucks in this market. In its study of Win-Win partnerships, the Center documented how Green Mountain, working with NGO partner TransFair USA, carved out a significant niche in the consumer marketplace for fair trade coffee.[15] This case illustrates some of the best practices in opening untapped markets.

Green Mountain added "Fair Trade" certified coffees to its product line in 2000. The aim was twofold: to differentiate its products line and to reach a new consumer base. The results so far: The Fair Trade and Organic certified line is now Green Mountain's fastest growing product line, accounting for approximately 29 percent of its sales in FY 2006 (versus 15 percent in 2004). Fair trade and organic coffee in its multiple forms—shade grown, rainforest, Newman's Own brand—along with fair trade chocolates, tea, and such have created significant business value for Green Mountain Coffee, which grew over 60 percent per annum from 2004 to 2007. This is not the whole story of its growth, of course. An aggressive move to online sales now accounts for one-third of its volume, and a move into single-cup brewing systems, with cups made from corn-based materials, have also been winners. The public has benefited too: not only from its coffees but also from its 5 percent pre-tax contributions to charity.

Starbucks' corporate social innovations in its supply chain have been matched by Green Mountain in intent if not scale, including a venture with EcoLogic in providing microlending to growers. Especially notable is Green Mountain's efforts on the demand side. Well before Fair Trade certification came into view, Green Mountain executives had had regular and deep contact with growers. Bob Stiller, CEO of Green Mountain, saw that there was a potential for a virtuous relationship between coffee quality, coffee price, and a better standard of living for the growers. Fair Trade certification offered the key to unlocking a better price for farmers and increased sales for the company. Certification provides critically important information to the company and the consumer, assuring that the coffee is being purchased on terms that benefit the farmers, and that the monetary benefits flow through to the individual growers.

While TransFair's certification was useful, it came at a cost, and would require some changes in Green Mountain Coffee's business model. The first and biggest change was paying more for coffee. As Green Mountain Coffee struggled to decide whether and how to launch its Fair Trade line; there were many heated discussions among staff: Would it sell? Would it ever be profitable? If only some of Green Mountain Coffee's lines were certified as "Fair Trade," wouldn't that imply that the rest were "UnFair Trade"? These and many other issues were not easy to resolve.

In order to launch the line, Green Mountain had to think through how to package and promote the product to its own sales force, skeptical about the market. The CEO set up an internal team to manage the product development process. With the help of Oxfam America, TransFair provided information that showed how concerned students across the United States were championing fair trade coffee and launching campaigns to influence the policies of university purchasing departments. The team used success stories to show that there was a market for the product, and that it could help increase sales. Whenever there was a meeting, they put this topic on the agenda. Eventually, the decision was made to launch the line by focusing on accounts in which there was likely to be a very high customer interest in the Fair Trade label, and to start with a limited number of products.

Then there were questions about how to educate employees, customers, and ultimately individual coffee drinkers about why Fair Trade mattered and about why the Green Mountain Coffee line was worth the extra cost. The key was finding channels where the customer demand would drive acceptance of the product, and where there was a lower degree of price sensitivity (e.g., in organic and whole food stores and with university food services). When Fair Trade was launched in the United States, TransFair worked with Oxfam America's campus chapters to create a postcard campaign for students to request Fair Trade coffee. TransFair also began a campaign of public relations and community engagement with a variety of environmental, faith-based, student, and consumer organizations to generate grassroots consumer demand and promotional support for Fair Trade products on a national level. This, in effect, transformed a loose stakeholder web into an advocacy net.

Back to the Future: A New Generation of Companies with a Conscience

Even as Starbucks and Green Mountain garner praise in both the CSR and mainline business press for taking citizenship to the marketplace in their profitable fair trade and organic end-to-end business lines, we are reminded of their forebears: Ben & Jerry's, the Body Shop, Smith & Hawken, Seventh Generation, and others. B&J's, for example, paid a premium to Vermont family farmers whose cows supplied its cream and then recycled leftover ice cream for consumption by pigs—a variation on closed-loop manufacturing. The Body Shop built a soap-making plant in Glasgow, at some cost to the company but great benefit to an economically depressed community. It also sourced some of its ingredients from Brazilian rainforests to save them from clearing, used recycled materials in its packaging and many product offerings, and offered its customers biodegradable, multi-use bottles long before Natura, a Brazilian cosmetic maker of the same ilk, came on the scene. Both companies famously linked specific products to social causes and the founders are linked to many and varied social campaigns.

Mention should also be made of Patagonia who, in 1985, pledged 1 percent of its total revenue (not profits!) to the preservation and restoration of the natural environment and has since enlisted hundreds of small, environmentally intensive firms like builders, contractors, and building supply companies, plus a few big ones like Hyatt International, to the cause. It made the decision early on to take their cotton sportswear 100 percent organic and has been a leader in fiber-to-fiber recycling in many of its goods. Everything from the wood and lighting in Patagonia's retail stores to the food in the corporate cafeteria has been scrutinized to reduce environmental harm. And Patagonia customers are routinely challenged to get involved in environmental cleanup and improvement campaigns.

Many of these kinds of companies, ahead of their time in the 1960s through 1980s, have since grown up and some have joined larger corporations. But the next generation of their kind is cropping up throughout the world. One exemplar is Frog's Leap Winery, which grows its grapes organically, practices dry farming, and is 100 percent solar powered. CEO John Williams, interestingly, learned about these things with help from the much larger Fetzer winery. Although members of the Center tend to be large, public companies, they do business with a variety of companies that exemplify an innovative, small- and mid-size company version of next generation citizenship. The Web site of

Business as an Agent of World Benefit has profiles of many of these suppliers and stand-alone firms.[16] A roster of some of the best of these socio-commercial entrepreneurs appears in Appendix 5.

Meanwhile, it is evident that some fast-growing companies are profiting from the confluence of social and marketplace trends. We have noted that in the United States a significant number of consumers have "lifestyles of health and sustainability." This is the market of Whole Foods, the grocer that specializes in locally sourced, organic, and fair trade produce and goods. Inside, the company, like B&J's long ago, has a salary cap on top executives' salaries (nineteen times the average full-time pay) and regularly ranks among the top ten best places to work in the United States. For its customers, who pay a premium for its offerings and the unmatched customer experience, the deal seems to be worth it. Whole Foods has grown 20 percent per annum the past five years, and leads the grocery industry in comparable store growth and sales per square foot. All of this is built on the back of "The Whole Philosophy," which stresses the sale of all natural and organic products and strong commitments to employees, customers, communities, and the natural environment.

Recall, however, that the evidence is slim that consumers will pay a premium for goods and services from CSR leaders when they can find those of equal quality at a better price from companies who lack credentials in this arena. On the other hand, there are indications that increasing numbers will switch from one brand to another of same price and quality if the other brand is associated with a cause. A 2007 survey by Cone, Inc. shows that 87 percent of consumers would switch under such conditions versus 65 percent in 1999.[17] Another survey finds that members of today's Millennial Generation, at least in the United States, are "the most socially conscious consumers to date."[18] In this study, some 61 percent of thirteen- to twenty-five-year-olds feel personally responsible for making a difference in the world; 69 percent consider a company's social and environmental commitment when deciding where to shop; and 83 percent trust a company more if it is socially-and-environmentally responsible.

Next Generation Consumers

U2 lead singer Bono's Product Red campaign is aimed at Internet-savvy young people with a social conscience. It has companies donate a portion of profits from the sale of their Red-branded products to the Global Fund, a multisector partnership, which dispenses the money to groups fighting diseases in Africa. The Web site encourages consumers to download Red Brand icons to identify themselves, upload personal videos about what the campaign means to them, and connect to like-minded "buddies." It also has consumers calculate the impact of their purchases, which, as of mid-2007 was well over $8 billion contributed translating into 6 million people tested and six hundred thousand treated for HIV and AIDS, 1.5 million for tuberculosis, and 8 million for malaria, plus 12 million receiving insecticide-treated mosquito nets.

The campaign, as of this writing, has been a mixed success for some of its sponsors but a real winner at the clothing retailer, the Gap.[19] There, rather than simply market goods branded as Red products, à la simple cause marketing, the company developed a whole new line of clothing, sourced sustainably from Africa, where the proceeds from its sale return to fight HIV/AIDS. As Dan Henkle, SVP of social responsibility at the Gap, describes it, he was interviewed carefully by Bono, even as the Gap itself questioned its involvement in the campaign, and afterwards found himself winging to Lesotho in sub-Saharan Africa to see a region whose fledgling manufacturing sector was in rapid decline as production was shifting to China. Upon arrival, Henkle entered one of the factories, was mistaken for the rock star, and was greeted with a chorus of song, clicks, and cheers. Shortly thereafter, he, Bono, and Bobby Schriver, co-founders of the campaign, and several other suppliers met local managers and workers, spent an evening in song and good spirit, and then vetted the manufacturing practices to check that they were in line with supply-chain labor standards and examined finished goods to ensure they were in synch with consumer tastes.

Red T-shirts, with the Inspi(Red) logo went on sale in October 2006 and sold out promptly. Oprah Winfrey featured the product and gave shirts to all her audience. A Desi(Red) shirt as well as a line of baby clothing, Diape(Red), followed. Soon Gap brands Banana Republic and Old Navy began to outline their campaigns. Why so successful at the Gap versus other companies? A special marketing team was put together to conceive and activate this business line; Gap marketers were consulted about the program at every step; and store staffers were specially trained to communicate about the entire effort to their young customers. Many in fact searched on line to develop their own unique sales pitch about AIDS in Africa, life in Lesotho, and the Global Fund. It was this beginning-to-end business model, augmented by the passion of staff, that spelled success for Gap's Red Campaign and, not coincidentally, added significantly to the brand's bottom line.

Co-creating Value for
Business and Society

Corporate philanthropy in the United States was estimated at $12.7 billion in 2006, according to the most recent data collected by the Giving USA Foundation, representing 4.3 percent of total charitable gifts in the nation. Although this was a decline from 2005, when giving was inflated by funds, goods, and services for disaster relief, more detailed analyses from the Committee to Encourage Corporate Philanthropy (CECP), a forum of business leaders focused on this subject, revealed that a majority of American companies actually increased their overall financial contributions in 2006 (while a minority decreased them) and that international corporate giving rose substantially.[1]

To better understand the nature of this funding and the intent behind it, the Center has partnered with the CECP to analyze patterns of giving in a sample of seventy-five companies (including thirty in the Fortune 500). Here's a sample of the findings:

- Fortune 500 companies make bigger contributions overall, but smaller companies' gifts represent a larger share of pre-tax profits.
- The largest share of contributions is in the form of cash (72 percent), with non-cash contributions coming in just under 30 percent.
- As for budget source, the majority are from corporate headquarters (38.2 percent), followed by corporate foundations (31.3 percent) and "all other groups" (30.5 percent from business units or branch offices).
- Some 81 percent of the companies examined had a formal volunteer program in place for domestic employees, among them paid time off, flexible scheduling, dollars-for-doers, employee volunteer recognition awards, retiree and family volunteering.

Interestingly, almost nine in ten companies studied had one or more business-related goals associated with their philanthropic efforts. This is a huge jump from two decades ago, when most companies tried to choose areas for their efforts that were distant enough from their business objectives to eliminate the appearance of conflicts or self-interest. A breakdown of total cash and non-cash contributions found that roughly half of the contributions were described as purely charitable giving, where a company anticipated no direct business bene-fits, whereas 36 percent was defined as strategic giving and another 15 percent as commercially motivated. Giving professionals cited more than twenty benefits from their engagement with communities, among the strongest being a greater capacity to recruit and retain employees, enhance the brand, develop relation-ships both within the company and with communities and governments, and smooth expansion into new geographical areas.

Michael Porter and Mark Kramer crystallized a growing trend in U.S. compa-nies with an article in the *Harvard Business Review* on "the competitive advan-tage of corporate philanthropy."[2] They argued that the competitive context today is focusing on the "convergence of social and business interests and shifts some corporate resources away from communal and goodwill-only initiatives to more strategic activities and investments." They depict this in the form a two-by-two grid where corporate giving aims to provide value for business *and* society.

There are many fine accounts of strategic corporate philanthropy in the United States, among them being a selection of best-practice examples in cause marketing and in social entrepreneurship and firsthand reports of community investments by corporate leaders in a volume entitled aptly *The Business of Changing the World*.[3] There is no need here to work this familiar ground. Instead, we turn our attention to three subjects not as thoroughly studied or well documented: (1) the spread of strategic philanthropy to companies around the globe; (2) the trend toward partnerships between companies and nonprofits to co-create value for business and society; and (3) the increase in multibusiness and multisector collaboration to address major global concerns. We begin with the development of corporate philanthropy in Korea and the case of a company that seeks to strategically transform what it calls its corporate community involvement (CCI).

Corporate Community Involvement (CCI)—SK Group

The SK Group is a South Korean chaebol (conglomerate) that was founded in the early 1950s as a small textile manufacturer. It was incorporated in the 1960s as a gasoline retailer, when it took over the privatized national company, then moved into upstream production in the 1980s, and in the 1990s completed its petroleum-to-fibers vertical integration by establishing SK Telecom (SKT), a mobile communication company that provides wireless and long-distance serv-ice. Since then, the company has expanded into China, Vietnam, and other parts of Asia and into the United States with Helio, a joint venture between SKT and Earthlink. SK earned revenues of USD $70 billion in 2006 with more than forty-three thousand employees.

SK Group created its CCI function in 2002 and was one of the first Korean companies to promote employee volunteerism. In just a few short years, over 70 percent of its employees joined what are, in effect, company-sponsored teams that define their own specific volunteer activities and join in on company efforts that range from disaster relief to hosting the televised showing, in a downtown square in Seoul, of the country's national team's World Cup games.

The Center's Korean CCI affiliate Angela Joo-Hyun Kang and researcher Kwang Yong Ryu, among others, worked with SK through 2006 to study the implications of globalization for the company's CCI efforts and to assess the ins and outs of creating a more strategic, business-relevant CCI thrust.

Background

Overall, SK currently spends about 2 percent of pre-tax profits on CCI, a percentage nearly double that of U.S. corporations and higher than the norm among large corporations in Korea and Japan. Roughly 58 percent of these funds is reserved for ongoing investments in social welfare and education. The remaining 42 percent is more discretionary.

The company's CCI profile needs to be put into a Korean context. One difference from the United States is that the Korean national government exerts a strong influence over corporate involvement in society, requesting funding, for example, for specific community economic development, poverty relief, and education projects. This defines a portion of the CCI playing field. Second, there are strong anticorporate feelings in the Korean public that raise red flags when charitable works hint at some benefit for companies. Thus there was concern among management, and among stakeholders, that SK not go "too far, too fast" in its move toward more strategic philanthropy.

SK has some significant and visible national investments in Korea, including its support of a foundation that sends students to universities around the world, sponsorship of the popular television program "Scholarship Quiz," and the reclamation and transformation of an old industrial site into an eco-park. The company has a strong reputation in Korea—number three behind Samsung and LG. One of the first studies undertaken through the Reputation Institute was to determine to what extent SK's reputation was influenced by its corporate citizenship and community activities. Interestingly, the research found that while its products and services accounted for nearly 60 percent of the public's opinion of SK, perceptions of its citizenship accounted for only 11 percent. This was a stimulus to look at how citizenship might link to the SK brand.

Vision, Culture, Image

SK had achieved a great deal in a short time from its start up in CCI, but there were several factors that limited the impact of its programs and their relevance for globalization. For one, SK did not have a clear vision of what it wanted to achieve with its CCI—save to give back to society and be responsive to requests from the government, charities, and NGOs. Second, it had a fragmented set of social programs. This is to some extent a function of the conglomerate group structure, with each subsidiary having its own budget and wanting to sponsor its own programs. But the combination of small investments in many programs diluted their impact and visibility. As one top executive lamented, this fragmentation made it difficult to see SK's "color" in society.

It should be noted that, given the age-and-stage of CCI in SK, this pattern is not unusual. Twenty years ago, most American companies wrote big checks to the United Way, had a broad variety of CCI programs, and did not link their philanthropy to their business interests or competencies. Since then, many have taken a more strategic outlook on CCI and developed "signature" programs.

In essence, a strategic CCI program builds off of and expresses the corporate brand. Professors Mary Jo Hatch and Majken Schultz have developed a model of corporate branding that poises it in the alignment of a company's strategic vision, organizational culture, and stakeholder images of the firm.[4] The research team applied this VCI model, through a series of questions, to SK's CCI activity (see Figure 12.1).

Input 1. What are the expectations and interests of SK's stakeholders when it comes to CCI? What does SK mean to them and what do they want to see in your CCI program? SK CCI has conducted research on stakeholder expectations and has an advisory group of outside experts. By a large margin, the Korean public wants SK, like all Korean corporations, to invest in public welfare. A survey of opinion leaders sharpened this to mean that SK should focus on aiding the disadvantaged. The next two items on stakeholders' list are the natural environment and education. Such input, while directional, could apply to most any Korean company and yields many possible ways for SK to contribute to society.

Input 2. How does SK want to express its culture and competencies in CCI? What shared social value do you propose to deliver to society? Many we spoke to in SK stressed the importance of its management system (SKMS) as the guiding

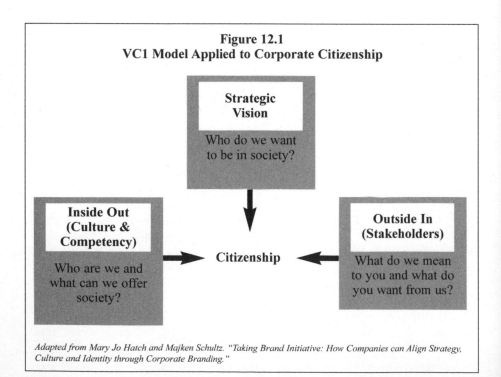

Figure 12.1
VC1 Model Applied to Corporate Citizenship

Strategic Vision — Who do we want to be in society?

Inside Out (Culture & Competency) — Who are we and what can we offer society?

Citizenship

Outside In (Stakeholders) — What do we mean to you and what do you want from us?

Adapted from Mary Jo Hatch and Majken Schultz. "Taking Brand Initiative: How Companies can Align Strategy, Culture and Identity through Corporate Branding."

philosophy—the bible—of the company. Created in the early days of the company, as industry was recovering from war, this philosophy has been updated periodically and underwent a significant shift as Korean companies gained financial stature; recently SK's "profit maximization" intent, aimed at building the national economy, shifted to "happiness maximization." The SKMS says that the company's mission today is to "contribute to mankind's happiness" and speaks to creating value for customers, employees, and shareholders. Look at some reflections on the implications for CCI from senior executives throughout the firm (see Figure 12.2).

These comments variously reflect the executives' intent to spread happiness, consistent with SK's new brand identity the "wings of happiness," along with a sense of obligation to contribute to society. They also highlighted some themes that extend from the company's main business lines—telecommunication and energy—that might inform a more focused set of social investments that draw

Figure 12.2
Corporate Community Involvement (CCI) Implications at SK Group

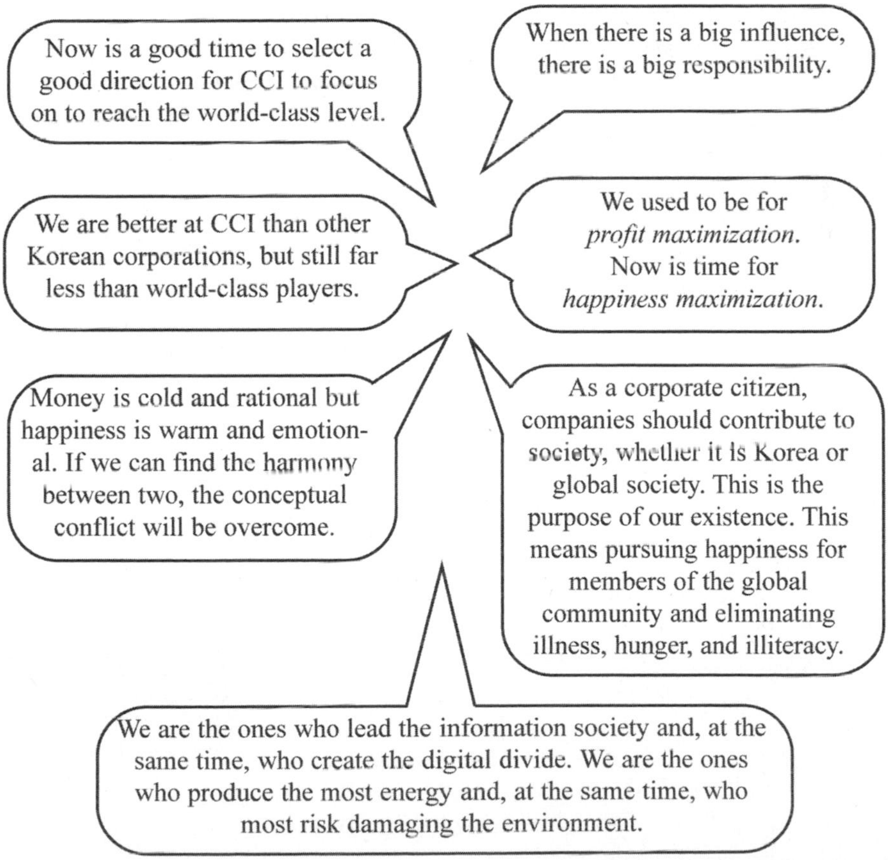

Now is a good time to select a good direction for CCI to focus on to reach the world-class level.

When there is a big influence, there is a big responsibility.

We are better at CCI than other Korean corporations, but still far less than world-class players.

We used to be for *profit maximization.* Now is time for *happiness maximization.*

Money is cold and rational but happiness is warm and emotional. If we can find the harmony between two, the conceptual conflict will be overcome.

As a corporate citizen, companies should contribute to society, whether it is Korea or global society. This is the purpose of our existence. This means pursuing happiness for members of the global community and eliminating illness, hunger, and illiteracy.

We are the ones who lead the information society and, at the same time, who create the digital divide. We are the ones who produce the most energy and, at the same time, who most risk damaging the environment.

on the company's skills *and* society's interests in high technology and in environmental protection.

Input 3. What is your strategic vision for SK? What does this mean for your CCI activities? We asked several interviewees whether SK would become a "Korean company with extension in Asia and global outreach" or a "global company with its heart in Korea?" Almost everyone said that the strategic vision was to retain SK's unique culture but to become a truly global company through growth in China and in global acquisitions. On this count, we were referred to the founder's philosophy: "Your real power comes not from wealth but from knowledge. What I want to inherit is knowledge, not wealth. If you have knowledge, wealth will follow. Wealth without knowledge will make others unhappy."[5] This highlighted a signature theme that might represent the trio of SK's culture and competencies, the interests and needs of its stakeholders, and the core of its strategic vision: Spreading Knowledge.

Toward a More Strategic Approach to Society

The Center's benchmarking team led by Guy Morgan and Kwang Yong Ryu did a benchmark study of what characterizes the CCI program of companies around the world that have adopted a more strategic approach to social investments. This yielded five defining features:

1. *Shared Value*. Investments aimed at benefiting the society *and* the business.
2. *Competency-Based*. Investments that make more use of a company's skills, technology, and scale.
3. *Brand-Related*. Investments that carry brand associations, express company culture, and help in brand building.
4. *Employee Engagement*. Active, hands-on involvement of employees in service.
5. *Capacity-Building*. Working with NGO/government partners, suppliers, customers, and other stakeholders to build their capacities to better deliver value to society.

Each of these characteristics seemed to be relevant to SK's agenda to move from its current status toward a more strategic profile.

Create Shared Value

On the one hand, it seems evident that SK has made the choice to adopt a more strategic approach to CCI as an increasing percentage of its budget is available for discretionary investment as defined by SK's interest and values. On the other hand, many we spoke to emphasized the importance of "purity" when it comes to CCI—to both internal and critical external audiences. What is key, as one executive said it, is to combine "sincerity and integrity," or as another stated, "sincerity and a business mind."

Serve through Competencies

Many top companies serve society through CCI that draws on the interests and capabilities of their business. This means applying the skills, technology, and scale of the business in addressing social problems. We have noted IBM's application of its computing know-how to reinventing education and Cisco's creation of academies to train and certify disadvantaged youth in IT competency as examples. SK identified some of the strengths it might share with society: (1) knowledge workers, (2) business knowledge, (3) innovative skills and spirit, (4) advanced technologies, and (5) identification with youth and passion.

Build Brand-Relevance

Companies are also making social investments that are brand-relevant and help in brand building; we have noted Nokia, Johnson & Johnson, and IBM among others. One recent poll found that 79 percent of Asian executives believe that CCI activities can make an important contribution to corporate reputation. Another found that 68 percent of Koreans are interested in learning more about ways companies are trying to become more socially responsible—a figure that rises to 82 percent in China.[6] All of this pointed to the potential of brand building through CCI.

Employee Engagement

American companies and their people excel at volunteerism. SK was a leader in this regard in Korea. One question at hand was how to activate employee engagement in its investments in China.

Partnering

Finally, leading companies today are working with NGO and government partners in these programs, as well as suppliers, customers, and other stakeholders. SK has developed a number of these relationships in its CCI efforts to date. What top companies are doing, however, is using their business knowledge and skills to develop the capacities of their CCI partners to deliver better value to society. Funding is only a part of this. It also includes technical and managerial support, coaching, joint learning, and so on. SK has applied this capacity-building expertise in its work with business customers and suppliers. Perhaps this could also be extended to its partners in CCI efforts?

Four Types of Strategic Corporate Philanthropy

As part of the research, the Center developed a framework to differentiate between four types of strategic corporate philanthropy. The framework is built on two strategic dimensions: (1) *core competencies* (to what extent CCI programs align with a firm's business strategy and draw on its knowledge, experiences, resources, and people) and (2) *core markets* (to what extent CCI programs align with the interests of a firm's customers and other key stakeholders and build relationships to them). The research team then analyzed SK's programs in terms of their competence- and market-orientation to help the company distinguish four types of CCI investments (see Figure 12.3).

Reputation-type CCI

Several SK programs were seen more or less as gifts to society in that they had broad-based benefits and did not draw on any special expertise from the company. These represented the "pure" philanthropy favored by some in SK and by some stakeholders too. They did, however, help to burnish the company's image and enhance its reputation.

Relationship-type CCI

Other programs had SK working with the government, social service agencies, and other key stakeholders to address important social needs. This type of philanthropy included, for instance, community-based lunch programs and education investments, as well as many of the volunteer initiatives of SK teams. These programs helped to build relationships to the community while capitalizing more on SK's competencies and technologies.

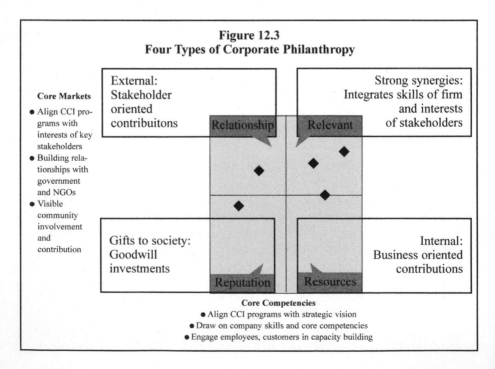

Figure 12.3
Four Types of Corporate Philanthropy

Core Markets
- Align CCI programs with interests of key stakeholders
- Building relationships with government and NGOs
- Visible community involvement and contribution

External: Stakeholder oriented contribuitons

Relationship

Relevant

Strong synergies: Integrates skills of firm and interests of stakeholders

Gifts to society: Goodwill investments

Reputation

Resources

Internal: Business oriented contributions

Core Competencies
- Align CCI programs with strategic vision
- Draw on company skills and core competencies
- Engage employees, customers in capacity building

Resource-type CCI

By contrast, a third set of programs employed SK-specific knowledge and resources in service to society. These included job creation for the hard to employ, small-scale IT and auto mechanic training for youth, and other such programs that, while beneficial to society, lacked scope and large-scale impact.

Relevant-type CCI

What kinds of programs fit in this category? Those that are business-relevant and that enable SK to engage its stakeholders and society in a unique, brand-relevant way. One such set of programs engages employee family and customers in large-scale company-sponsored volunteer days. Along this same line, university students who are customers of SK Telecom can participate in the company-sponsored "Sunny" volunteer program. This program enlists thirty thousand offline and five thousand online Korean students in community volunteerism nationwide. Another set of programs makes use of SK's technology. SK Telecom's "mobile social safety net," as an example, makes unique and compelling use of the company's core technology. Through their cell phones, customers can access Web sites to help find missing children, provide mobile mentoring to youth, and make donations to worthy causes ("beautiful call"). The company also uses its cell phones to provide disaster warnings and has services that make it easier for the disabled to use a mobile phone. These services have broad reach and brand relevance, make good and innovative use of SK tools, involve many relevant partners, including police, fire departments, and social services agencies, provide a valuable public service, are distinctive, and deliver real sustainable value.

This analysis was not intended to promote the idea that all SK programs should fit into this final category. Indeed, the Center's analysis of CCI programs in several best-practice companies shows that their portfolios also cover each quadrant. But the SK CCI team did see promise in developing a stronger set of programs in the business-relevant sector—and a signature theme.

Next Steps

As of this writing, the SK CCI program is moving forward on three fronts. First, SK's CCI Director, Do Young Kim, has gained top management's agreement to focus the company's strategic social programs under the theme of knowledge sharing. Each of the firm's businesses has been challenged to refocus on programs that make use of their core competencies and reach key societal stakeholders, moving more investment into the business-relevant quadrant that SK terms the "Happy Zone." Second, the company is stressing the importance of knowledge sharing in its volunteer service. This is modeled loosely on General Electric's "Elfun" program that links employees' skills and interests to volunteering opportunities.

Finally, on its globalization agenda, SK has increased its knowledge investments in Mongolia and Vietnam, there taking the form of creating village-level libraries, in partnership with NGOs and government. In China, meanwhile, the company is benchmarking the experience of first-mover multinationals that have hands-on programs and partnerships in line with SK's interests and competencies. This sample includes Motorola and IBM (education), Microsoft, Cisco, and Dell (digital divide), British Petroleum (environmental education), and Unilever and GE (employee volunteerism), plus many leading Chinese firms (see Appendix 6 for illustrations). SK is also navigating through three government ministries and in contact with international and domestic NGOs about partnering possibilities. On this count, it is worth noting that as of 2006, China had 110,000 registered private nonprofits and another 129,000 registered social service organizations.[7]

Business–NGO Partnerships

Who does the public trust to operate in the best interests of society? On a global scale, NGOs earn far more trust than global companies in both the northern (68 versus 38 percent) and the southern hemispheres (63 versus 46 percent); and in both NGOs are more trusted than national governments, domestic companies, trade unions, and the media.[8] Who is most trusted to do what's right? In the United States, where trust in business in this regard has been relatively constant since 2001, trust in NGOs has increased dramatically (from 36 percent in 2001 to 54 percent in 2006), moving well ahead of business. NGOs are now the most trusted institution in every country except Japan and Brazil.

This is only one reason, albeit an important one, that companies are partnering with NGOs to contribute to society, a trend we defined as one of the new rules for business success for twenty-first-century companies. Three other reasons are relatively straightforward. First, traditions of checkbook philanthropy are giving way to the active engagement of companies in social problems. The public all over the world says that the best way for companies to make a positive contribution to society is by working to solve a specific social problem, rather than donating monies to charity (although both rank below their primary contribution of developing safer and healthier products and services).[9] This perception is often activated by companies in the form of corporate community initiatives and hands-on volunteer work.

Second, in this era where companies focus on their core business and outsource whole functions, few firms choose to dedicate extensive resources and staff to community relations and the fieldwork associated with active involvement in communities. Nor do many have the in-house expertise, capacity, and local connections to deliver high-quality services. As a result, NGOs are the go-to providers of service.

Third, there is some evidence that partnering with NGOs is itself a source of legitimacy for companies in society. A GlobeScan survey found that 85 percent of the public reported that its respect for a company would go up if it partnered with a charity or NGO.[10] Furthermore, a growing segment of the public says that a key indication that a company is socially responsible is that it works directly with a charity group or NGO.[11] This perception increased in the United States from 16 to 30 percent from 2002 to 2005 and, it should be noted, from 19 to 33 percent in South Korea.

None of this works, however, unless NGOs develop the capacities to address social problems at a larger scale and the motivations to work in partnership with business. We have noted how some NGOs are partnering with companies in social service and socio-commercial ventures—ushering in the next generation of corporate citizenship. Here are some of the examples that arise from the Center's community involvement research on partnerships between business, NGOs, and in some cases government.[12]

Community Service

The Home Depot chose to form a partnership with KaBOOM! in the mid-nineties in order to enhance its community impact.[13] The Home Depot, the world's largest home improvement specialty retailer, realized that it could offer its unique capabilities— building and home construction materials, tools, and expertise—to communities in which it does business. In KaBOOM!, a national nonprofit, the company found a partner that had a presence in these communities and a worthwhile cause to focus on, providing play spaces for American children, particularly those in low-income or disaster-affected neighborhoods.

As KaBOOM! sees it, the lack of play is linked to problems ranging from childhood obesity to underachievement in schools to youth violence. Recent studies show that nearly two out of three U.S. children aged 9–13 do not participate in any organized physical activity during non-school hours. Furthermore, many local communities are not well organized to develop or improve neighborhood play spaces. Together, The Home Depot and KaBOOM!, pooling their complementary capabilities, have created a community-build model, akin to an old-fashioned barn raising, that helps communities to get organized and create playgrounds for kids.

The partnership has sponsored initiatives, such as "Operation Playground," that have resulted in the creation or improvement of five hundred playgrounds, skate parks, and sports fields across North America. In an impoverished area of Chicago, for example, where racial tensions racked the community, KaBOOM! helped The Home Depot to locate playground building sites and join with a local nonprofit, the Chicago Youth Center's Fellowship House in Bridgeport, to activate community and company volunteers in design and construction, and to bring children of all racial backgrounds together to play and learn about sharing and cooperation.

Education

The Center's biennial surveys of American business firms find that K–12 education is by far their number one priority for community investment, expressed in the form of cash and equipment contributions, business–education partnerships, adopt-a-school programs, sponsorship of science fairs and competitions, as well as volunteer mentoring, sports coaching, and the like.[14] Companies have partnerships in approximately 70 percent of U.S. school districts; they contribute roughly $2.5 billion to education annually, as well as over 100 million volunteer hours.[15] All of this for good reason: as Stephen Jordan, from the U.S. Chamber of Commerce's Business Civic Leadership Center reminds, there is a daunting gap between employers' job requirements and the skills of today's students, particularly in science and math, but also basic literacy. Employers say that this gap is a prime factor affecting America's and their own long term competitiveness.

Many high-tech companies in addition to IBM and Cisco, including Microsoft, HP, Intel, and Honeywell, are attempting to bridge this gap by drawing on their distinctive knowledge, personnel, and tools to help to educate millions of students in the United States and around the world. Now Dell Computer, a comparative newcomer, is partnering with American school districts to bring computers and computer literacy to middle school students across the country.[16] The program, called TechKnow, connects Dell and middle school teachers in providing hands-on technology instruction to low-income or underserved students. In after-school learning sessions, the students learn to disassemble and assemble a computer, to identify and correct basic hardware problems, to load and use Microsoft Office software, and to use the Internet. Through Dell's product donations, each student participating also earns his or her own home computer.

The program enabled 16,800 students from sixty participating school districts in the United States and Canada to complete the forty-hour course and graduated eighty-five hundred students in the 2006–07 school year. Of all participants, more than 80 percent are Hispanic or African American and 46 percent are young women. Also indicative of the success of the program is the number of new partners that have joined in, including Microsoft (operating systems and software), America Online (Internet access), and EGL Eagle Global Logistics (free transport of equipment).

Equity and Social Justice

In order to extend its insurance services and live up to its "Good Neighbor" reputation, State Farm Insurance teamed up with Neighborhood Housing Services (NHS) of Chicago to deliver insurance and financial education to low-income communities.[17] NHS, a local NGO focused on increasing the availability of insurance services in low-income communities in Chicago, was a natural match for State Farm that wanted to build those communities into sustainable business markets. In addition to mutual goals, the partners also had complementary capabilities: State Farm had the products, sales force, and analytic services, while NHS was able to introduce agents to local residents and help the insurer to adapt its underwriting guidelines and pricing structure for low-income markets. Most recently, the partners have worked together to provide over eight hundred home inspections and three hundred low-interest home improvement loans for residents of low-income neighborhoods.

As with most cross-sector partnerships, this one faced challenges. At first State Farm questioned whether serving low-income areas would yield profits for the company, but later realized the business case. "Strengthening neighborhoods eventually strengthens your company," concluded Clayton Adams, State Farm's vice president of community development. In addition, language proved to be an initial source of misunderstanding. When an NHS official talked about "community development," for instance, she was thinking in nonprofit terms of equity and social justice. The insurer, in business terms, characterized this as "loss mitigation." Eventually, the partners understood one another and the value of their respective points of view.

The effort has proven to be successful for a number of reasons. First, the partnership was integrated fully into State Farm, embedding it into the company's business practice. Adding new programs has helped both organizations build new capabilities, penetrate new markets, and remain fresh and innovative. Finally, and perhaps most importantly, each partner has been willing to understand the other's point of view. Seeing the success of this joint effort, State Farm has expanded its commitment to neighborhood development on a nationwide scale by partnering with NeighborWorks America, a national network of community-based organizations that works with community residents, business people, government officials, and other partners.

Digital Divide

A partnership between Nokia, one of the world's leaders in mobile communications technology, and the Grameen Foundation, an innovator in microfinance for the poor, has produced significant benefits for some of the world's downtrodden rural communities.[18] By pooling their respective strengths, these two organizations are providing rural areas with access to affordable telecommunications service through a joint program called Village Phone.

The idea for this partnership grew from the pioneering work of Muhammad Yunus and the Grameen Bank in Bangladesh, which revolutionized banking by providing microloans to would-be small business owners in poor communities. The Grameen Foundation next aimed to improve their access to telecommunications, a vital tool for a growing microenterprise. Closing the gap between widespread access to technology in the West and the far more limited access in the developing world, known as the digital divide, has been a longstanding goal for Nokia. This gap prevents poor countries from accessing tools and ideas that could help them improve education, healthcare, and productive enterprise. That's the social motive behind Nokia's engagement with the digital divide, as well as that by AMD (50x15), HP (e-inclusion), and other companies we have noted.

But there are market motives here, too. The market for mobile phones is projected to reach four billion subscribers by 2012. Mobile technology has been accessible for some time in remote, underdeveloped areas of the world where it is difficult and costly to build fixed-line infrastructure and Internet access. However, while capacity for greater access to this technology is available—80 percent of the world has mobile coverage—only 25 percent of the world is now accessing it. Veli Sundbäck, head of CR at Nokia, expressed the market logic this way: "It is clear that socio-economic development and telecommunications growth are intimately linked."

The way Village Phone works is simple. The program provides a loan of approximately $200 to a village operator so that he or she may purchase a mobile phone kit, including a Nokia handset, SIM card, prepaid airtime, and antenna set, and marketing materials. The loan can be paid off over a long period, generally nine months, with an interest rate not to exceed 4 percent. The operators of Village Phone become small entrepreneurs, and earn revenue by renting out the provided air time to other villagers and business owners. Grameen has jokingly dubbed this program "a business in a box." From 2003 to early 2007, five thousand new businesses have been created in Uganda as a result, and three thousand are expected in Rwanda, the program's first two pilot nations. Beginning in 2005, the creators of Village Phone began to replicate the program in Cameroon, the Philippines, and elsewhere.

Environment

One of the more innovative partnership stories is the alliance formed between international fruit giant Chiquita and the ecology-minded NGO Rainforest Alliance. The partnership, based on the NGO's expertise in sustainable agriculture and the company's need to improve its reputation and social performance, was borne of conflict and exemplifies the value of cross-sectoral cooperation and diplomacy.[19]

David McLaughlin, senior director of environmental affairs for Chiquita, and Tensie Whelan, executive director of the Rainforest Alliance, tell us this story. Chiquita is a company steeped in history. More than a hundred years ago, Captain Lorenzo Dow Baker bought a hundred sixty bunches of bananas in Jamaica, sailed them to Jersey City, and sold them for a profit. Since then, Chiquita has expanded operations into some sixty countries, with Latin America providing the bulk of the produce for the company's $4 billion global sales. Like many multinationals operating in developing countries during the colonial era, the company established a patriarchal base and took care of everything from telecommunications to road maintenance. Later this was judged as corporate imperialism, and the firm was charged with creating jungle fiefdoms and sustaining banana republics in Central and South America.

Early in the 1990s, Chiquita faced serious protest over its practices. "Our license to operate was being severely questioned by a lot of environmental activists," recalls McLaughlin.

After many months on the defensive, Chiquita's management opened the door to the Rainforest Alliance, a New York-based NGO committed to protecting ecosystems and the people and wildlife that depend on them, by transforming land-use practices, business practices, and consumer behavior. "We really had to go beyond any traditional boundaries that we had in our corporate culture," says McLaughlin, a twenty-seven-year veteran of the company. "We had to change our decision framework, completely open up, accept these viewpoints, and figure out whether we could accept them and fit them into our production process. We also recognized the need for a credible standard."

This engagement between the two organizations, while often uncomfortable and confrontational, led Chiquita's management to a greater understanding of the issues and grievances at play. It also led to their partnership in what was orig-inally called the "Better Banana" program, the Rainforest Alliance's certification standard. Broad areas covered by the certification include wildlife conservation, ecosystem health, soil erosion, water conservation, integrated waste and pest management, fair treatment and good conditions for workers, and the establish-ment of strong community relations.

Complying with these exacting standards has not been inexpensive for Chiquita. The company spent over $20 million from 1992 to 2000 to certify the environmental performance of its farms in Latin America. But certification has contributed to productivity and reduced costs—for all its farm operations from 1997–2005, the company has seen productivity increase by 27 percent and costs reduced by 12 percent. In terms of environmental performance, among other impacts, agrichemical use was greatly reduced and the incidence of pallet recy-cling increased. Today, some 93 percent of all the bananas Chiquita produces are Rainforest Alliance certified.

Lessons on Partnering

There are many lessons to learn from Chiquita's engagement with the Rainforest Alliance. Among those cited by McLaughlin and Whelan are:

- *The human element is very important.* Talking to people in person is a differ-ent experience from talking over the phone or via e-mail. Sitting down with the Rainforest Alliance in 1992 changed the dynamic of the relationship and put human faces to the partnership.
- *Third-party standards are tangible.* These allow goals to be set and in turn, allow both sides to establish accountabilities.
- *Buy-in from senior management is key.* Senior management buy in was fos-tered by the formation of a corporate responsibility steering committee at the corporate level within Chiquita and led to monthly meetings with NGOs and activist organizations. This exposed senior managers within the company to stakeholder issues and helped them face their so-called adversaries on a per-sonal level.
- *The process of change is incremental.* These partners took baby steps in the development of their relationship, recognizing that cultures and processes do not change overnight.

The Center has conducted a number of other studies of corporate community involvement in education and youth development, community service and development, social justice, and the environment. Appendix 7 includes a roster of current "best practice" partnerships. Meanwhile, Jonathan Levine has culled these studies and devised a set of questions for partners to consider in assessing their efforts. For readers interested in what makes partnerships work, please consider Figure 12.4.

Multibusiness, Multiparty Alliances

In their authoritative volume on corporate practices in society, Jane Nelson, director of the Corporate Responsibility Initiative at Harvard, and her co-author Ira Jackson highlight how business-to-business (B2B) and multisector alliances are taking shape to address major economic, social, and environmental problems.[20] Most of the next generation citizenship companies we have profiled here have either helped to start or are members of several such alliances: GE (carbon trading, energy, and the environment), Unilever (fish, water, and agriculture, as well as food), AMD (electronic supply-chain management and the digital divide), Nike (fair labor practices), Diageo (responsible liquor consumption), Baxter, Pfizer, Novo Nordisk and nearly all of pharmaceutical companies (access to medicine, disease treatment, and prevention groups), and on and on.

The reasons are manifold, ranging from self-protection to leveling the playing field to leveraging each other's ideas and resources to shaping public opinion and public policy. And their impact can be profound. Nelson's recent research demonstrates how firms, NGOs, and governments are working together to combat trade in blood diamonds and to address corrupt business practices in developing countries; how multibusiness efforts are underway to establish transparency around oil payments so as to ensure fair dealings, to build national health and legal systems in African states, and to promote post-conflict reconciliation among peoples in Northern Ireland, South Africa, the Balkans, and Afghanistan; and how business and civil society partners promote peace through simple-but-difficult measures like creating jobs for youth growing up in lands ripe for conflict and terrorism.

There are many reports, Web sites, and studies that detail the variety and range of B2B and multiparty alliances. The Center has compiled a roster of partnerships and alliances that focus on corporate citizenship and CSR (see Appendix 8). Besides the UN Global Compact, these include AccountAbility, Asian Development Bank, Business for Social Responsibility, the Conference Board, the International Business Leaders Forum, and the World Business Council on Sustainable Development, not to mention our Boston College Center for Corporate Citizenship. To illustrate five-degrees-of-separation, the Center has, at present, working relationships with over fifty other associations, NGOs, consultancies, and academic bodies around the world focused on corporate citizenship that in turn connect to thousands of companies, and surely many millions of managers and students.

Citizenship Learning Forums

Finally, mention should be made about a new kind of multibusiness association: shared learning forums where companies speak openly about their practices and problems in hopes of learning something from their peers.[21] Why would

Figure 12.4
Elements of Sustainable Partnerships

Clarity of mission:
Is the common need or public purpose of the partnership well defined, and do all partners have a common understanding of it? Does a Memo of Understanding clearly lay out the goals, desired impacts and roles/responsibilities of each partner?

Congruency of strategy and values:
Do all partners buy into a common strategy of how to pursue the mission? Have you conducted due diligence of the partners' values to make sure they have no hidden agendas and that their activities won't harm you own reputation?

Value creation:
Does each partner's value complement the resources, skills or other assets of other collaborators? Is each partner the best one to supply that value, and will it make your targeted outcome more productive than if pursued with the partner?

Power-sharing:
Do all partners share equally in the design, implementation and reputation value of the partnership to ensure each has enough incentive and commitment to make it succeed?

Proper resources:
Is the financial and human capital committed to the partnership sufficient to ensure complete follow-through? This includes the political will of each partner's top management, identifiable leaders with time and passion to commit, and devoted budgetary resources.

Right size:
Is the proposed project or solution adequately scaled to the problem or need? If not, the intended impact may not be achievable.

Local involvement:
Does the conceptualization and implementation of the partnership include local people and institutions, and acknowledge realistic conditions of the target geography?

Measuring results:
Have the partners agreed to reasonable success factors and outcome metrics appropriate to the mission? Are there accurate information and baseline data, and adequate organizational capacity to track progress against the targeted outcomes?

Open communications:
Does communication among all partners enable frank and honest discussion of problems?

Good governance:
Have the partners set ground rules and agreed to roles and responsibilities to weather potential differences of opinion or unexpected difficulties down the road?

Continual learning:
Does the partnership include a process and resources for analyzing new data and absorbing key lessons to ensure ongoing improvement of the outcomes?

Courtesy of Jonathan Levine with contributions from James Austin, Harvard University; Mike Magee, World Medical Organization; and Elizabeth Sobel, Management Systems International.

companies work and learn together in this arena? It is well established that new situations, particularly when they pose potential risks or opportunities to an organization, spur a search for a better understanding of what is happening and ways to respond to it. In the GLN and Executive Forum, every company was facing new expectations from stakeholders, reporting requirements, and increasing calls for transparency and responsiveness, all in the context of heightened mistrust of business overall. At the same time, there has been growing recognition of the social-and-business case for corporate citizenship, and of the cost savings, market potential, and sheer necessity of sustainable business practices. This amalgam of heightened risk and opportunity, given a paucity of past experience and even best practice to draw upon, made the members of these study groups especially responsive to the call to join with other companies in an academic research forum.

Knowledge about citizenship has both explicit and implicit dimensions. Models, case studies, and practical guidelines for citizenship can be found on both the academic and practice sides of these consortia. To get at some of the implicit "know what" information, however, requires more intensive and sustained dialogue among the practitioners and academics. Just as important is the "know-how." Responsibilities for citizenship in companies span hierarchical and functional boundaries. To be successful in their endeavors, practitioners not only need subject matter expertise, but also a sense of organizational politics and culture. To get at this kind of implicit knowledge requires thick description, storytelling, reciprocal interaction, even visits to one another's organizations. Thus considerable time would be spent in each forum developing open work processes and increasing levels of trust and engagement among the participants.

There are, of course, other learning forums on aspects of corporate citizenship. As an example, Peter Senge, MIT lecturer and founder of the Society for Organizational Learning (SoL), has helped to establish a SoL Sustainability Consortium of companies and consultants who belong to SoL.[22] Specialists from Ford, BP, and Nike, as well as Schlumberger, Harley-Davidson, United Technologies, Plug Power, and other companies, have been sharing ideas and practices for the past several years in the consortium. Versed in the tools of organization learning, these experts are learning from one another how to develop system dynamics models of, say, the interactive effects of energy, water, transportation, materials, and such as these flow into and out of their firm's production processes. Increasingly, their dynamic models are incorporating social factors related to poverty, human rights, and the business climate.

It is important to note that complex model building of this sort is not just a byproduct of getting smart people together. A team reviewing the effectiveness of "knowledge-exchange" in the Sustainability Consortium stressed the importance of the "relational space" for fostering open dialogue. One forum member commented: "This is a special group of people with high capacity for telling the truth, thinking about complexities without oversimplifying. They can see the big picture." Another reported: "I didn't understand before the Sustainability Consortium the real power of getting in the room with other folks and actually speaking the truth rather than trying to bullshit each other like we do at conventional business meetings."

Conclusion

Can Business Step Up?

L isten to Hector Ruiz, Chairman and CEO of AMD, pose a fundamental choice to fellow business leaders at the Detroit Economic Club in
March 2007:

> We've all heard the terms; we all know what they mean for our businesses: The
> Internet; globalization, the spread of democracy; the rule of law and science-driven
> technologies. These forces have combined to allow businesses, and their products
> and services to have a deeper impact on society than at any other time in our his-
> tory. And the evidence suggests our influence will only strengthen.
>
> With every innovation in manufacturing and packaging, we extend the reach of
> our products around the world. With every gain in productivity, we make our
> goods and services cheaper and more accessible. With every advance in technology,
> we empower more people to participate in the global economy and lead healthier
> and wealthier lives.
>
> Yet, across the world it is a hotly debated question on whether this growing
> influence of business on people's lives is healthy. While I respect this concern, I
> believe it is the wrong question to ask. The power of its influence, like the power of
> technology or the power of wealth, is at its core neutral in its effects. It is only how
> that influence is applied that makes it positive or negative. So as business leaders,
> with such great influence at our disposal, we have a choice.
>
> Do we accept this growing power to influence simply as a sign of success? Or,
> do we acknowledge that with greater power comes greater responsibility, and lever-
> age our influence to better serve the world as we've never done before?[1]

In this volume, Chapter 7 highlighted how AMD is making an affirmative choice
by integrating citizenship fully into its business, joining with other high-tech
firms in The Green Grid to bring energy- and eco-efficiency to power-drinking
data centers, launching its 50x15 initiative to get 50 percent of the world on the
Internet by 2015, and partnering with Nicholas Negroponte from MIT's Media
Lab in the nonprofit venture One Laptop per Child, which aims to produce a
low-energy, high-performance personal computer, chock-full of interactive educational software and Internet tools, for sale at less than $100.

In testimony to its achievements as a corporate citizen, *CRO* (Corporate
Responsibility Officer) magazine ranked AMD number two in its America's 100
Best Corporate Citizens in 2007.[2] Who was number one? Green Mountain

Coffee Roasters, covered in Chapter 11, whose commitments to coffee cooperatives and leadership in the fair trade movement have also earned it high marks from consumers and a substantial financial return. "This is not rocket science," says Green Mountain CEO Bob Stiller, speaking about his company's beginning-to-end business model. "We started going to coffee farms to see people and in company meetings would announce what we're doing and get applause. Talking to the employees when they came back from these trips—it changed their lives! You know, a lot of people just have no idea; you can read about it; you can watch videos but when you're there and interact with the growers and understand the whole connection, it really changes your perspective about what's needed." "Leadership is about engaging people," he reminds, "making them part of the solution."

Interestingly, in third place in the 2007 *CRO* rankings was Nike. We summarized in Chapter 6 its shift from defense to offense in dealings with its supply chain. Today the company has a number of social ventures in China, including partnerships with Mercy Corps in micro-enterprise development and with Special Olympics International to promote participation by the handicapped in sports. It has also launched its NikeGO community program in several cities, and to support the 2008 Olympics in Beijing Nike has donated funds and material to construct the first playing field ever built of 100 percent Nike Grind, a substance made from recycled rubber from tennis shoes. The *CRO* ranking experts credit Nike with a full turnaround on its social and environmental performance. Even its longstanding critics give it a begrudging nod. *Doonesbury* cartoonist Gary Trudeau, who took the company to task in the 1990s over its supply-chain lapses, gave the company a head nod in a recent strip. See a wounded Iraq war vet say it's okay now to identify with the company (Figure 13.1).

Figure 13.1
Things Change

DOONESBURY © 2006 G. B. Trudeau. Reprinted with permission of UNIVERSAL PRESS SYNDICATE. All rights reserved.

Critical Success Factors

General Electric, IBM, and Unilever have been described throughout this book as big-company exemplars of next generation citizenship. We've singled them out because they have gone beyond "good company" to build corporate citizenship into their operating processes and business models. They are also companies that we have studied for several years, making it possible to report some of the details of how and why they made their game-changing moves. But there are several other corporations at the frontiers of socio-commerce that are noteworthy exemplars of three critical success factors.

Competing on Foresight

Japanese carmaker Toyota stands out for introducing the hybrid engine automobile to the United States, which, combined with its legendary commitment to quality and affordable design, has made it the worldwide sales leader.[3] Toyota is today greening its auto dealerships and pledging to offer an all-hybrid lineup within the next few years. Compare its market foresight with, say, Ford Motor Company's, whose chairman was preaching about sustainability while its operators chose instead to rake in profits from gas-guzzling SUVs. Shrinking revenues, a substantial loss of market capital, and massive layoffs are the legacy of betting against the future.

We noted in Chapter 10 how 3M was ahead of its time with its Pollution Prevention Pays program and continues to lead the way in environmentally sound practices. DuPont has an equally prescient and compelling story to tell. *Fortune* features it in its list of ten "Green Giants" selected by a panel of environmentalists and consultants.[4] In Chapter 3 we detailed how Unilever has forged partnerships for sustainable agriculture and industrial water use. Its global competitor Nestlé has been a leader in these areas too.[5] But note how leading companies are reformulating their products, such as washing powder, to reduce water use. When it comes to bringing environmentalism to the consumer marketplace, Wal-Mart's 360-degree sustainability strategy whereby it scores suppliers' products on sustainability, promises to speed the movement forward.

Throughout this volume we have illustrated how, through new business models and strategic philanthropy, several next generation companies are reaching out to youth around the world. Their innovations include e-training in new technologies; hands-on training and internships in retail, banking, and manufacture; social programs aimed at fitness and self-esteem; and countless more. But Western societies (plus Japan) have an aging population and face a future of record numbers of persons aged sixty to over one hundred. This is the growing market and social space served by Grand Circle Corporation, a travel agency specializing in meeting the needs of older clients. The company was founded by Ethel Andrus, a retired teacher and principal, who had a vision of helping Americans lead more vital, challenging, and politically active lives. Pursuing this dream, she founded the American Association of Retired Persons (AARP) in 1958 and created Grand Circle to offer tours to her peer group. What followed over the next decades were thousands of innovative travel programs designed to fit the needs of the most mature passengers, and today it offers hundreds of vacation packages that aim to energize, stimulate, and prepare the "young old" for the next stage of their lives.

Not surprisingly, Grand Circle also promotes employee volunteerism, has programs that engage the elderly in community service, and measures its triple bottom line performance. Current Chairman and CEO Alan E. Lewis and his wife Harriet established the Grand Circle Foundation, which donates millions to causes and recently launched its $10 million World Classroom initiative that supports more than seventy schools in developing countries. In so doing, the Foundation is helping these schools employ retired persons as teachers.

Corporate Social Innovation

Whether it's the eco-wear of Patagonia, the cool carpets of Interface, the many thousands of high-tech solutions opening new vistas for kids in U.S. cities and farmers in Africa, or the myriad high-touch consciousness-raising volunteer and training programs, the success of tomorrow's business models depend on innovation. We have seen how companies must innovate to tap untapped markets and reach the bottom of the pyramid. C. K. Prahalad is now promulgating the "innovation sandbox"—a toolkit that helps firms craft low-cost, high-quality new business models that rely on a combination of new supply and distribution channels, high technology applications, and consumer education.[6] His former student and BoP co-developer, Stuart Hart, has advanced a "sustainable value framework" that identifies a range of current business opportunities where social and environmental investments today might yield cost savings or risk reductions.[7] The real payoff comes next generation, when clean technologies portend disruptive innovation and new opportunities for firms to meet unmet needs. Hart and colleagues at Cornell University run a base-of-the-pyramid learning laboratory where companies swap innovative ideas and practices. The aim is to create a more "inclusive commerce"—in line with the new rule for business success: Global growth requires global gains.

CEMEX, Nokia, and many of the other companies we have covered are practicing inclusive commerce with the aid of various new forms of microlending. This space, pioneered by the Grameen Bank, is attracting social entrepreneurs and commercial insurers, lenders, and the world's largest financial institutions. There is also innovation afoot in global capital markets. Goldman Sachs, mentioned for incorporating social and environmental criteria into its weighty financial analyses of companies, is also investing big time in alternative energy and clean technology and was a key player in the buyout of Texas energy company TXU that scrapped some of its plans to build coal-fired power plants.[8] Meanwhile, global carbon trading is in the offing.

We've talked about the problems of over- and under-nutrition and how these social issues are being factored into corporate responsibilities. Foods producers and purveyors are innovating throughout this value chain. Fortified foods and beverages? Companies are capitalizing on the healthful attributes of tea and yogurt cultures, and food laboratories are experimenting with micronutrients that can improve diets in the developing world. Beyond the usual additions of vitamins and minerals, there are already energy-increasing, cholesterol-lowering, and anti-aging formulations on the market. Isotope-enhanced chicken and steak are not far behind.

There are considerable corporate and societal risks associated with innovations ranging from animal cloning to growth hormones to the genetic modification of plants. Consumer movements concerning food safety, sustainable agriculture and aquaculture, and animal rights also feature here. All these issues are leading next generation companies toward more transparency about sourcing and ingredients, the start of a food certification movement, and the cleanup of the most unsustainable farming and inhumane animal handling practices. After the unhappy experiences of Monsanto, the company that wanted to genetically modify crops and was charged with possibly creating monstrous "frankenfoods," other innovators are wondering: Will the public accept biotechnology breakthroughs in its diet?[9]

Besides IBM, AMD, and Nokia highlighted here, much more could be said about how Cisco, Intel, Dell, and others are innovating on the high-tech sociocommercial front. How about the dot-com companies? As of this writing, neither Google, eBay, nor Yahoo, to pick the biggest, has as yet distinguished itself beyond innovative philanthropy, though Google is making its applications for email, messaging, and such available to government ministries and universities in several countries in Africa along with technical support. It also has pledged 1 percent of its profits to support philanthropy, and its foundation funds a TechnoServe training program for youth and other more commercially oriented ventures.

We have noted how salesforce.com is a role model of philanthropy and citizenship for other dot-com companies. Also notable is creativegood.com for its work with Web site designers. CEO Phil Terry has formed multicompany, multisector councils that bring the designers and their bosses together to talk about enhancing the customer experience. Meanwhile, co-founder and President Mark Hurst hosts an annual "Good Experience Live" conference that raises the consciousness of this e-commerce community about, among other subjects, aesthetics, ethics, and spirituality as well as their social responsibilities and opportunities.[10]

Finally, while in this sector note the emergence of "philanthropreneurs," such as Pierre Omidyar, founder of eBay, and Jeffrey Skoll, its former president; Stephen Case, from America Online; and Richard Branson of Virgin. Each has redefined philanthropy as social investment, with expected financial returns.[11] Through venture capital funding and business acumen, plus an eye for opportunity, their sociocommercial involvements include microfinance, filmmaking, alternative energy, and manufacture of low-tech equipment in developing countries.

Leading with Values

While foresight and innovation carry companies to the leading edge of corporate citizenship, values provide a reason to go there and bring employees, and even customers, along. As we studied the many companies profiled here we were struck by how often they moved forward by referencing their past. Managers at Unilever and Levi Strauss & Co., for instance, harkened back to their generous and generative founders when explaining their new value propositions. GE and IBM returned to their innovative origins and revitalized their laboratories to tackle the world's biggest problems. Even Wal-Mart would have you believe that Sam Walton would have approved of its eco-initiatives.

A nagging question is whether or not companies turn away from citizenship when their fortunes decline. Interestingly, our surveys find only a small correlation between how well a company performs financially in a given year and its investments in citizenship in the next year—based on self-reported data from executives. That said, it was our impression that Hewlett Packard's work as a leading corporate citizen declined with its financial losses and change of leadership the past several years. And that Levi's social agenda had stalled. There are reasons to believe, however, that HP is innovating again in this arena and that Levi Strauss, as described, is moving forward. Robert Hanson, president of the North American Division, explains why: "When you hit difficult times it's important to be able to look at the roots of what has driven the company's behavior in great times and make sure that even during difficult times that the essence of your corporate citizenship efforts—the essence of your values— remains intact."

Timberland CEO Jeff Swartz also saw his firm suffer a downturn in sales. But, as Swartz told us, the company's process for dealing with the slump reaffirmed its values: "When we went into the communities we served, we saw our potential in a different context. We saw that serving the community was central to our identity—it was who we are, not just what we do." Timberland has deepened the connection between the company's mission and its role in the community. "By inviting the engine of commerce to fit into the chassis of civil society," Swartz says, "we could bring the free market to bear in order to feed, educate, and inoculate children even as we made the quarter." Still, he stresses that the company's overall impact in society is modest. He, like other CEOs we talked to, sees a need for systemic solutions, where private sector leaders overall "must be implicated, not in a casual way, but up to their elbows in the building of community."

Toward a New Social Contract

Part I of this volume illustrated how the social contract between business and government in the United States has changed dramatically in the past twenty-five years. In the 1960s and 1970s, for instance, government took care of society, redistributed wealth, and set the rules of the game; business took care of business and growing the economy; and nonprofits and charities filled the chinks in the social fabric that government missed. Corporate social responsibility in this contract was fairly simple to understand: You paid your taxes, obeyed the law, employed and treated people fairly, and gave something back through philanthropy.

We saw how this contract shifted with the decline of government in the social sphere, the rising power and voice of community activists and NGOs, and new responsibilities being thrust on companies. And while historically the pendulum of power swings between business and government, there are many reasons to believe that, in the foreseeable future, the tendency toward market-based activity will continue.

It is evident, for example, that growing entitlements and debt interest payments are consuming more and more of the U.S. fiscal budget, leaving fewer resources for social programs. Discretionary federal spending on social programs has shrunk from 70 percent of the budget in the 1960s to roughly 25 percent today and, with social security, Medicare, and interest expenses all growing, is not apt to increase anytime soon and may decline further.[12] In addition to resources and flexibility, the state is losing its legitimacy. Disaffected voters have demanded the rollback of an inefficient and bureaucratic welfare state. Political capital has continued to erode amidst reports of corruption and manipulation in government, as well as the state's failure to protect its citizens from catastrophe. Trust in government has plummeted from over 70 percent in the early 1960s to 20 percent today. Cynicism about government has increased in kind.[13]

Speculating on the future of the social contract, the Center's Chris Pinney believes that the role of government may change from that of primary agent to one of enabling and convening other groups, notably business and NGOs, which have greater capacity to affect social issues. In many respects, this is taking shape through deregulation, a pullback of government, and the contracting of social services. Indeed, nonprofit employment in the United States has doubled in the past twenty-five years and today accounts for 10 percent of the workforce.[14] We noted the growth in the number and scale of NGOs, which the public deems far more trustworthy than government when it comes to addressing environmental issues (65 versus 16 percent), human rights issues (69 versus 14 percent), and health issues (64 versus 17 percent).[15] Pinney believes that these groups will continue to be the champions of social issues and leading advocates for underserved segments of society. At the same time, he sees them partnering with government and with business in social service delivery. This is their transition from corporate watchdogs to co-creators of business and social value that we described.

The New Role of Business

In our model of the stages of corporate citizenship in Chapter 5, we showed businesses progressively stepping up to greater responsibilities. Some of this has been stimulated by government regulation in health, safety, employment, the environment, and most recently financial accountability; and some is attributable to "civil regulation"—the collective pressure that society imposes on business through its expectations and sanctions. The Center's national business surveys show that mainstream company leaders resist these pressures, and many big-company CEOs we interviewed chafe at the idea of external intrusions into their realms. Said one in knee-jerk reaction, "I would break out in hives if someone said, 'Here is a rule book of how you should contribute to society.'" Another questioned: "If corporations are asked to pay for things that we haven't been previously asked to pay for, will the shareholder appreciate that?"

The attitude toward NGOs is no more sanguine among these kinds of executives. One told us, "The greater good of the enterprise is somehow being lost because of its most vocal opponents. If you ask me what executives talk about, it's how can a group of fifty people be causing us ten million bucks a year of distraction when their issues have no substance?" Another said of NGOs: "They're activists, they're not partners naturally."

Allen L. White, GRI founder and Tellus Institute senior fellow, asks, "Is it time to rewrite the social contract?"[16] In answering affirmatively, he proposes a bold notion that "the purpose of the corporation is to harness private interests and to serve the public interest." Plainly, segments of the U.S. public are fed up with business-as-usual. A 2007 poll by Fleishman-Hillard and the National Consumers League found that four out of five Americans—majorities of Democrats, Independents, and Republicans—say it is "extremely" or "very" important for the Congress to work to ensure that corporations address social issues such as energy, the environment, and healthcare. Majorities also call for more governmental oversight of the pharmaceutical, chemical, food, and healthcare industries. It is foreseeable, then, that unless business steps up, governmental and civil regulation will set the next citizenship agenda.[17]

Parts II and III of this volume showed next generation companies crafting socially relevant value propositions, taking an integrated, strategic approach to citizenship, and putting it all to work in their governance and in their commercial and societal strategies. All of this fits within the rubric of the free market system. And these illustrate the power of individual and corporate foresight, innovativeness, and values to serve society's interests. But in so doing, leading firms are increasingly working in partnership with NGOs and local and state governments in the United States and abroad. A question unaddressed: How does business best fit alongside national governments in filling a socially responsible role?

Spotlighting the situation in the United States, there is frustration that government refuses to take on more of a leadership role; one CEO we interviewed commented that too many in government see their job as keeping government out of business when in fact in many policy areas—from energy to global warming to education to healthcare—government needs to step up and go into partnership with business and community groups. But some also acknowledge that notions of corporate responsibility and citizenship do not fully capture all of the dimensions of the business–society relationship. For the most part, socially responsive companies embrace issues having to do with risk and reputation, and produce new goods and services related to social and environmental need. This is a significant development in how companies relate to wider society. However, major issues of social concern, such as employment and retirement policies, immigration, climate change, and healthcare, do not often register on the citizenship radar screen—nor does the influence business has over government.

Indeed, if you think about the breadth and depth of the business–society relationship, and then consider what corporate citizenship traditionally tries to address, it is readily apparent that there are significant gaps and inconsistencies. Citizenship strategies and social reports do not often deal with or fully account for companies' lobbying activities and political contributions, their stands on taxation and tort reform, or positions on immigration, offshoring, and labor. Moreover, it is often the case that even as companies take some strides toward affirmative leadership on corporate citizenship, they apply their political contributions and legal muscles to block progressive legislation and thwart remedies to misconduct.

There is movement today to create more transparency about corporate lobbying and public policy activity.[18] One study finds that 50 percent of major companies are disclosing some information in these regards. And governance reform adds at least an external check on how a firm operates vis à-vis society. But the broader questions are: Should corporate citizenship focus on the full relationship of business to society? Should business leaders be shaping public policy? Of course, business attempts to influence public policy are nothing new, and one of the reasons often cited for loss of trust is that companies can appear to be lobbying against the public good and for their financial self-interest. Clearly, any attempt to engage in public policy in a different way will be affected by this legacy, and as one executive remarked: "Government needs to be extremely, extremely careful of companies with strong views of what the public interest is, because it's remarkable how often it's in alliance with their own interests, and especially those of their senior people."

At the same time, a number of executives have begun to speak out publicly about public affairs. As GE's Jeffrey Immelt, who has been vocal about climate change, told us: "It's not an easy time to stick your head up, because there's a sense that any corporation is evil or is Enron or something like that. But I think companies are finding their voice in terms of where we should take a stand." Mike Harrison of Timberland adds: "If you're talking about the many aspects of public policy business is inextricably linked with, it seems like we should take the lead. Environmental policy is a good example; human rights in the supply chain is another; and the whole debate over underfunded pensions. If business just waits for government to try to find the answers to those kinds of issues, (a) we won't get the best answers and (b) it'll be more of an adversarial relationship, and probably not to anybody's best interest."

Multisector Cooperation

The multisector engagement of business, government, and NGOs is a hallmark of the next stage of corporate citizenship, as Simon Zadek sees it.[19] We have seen this aplenty in on the-ground partnerships and multisectoral associations. On a national scale, as one executive put it succinctly: "Businesses and governments now have a much more well-defined love–hate relationship. They both need each other and they both hate each other." "I think some people in business still say, as they would have done twenty or forty years ago, 'My job is to create value for my shareholders. The government will do what the government does; it all just happens,'" says Susan Rice of Lloyds TSB. "Now, I think you've got more companies saying, 'Well, actually, it's not enough. The government can't do it and actually is not very capable at doing it on its own. . . . Therefore it's our place as a private-sector business to be involved.'"

This call for collaboration has implications beyond the confines of any one company or country. China, for example, has eight of the ten most polluted cities in the world and a huge pent-up demand for energy and automobiles. Leaders from all levels of government, domestic business, and multinationals are together trying to devise environmental principles that fit into the nation's model of a Harmonious Society. John Anderson, president of Levi Strauss, has a view on the corporate role in this exchange: "I think corporate responsibility gives companies the opportunity to have influence on how societies are led. I'm not talking from a political point of view as much as from a point of view on human rights, the environment, or working standards. If companies are going to be committed to a level of what's acceptable, I think they then can encourage political leaders to move along that path to a more open society or to some of the things that we take for granted in the Western world."

It seems likely that companies will increasingly come together to think about major societal challenges, but not always in formal or systematic ways. There is a sense that the time is right for this kind of out-of-the-box thinking where, for example, a medical company partners with a coffee company to see what they can do together to address village-level poverty in Latin America. What is more, this kind of multicompany collaboration, tough though it can be, is needed because it ultimately becomes too difficult for any one company to constantly take the lead on any given issue.

Global Corporate Citizenship

On the global stage, corporate citizenship principles are no longer optional, they are essential to business survival. Global corporate citizenship calls on companies to become engaged in social issues, align operations in a responsible and sustainable manner, and innovate to create the greatest possible social value. Businesses are already in the driver's seat of globalization, and the world is depending on them to be responsible drivers.

On the other hand, while business activity is adding value in terms of employment and production, it can also exacerbate social ills by externalizing costs such as pollution, supporting abusive regimes, or mistreating workers. Companies have been repeatedly criticized for taking advantage of and even exploiting poorer nations, communities, and individuals. In this age of globalization, society will not allow detached and irresponsible management even if there is no global body to control it. A wider scope of self-imposed responsibility is expected, one that will encompass fairness along the entire supply chain, environmental awareness, and greater standards of accountability and transparency.

We've seen this self-regulation in the form of industry-wide supply-chain principles, human rights policies, and fair trade practices and products.

Companies can also now look to international collective agreements and global performance standards to align their operations with expectations worldwide. There is also great potential in multibusiness collaboration. As an example, the Extractive Industries Transparency Initiative (EITI) is a collaborative effort that includes BP, Chevron Texaco, Exxon Mobil, Shell, Rio Tinto, Total, and other major oil and gas providers. EITI specifically aims to reduce the embezzlement of oil and natural resource revenues and allow others to monitor and influence governmental spending priorities by promoting the transparent reporting of payments.

Finally, certification is an area ripe for collective action. The U.S. Environmental Protection Agency's Energy Star program, for example, includes product certification and a wide-ranging educational campaign. Standards for organic produce and fair trade products are taking shape. Interestingly, Wal-Mart has become a force here, most recently by scoring electronic products on their sustainability.

Companies have proven over the past century that they are the most powerful and effective sources of change and innovation. In Chapter 4 we laid out new rules for business success in the twenty-first century. And we have shown how next generation companies are moving toward socio-commercial business models that provide innovative solutions to new management challenges such environmental and health problems, inequities in education, and the digital divide at home and in the developing countries where businesses now work. All of this translates into an easy-to-articulate but difficult-to-execute business agenda (see Figure 13.2). Again, the key driver of this agenda is leadership.

The Call for Courageous Leadership

We are at a junction where companies are driven by short-term demands while the challenges of new societal expectations require business to address long-term issues. In this climate, the role of business is being redefined but is still a work in progress. What we are seeing played out are a number of experiments involving the role of business and how it should be managed. For instance, executives are struggling with the extent to which business can regulate itself or is in need of more regulation. To what extent can it be organized through principles and how much through rules? How much should profit be used to validate business's actions, and how much should alternative notions of value figure into the equation?

These experiments are at different stages, and some will prove more important than others. Sometimes it will prove vital to have a single answer, and at other times it might be viable to have alternative models running in tandem. But we cannot ignore the reality that the outcomes of these experiments will shape not only business but the very nature of society. We have seen that the public is calling on business to better care for society, take care of the natural environment and, in certain arenas, to exercise a leadership role. More than just wealth, companies have technical, infrastructure, and human resources that exceed anything at the disposal of other sectors in society. Moreover, business leaders

---

Figure 13.2
Moving the Business Agenda in the 21st Century

Forward-looking agenda for 21st Century companies will:

1) Invest in products that address societal needs.

2) Create business models that explore the limits of what the principled enterprise can achieve.

3) Make corporate responsibility a distinct business management competency.

4) Build a long-term perspective for the capital markets.

5) Work with non-business organizations to find solutions to societal issues that go beyond a narrow definition of business self-interest.

6) Engage in public policy in ways that take place at different levels on a wider range of issues, and that seek to represent the interests of a wider range of stakeholders.

7) Build new ways to understand and communicate the impact business's relationship with society has on company value.

8) Actively seek to rework the social contract to maintain and maximize their wealth creation function.

---

are often in a better position to bring together leading thinkers from all sectors on issues as diverse as globalization, climate change, and poverty reduction.

Put simply, business has the ingredients of power, resources, and global reach. But there is no consensus among its top executives about if, when, and how to use them. As is to be expected, critics of big business fear the influence of major corporations.[20] More surprisingly, the executives from those very companies, certainly some of the strongest supporters of free enterprise, echo fears about imperial capitalism and investor short-termism. Remember the cautionary remarks of one CEO: "Capitalism, if unchecked, could eat us alive." Several other business leaders we interviewed looked askance at the way so many in business and government trust the market to be the primary arbitrator of the public good. As one CEO expressed his frustration with the current state of play: "You got a government that says, 'We don't need any more government in corporate American business.' And you got a bunch of sheep who say, 'Well, we don't need government in our business.'"

The bulk of today's business leaders are often uncertain, confused, and timid about exerting leadership beyond the confines of the corporation. This is especially true where the challenges require them to look beyond the business case, when decisions and success cannot be measured by reference to share price or other financial indicators. Even when corporate executives recognize the need to engage with society to address common challenges, and acknowledge their ability to do so, they point to short-term profit pressures and a lack of interest among financial analysts and some institutional investors as barriers to social action.

On these counts, a few companies are eschewing quarterly forecasts and some publicly owned firms are going private. Private ownership, especially through private equity firms, brings its own unique pressures and demands, yet some leaders we talked with believe it is much easier for privately owned companies and limited liability partnerships to talk to their owners about their long-term perspectives when compared to publicly held companies. On the flip side, another felt it *"was just specious"* for a CEO to say that being publicly held prevented the company from taking certain courses of action.

Fiscal pragmatism is another barrier: Companies that are struggling to remain financially solvent may not have enough resources to experiment and engage in social innovation. And some leaders simply do not see this as their job. These two factors seem to be behind the ugly decision of the U.S. retailer Circuit City to lay off their longer-term sales clerks, and then open up their hiring at entry-level wages. Competitors like Best Buy have instead invested in their staff and devised a different business model.[21]

Breaking out of this diminishing mindset requires what one executive calls "courageous leadership"—which does not mean forsaking financial imperatives, but rather building a prosperous business that also meets standards of integrity and social innovation. While the day when corporate citizenship was synonymous with the acts of individual corporate leaders has transitioned to a situation where companies themselves are expected to add value in new ways, the individual leader nonetheless has an important contribution to make. Mike Rake, Chair of KPMG, spells out the implications for his peer group: "We need chairmen and chief executives to have the courage to run their businesses in very difficult, different ways. They have to be leaders. They can hire managers. But they need to be leaders of the business in a sense that really engages their people, their stakeholders, their shareholders, their communities, in believing that what they're doing is good for their business, good for their communities, and that these are inextricably intertwined."

This was the leadership role embraced by the pioneers of a new model of corporate citizenship—Ben and Jerry, Anita Roddick, Jeffrey Hollender, and others profiled in Chapter 8. It is today the leadership role being embraced by Jeffrey Immelt, Ray Anderson, Sam Palmisano, and Hector Ruiz, those whom we have characterized as next generation corporate citizens. How does Timberland's Jeff Swartz justify his getting up to his elbows in building community to skeptical shareholders and doubtful financial analysts?

I say, "I want these questions that say 'prove that our model works,' because otherwise it's not a scalable model." That's why being on the *Fortune* "100 Best Companies to Work For" list is nice, but being on the *Forbes* Platinum list of the best-performing public companies is not nice, it's essential. I insist on being a public company. I want to be in the crucible where innovation gets wrung out. There shouldn't be any room for flabbiness in this argument about business and social justice, because flabbiness defeats the argument.

The call for courageous leadership embraces not only top executives, but employees at every level and the next generation of corporate leadership. We saw in Chapter 9 how leading companies are engaging their employees as citizens and grooming their next generation of leaders to run sustainable businesses. Movement is afoot in M.B.A. curriculums and management education programs throughout the world on this front. But academic leadership from business school deans, college presidents, and business leaders on university boards of trustees might hasten the pace. For example, the Harvard Business School recently joined with the Kennedy School of Government to form a partnership in training the next generation for a broader, multisector leadership role; this was years after Yale University innovated in this space. Why not the nation's and world's other leading universities?

The call extends to our academic colleagues to devise the next generation of theories needed for twenty-first-century business. In his dying days, Sumantra Ghoshal published an eloquent and urgent essay about how "bad management theories are destroying good management practice."[22] He chastised the academy for uncritically embracing agency theory and its notions that managers are simply agents for the owners of the firm, its shareholders. In so doing, he made the point that firms are more than financial capital and that managers serve as agents for multiple interests, including societies and the planet. Stakeholder theory may not be as lean as agency theory, but it properly reflects the complexity of the new operating environment for business. But the next stage of corporate citizenship is, at this point, a work in progress and open to new theorizing and research, particularly as concerns its holistic character and positive potential. Given the animating power and practical import of theory, courageous scholarship is needed here.

The call for courage extends as well to leaders in government at all levels and in civil society and NGOs. Even as the pendulum swings toward an ever-larger role for business in addressing societal and environmental ills around the globe, the need for collaboration and partnership among all sectors of our world has never been greater. As Tom McCoy of AMD reminds us all: "You know, the problems that we face in the world are very huge, very complex. No one company can do it alone. IBM cannot fix the educational problem, but in unity with other big corporations, with government, with local communities, the leveraging effect of what they can accomplish with their leadership is extraordinary."

Hector Ruiz laid down the gauntlet; there are choices to be made for leaders at every level—whether in a giant global corporation or a dot-com start-up, in governmental units in a nation rich or poor, in a formal NGO or neighborhood association, as a B-school professor or beginning business student, as a corporate citizenship professional or line manager: Do you want to leverage your influence to better serve the world as you've never done before?

Appendix 1

Business in Society Interviews

Company	Interviewee	Position**
AMD	Hector Ruiz	Chairman & CEO
AMD	Tom McCoy	EVP—Legal Affairs & Chief Administrative Officer
Apache	Raymond Plank	President
Apache	Steve Farris	Chairman & CEO
Aramark	Joe Neubauer	Chairman & CEO
Aramark	Tim Cost	VP—Corporate Affairs
Baxter	Bob Parkinson	Chairman & CEO
Baxter	John Greisch	CFO
BD	Ed Ludwig	Chairman, President & CEO
BD	Pat Shrader	Corporate Vice President, Regulatory Affairs & Compliance
Booz Allen Hamilton	Ralph Shrader	Chairman & CEO
Booz Allen Hamilton	Chris Kelly	Vice President
Citigroup	Chuck Prince	Chairman & CEO
Citigroup	Todd Thomson	Chairman & CEO - Global Wealth Management Division
Ernst & Young	Jim Turley	Chairman & CEO
Ernst & Young	Steve Howe	Managing Partner—Financial Services Office
GE	Jeff Immelt	Chairman & CEO
GE	Ben Heineman	Senior Vice President for Law and Public Affairs
Georgia Pacific	Pete Corell	Chairman & CEO
Georgia Pacific	James Bostic	EVP Government Affairs, Environmental, and Adminstrative Services
IBM	Sam Palmisano	Chairman & CEO
InBev	John Brock	CEO
Johnson Controls	Steve Roell	Vice Chairman & Executive Vice President

(continued)

Company	Interviewee	Position**
Johnson Controls	John Kennedy	Executive Vice President
Keyspan	Bob Catell	Chairman & CEO
Keyspan	David Manning	SVP Corporate Affairs
KPMG	Mike Rake	Chairman
KPMG	John Griffith-Jones	CEO UK
Levi Strauss	Phil Marineau	President & CEO
Levi Strauss	John Anderson	President, Asia Pacific Division
Lloyds TSB (Scotland)	Susan Rice	CEO
Lloyds TSB (Scotland)	Manus Fullerton	Corporate and Commercial Director
Manpower	Jeff Joerres	Chairman & CEO
Manpower	Mike van Handel	CFO
Nestlé	Peter Brabeck-Letmathe	Chairman & CEO
Raytheon	Bill Swanson	Chairman & CEO
Raytheon	Jay Stephens	General Counsel
State Street	Ron Logue	Chairman & CEO
Timberland	Jeff Swartz	Chairman & CEO
Timberland	Mike Harrison	Senior Vice President & General Manager—International
Turner Construction	Tom Leppert	Chairman & CEO
Turner Construction	Jeff Herriman	SVP—Strategic Planning and Corporate Development
Unocal	Chuck Williamson	Chairman & CEO
Unocal	Jo Bryant	President & COO
Verizon	Ivan Seidenberg	Chairman & CEO
Verizon	Doreen Toben	CFO
Others Holiday	Jack Connors	Chairman and former CEO, Hill
Others Airlines	Jack Creighton	Ex-CEO Weyerhaeuser, United

**Position held at time of interview

Appendix 2

Business Case for Corporate Citizenship

Core Asset or Function	Cost Reduction	Value Creation
License to Operate	Reduced project risk	Increased community support for the company's operations ("bank account of goodwill")
	Reduced risk of crisis escalation	
	More favorable government relations and regulatory rulings	
	Faster permitting and building approval	
	Reduced shareholder activism	
	Reduced risk of lawsuits	
	Reduced risks posed by social issues (e.g., lack of skilled work force)	
	Reduced work stoppages	
	Easier entry into markets and operating locales	
	Easier exit from markets and operating locales	
Customer Marketing	Reduced negative consumer activism and boycotts	Increased customer attraction
	Positive media coverage and "free advertising"	Increased customer retention
	Positive "word-of-mouth" advertising	
Human Resources	Increased employee retention and morale	Enhanced professional development
		Enhanced recruitment
		Increased productivity
		Development of diverse workforce
Reputational Capital	Reduced negative media coverage	Enhanced professional development
	Dampened effect of crises or negative events	Enhanced recruitment
		Increased productivity
		Development of diverse workforce

(continued)

Core Asset or Function	Cost Reduction	Value Creation
Innovation and Market	More efficient use of products and services (i.e. companies have learned from Corporate Citizenship programs and make improvements on products. (for example, certain insurance companies have used their citizenship experience in low-income communities to create programs that reduce property damage and insurance claims, making underwriting less risky and more profitable.) More efficient production processes (e.g., some companies have used disputes with community and environmental groups to learn how to improve overall manufacturing efficiencies).	Enhanced knowledge of markets Support for marketing efforts (relationship marketing) Development of new non-traditional market opportunities Opportunities to test new products and services. Asset diversification that mitigates risk
Corporate Financial	Effective management of community-based stakeholders—noted in the categories above—helps reduce operating costs.	Efficient operations and the creation of new opportunities (defined in the categories above) adds to the bottom line
Social Investing		Social screens and investment funds are attracted to companies perceived as good social performers

Appendix 3

Stages of Corporate Citizenship—Self-Assessment Survey

What the survey is. This survey asks about the current "landscape" of corporate citizenship in your company. It focuses on eight important aspects of corporate citizenship according to The Center's research and experiences. Depending on the company, we've often found that some aspects of corporate citizenship are more developed than others. The survey can help you gauge your company's development along each key dimension.

This survey is not intended to provide an in-depth assessment of the state of corporate citizenship in your company or how well it is managed. Rather, it is a first-pass diagnostic that can provoke thinking and be a basis for discussion with your colleagues.

How to complete the survey. To complete the survey, read the questions in each section to get a flavor for the topic and then place an "X" by the one statement that best describes citizenship in your company.

Corporate Citizenship Concept: What best describes corporate citizenship in your company? How broad is your citizenship concept?	
The concept of corporate citizenship in my company primarily focuses on:	
	Just the Basics: Jobs, profit, taxes
	Functional Focus: Philanthropy, community relations, environmental protection
	Stakeholder engagement and management
	An Integrated Concept: Triple bottom line, with equal importance assigned to economic, social and environmental factors
	Embedded in the corporate DNA: It is the way we define and do business.

Strategic Intent: What is your company's strategy with regard to corporate citizenship? Does your company believe that citizenship has an impact on reputation? On recruiting and retention? On bottom line performance? Is corporate citizenship integrated into your company's business model?

My company's strategic intent with regard to corporate citizenship focuses on:

	Legal compliance
	Preserving our reputation and license to operate
	The Business Case: Traditional ROI criteria
	Business Case plus Value Proposition: In addition to traditional ROI criteria, company values are seen as a key driver for assessing risk and opportunity.
	Corporate citizenship is a part of our business model: A focus on market opportunity and creation

Leadership: How engaged are your CEO and other top company leaders about corporate citizenship? What type of leadership do they exercise in this area? Are their efforts visible outside the company? Is your company's Board of Directors active in citizenship?

I would characterize my company's leadership as:

	Lip service, out of touch
	Supporters: Leaders are in the loop, but not driving it.
	Stewards: Leaders are on top of it.
	Champions: Leaders are out in front, leading our industry.
	Visionaries: Leaders aim to change the game of business.

Operations: Are there people or units with specific responsibilities for citizenship activities in your company? Do they exchange information across units? Coordinate actions? Work together? Are there cross functional committees or groups that address social and environmental performance? Is citizenship integrated into line business operations?

The extent to which corporate citizenship is embedded in my company's structure and business operations is:

	Marginal: Functional heads "do their bit." Citizenship responsibility is fragmented or nonexistent.
	Functional: There are units with specific citizenship-related responsibilities, but activity is still mostly siloed.
	Cross-Functional Coordination: Citizenship responsibility is coordinated across units.
	Aligned: There is vertical buy-in across the company and lines of business are engaged.
	Integrated: Corporate citizenship is driven by the business, and activities cut across and are owned by functions and business units.

	Issues Management: How does your company handle social and environmental issues that arise? Are there clear policies on these matters? Effective programs? Goals and measurements? Are citizenship-related issues managed as other vital activities in the company? Is there a proactive approach to issues as opportunities?
	I would characterize my company's approach to issues management as:
	Defensive: Issues are handled as one-offs.
	Reactive: We have programs on paper, but many are not fully implemented.
	Responsive: We have operationalized policies and programs on key issues relevant to the company.
	Responsible: We have programs along with plans, goals and performance measures on the management of issues we face.
	Proactive: Plans and actions are ahead of the curve. We anticipate and prepare for emerging issues—both risks and opportunities.

	Stakeholder Relations: How does your company relate to its stakeholders? Does it communicate openly and regularly? Are there good working relationships with stakeholders? A relationship of mutual benefit? A relationship of partnership?
	I would characterize my company's approach to stakeholder relations as:
	Unilateral: We generally have one-way communication with stakeholders.
	Interactive: We generally have two-way communication with stakeholders.
	Consultation: We have a relationship of mutual influence, in which stakeholders influence the business and the business influences stakeholders.
	Win-Win: We have a shared agenda with stakeholders and we all do our part.
	Partnership: We work together with stakeholders on important issues and learn from them as equal partners.

	Accountability: To what extent does your company measure the quality and impact of its social, environmental, and economic efforts on the business and on society?
	I would characterize my company's accountability mechanisms as:
	Minimal: Only that which is required for legal compliance
	Sporadic: Mostly when a high-profile issue arises
	Systematic: But *only in a few* line and staff functions
	Systematic: In *many* functions of the business
	This is core to how we run the business.

Transparency: To what extent does your company communicate about it its financial, social, and environmental performance? Is there public reporting? Outside verification of performance results?	
I would characterize my company's approach to transparency about its social, environmental, and financial performance as:	
	Flank protection: Minimal disclosure
	Public relations: Some disclosure, emphasizing good news
	Public reporting on citizenship-related issues
	Full disclosure of goals and results
	We seek third party assurance and verification for our reported results.

Appendix 4

Roster of Founder/ CEO Citizenship Trailblazers

Individual Leader	Organization	Location
Ray Anderson	Interface, Inc	GA, USA
Godric Bader	Scott Bader	United Kingdom
Joan Bavaria	Trillium Asset Management	MA, USA
Mike Gilliland	Wild Oats & Sunflower Markets	CO, USA
Seth Goldman	Honest Tea	MD, USA
Ron Grzywinski	ShoreBank Corporation	IL, USA
Gary Hirshberg	Stoneyfield Farm	NH, USA
Jeffrey Hollender	Seventh Generation	VT, USA
Mary Houghton	ShoreBank Corporation	IL, USA
Jim Kelly	Rejuvenation	OR, USA
Laura Markham	Dragonfly Media	NY, USA
Anita Roddick	The Body Shop	United Kingdom
George Siemon	Organic Valley Farms	WI, USA
D. Wayne Silby	Calvert Group, Ltd.	MD, USA
Rory Stear	Freeplay Energy Plc.	South Africa
Bob Stiller	Green Mountain Coffee Roasters	VT, USA
Hal Tausigg	Idyll, Ltd.	PA, USA
Judy Wicks	White Dog Café	PA, USA

Appendix 5

Today's Socio-commerical Entrepreneurs: Select Examples

In contrast to "social entrepreneurs," who are mainly focused on providing a missing social need, socio-economic entrepreneurs began their enterprises with a dual focus in mind, profits and social benefit. We mentioned Natura, The Greyston Bakery, and Hemisphere Development in the opening chapter. Here are some others:

Company Name	Value Proposition
TerraCycle	Terracycle has created a business from an innovative process for creating organic non-toxic fertilizers. TerraCycle fertilizers are made completely from waste, and are also packaged in waste. In this way, the company utilizes an ecologically sound, chemically-free method for delivering a product that assures the superior growth of vegetation. TerraCycle has also connected to consumers through urban community gardens and school-wide recycling events.
Bamboo Hardwoods	This successful and environmentally sustainable company is working to slow deforestation. Bamboo Hardwoods sells bamboo (which is a grass) as an alternative source material for flooring. The company ensures a steady source of income (50–100% above market rates) to farmers, and provides a healthy work environment in regions where the wood is sourced, primarily in Vietnam.
Blue Sky Hauling	This Oakland, California-based hauling company has found an innovative way to help underserved populations by removing unwanted items and materials from homes and businesses and then delivering them to local, national, and international NGOs serving the poor. The company charges customers up to $495 for a full 15-cubic-yard truck-load removal, and to date it has diverted 128,643 tons of recyclable materials from landfills.

(continued)

Company Name	Value Proposition
The Lusty Wrench	This "not-your-ordinary" auto repair shop combines reliable auto repair services with innovative, environmentally-friendly business practices. The Lusty Wrench recycles waste products, purchases auto parts from socially-responsible countries, and educates customers on auto-related sustainability issues. It is devoted to keeping cars running for as long as it makes "good ecological and economical sense." For these activities, the auto repair shop has won awards for its "eco-consciousness."
Honey Care Africa	Honey Care Africa was established as an enterprise in order to increase the income of rural farmers in Kenya. The company has achieved this goal by training rural farmers in commercial beekeeping, buying their output at a guaranteed price, and selling it as premium high-quality African honey. This small enterprise earns revenues of about $110,000 per year. Today, Honey Care has the largest domestic market share of its honey products in Kenya and it was named the top small- to medium-sized business in Africa in October 2005.

Source: The Center for Business as an Agent of World Benefit, The Case Weatherhead School of Management, "Innovation Bank": http://worldbenefit.cwru.edu/innovation.

Appendix 6

Corporate Community Involvement in China: Select Examples

MICROSOFT

Focus: *Digital Divide*

Invested $500K+ for computer training for laid off and migrant workers. Their "Unlimited Potential" grant program transforms local community centers to tech-enabled centers for learning and collaboration.

BOEING

Focus: *Youth Development*

Boeing developed a Junior Achievement business plan program which engaged 1,020 Chinese teens. They maintained active involvement through mentoring and financial support of the programs and business ventures themselves.

BAYER

Focus: *Core Values for Kids*

Donates "soccer in a box" to children in poor areas, helping them organize teams. Early Bayer established soccer clubs to help retain employees. Soccer brings their culture and spreads their values: fair competition, teamwork, and education.

DAIMLER CHRYSLER

Focus: *Knowledge Transfer*

DC produces a bilingual insert for the Beida newspaper that reaches the young elite at 100+ universities. They also host roundtables with officials to exchange ideas related to policies, new technologies and products, market trends, etc.

BP

Focus: *Environmental Education*

World Wide Fund for Nature is a JV (BP, Government, World Wildlife Fund) to develop and test environmental education materials and methodologies with the aim of transforming the existing primary and secondary school curriculum.

INTEL

Focus: *Education*

Funds scholarships and equipment; assists government educational organizations build Web sites with course materials for teachers, sending a Chinese team to the Intel International Science and Engineering fair in the United States.

HSBC

Focus: *Local Involvement*

HSBC has set in place an integrated community relations program: Volunteers from the banks help in retirement homes that were established with HSBC's financial support. The bank also funds professional training for the full-time care staff.

IBM

Focus: *Technology Training*

IBM has made investments in the order of $10–20M in IBM technology centers in Chinese universities around the country, as well as setting aside significant funds for teacher and scholar training and student scholarship programs.

MOTOROLA & COCA COLA

Focus: *Education*

Motorola and Coca-Cola have each donated $2M to Project Hope through the Youth Development Foundation, which has used most of the funds to build primary schools and fund primary education in poor rural China.

GE

Focus: *Quality of Education*

GE is the primary sponsor of a local Chinese version of Sesame Street, "Zhima Jie," with local partners, Children's Television Workshop, and Shanghai TV. It was written and produced in China to support a commitment to enhance the quality of children's TV in China and the education of Chinese children.

HP, GAP, FORD, TARGET, PFIZER,

Focus: *Social Accountability*

With academic and NGO partners, the Global Supplier Institute has a "beyond audit" strategy, where they will be offering training programs on management, health and safety, and HIV/AIDS, among other compliance curricula.

Other Broad Areas for Philanthropic Activity:

- Community Activism and Empowerment
- University Scholarships
- Educational International Exchange Programs
- Joint Technology Institutes
- Disaster Relief
- Health/Medical Care
- Training/Tutoring/Mentoring
- Primary Education

Corporate-Nonprofit Partnerships: Select Examples

Partnerships in the Environment

Starbucks & Conservation International

- In 1998, Starbucks partnered with Conservation International (CI), an NGO concerned with sustainable agricultural practices.
- The two parties agreed to work together to reduce environmental impact from coffee production and improve the quality of the product.
- CI provides farmers with technical assistance in producing high quality, shade-grown coffee for Starbucks and in turn Starbucks provides CI with financial support for its work.
- The project has expanded from its original site in Chiapas, Mexico to additional sites in Colombia and Peru and the number of cooperatives involved in the program has doubled.

Chiquita & Rainforest Alliance

- Facing serious challenges to its practices, Chiquita turned to the NGO, Rainforest Alliance.
- A partnership was founded on what was known as the "Better Banana Program," Rain Forest Alliance's certification standard.
- The standard covers areas such as wildlife conservation, soil erosion, water conservation, good conditions for workers, and strong community relations.
- Chiquita began with two test farms in order to determine the business case for certification.
- Certification contributed to increased productivity and reduced costs for Chiquita, and Chiquita has been able to significantly improve its reputation.
- Chiquita has spent over $20 million to certify its farms in Latin America.
- Rain Forest Alliance has learned lessons applicable to further developing corporate partnerships.

HSBC & Earthwatch

- In February 2002, HSBC created a partnership with Earthwatch, the World Wildlife Fund, and Botanic Gardens International to create a conservation program called "Investing in Nature."
- The company pledged an initial $16 million to a five-year, $50 million project designed to fund conservation research initiatives around the world.

- As a result of the funding, two hundred young scientists will be trained to conduct research in biological hotspots.
- In addition to monetary support, two thousand HSBC employees are engaged in voluntary fieldwork projects targeted at cleaning up three of the world's major river systems, saving twenty thousand rare plants from extinction, and conserving biological hotspots worldwide.

McDonald's and the Environmental Defense Fund

- McDonald's and the Environmental Defense Fund have been working together to reduce waste generated from fast food and to develop environment-friendly packaging.
- McDonald's has succeeded in reducing its packaging volume by more than 70%, has begun recycling, and has switched to paper packaging.
- As a result of this partnership, McDonald's also now requests that suppliers use recycled materials.

Partnerships in Community Service and Development

Whirlpool & Habitat for Humanity

- Realizing that the firm's ideals of home, family, inclusion, integrity, respect, and teamwork matched those of Habitat for Humanity, Whirlpool has become one of Habitat's most involved corporate partners in addressing the housing crisis in the United States and around the world.
- Whirlpool donates an Energy Star model refrigerator and freestanding range to every home in North America built by Habitat volunteers.
- The company also assists financially in the home-building process and inspires employees, trade partners, and consumers to volunteer with the organization.
- The partners also engage in a co-marketing and advocacy campaign involving a Reba McEntire concert tour and promotion.

Home Depot & Kaboom!

- KaBOOM! and The Home Depot have worked together over the last ten years to develop a community-build model that encourages civic leadership and revitalizes communities through creating great playspaces for children.
- The partnership sponsors initiatives such as: 1,000 Playgrounds in 1,000 Day, Operation Playground, and Racing to Play, and has built or improved more than five hundred community playgrounds, skateparks, and sports fields across North America
- The two partners were recognized in 2006 with a Excellence Award from the Committee to Encourage Corporate Philanthropy

Timberland & City Year

- A partnership between Timberland and City Year began through product donations and quickly expanded.
- The relationship sparked a commitment on the part of Timberland and its CEO, Jeffrey Swartz, to community service.
- Timberland sponsored City Year teams, provided uniforms, and offered marketing expertise and management systems.
- City Year has provided Timberland employees with team-building and diversity training, as well as service opportunities and planning.

- Jeff Swartz was chairman of City Year's national board until 2003.
- In 2000, City Year established a local New Hampshire site within the Timberland headquarters.

Partnerships in Social Justice

Green Mountain Coffee & TransFair USA

- Green Mountain signed on as a licensee of national fair trade certifier, TransFair USA.
- Green Mountain pays a royalty of $0.10/lb for certification.
- Green Mountain enhances its brand with the Fair Trade certification label.
- TransFair gained a "flag carrier" in the East to grow its concept.
- Fair Trade grew to over 14% of Green Mountain's coffee purchases in four years.

Union Bank & Operation Hope

- Union Bank and Operation Hope shared a mission to provide financial services to low income communities.
- The partnership began in the mortgage-lending arena, and extended to Union's "Cash & Save" check cashing program.
- Union provided equipment, management, marketing, and operations support for Hope Center banking facilities.
- The partnership enables Union to better deal with regulation and scrutiny and has created a new consumer market.

The TJX Companies & Goodwill Industries

- TJX publicly pledged to hire five thousand individuals on welfare by 2000.
- Goodwill and TJX were both off-price retailers and Goodwill had experience in finding work for the difficult to employ.
- The partners joined forces to develop a welfare-to-work program, "The First Step."
- Goodwill oriented managers and developed the program design and curriculum tailored to TJX: three weeks of classroom training, two- to five-week paid internship, and a full year of case management; Goodwill hired half of graduates.
- Goodwill gained an opportunity to expand its reputation and its ability to serve its clientele and received funding from the government and later from TJX.
- TJX gained positive publicity and a reliable workforce.

State Farm Insurance & Neighborhood Services of Chicago (NHS)

- Facing pressure to provide services in low-income communities, State Farm management decided to address the issue strategically, beginning a twenty-five year partnership with NHS.
- While State Farm initially envisioned the relationship as philanthropic, it became a mutually beneficial partnership where competencies could be shared.
- NHS helped State Farm understand low-income communities and how to develop the company's competitive advantage there.
- State Farm has collaborated with NHS to develop new insurance services and pricing structures for low-income communities.
- NHS and State Farm also produce an annual volunteer day of neighborhood rejuvenation together, including three hundred State Farm employees, and have developed a home safety education initiative.

Partnerships in Education and Youth Development

Advanced Micro Devices (AMD) & Capital Area Training Foundation (CATF)

- When AMD was faced with a lack of qualified technicians, it approached the Capital Area Training Foundation (CATF) to create a workforce development partnership.
- Together AMD and CATF developed a comprehensive school-to-work initiative, the Accelerated Careers in Electronics (ACE) program, to expose high school students to careers in semiconductor manufacturing.
- The scope of this partnership expanded regionally and incorporated other companies and schools to become the Semiconductor Executive Council.
- When the economy took a downturn, the partnership showed its flexibility by shifting its focus toward the promotion of science and math education.

Hewlett-Packard & Kuppam i-community

- In 2002, HP launched a three-year partnership with the state of Andhra Pradesh to build an HP i-community in Kuppam, India.
- An i-community is a concept that strategically deploys information and communications technology to help improve job creation, income opportunity, access to government, education and healthcare services.
- The program also provides technology to support job creation and develop the economic infrastructure of the community.
- HP has utilized its core business competencies to develop and implement the program in the following ways: determining customer needs, developing a diverse management team, and developing a systems approach to addressing problems.
- Local groups now use technology in innovative ways to address everything from pest management to increasing literacy among the population.

Nokia & International Youth Foundation (IYF)

- Nokia has partnered with a nonprofit organization focused on youth in order to develop global youth development program.
- The program empowers youth through structured life skills growth opportunities and provides training for adults to work with young people.
- To date, Nokia has invested US $26,000,000 in twenty-four countries and directly benefited more than 330,000 young people.

Intel & Museum of Science Boston

- The Intel Computer Clubhouse, a community-based after-school program that gives kids access to innovative technology, was first developed by the Museum of Science in Boston in collaboration with the MIT Media Laboratory.
- Financial support along with knowledge and expertise from Intel Corporation made the first Computer Clubhouse possible, and then supported its expansion worldwide.
- Intel currently funds two-thirds of the clubhouses, while the Museum of Science manages the network and provides technical innovation and expertise.

Unilever & Girl Scouts of the USA

- As a part of Unilever's Dove Self Esteem Fund, since 2002 Unilever has invested in "uniquely ME! The Girl Scout Dove Self-Esteem Fund."
- Girl Scouts of the USA has provided its unique resources and network to help the Fund strengthen the self-esteem of young girls.
- Unilever has invested $3.6 million to fund an educational program and mentoring, community service, and sports activities.

Appendix 8

Global Citizenship Organizations: Select Examples

1. Account Ability
2. Asian Development Bank (ADB)
3. Boston College Center for Corporate Citizenship
4. Business for Social Responsibility (BSR)
5. Business in the Community (BIC)
6. Corporate Responsibility Initiative at the Kennedy School of Government, Harvard University
7. European Economic Community (EEC)
8. Global Compact (GC)
9. Global Reporting Initiative (GRI)
10. Inter-American Development Bank (IADB)
11. International Business Leaders Forum (IBLF)
12. International Finance Corporation (IFC)
13. International Labor Organization (ILO)
14. International Organization for Standardization (ISO)
15. Organization for Economic Co-operation and Development (OECD)
16. Sustainability
17. The Conference Board
18. World Bank (WB)
19. World Business Council for Sustainable Development (WBCSD)
20. World Economic Forum

1. AccountAbility

Kind of Organization: *Nonprofit*
Founded: *1995*
Headquarters: *London, United Kingdom*
Web Page: *http://www.accountability.org.uk*
Members: *350 (businesses, NGOs, research entities)*

- Promotes accountability innovations that advance responsible business practices.
- AccountAbility innovations: Sustainability Assurance and Stakeholder Engagement Standards; Partnership Governance and Accountability Framework; Responsible Competitiveness Index; Accountability Rating of world's largest companies, published annually with Fortune International.
- Co-founder with CCC and conveners with IBM and GE of Global Leadership Network.

2. Asian Development Bank

Kind of Organization: *Multilateral Development Financial Institution*
Founded: *1966*
Headquarters: *Manila, Philippines*
Web Page: *http://www.adb.org*
Members: *66 members*

- Tries to improve welfare of people in Asia and Pacific.
- Helps its developing member countries reduce poverty and improve quality of life of their citizens.
- Key instruments for providing help to its members are: policy dialogue, loans, technical assistance, grants, guarantees and equity investments.

3. Boston College Center for Corporate Citizenship

Kind of Organization: *Academic Global Nonprofit*
Founded: *1985*
Headquarters: *Chestnut Hill, MA United States*
Web Page: *http://www.bcccc.net*
Members: *350 corporate-only*

- Educational institution, think tank and information resource for global companies.
- Engages companies to redefine business success as creating measurable gains for business and society.
- As part of the Carroll School of Management, the Center achieves results through the power of research, education and member engagement. Promotes cross-sector collaboration and contributes to global efforts to advance field of CSR.
- Provides only certificate-level training programs in Corporate Community Involvement and Corporate Citizenship
- Offers custom training, custom research, and benchmarking for corporate members.

4. Business for Social Responsibility (BSR)

Kind of Organization: *Global Nonprofit*
Founded: *1992*
Headquarters: *San Francisco, United States*
Web Page: *http://www.bsr.org*
Members: *Membership List*

- Helps members achieve success in ways that respect ethical values, people, communities, and environment.
- Promotes cross-sector collaboration and contributes to global efforts to advance field of CSR.
- Provides practical resources, issue expertise, advisory services, training, and timely insight on news, trends and innovations; services accessible through consultation, custom reports, and publications.
- Web also acts as intermediary between business and civil society.
- Maintains strong relationships with other key stakeholders and opinion leaders in civic and public sectors.

5. Business in the Community

Kind of Organization: *Private*
Founded: *1982*
Headquarters: *London, United Kingdom*
Web Page: *http://www.bitc.org.uk*
Members: *750+*

- Creates public benefit by inspiring companies to improve positive impact of business in society.
- Initiatives focus on different social issues; delivered through Partnership Academy.
- Specific professional service support, such as marketing or legal advice, delivered through Pro Help campaign.

6. Corporate Responsibility Initiative at the Kennedy School of Government, Harvard University

Kind of Organization: *International, Educational*
Founded: *2004*
Headquarters: *Cambridge, MA United States*
Web Page: *http://www.ksg.harvard.ed/m-rcbg/CSRI/index.html*

- Examines the changing roles in society related to the public and private sectors.

- Promotes multi-stakeholder alliances in the area of international development.
- Focus on issues related to governance and accountability.
- Supports scholarship on corporate social responsibility through publications and events.

7. European Economic Community (EEC)

Kind of Organization: *Intergovernmental and Supranational Union*
Founded: *1992*
Headquarters: *Brussels, Strasbourg, and Luxembourg City*
Web Page: *http://www.europa.eu*
Members: *25 Democratic States*

- Known since ratification in 1993 of Maastricht Treaty as European Union, EU.
- Activities cover topics such as economic policy, foreign affairs, defense, agriculture, and trade.
- Members have set up common institutions to which they delegate some of their sovereignty so that decisions on specific matters of joint interest can be made democratically.

8. Global Compact

Kind of Organization: *International Initiative*
Founded: *1999*
Headquarters: *New York, United States.*
Web: *http://www.unglobalcompact.org/*
Members: Global Compact

- International initiative launched through the United Nations.
- Membership includes companies and international labor and civil society organizations from all regions of the world engaged in Global Compact.
- Working to advance ten universal principles in areas of human rights, labor, environment, and anti-corruption.
- Offers facilitation and engagement through policy dialogues, learning, country/regional networks, and projects.

9. Global Reporting Initiative (GRI)

Kind of Organization: International Institution
Founded: *1997*
Headquarters: *Amsterdam, The Netherlands*
Web Page: *http://www.globalreporting.org*
Members: *no formal membership*

- Mission is to develop and disseminate a globally applicable framework for reporting an organization's sustainability performance.
- Intended for voluntary use by organizations reporting on economic, environmental, and social dimensions of their activities, products, and services.
- Most recent Guidelines are 2002 Sustainability Reporting Guidelines.
- Cooperates with former UN Secretary-General Kofi Annan's Global Compact.

10. Inter-American Development Bank

Kind of Organization: *Regional Development Bank*
Founded: *1959*
Headquarters: *Washington, D.C. United States*
Web Page: *http://www.iadb.org*
Members: 47 Countries

- Helps foster sustainable economic and social development in Latin America and Caribbean through its lending operations.
- Leadership in regional initiatives, research and knowledge dissemination activities, institutes, and programs.
- Assists its Latin American and Caribbean borrowing member countries in formulating development policies, and providing financing and technical assistance to achieve environmentally sustainable economic growth and increase competitiveness.

11. International Business Leaders Forum

Kind of Organization: International Not-for-Profit
Founded: 1990
Headquarters: London, United Kingdom.
Web Page: http://www.iblf.org
Members: No formal membership

- Works with businesses, governments, international agencies, and other stakeholders to create partnerships.
- Focuses on three areas: *Visionary leadership, innovative cross-sector partnerships*, and *development solutions*.
- Supported by corporate resources from over a hundred of the world's most influential international companies and private investors.

12. International Finance Corporation

Kind of Organization: Intergovernmental
Founded: 1956
Headquarters: Washington, D.C. United States.

Web Page: http://www.ifc.org
Members: 178 Countries

- Private sector arm of the World Bank Group.
- Promotes sustainable private sector investment in developing countries.
- Global investor and advisor committed to promoting sustainable projects in developing member countries.
- Focuses on frontier markets, building long-term partnerships with emerging global players, developing domestic financial markets through institution building, and use of innovative financial products.

13. International Labour Organization

Kind of Organization: United Nations Specialized Agency
Founded: 1919
Headquarters: Geneva, Switzerland.
Web Page: http://www.ilo.org
Members: 179 Countries

- Seeks promotion of social justice and internationally recognized human and labor rights.
- Formulates international labor standards in form of conventions and recommendations.
- Sets minimum standards of basic labor rights such as freedom of association, right to organize, collective bargaining, abolition of forced labor, and equality of opportunity and treatment.
- Promotes development of independent employers' and workers' organizations, and provides training and advisory services.

14. International Organization for Standardization

Kind of Organization: Non-Governmental Organization
Founded: 1947
Headquarters: Geneva, Switzerland
Web Page: http://www.iso.org
Members: 157 Countries

- Principal activity is the development of technical standards.
- The International Standards are useful to industrial and business organizations, governments, other regulatory bodies, trade officials, conformity assessment professionals, and to suppliers and customers of products and services in both public and private sectors.
- Provides governments with a technical base for health, safety, and environmental legislation. They aid in transferring technology to developing countries. ISO standards also serve to safeguard consumers.

15. Organization for Economic Co-operation and Development

Kind of Organization: Global Organization
Founded: 1961
Headquarters: Paris, France
Web Page: http://www.oecd.org
Members: 30 Countries

- Mission has been to build strong economies in its member countries, improve efficiency, expand free trade, and contribute to development in industrialized as well as developing countries.
- Active relationships with 70+ non-member countries and NGOs.
- Plays a prominent role in fostering good governance in public service and in corporate activity.
- Creates internationally agreed instruments, decisions, and recommendations in areas where multilateral agreement is necessary and not available.

16. Sustainability

Kind of Organization: Independent Organization
Founded: 1987
Headquarters: London, United Kingdom.
Web: http://www.sustainability.com
Members: no formal membership

- Independent think tank specializing in market opportunities for corporate responsibility and sustainable development.
- Coined terms "green consumer" and "triple bottom line" to describe new types of markets and business approaches.
- Strategic counsel and consultancy services for corporate clients; pro-bono work for NGOs and others.

17. The Conference Board

Kind of Organization: Not-for-profit Organization
Founded: 1916
Headquarters: New York, United States.
Web: http://www.conference-board.org
Members: Top executives and industry leaders from large corporations

- Not-for-profit nonpartisan organization that brings leaders together to examine major issues having an impact on business and society and to find solutions to common problems.

- Best known for Consumer Confidence Index and Leading Economic Indicators; practical knowledge through issues-oriented research and senior executive peer-to-peer meetings.

18. World Bank

Kind of Organization: Development Bank
Founded: 1944
Headquarters: Washington, D.C. United States.
Web Page: http://www.worldbank.org
Members: 184 Countries

- Cooperative with member countries as shareholders who are represented by a Board of Governors.
- Board of Governors are ultimate policymakers at World Bank; vital source of financial and technical assistance to developing countries around the world.
- Comprised of two unique development institutions—International Bank for Reconstruction and Development (IBRD) and the International Development Association (IDA).
- IBRD and IDA each play a different role in organization's mission of global poverty reduction and improvement of living standards. IBRD focuses on middle income and creditworthy poor countries; IDA focuses on the poorest countries in the world.
- Together, IBRD and IDA provide low-interest loans, interest-free credit, and grants for education, health, infrastructure, communications, etc.

19. World Business Council for Sustainable Development (WBCSD)

Kind of Organization: International Organization
Founded: 1991
Headquarters: Geneva, Switzerland
Web Page: http://www.wbcsd.org
Members: 180 International Companies

- 180 international companies in a shared commitment to sustainable development through economic growth, ecological balance and social progress.
- Members represent more than thirty countries and twenty major industrial sectors.
- Mission is to provide business leadership as a catalyst for change toward sustainable development.
- Objectives: *Business Leadership, Policy Development, The Business Case, Best Practices, and Global Outreach.*

20. World Economic Forum

Kind of Organization: Independent International Organization
Founded: 1971
Headquarters: Geneva, Switzerland
Web Page: http://www.weforum.org
Members: No formal membership

• Nonprofit, tied to no political, partisan. or national interests.
• Under supervision of Swiss Federal Government.
• Committed to improving state of the world by engaging leaders in partnerships to shape global, regional, and industry agendas.
• Three-fold vision:
  1. To be the leading organization that builds and energizes leading global communities.
  2. To be a creative force in shaping global, regional, and industry strategies.
  3. To be the catalyst of choice when undertaking global initiatives to improve the state of the world.

Notes

Introduction

1. All quotes used in this volume come from the Boston College Center for Corporate Citizenship research unless otherwise referenced. The Center's main research studies (see bbccc.net) cited throughout this volume include:

    Biennial surveys of business leaders, *The State of Corporate Citizenship in the U.S.: A View from Inside 2003–2004. The State of Corporate Citizenship in the U.S.: Business Perspectives in 2005* (Boston: Boston College Center for Corporate Citizenship, 2004, 2005, 2007);

    The Executive Forum, a multiyear research body, involving Abbott, AMD, Agilent, JP Morgan Chase, Levi Strauss & Co., Petro-Canada, and Verizon, reported in *Integration: Critical Link for Corporate Citizenship* (Boston: Boston College Center for Corporate Citizenship, 2005);

    The Global Leadership Network, a strategic citizenship forum, including IBM, GE, 3M, FedEx, Diageo, Cargill, Manpower, Omron, GM, and CEMEX, *Putting the Corporate into Corporate Responsibility.* (London: Accountability Forum, 2005),

    The Business Leadership in Society study, interviews with CEOs and senior executives, *Step Up: A Call for Business Leadership in Society* (Boston: Boston College Center for Corporate Citizenship, 2006); plus many In Practice and In Focus case studies.

2. See Edmund M. Burke, *Managing a Company in an Activist World: The Leadership Challenge of Corporate Citizenship* (Westport, CT: Praeger, 2005); Daniel C. Esty and Andrew S. Winston, *Green to Gold: How Smart Companies Use Environmental Strategy to Innovate, Create Value, and Build Competitive Advantage* (New Haven: Yale University Press, 2006); critiques and limitations include "Survey: Corporate Social Responsibility." *The Economist* (January 25, 2005); and David Vogel, *The Market for Virtue: The Potential and Limits of Corporate Responsibility* (Washington, D.C.: Brookings, 2005).

3. For *model of stages* see Philip H. Mirvis and Bradley Googins, "The Best of the Good." *Harvard Business Review* (December, 2004): 20–21; Philip H. Mirvis and Bradley Googins, "Stages of Corporate Citizenship: A Developmental Framework." *California Management Review 48*, 2 (2006): 104–126.

4. For *Unilever* see Pete Engardio, "Beyond the Green Corporation." *Business Week* (January 29, 2007), online edition, http://www.businessweek.com/magazine/content/07_05/b4019001.htm.

5. Mirvis and Googins. "The Best of the Good."

6. For *Wal-Mart* see Marc Gunther, "The Green Machine." *Fortune*, (July 31, 2006), online at money.cnn.com.

7. For *surveys on interest in CSR* see the Reputation Institute, RepTrak Pulse 2006: Social Responsibility Report at http://www.reputationinstitute.com. For the most comprehensive, longitudinal surveys of public opinion about corporate citizenship, see global polls from Globescan, *Corporate Social Responsibility Monitor (2001–2007)*, at www.globescan.com and U.S. domestic opinion by GolinHarris, *Doing Well by Doing Good: The Trajectory of Corporate Citizenship in American Business*, at www.golinharris.com. We will cite specific surveys throughout this volume.

Chapter 1

1. For *Jack Welch as "manager of the century,"* see Peter Petre, Brent Schlender, Thomas Stewart, and Alex Taylor III "Businessman of the Century," *Fortune* (November 01, 1999).

2. For *GE and the Hudson*, see Natural Resources Defense Council, "Healing the Hudson," online at www.nrdc.org; Clearwater, "The Hudson River PCB story," online at www.clearwater.org.

3. For *what are companies' responsibilities?*, see Sandra Waddock, *Leading Corporate Citizens: Visions, Values, Value Added, 2nd edition* (New York: Irwin, 2005).

4. For *three tactics*, see "Global Survey of Business Executives," *The McKinsey Quarterly* (January, 2006), online at www.mckinseyquarterly.

5. For *reputation and market value*, see Charles J. Fombrun and Cees Van Riel, *Fame and Fortune: How Successful Companies Build Winning Reputations* (New York: Financial Times Prentice-Hall, 2003).

6. For *CEO's primary social responsibility*, see John Welch, *Jack: Straight from the Gut* (New York: Warner Business Books, 2003).

7. For *saving the planet*, see "The Greening of General Electric," *The Economist* (December 8, 2005).

8. For *turned IBM around*, see Louis V. Gerstner, Jr., *Who Says Elephants Can't Dance? Inside IBM's Historic Turnaround* (New York: HarperBusiness, 2002).

9. For *firms like Ben & Jerry's*, see Howard Rothman and Mary Scott, *Companies with a Conscience, 3rd edition* (San Francisco: Myers Templeton Publishers, 2004).

10. *Ben Cohen* coined the term "caring capitalists." Quote from interview with Hannah Clark, "New Taste for Activism" (January 9, 2007), online at Forbes.com.

11. Jeffrey Hollender and Stephen Fenichell, *What Matters Most: How a Small Group of Pioneers Is Teaching Social Responsibility to Big Business, and Why Big Business Is Listening* (New York: Basic Books, 2003).

12. For *hybrid enterprises*, go to the Center's Web site: bcccc.net and also to The Center for Business as an Agent of World Benefit, The Case Weatherhead School of Management, "Innovation Bank," http://worldbenefit.cwru.edu/innovation.

13. For *over 200,000 new citizen groups* and other statistics on NGOs, see John Hopkins Institute for Policy Studies, Center for Civil Society Studies, online at www .jhu.edu/~ccss; on growing sociocommercial work on NGOs see The Democracy Collaborative of the University of Maryland, *The New Asset-Based Approach to Solving Social and Economic Problems* (Washington, D.C.: Aspen Institute, April, 2005).

14. For *multisector partnerships*, see World Economic Forum, *Partnering for Success: Business Perspectives on Multistakeholder Partnerships* (Geneva, Switzerland: WEF, 2005); also see Business Civic Leadership Center, "Strengthening Public-Private

Partnerships for Social and Economic Development" (Washington, D.C.: BCLC, September 2006).

15. For *myths and lapdogs,* see Deborah Doane, "The Myth of CSR," *Stanford Social Innovation Review* (Fall, 2005), and Mark Kramer and John Kania, "Changing the Game," *Stanford Social Innovation Review* (Spring, 2006), both online at www.ssireview.org.

16. For *preparadigmatic phase,* see Dirk Matten and Andrew Crane, "Corporate Citizenship: Toward an Extended Theoretical Conceptualization," *Academy of Management Review* 30, no. 1 (2005): 166–79.

17. For *a big corporation view,* see Niall Fitgerald and Mandy Cormack, *The Role of Business in Society: An Agenda for Action,* The Conference Board, Harvard University's Kennedy School of Government and International Business Leaders Forum (October 3, 2006).

18. For *studying centuries of discoveries,* see Gunther S. Stent, "Prematurity and Uniqueness in Scientific Discovery," *Scientific American* 227 (1972): 84–93.

19. For *stakeholder theory,* see R. Edward Freeman, *Strategic Management: A Stakeholder Approach* (Boston: Pitman, 1984).

20. For *term has gained traction,* see stakeholder citations reported by James Walsh, "The Rise of Stakeholder Thinking: A Theory and Practice Keyword Search," *Business as an Agent of World Benefit Global Forum.* Case Western Reserve University (October 25, 2006).

21. For *TBL,* see John Elkington, *Cannibals with Forks: The Triple-Bottom Line of 21st Century Business* (London: Capstone/John Wiley, 1997).

22. For *integrative logic of citizenship,* see Henri C. de Bettignies, "Reviewing Meanings and Contexts of Role of Business in Society." Presentation at the launch of the European Academy of Business in Society (Fontainebleau, France, July 5, 2002). One sign of acceptance of new and more encompassing ideas is their shortening in everyday language: think "e-commerce" or "flex-time" or "C-suite." Another indicator is their expression via an acronym: in this field see CSR, CC, CR, TBL (or 3BL), and the latest, Corporate Social Innovation or CSI.

23. For *best of both worlds,* see Gerald F. Davis, Marina van N. Whitman, and Mayer N. Zald, "The Responsibility Paradox: Multinational Firms and Global Corporate Social Responsibility," Social Science Research Network (SSRN), http://ssrn.com/abstract=899112.

24. For *CSR is limited as an agenda,* see Ian Davis, "The Biggest Contract," *The Economist* (May 16, 2005); see also Sheila M. J. Bonini, Lenny T. Mendonca, and Jeremy M. Oppenheim, "When Social Issues Become Strategic," *McKinsey Quarterly* 2 (2006), both online at www.mckinseyquarterly.com

25. For *this implicates the whole value chain,* see Steven Rochlin, "Llevar la responsabilidad corporativiva al AND de su empresa," *Harvard Business Review* (Latin America) (August, 2005).

26. Charles Handy, *The Elephant and the Flea: Reflections of a Reluctant Capitalist* (Boston: Harvard Business School Press, 2002).

27. For *Revolutionary Renewal,* see David S. Bright, Ronald E. Fry, and David L. Cooperrider, "Transformative Innovations for the Mutual Benefit of Business, Society, and Environment." Business as an Agent of World Benefit Global Forum. Case Western Reserve University (October 25, 2006).

Chapter 2

1. For the *infamous 1970 article,* see Milton Friedman. "The Social Responsibility of Business Is to Increase Its Profits." *New York Times,* September 13, 1970.

2. For *agency theory,* see Michael C. Jensen and William H. Meckling, "Theory of the Firm: Managerial Behavior, Agency Costs, and Ownership Structure," *The Journal of Financial Economics* (1976) and Michael C. Jensen, *A Theory of the Firm: Governance, Residual Claims, and Organizational Forms* (Boston: Harvard University Press, 2000), online at SSRN: http://ssrn.com/abstract=94043.

3. "Global Survey of Business Executives," *The McKinsey Quarterly* (January, 2006), online at www.mckinseyquarterly.

4. For *the term "social responsibility,"* see Frank Abrams in Anthony F. Buono, "Book Review: *Corporation, Be Good! The Story of Corporate Social Responsibility,"* *Business and Society Review* 111, no. 2 (2006): 235–40.

5. For *it gained a following,* see Howard Bowen, *Social Responsibilities of the Businessman* (New York: Harper and Brothers, 1953).

6. For *some argue CSR is a function of regulation,* see Michael Blowfield, "Does Society Want Business Leadership?" Center for Corporate Citizenship Working Paper. (December, 2005), online at bcccc.net.

7. For *survey of professions,* see The Gallup Poll, "Honesty/Ethics in Professions" (December 8–10, 2006), online at www.galluppoll.com.

8. For *reaction to financial misdeeds,* see poll by *Los Angeles Times* (March, 2004).

9. For *public opinion about company's citizenship,* see GolinHarris, *Doing Well by Doing Good: The Trajectory of Corporate Citizenship in American Business,* online at GolinHarris.com; Reputation Institute, RepTrak Pulse 2006: Social Responsibility Report, online at Reputationinstitute.com.

10. For *punitive view of bad corporate behavior,* see Cone, Inc., "2004 Corporate Citizenship Study" (December, 2004), online at Coneinc.com.

11. For *citizenship programs effect on reputation,* see Reputation Institute, RepTrak Pulse 2006: Social Responsibility Report, online at Reputationinstitute.com; also see Antonio Márquez and Charles J. Fombrun, "Measuring Corporate Social Responsibility" *Corporate Reputation Review* 7, no. 4 (January, 2005): 304–08.

12. Hill and Knowlton and Crown Ferry International, "Corporate Reputation Watch" (September, 2003). See also *Return on Reputation: Corporate Reputation Watch 2006,* online at HillandKnowlton.com.

13. For *research by* British Telecom, see *"Just Values: Beyond the Business Case for Sustainable Development"* (2003), online at BT.com.

14. *Mirvis on B&J surveys,* reported in Philip H. Mirvis, "Ben & Jerry's: Team Development Intervention (A and B)," in *Cases in Organization Development,* eds. A. Glassman and T. Cummings (Homewood, IL: Irwin, 1991).

15. *A comparison on total returns with DGSI data,* reported in World Economic Forum Annual Report 2005–2006, Geneva, Switzerland. Online at Weforum.org.

16. For *a compilation of studies* by United Nations Global Compact, see *Who Cares Wins: Connecting Financial Markets to a Changing World* (December, 2004), online at Unglobalcompact.org.

17. For *meta analysis,* see Marc Orlitzky, Frank L. Schmidt, and Sara L. Rynes, "Corporate Social and Financial Performance: A Meta-analysis," In *Organization Studies* 24, no. 3 (2003): 403–41; also see J. D. Margolis and J. P. Walsh, *People and Profits? The Search for a Link between a Company's Social and Financial Performance* (Mahwah, NJ: Lawrence Erlbaum Associates, 2001).

18. Marjorie Kelley, "Holy Grail Found," *Business Ethics* 18, no. 4 (2004): 4–5.

19. For *antiglobalization rallies and anticorporate notes*, see Naomi Klein, *No Logo: Taking Aim at the Brand Bullies* (New York: Picador, 2000); also see Paul Kingsnorth, *One No, Many Yeses: A Journey to the Heart of the Global Resistance Movement* (New York: Free Press, 2004); and Charles Derber, *Corporation Nation: How Corporations Are Taking Over Our Lives and What We Can Do About It* (New York: Griffin Trade Paperback, 2000).

20. For *of the world's one hundred economies*, see the size of corporations in Medard Gabel and Henry Bruner, *Globalinc: An Atlas of the Multinational Corporation* (New York: The New York Press, 2003); and Sarah Anderson and John Cavanaugh, "Top 200: The Rise of Corporate Global Power," the Institute for Policy Studies, December 2000.

21. For *globalization issues* such as income inequality, see World Bank PREM Economic Policy Group and Development Economics Group, "Assessing Globalization" (2000), online at worldbank.org; outsourcing, Forrester Research in Daniel Drezner. "The Outsourcing Bogeyman," *Foreign Affairs*, May/June 2004; spread of democracy in Nayan Chanda, "Coming Together: Globalization Means Reconnecting the Human Community," *Yale Global*, November 19, 2002; energy demand, in World Business Council for Sustainable Development, "From Challenge to Opportunity: The Role of Business in Tomorrow's Society" (February, 2006), online at Wbcsd.org.

22. For *the world's worst problems*, see Thomas Friedman, *The World Is Flat: A Brief History of the Twenty-first Century* (New York: Farrar, Straus, Reese, and Giroux, 2005).

23. For *business challenges*, see Ian Davis and Elizabeth Stephenson, "Ten Trends to Watch in 2006," in *The McKinsey Quarterly* (March 30, 2006); also see "CEOs as Public Leaders: A McKinsey Survey," *The McKinsey Quarterly* (April 24, 2007).

24. For *government serves the common good poll*, see Edelman Trust Barometer 2007, online at Edelman.com; also for data on cynicism see Donald L. Kanter and Philip H. Mirvis, *The Cynical Americans: Living and Working in an Age of Discontent and Disillusion* (San Francisco: Jossey Bass, 1989).

25. Among the firms we visited in our interviews, hundreds of multisector partnerships are already taking shape on many fronts—to address human rights in supply chains (Levi Strauss, Manpower), HIV/AIDs (Baxter, BD), agriculture and water (Nestlé), timber (Georgia-Pacific), climate change (GE), access to technology (AMD, IBM), credit (Citigroup, Lloyd's), and the development of principle-based accounting (KPMG, Ernst & Young).

26. For *business environmental agenda*, see Daniel C. Esty and Andrew S. Winston, *Green to Gold* (2006); Stuart Hart, *Capitalism at the Crossroads: From Obligation to Opportunity, 2nd Edition* (Upper Saddle River, NJ: Wharton School Publishing, 2007).

Chapter 3

1. For *Unilever's corporate history*, see Geoffrey Jones, *Renewing Unilever: Transformation and Tradition* (Oxford: Oxford University Press, 2005).

2. For *biographers report*, see Adam MacQueen, *The King of Sunlight: How William Lever Cleaned Up the World* (New York: Bantam Press, 2004).

3. For *witness Michael Moore*, go to michaelmoore.com; industry critiques by Eric Schlosser, *Fast Food Nation: The Dark Side of the All-American Meal* (New York: Houghton Mifflin, 2001) and the film *Fast Food Nation* (2006); and antiglobalization

work by Joel Bakan, *The Corporation: The Pathological Pursuit of Profit and Power* (New York: Free Press, 2004) and the film *The Corporation* (2005); also a 2005 GlobeScan poll plus multiyear comparisons in *Corporate Social Responsibility Monitor* (2001–2006).

4. For *use of natural resource at Unilever,* see reports on agriculture, water, palm oil, soy, and food lab at unilever.com; on status of water see World Water Council at worldwatercouncil.com; on agriculture see Food and Agricultural Organization of the United Nations at fao.org.

5. For *threats involve consumption,* see information on obesity at International Obesity Task Force iotf.org and news citations on obesity from Regina G. Lawrence, "Framing Obesity: The Evolution of News Discourse on a Public Health Issue," The Joan Shorenstein Center on the Press, Politics, and Public Policy, Harvard University, 2004–2005, at ksg.harvard.edu.

6. For *particularly in the West a move toward healthy and sustainable consumption,* see Anthony Kleanthous and Jules Peck, "Let them Eat Cake," World Wildlife Fund, (WWF-UK, 2006).

7. For d*ebate about gap between expressed and actual buying behavior,* see Timothy Devinney, Patrice Auger, Giana Eckhardt, and Thomas Birtchnell, "The Other CSR," *Stanford Social Innovation Review* (Fall 2006) and United Nations Environmental Program, "Talk the Walk" (UNEP, 2005), available at Uneptie.org.

8. For *evidence when a brand's social content aligns,* see C. B. Bhattacharya and Sankar Sen, "Doing Better at Doing Good: When, Why, and How Consumers Respond to Corporate Social Initiatives.," *California Management Review* 47, no. 1 (2004): 9–24.

9. C. K. Prahalad, *The Fortune at the Bottom of the Pyramid* (Upper Saddle River, NJ: Wharton School Publishing, 2005).

10. For *many of the leaders shaping BAWB,* see http://worldbenefit.cwru.edu/forum2006.

11. For *appreciative inquiry and positive psychology,* see James D. Ludema, Bernard Mohr, Diane Whitney, and Thomas J. Griffin, *The Appreciative Inquiry Summit: A Practitioner's Guide for Leading Large-Group Change* (San Francisco: Berrett-Koehler, 2003); and David E. Cooperrider and L. E. Sekerka, "Toward a theory of positive organizational change," in K. S. Cameron, J. E. Dutton, and R. E. Quinn, eds., Positive Organizational Scholarship (San Francisco: Jossey-Bass, 2003).

12. For *Social Investment in the United States,* see *Reports on Social Investing Trends in the United States: 10 Year Review* (Washington, D.C.: Social Investment Forum, January 4, 2006).

13. *Walsh, People and Profits?* (2001).

14. For *the group's most recent survey of business students,* see "New Leaders, New Perspectives: A Net Impact Survey of M.B.A. Student Opinions on the Relationship between Business and Social/Environmental Issues" (San Francisco: Net Impact, October 2006).

15. For *scholars who study development of social issues,* see John J. Mahon and Sandra A. Waddock, "Strategic Issues Management: An Integration of Issue Life Cycle Perspectives," *Business & Society* 31, no. 1 (1992): 19–32.

16. For *research on the diffusion of new ideas,* see Everett M. Rogers, *Diffusion of Innovation, fifth edition* (New York: Free Press, 2003); on tipping point, see Malcolm Gladwell, *Tipping Point: How Little Things Can Make a Big Difference* (Boston: Little, Brown & Company, 2000); statistics on spending from CRO (Corporate Responsibility Officers), Jay Whitehead of TheCRO.com.

Chapter 4

1. For *in October, 2005 Lee Scott,* see "Twenty First Century Leadership" (October 24, 2005), online at walmartstores.com.

2. On companies doing best and worst job fulfilling social responsibilities *for seven years running, this survey house,* see Globescan, "Corporate Social Responsibility Monitor" (2006).

3. See *Sam Walton* with John Huey, *Sam Walton, Made in America* (New York: Doubleday, 1992).

4. For *Anderson is a credible corporate spokesman,* see Ray C. Anderson, *Mid-course Correction* (White River Junction, VT: Chelsea Green Publishing, 1998).

5. *Paul Hawken, The Ecology of Commerce: A Declaration of Sustainability* (New York: HarperCollins, 1993).

6. For *he also spoke of,* see Paul Hawken, Amory Lovins, and L. Hunter Lovins, *Natural Capitalism: Creating the Next Industrial Revolution* (Boston: Little, Brown & Company 1999); Interface Web site at interfaceinc.com.

7. For *these methodologies,* see description in Philip H. Mirvis, "Revolutions in OD: The New and New, New Things," in *Organization Development: A Jossey-Bass Reader,* Joan Gallos (ed.) (San Francisco: Jossey-Bass, 2006).

8. For *a series of "quick wins"* updates, go to walmartfacts.com.

9. *Good places to locate sources for countless critical academic studies* are the union-hosted site, walmartwatch.com and www.pbs.org/wgbh/pages/frontline/shows/walmart/secrets/.

10. For *a company that hitherto "hit the sandbags,"* see Edelman Group campaign in Kris Hudson, "PR Firm Remakes Wal-Mart's Image," *The Wall Street Journal* (December 7, 2006); and Geoffrey Goldberg, "Selling Wal-Mart," *The New Yorker,* (April 2, 2007), at Newyorker.com.

11. For *critics of the PR point out,* see the comprehensive work by Charles Fishman, *The Wal-Mart Effect: How the World's Most Powerful Company Really Works—and How It's Transforming the American Economy* (New York: Penguin Press, 2006).

12. For poll after poll, see Globescan, "Corporate Social Responsibility Monitor" (2006).

13. For *it also announced its Sustainability 360 strategy,* see Lee Scott at Prince of Wale's Business and the Environment Programme, London (February 1, 2007), at Walmartfacts.com.

14. For *yet a late-2006 Business Week survey of factory practices in China,* see Dexter Roberts and Pete Engardio, "Secrets, Lies and Sweatshops," *Business Week* (November 27, 2006), online at businessweek.com.

15. For *in a compelling account,* see *The Wal-Mart Effect* (2006).

16. For *the utter incompetence of FEMA,* see Douglas Brinkley, *The Great Deluge: Hurricane Katrina, New Orleans, and the Mississippi Gulf Coast* (New York: Morrow, 2006).

17. For *meanwhile, big business was at its best,* see cover story "After Katrina: Government Broke Down. Business Stepped Up," *Fortune* (September 21, 2005).

18. For *recall that, after Katrina,* see Alex Parry, "Unnatural Disaster," *Time Magazine* (August 2, 2004); Jeffrey Sachs, "How to End Poverty," *Time Magazine.* (March 14, 2005).

19. Jeffrey Sachs, *The End of Poverty: Economic Possibilities for Our Time* (New York: Penguin Press, 2005).

20. For *the evidence is that income gaps,* see World Bank, World Development Indicators, 2007, at worldbank.org.

21. Don Tapscott and David Ticoll, *The Naked Corporation: How the Age of Transparency Will Revolutionize Business* (New York: Free Press, 2003).

22. For *experts say that cost cutting was behind accident,* see "U.S. Chemical Safety Board Concludes 'Organizational and Safety Deficiencies at All Levels of the BP Corporation' Caused March 2005 Texas City Disaster That Killed 15, Injured 180," released by U.S. Chemical Safety and Hazard Investigation Board (April 20, 2007), at www.chemsafety.gov.

23. For *there is in the United States an estimated fifty million people,* see lohas.com; for more insight try Andrew Zolli, "Business 3.0," *Fast Company* (March, 2007), at Fastcompany.com.

24. For *Unilever, testing its commitment in,* see Jayson W. Clay, *Exploring the Links Between International Business and Poverty Reduction: A Case Study of Unilever in Indonesia* (Oxford, UK: Oxfam Publishing, 2005).

25. For *within five years it is estimated that mobile phones,* from World Scan by nokia .com.

26. For *World Health Organization predicts,* see Colin D. Mathers and Dejan Loncar, *Updated Projections of Global Mortality and Burden of Disease, 2002–2030: Data Sources, Methods, and Results,* World Health Organization (October, 2005).

Chapter 5

1. Jean Piaget's theory, for example, has children progress through developmental stages that entail more complex thinking and finer judgments about how to negotiate the social world around them. Similarly, groups mature along a developmental path as they confront emotional and task challenges that require more socially sensitive interaction and complex problem solving. This progression is represented in a sequence of stages that has a group first forming itself, storming through conflicts, then getting organized or norming, and finally performing effectively. See Jean Piaget, *The Psychology of the Child* (New York: John Wiley, 1969) and Susan A. Wheelan, *Group Processes: a Developmental Perspective* (Sydney: Allyn & Bacon, 2004).

2. Larry Greiner, "Evolution and Revolution as Organizations Grow," *Harvard Business Review* (July–August, 1972): 37–46.

3. For macro scale, see William C. Frederick, *Corporation, Be Good! The Story of Corporate Social Responsibility* (Indianapolis, IN: Dog Ear Publishing, Inc., 2006), and Donna J. Wood, "Corporate Social Performance Revisited," *Academy of Management Review* 16, no. 4 (1991): 171–81; for micro scale see James Post and Barbara Altman, "Models of Corporate Greening: How Corporate Social Policy and Organizational Learning Inform Leading Edge Environmental Management," *Research in Corporate Social Performance and Policy* 13 (1992): 3–29, and Simon Zadek, "The Path to Corporate Responsibility," *Harvard Business Review* (December, 2004): 125–33.

4. For a provocative interpretation of Friedman's message, see T. J. Rodgers in "Rethinking the Social Responsibility of Business. A Reason Debate featuring Milton Friedman, Whole Foods' John Mackey, and Cypress Semiconductor's T. J. Rodgers," *Reason Magazine* (October 2005).

5. For *it's clear that society expects more from companies today,* see surveys in *Millennium Report* (Toronto, CA: Environics, 1999; 2003).

6. For *one of our team began working with Royal Dutch Shell*, see Philip H. Mirvis, "Transformation at Shell: Commerce and citizenship," *Business and Society Review* 105, no. 1 (2000): 63–84.

7. Many companies today are members of the Coalition for Environmentally Responsible Economies (CERES) and have adopted its CERES Principles, a corporate code of environmental conduct, developed in 1989 after the Valdez oil spill. On Baxter, see Keith H. Hammond, "Harry Kraemer's Moment of Truth," *Fast Company* 64 (2002): 93.

8. See Svendsen and Laberge's work online at www.collectivewisdominitiative.org.

9. For *an analysis of firms* with Board-level CSR committees, see *2003 Sustainability Assessment* (Zurich: Sustainability Asset Management, 2003).

10. See the Environment and Society section of British Petroleum's Web site at bp.com; note the paradox facing BP for despite its supportive systems, strategies, and rhetoric on sustainability, its industry is one of the central contributors to global warming. BP's plans to change its business model will take decades, not years, and depends on complementary moves from the transportation industries and governments.

11. For *estimates* on verification from KPMG, see *International Survey of Corporate Responsibility Reporting 2005* (KPMG, 2005); also see KPMG *Beyond Numbers* (KPMG: 2004); and studies on sustainability through the Pacific Sustainability Index (PSI) at http://roberts.cmc.edu/.

12. For *Anderson, "we have found a way to win,"* quoted in Bennett Davis, "Profits from Principle: Five Forces Redefining Business," *The Futurist* (March 1999): 28–33.

13. See John Weiser, Michele Kahane, Steve Rochlin, and Jessica Landis, *Untapped: Creating Value in Underserved Markets* (San Francisco: Berrett-Koehler, 2006).

14. For positive deviants, see Jerry Sternin "Positive Deviance: A New Paradigm for Addressing Today's Problems Today," *Journal of Corporate Citizenship* 5:57–62, 2002.

Chapter 6

1. For *throughout the 1990s, as Nike's fortunes grew, its sociopolitical troubles*, see summary in the HBS teaching case, "Hitting the Wall: Nike and International Labor Practices" (Boston: Harvard Business School, 9-700-047, 2000).

2. *Zadek*, "The Path to Corporate Responsibility" (2004).

3. See *Mike McBreen*, "Beyond the Wall: Moving from Defensive to Defining," presentation at Harvard Business School, Corporate Social Responsibility Program, (October 25, 2005); see also Kramer and Kania, "Changing the Game" (2006)

4. For *PricewaterhouseCoopers* survey of CEO's on social issues, see "Globalization and Complexity: Inevitable Forces in a Changing Economy" (PricewaterhouseCoopers: 2006); find ten years of CEO surveys at pwc.com; for *McKinsey & Co.*, see "Global Survey of Business Executives" (March 2007).

5. See *McKinsey & Co.*, "Global Survey of Business Executives" (January 2006).

6. For *Public Relations firm GolinHarris*, see "2006 Corporate Citizenship Survey," *Fast Facts: GolinHarris Change!* Golinharris.com.

7. See *Globescan, Corporate Social Responsibility Monitor* (2006).

8. For *the main facts about the state of the world* and details on the Millennium Development Goals, see www.developmentgoals.org; and for world development indicators go to www.worldbank.org/data/; on U.S. domestic earnings gaps, a new Pew Charitable Trusts study finds that between 1979 and 2004, the income of the poorest one-fifth of Americans rose 9 percent while the income of the richest one-fifth rose 69 percent. The income of the top 1 percent rose 167 percent during

this period. See Isabel Sawhill and John E. Morton, "Economic Mobility: Is the American Dream Alive and Well?" Online at www.economicmobility.org.

9. For *models and frameworks*, see Michael Porter and Mark Kramer, "Strategy & Society: The Link between Competitive Advantage and Corporate Social Responsibility," *Harvard Business Review* (December, 2006); Scott C. Beardsley, Sheila Bonini, Lenny Mendonca and Jerry Oppenheim, "A New Era for Business," *Stanford Innovation Review*, (Summer, 2007); for more see Robert S. Kaplan and David Norton *Strategy Maps: Converting Intangible Assets into Tangible Outcomes* (Boston: HBS Press, 2004); also the HBS teaching case by Robert Kaplan and Ricardo Reisen de Pinho, "Amanco: Developing the Sustainability Scorecard" (Boston: Harvard Business School, 9-107-038, 2007).

10. For *sustainability specialist*, see Andrew W. Savitz, *The Triple Bottom Line: How Today's Best Run Companies are Achieving Economic, Social, and Environmental Success—and How You Can Too* (San Francisco: John Wiley & Sons, Inc., 2006).

11. For *on the broadest strategic scale,* see Shell Global Scenarios to 2025, "The Future Business Environment: Trends, Tradeoffs, and Choices," June 28, 2005, available at www.shell.com.

12. For *Booz Allen Hamilton/Aspen Institute* study, see Chris Kelly, Paul Kocourek, Nancy McGaw, and Judith Samuelson, *Deriving Value from Corporate Values* (Washington: The Aspen Institute and Booz Allen Hamilton, 2005).

Chapter 7

1. For *in 1995, when computer chipmaker AMD*, see background information at www.amd.com; on trends in social reporting see KPMG *International Survey* (2005); on integration, see Philip H. Mirvis and Julie Manga, "Integrating Corporate Citizenship: Leading from the Middle" (Boston: Boston College Center for Corporate Citizenship, 2007).

2. For *the largest company in the $1.2 trillion IT world*, see background information at www.ibm.com; see especially IBM Corporate Responsibility Reports at ibm.com/ibm/responsibility.

3. See James C. Collins and Jerry I. Porras, *Built to Last: Successful Habits of Visionary Companies* (New York: HarperBusiness, 1994).

4. See Samuel B. Graves and Sandra A. Waddock, "Beyond Built to Last: Stakeholder Relations in 'Built-to-Last' Companies," *Business and Society Review* 105, no. 4 (2006): 393–418.

5. See Joseph H. Bragdon, *Profit for Life: How Capitalism Excels* (Cambridge, MA: Society for Organization Learning, 2006).

6. For *in 2003, under Palmisano's lead, IBM held an important conversation*, see "Leading Change When Business Is Good: The HBR Interview—Samuel J. Palmisano," *Harvard Business Review* (December, 2004).

7. For *in 2006, IBM went where*, see Global Innovation Outlook 2.0 (IBM, 2006); Donofrio quoted in "Innovation: A Spark to Ignite the 21st Century" (June 11, 2006), online at www.bcccc.net; Palmisano quoted in "Big Blue Brainstorm," *Business Week* (August 7, 2006), online at www.businessweek.com.

8. For *the company hosted HabitatJam*, see "Collaboration that Matters: IBM 2006 Corporate Responsibility Report"; for World urban forum sponsored by United Nations Human Settlements Programs at http://www.unhabitat.org.

9. For *the World Community Grid*, see "Collaboration that Matters."

10. For *some years ago,* see Rosabeth Moss Kanter, "From Spare Change to Real Change: The Social Sector as a Beta Site for Business Innovation," *Harvard Business Review* (December, 1999).

11. For *differentiation is a key feature in development,* see Andrew H. Van de Ven and M. Scott Poole, "Explaining Development and Change in Organizations," *Academy of Management Review* 20 (1995): 510–40

12. For *as Palmisano puts it,* quoted in "Leveraging Business Strategy to Increase Employee Engagement" (August 3, 2004), online at www.bcccc.net.

13. For updates on AMD's 50x15 initiative, see http://50x15.amd.com.

Chapter 8

1. Quotes from big company CEOs come from the Center's Business Leadership in Society Study, *Step up* (2006); on the bulls-eye on CEOs, a 2007 Bloomberg/LA Times polls finds that six in ten Americans don't find CEOs to be ethical and eight in ten say that they are paid too much (June, 2007) online at latimes.com.

2. Paul Hawken, *The Ecology of Commerce* (1993).

3. Ben Cohen and Jerry Greenfield, *Ben & Jerry's Double Dip: How to Run a Values-led Business and Make Money, Too* (New York: Simon & Schuster, 1997); also see Fred Lager, *Ben & Jerry's: The Inside Scoop* (New York: Crown, 1994).

4. *Anita Roddick,* quoted from *Business as Unusual: The Journey of Anita Roddick and The Body Shop* (London: Thorsons, 2001).

5. See Hollender and Fenichell, *What Matters Most* (2003); also Hollender, "What Matters Most: Corporate Values and Social Responsibility," *California Management Review* 46, no. 4 (2004): 111–19;

6. Quotes from pioneering company founders are from Keith Cox, *Organic Leadership: The Co-creation of Good Business, Global Prosperity and a Greener Future* (Lisle, IL: Benedictine University, 2005); also Keith Cox and Phillp H. Mirvis, "Leadership for Global Sustainability" (2006), BAWB, http://worldbenefit.cwru.edu/forum2006.

7. For *biographical studies by psychologist,* see Howard Gardner, *Leading Minds: An Anatomy of Leadership* (New York: Basic Books, 1995).

8. For *many trace themselves to the cultural shifts of 1960s,* see Donella H. Meadows, Dennis L. Meadows, Jorgen Randers, and W. H. Behrens III, *The Limits to Growth: A Report for the Club of Rome's Project on the Predicament of Mankind,* first ed. (New York: Universe Books, 1972); Daniel Yankelovich, *New Rules: Searching for Self-Fulfillment in a World Turned Upside Down* (New York: Random House, 1981); Landon Jones, *Great Expectations: America and the Baby Boom Generation* (New York: Ballantine, 1986).

9. For *in her autobiography,* see Anita Roddick, *Body and Soul: Profits with Principles—The Amazing Story of Anita Roddick & The Body Shop* (New York: Crown Publishers, 1991).

10. For *Mirvis's hands on studies,* see Philip H. Mirvis, "Environmentalism in Progressive Businesses," *Journal of Organizational Change Management* 7, no. 4 (1994): 82–100.

11. See Joe Queenan, "Purveying Yuppie Porn," *Forbes* (November 13, 1989): 60–64); and John Entine, "The Stranger than Truth Story of the Body Shop," in *Killed: Great Journalism Too Hot to Print* (Nation Books, June, 2004).

12. For *this is the intellectual side of leadership,* see Peter F. Drucker, "The Theory of the Business," *Harvard Business Review* (September–October, 1994).

13. See *Ray C. Anderson, Mid-Course Correction* (1998).

14. See Ramona Amodeo, *Becoming Sustainable: Identity Dynamics Within Transform-ational Culture Change at Interface, Inc.* (Lisle, IL: Benedictine University, 2005); Guy Vaccaro, *The Story of Interface, Inc.: How a Large Manufacturing Organization Became Both Ecologically Sustainable and Profitable* (Lisle, IL: Benedictine University, 2007); quotes from Interface by Amodeo and Vaccaro.

15. For *behind the social, environmental, and political shifts*, see Willis Harman, *Global Mind Change* (Indianapolis, IN: Knowledge Systems, 1988); Fritjof Capra, *The Turning-Point: Science, Society and the Rising Culture* (New York: Bantam, 1982).

16. For *his literary journey traced the arc of ideas about sustainability*, see, for example, Wendell Berry, *The Unsettling of America: Culture and Agriculture* (New York: Avon/Sierra Club Books, 1978); Kenneth Boulding, "Economics of the Coming Spaceship Earth," in *The Environmental Handbook*, G. de Bell, ed. (New York: Ballantine, 1970); Lester Brown, *Building a Sustainable Society* (New York: W. W. Norton, 1981); Rachel Carson, *Silent Spring* (Cambridge, MA: Riverside Press, 1962); Aldo Leopold, *A Sand Country Almanac* (New York: Ballantine, 1966); E. F. Schumacher, *Small Is Beautiful: Economies as if People Mattered* (New York: Harper & Row, 1973).

17. For more on "cultural creatives," see Paul H. Ray and Sherry R. Anderson, *The Culture Creatives: How 50 Million People Are Changing the World* (New York: Three Rivers Press, 2000).

18. For *these complex models*, go to http://www.interfacesustainability.com/model.html; also see Bill McDonough and Michael Braungart, *Cradle to Cradle: Remaking the Way We Make Things* (New York: North Point Press, 2002).

19. For *the Natural Step*, go to naturalstep.org; also see Hilary Bradbury and J. A. Clair, "Promoting Sustainable Organizations with Sweden's Natural Step," *The Academy of Management Executive 13*, no. 4 (1999): 63–74.

20. For *in many respects, CSR fits into the class of situations*, see Fred E. Emery and Eric L. Trist, "The Causal Texture of Organizational Environments," *Human Relations* 18 (1965): 21–32; on incremental strategy and small wins, see Debra E. Meyerson, *Tempered Radicals: How Everyday Leaders Inspire Change at Work* (Boston: Harvard Business School Press, 2003).

21. See Peter F. Drucker, *The Daily Drucker: 366 Days of Insight and Motivation for Getting the Right Things Done* (New York: HarperCollins, 2004).

22. For *it is speculative, some of the sensibilities*, see Judy B. Rosner, "Ways Women Lead," *Harvard Business Review* (November–December, 1990); also Barbara Kantrowitz, "When Women Lead," *Newsweek* (October 24, 2005).

Chapter 9

1. For *in the United States, three of four young people* want to work for a company that cares, from "The 2006 Cone Millennial Cause Study" (October 24, 2006), at www.coneinc.com.

2. See *GolinHarris surveys, Doing Well by Doing Good* (2001–2006).

3. See Marcie Pitt-Catsouphes and Bradley Googins, "Recasting the Work–family Agenda as a Corporate Responsibility," in *Managing Work-Life Integration in Organizations: Future Directions for Research and Practice* (Boston: Erlbaum, 2005).

4. See The Reputation Institute, "RepTrak Pulse 2006: Social Responsibility Report" at http://www.reputationinstitute.com; also *a recent MORI poll found that 58 percent of employees in the United Kingdom say that the social and environmental behavior of their organizations is important to them*, see "Feel Good Factories," *The Guardian*

(January 21, 2006); on UK trends see also Institute of Business Ethics, "Survey Findings 2005: Ethical conduct within business" (March, 2006), at www.ibe.org.uk.

5. See "The 2006 Cone Millennial Cause Study" (October 2006), at www.coneinc.com; CSR minus HR = PR from "Management issues news" (August 7, 2003), at www .management-ssues.com.

6. *For the appeal of corporate citizenship to employees is by no means limited to the United States*, see The Reputation Institute, "RepTrak Pulse 2006: Social Responsibility Report" at http://www.reputationinstitute.com and Globescan *Corporate Social Responsibility Monitor* (2006), http://www.globescan.com.

7. See Deborah E. S. Frable, "Gender, Racial Ethnic, Sexual and Class Identities," *Annual Review of Psychology* 48 (1997).

8. For *in top companies today, diversity is valued*, see David A. Thomas and Robin J. Ely, "Making Differences Matter: A New Paradigm for Managing Diversity," *Harvard Business Review* (September–October 1996): 80–90.

9. Find *this yields more commitment* in Douglas T. Hall and Philip H. Mirvis, "The New Protean Career: Psychological Success and the Path with a Heart," in The *Career Is Dead—Long Live the Career by* D. T. Hall and Associates, eds. (San Francisco: Jossey-Bass 1996); a 2007 Sirota Survey Intelligence survey, of 1.6 million employees in seventy companies, found that 71 percent of employees who approve of their company's commitments have favorable perceptions of their management's integrity versus 21 percent of those who do not approve. Those who favor their company's commitments are also more apt to believe that their employers are interested in their well-being (75 versus 17 percent), see Sirota Survey Intelligence, online at Sirota.com.

10. For *studies find the prime source of information*, see the 2007 Fleishman-Hillard/National Consumers League survey that found that some 54 percent of consumers seek out information "sometimes" about the social responsibility of particular companies. Increasingly, they are turning to the Internet to search for information. Interestingly, over half of the consumers surveyed turned to the Web sites of independent groups, such as consumer-watch groups or accrediting agencies, to garner data, a substantial increase over prior years. When it comes to judging the credibility of data, consumers favor independent (cited by 43 percent as credible) versus company Web sites (cited by 29 percent). The most credible sources are personal experience (cited by 60 percent) and word of mouth (56 percent); see two surveys "Rethinking Corporate Social Responsibility" (National Consumers League Study, 2006 and 2007).

11. For *IBM On Demand community*, see ibm.com; also, "Employee Engagement: On Demand Community" (Boston College Center for Corporate Citizenship Conference Presentation, October 14, 2004); John A. Quelch, "IBM On Demand Community," Harvard Business School Case no. 9-504-103 (May 21, 2004).

12. For *Timberland is another company*, and volunteerism go to www.timberland.com; also see "Timberland Partners with City Year, SOS, and SkillsUSA" (Boston College Center for Corporate Citizenship, In Practice Brief, March 14, 2004); James E. Austin, Herman B. Leonard, and James W. Quinn, "Timberland: Commerce and Justice," Harvard Business School Case no. 9-305-002 (July 19, 2004).

13. *On a global scale Nokia*, on societal engagement see www.nokia.com; also "The Real Story: What Works in Effective Corporate and NGO Collaboration" (Boston College Center for Corporate Citizenship Conference Presentation, October 14, 2004).

14. *In PricewaterhouseCoopers 10th Annual Global CEO Survey:* "Was: Within borders Is: Across borders Will be: Without borders?" (PwC: 2007).

15. For *recognizing the power of these kinds of consciousness-raising experiences*, see service learning in Karen Ayas and Philip H. Mirvis, "Educating Managers Through Service Learning Projects," in *Educating Managers Through Real-World Projects*, C. Wankel and R. DeFillippi, eds. (Greenwich, CT: IAP, 2005).

16. For *yet, the case can be made*, see Philip H. Mirvis, "Executive Development Through Consciousness Raising Experiences," in *Academy of Management Learning & Education* (2007); Unilever story in Philip H. Mirvis and Willem L. Gunning, "Creating a Community of Leaders," *Organizational Dynamics 35*, no. 1 (2006): 69–82.

17. For *a more sustained example* from Unilever's Young Leader Forum, see Karen Ayas and Philip H. Mirvis, "Young Leaders' Forum in Asia: Learning About Leadership, Abundance, and Growth," *Reflections* 4, no. 1 (2002): 33–42.

18. Gardner, *Leading Minds* (1995).

19. For *consciousness raising requires some degree of internalization*, see James O. Prochaska, John Norcross, and Carlo DiClemente, *Changing for Good* (New York: William Morrow, 1994).

Chapter 10

1. For *progressive trend documented*, the Conference Board's 2006 survey of medium to large size multinationals (a select sample of 198 member companies) finds that over 60 percent of companies say that they have formal programs to manage citizenship and sustainability and nearly half of this sample says that their Boards routinely review citizenship efforts in their companies. The Global Environmental Management Initiative (GEMI) and Businesses for Social Responsibility (BSR) surveyed 54 business professionals in 2006 from their respective member companies. In that study, over 60 percent report that their citizenship efforts are aligned and coordinated with overall company strategy. Finally, McKinsey & Co.'s 2007 survey of companies participating in the Global Compact finds that 90 percent of CEOs are doing more than they did in five years ago to incorporate environmental, social, and governance issues into strategy and operations. But gaps are notable: 72 percent of CEOs agree that corporate responsibility should be embedded into strategy and operations, but only 50 percent think their firms do so. And six in ten say that corporate responsibility should be infused into global supply chains, but only twenty-seven say they are doing so. See The Conference Board. "Reward Trumps Risk: How Business Perspectives on Corporate Citizenship and Sustainability are Changing its Bottom Line." Executiveaction #216, November, 2006. Online at conferenceboard.org; GEMI/BSR. "Sustainable Business & Strategy: A View from the Inside" (September 15, 2006). Online at bsr.org; McKinsey & Co., "Shaping the New Rules of Competition: UN Global Compact Participant Mirror." (July, 2007). Online at McKinsey.com.

2. For *GE publishes an enumeration of these concerns* and statistics, see "GE 2007 Citizenship Report—Investing in a Sustainable Future," at www.ge.com.

3. In a *2002 public opinion poll, GE . . . slipped*, reported by Ronald Alsop in, "Scandal Filled Year Takes Toll on Firms' Good Names," *The Wall Street Journal* (February 12, 2003).

4. *Interestingly, Corcoran insists that making money*, reported by Nicola West-Jones in, "Top 10 and Counting . . . How GE Became a Good Corporate Citizen and How You Can Too," *On Philanthropy* (April 4, 2007).

5. On British Telecom see www.btplc.com; and Chris Tuppen, "From Focus on Environmental Compliance to Integrated Corporate Citizenship Program" (Boston

College Center for Corporate Citizenship: The Voice of Corporate Citizenship, December 15, 2004).

6. *It issued a provocative . . . report*, "*Just Values*" (London: British Telecom, 2003) online at bt.com; see BT's other writings on values in the Society and Environment section of their Web site and *The Materiality Report: Aligning Strategy, Performance, and Reporting*, (London: AccountAbility, BT, LRQA, November, 2006).

7. See KPMG *International Survey of Corporate Responsibility Reporting 2005 (KPMG, 2005); also Reporting in Context, Global Reporting Trends 2006, (Context, 2007).*

8. For *decades of research into organizational change*, see Mirvis, "Revolutions in OD," *(2006).*

9. Bradley Googins and Steven Rochlin, "Corporate Citizenship Top to Bottom: Vision Strategy and Execution," in *The Accountable Corporation Vol. 3: Corporate Social Responsibility*, Marc J. Epstein and Kirk O. Hanson, eds. (Westport, CT: Praeger, 2006): 111–29.

10. McKinsey & Co., "Shaping the New Rules of Competition: UN Global Compact Participant Mirror." (July, 2007).

11. For *One company that continues to infuse its culture with corporate citizenship*, see Novo Nordisk at www.novonordisk.com; quotations from James Rubin, Susanna Beranova, Majken Schultz, and Mary Jo Hatch, "Novo Nordisk: Focusing the Corporate Brand," Darden Case No.: UVA-BC-0192 (October 11, 2006), SSRN: http://ssrn.com/abstract=907772.

Chapter 11

1. For *Jellu Sujatamma*, see Nancy Roberts, "Project Shakti: Growing the Market While Changing Lives," BAWB Newsletter 2, no. 2 (February, 2006), online at worldbenefit.case.edu.

2. See "District of Columbia Neighborhood Market Drill Down" (March 28, 2004), online at www.socialcompact.org.

3. For *In a recent survey by GlobeScan*, see "Corporate Social Responsibility Monitor," (2006).

4. For *David Vogel*, quoted from his letter to editor, see "Eco-Conscious Companies: Irrelevant or Inevitable?" *Business Week* (February 19, 2007).

5. Weiser, et al, *Untapped* (2006).

6. See the "Initiative for a Competitive Inner City" (April 25, 2004), online at icic.org.

7. See *Initiative for a Competitive Inner City: The Changing Models of Inner City Grocery Retailing* (Boston: ICIC, 2002).

8. See "SAFECO" (Boston College Center for Corporate Citizenship, Case Study, October 14, 2004).

9. From John M. Imperiale, "Aligning and Integrating Corporate Citizenship: Practitioners Speak About their Key Successes and Challenges" (Boston College Center for Corporate Citizenship Conference presentation, April 1, 2003).

10. Statistics from John Weiser, *Part of the Solution: Leveraging Business and Markets for Low-Income People: Lessons Learned from the Ford Foundation Corporate Involvement Initiative* (Ford Foundation, 2005).

11. See "Manpower's TechReach Program" (Boston College Center for Corporate Citizenship, In Practice Brief, February 10, 2003).

12. In "Turner Construction" (Boston College Center for Corporate Citizenship, Case Study, October 14, 2004); on Focus HOPE, see also Linda St. Clair, "A Global Model for the Business of Corporate Citizenship: The Success Story of Focus HOPE," in

Global Corporate Citizenship: Doing Business in the Public Eye by Noel Tichy, Andrew R. McGill, and Linda St. Clair (San Francisco: The New Lexington Press, 1997).

13. Statistics from Michel Kahane, "Making Markets Work for the Poor," (Boston College Center for Corporate Citizenship Conference Presentation, March 30, 2004).

14. See Jonathon Levine, "Coffee with a Conscience," *The Corporate Citizen 2006* (Boston College Center for Corporate Citizenship, January 5, 2007)

15. See "Green Mountain Coffee Roasters and TransFair" (Boston College Center for Corporate Citizenship, In Practice Brief, November 8, 2004); for more partnerships see *Business and Community Development: Aligning Corporate Performance with Community Economic Development to Achieve Win-Win Impacts* (Boston College Center for Corporate Citizenship, 2002).

16. *The Web site of BAWB*, "Innovation Bank," online at worldbenefit.case.edu.

17. See "The 2007 Cone Cause Evolution Survey" (July 9, 2007), at www.coneinc.com.

18. See "The 2006 Cone Millennial Cause Study" (October 24, 2006), at www.coneinc .com; also see Bruce Tulgan and Carolyn Martin, *Managing Generation Y* (Amherst, MA: HRD Press, 2001).

19. See Product RED campaign by Dan Henkle, "Taking Corporate Citizenship to Market: The Gap Story" (Boston College Center for Corporate Citizenship Conference Presentation, March 27, 2007).

Chapter 12

1. Estimate from The Giving USA Foundation, "Giving USA 2007: The Annual Report on Philanthropy for the Year 2006" (New York: American Association of Fundraising Counsel, 2007); see Committee to Encourage Philanthropy findings online at cecp.com.

2. Michael E. Porter and Mark R. Kramer, "The Competitive Advantage of Corporate Philanthropy," *Harvard Business Review* (December, 2002).

3. For many fine accounts, see Philip Kotler and Nancy Lee, *Corporate Social Responsibility: Doing the Most Good for Your Company and Your Cause* (New York: Wiley, 2005); David Bornstein, *How to Change the World: Social Entrepreneurs and the Power of Ideas* (New York: Oxford University Press, 2004); and Mark Benioff, *The Business of Changing the World* (New York: McGraw-Hill, 2007).

4. See Mary Jo Hatch and Majken Schultz. "Are the Strategic Stars Aligned for Your Corporate Brand?" *Harvard Business Review* (February, 2001): 128-134; see also *Taking Brand Initiative: How Companies can Align Strategy, Culture and Identity through Corporate Branding* (San Francisco: Jossey-Bass, due February, 2008).

5. *On this count, we were referred to the founder's philosophy*, quote by J. H. Chey in *SKMS* (Seoul: SK Corporation, 2003).

6. Asian polls by GlobeScan, "Corporate Social Responsibility Monitor" (2006); and The Reputation Institute, "RepTrak Pulse 2006."

7. See Mark Yu-Ting Chen, Lincoln J. Pan, and Hai Wu, "Developing China's Nonprofit Sector," *The McKinsey Quarterly* (August, 2006); on corporate involvement with NGOs in China and the D&E world, see Guy Morgan, "Building Trust, Guanxi, and Community" (Boston College Center for Corporate Citizenship, In Focus, December 8, 2004); *Going Global: Managers' Experiences Working with Worldwide Stakeholders* (Boston College Center for Corporate Citizenship, 2005).

8. See GlobeScan, "Report on Issues and Reputation" (2005).

9. For *the public all over the world says the best way for corporations to make a contribution*, see "Corporate Social Responsibility Monitor" (2006).

10. *On respect for partnering, ibid.*

11. See "Corporate Social Responsibility Monitor" (Trends 2001–2006).

12. *For examples of partnerships*, see Julie Engel Manga and Sapna Shah, *Enduring Partnerships: Resilience, Innovation, Success* (Boston College Center for Corporate Citizenship, 2005); also see Peter Asmus, "Special Report: NGO Engagement," *Ethical Corporation* (April 5, 2007).

13. *See* "KaBOOM! Partnership with the Home Depot Receives Award for Excellence" (February 27, 2006), at http://www.socialfunds.com/news/release.cgi?sfArticleId–5115; and "The Home Depot Joins KaBOOM! in America's Playgrounds," *Latino Leaders: The National Magazine of the Successful American Latino* (August–September, 2005).

14. Also see James Walsh, "Corporate Responsibility Initiatives in 86 of the top 100 U.S. Firms," Business as an Agent of World Benefit Global Forum, Case Western Reserve University (October 25, 2006).

15. See Stephen Jordan, "Next Steps for Business and Education Partnerships" (U.S. Chamber of Commerce's Business Civic Leadership Center, July 27, 2005).

16. See "Dell TechKnow Gears Up For Largest Class Ever; 10,000 Students Expected Nationally," *RTO Online* (August 30, 2006), at http://www.rtoonline.com/Content/Article/Aug_06/DellTechnow083006.asp.

17. See "State Farm Insurance and Neighborhood Housing Services of Chicago: Insuring a Future" (Boston College Center for Corporate Citizenship, Case Study, March 10, 2004).

18. For *a partnership between Nokia and the Grameen Foundation*, at http://www.nokia.com/; and in Joe Twist, "Pocket Answer to Digital Divide," *BBC News* (November 18, 2005), at http://news.bbc.co.uk/1/hi/technology/4446966 .stm?ls.

19. See Guy Morgan, "Chiquita and the Rainforest Alliance, a Fruitful Relationship," *The Corporate Citizen 2006* (Boston College Center for Corporate Citizenship, January 5, 2007)

20. See Ira A. Jackson and Jane Nelson, *Profits with Principles: Seven Strategies for Delivering Value with Values* (New York: Currency/Doubleday, 2004).

21. See account by Philip H. Mirvis, "Revolutions in OD: The New and New, New Things," in *Handbook of Collaborative Management Research by* A. B. Shani, N. Adler, S. A. Mohrman, W. A. Pasmore, and B. Stymne, eds. (Thousand Oaks, CA: Sage, 2007).

22. See Peter A. Senge, Art Kleiner, Joe Laur, Sara Schley, and Brian Smith, *Learning for Sustainability* (Cambridge, MA: Society for Organization Learning, 2006); quote from Hilary Bradbury, N. Powley, and John Carroll, "The Importance of Relational Space for Interorganizational Learning: Taking on a Broader Business Mandate" (Academy of Management Convention, August, 2003).

Chapter 13

1. For *listen to Hector Ruiz*, "The 21st Century CEO," Detroit Economic Club (February 20. 2007), online at www.bcccc.net.

2. See "100 Best Corporate Citizens," *CRO* (Jan/Feb, 2007).

3. See Alex Taylor III, "America's Best Car Company," *Fortune Magazine* (March 7 2007).

4. See Marc Gunther, "10 Green Giants," *Fortune* (March 16, 2007), online money.cnn .com/magazines/fortune.

5. For *Its global competitor*, see "The Nestlé Water Management Report" (March, 2007), online at www.water.nestle.com.

6. C. K. Prahalad, "The Innovation Sandbox," *Strategy + Business* (Autumn 2006); also see Jeb Brugman and C. K. Prahalad, "Co-creating Business's New Social Compact" *Harvard Business Review* (February, 2007).

7. See *Capitalism at the Crossroad*; also see Stuart L. Hart and Ted London, "Developing Native Capability: What multinational corporations can learn from the base of the pyramid," *Stanford Social Innovation Review* (Summer, 2005).

8. *Goldman Sachs* featured in Christopher Wright, "For Goldman Sachs, Long-Term Greed Means Going Green," *Ecosystem Marketplace* (January 23, 2007). http:// ecosystemmarketplace.com/pages/.

9. For *the latest on genetically modified crops and foods* go to http://www.monsanto .com/biotech-gmo/ and critics at http://www.gmwatch.org/.

10. For *Meanwhile, co-founder and president Mark Hurst*, go to goodexperience.com.

11. For *"philanthropreneurs,"* see Stephanie Strom, "What's Wrong with Profit?" *The New York Times* (November 13, 2006), online at http://www.nytimes.com/2006/11/13/ us/.

12. *Discretionary federal spending on social programs*, in "A series of issue summaries from the Congressional Budget Office" No. 1, June 14, 2002, revised July 3, 2002.

13. See American National Election Studies, Trust in Government Index, 1958–2004, online at http://www.electionstudies.org/nesguide/graphs/g5a_5_1.htm.

14. For *nonprofit employment in the United States*, see Independent Sector, "Employment in the Nonprofit Sector" (May 25, 2004), online at www.independentsector.org.

15. For *the growth in the number and scale of NGOs*, see *The 21st Century NGO: In the Market for Change* (London: Sustainability, 2003); on trust, see Richard Edelman, "Rebuilding Trust through Accountability and Responsibility" (Ethical Corporation Conference, 2002); GlobeScan, *Corporate Social Responsibility Monitor* (2006).

16. Allen L. White, "Is It Time to Rewrite the Social Contract?" (San Francisco: BSR, 2007) online at bsr.org.

17. Fleishman-Hillard/National Consumer League. Rethinking Corporate Social Responsibility. (May, 2007) online at www.fleishman.com.

18. See data in "Tomorrow's Value" (London: Sustainability, UNEP, Standard and Poors, November, 2006); also "Influencing Power: Reviewing the Conduct and Content of Corporate Lobbying" (London: Sustainability and WWF, July, 2005).

19. See Zadek, "The Path to Corporate Responsibility" (2004); see also Srilatha Batliwawa and L. David Brown, *Transnational Civil Society* (Bloomfield, CT: Kumarian Press, 2006).

20. See David Korten, *When Corporations Rule the World* (New York: Earthscan, 1995); and David Henderson, *Misguided Virtue: False Notions of Corporate Social Responsibility* (London: Institute of Economic Affairs, 2002).

21. On Circuit City see Harold Meyerson, "A Dream Short Circuited," *Washington Post* (April 11, 2007); also, on Wal-Mart versus Costco see Wayne F. Cascio, "The High Price of Low Wages," *Harvard Business Review* (December, 2006).

22. Sumantra Ghoshal, "Bad Management Theories Are Destroying Good Management Practices," *Academy of Management Learning & Education* 4, no. 1 (2005): 75–91.

About the Authors

Bradley K. Googins, Ph.D.

Bradley K. Googins, Ph.D. is executive director of the Center for Corporate Citizenship at Boston College, a leading voice in the U.S. on the role of business in society. Dr. Googins is also on the faculty of Boston College's Carroll School of Management. In 1990 he founded the Center for Work & Family at Boston University and directed it for six years before assuming his current position. He is the author of several books and monographs and sits on the review board of the *Journal of Corporate Citizenship*, the advisory board of Corporate Voices for Working Families, and the Brazilian research and education center Uni-Ethos. He is currently creating a global network of corporate citizenship institutions from China to Brazil.

Googins holds a Ph.D. in Social Policy from The Heller Graduate School at Brandeis University, an M.S.W. in social work, community organization, and social planning from Boston College, and a B.A. in philosophy and sociology from Boston College.

Philip H. Mirvis, Ph.D.

Philip Mirvis, Ph.D. is an organizational psychologist and senior research fellow at the Boston College Center for Corporate Citizenship. An advisor to businesses in the U.S., Europe, Asia, and Australia, he has worked with Ben & Jerry's, Royal Dutch Shell, Unilever, Novo Nordisk, and SK Corporation, among others on their citizenship agendas. Dr. Mirvis has authored ten books on his studies, including *The Cynical Americans* (social trends), *Building the Competitive Workforce* (human capital), and *Joining Forces* (the human side of mergers). His most recent is a business transformation story, *To the Desert and Back*. He is a fellow of the Work/Family Roundtable, a board member of the Foundation for Community Encouragement, and a trustee of the Society for Organization Learning.

Mirvis has a B.A. from Yale University and a Ph.D. in Organizational Psychology from the University of Michigan. He has taught at Boston University and has been a visiting faculty member at The University of Michigan, Jiao Tong University, Shanghai, China, and the London Business School.

Steven A. Rochlin

Steven Rochlin, formerly director of research and development for the Center for Corporate Citizenship, is now Head of the North American practice of AccountAbility, an international research and membership organization. Rochlin is the co-author of *Untapped: Creating Value in Underserved Markets* and frequently presents to and advises major corporate brands, NGOs, and multilateral organizations in the arena of business and society. Rochlin launched the Center's surveys of American business and helped to convene its multicompany forums on corporate practices. He works in Washington, D.C. and continues as a senior research fellow of The Center.

Rochlin holds a B.A. in political science from Brown University and an M.P.P. from Harvard University's John F. Kennedy School of Government. He has also worked in the areas of technology-based economic development for the National Academy of Sciences and the Center for Strategic and International Studies in Washington, D.C.

Index